Business Transformation
Management Methodology

Business Transformation Management Methodology

Edited by
AXEL UHL
LARS ALEXANDER GOLLENIA

GOWER

Gower Applied Business Research
Our programme provides leaders, practitioners, scholars and researchers with thought provoking, cutting edge books that combine conceptual insights, interdisciplinary rigour and practical relevance in key areas of business and management.

Published by
Gower Publishing Limited
Wey Court East
Union Road
Farnham
Surrey
GU9 7PT
England

Gower Publishing Company
110 Cherry Street
Suite 3-1
Burlington, VT 05401-3818
USA

www.gowerpublishing.com

Axel Uhl and Lars Alexander Gollenia have asserted their moral right under the Copyright, Designs and Patents Act, 1988, to be identified as the editors of this work.

British Library Cataloguing in Publication Data
Business transformation management
  methodology.
  1. Reengineering (Management) 2. Organizational change--
  Management.
  I. Uhl, Axel. II. Gollenia, Lars Alexander.
  658.4'063-dc23

Reprinted 2013

ISBN: 9781409449805 (hbk)
ISBN: 9781409449812 (ebk – PDF)
ISBN: 9781409483984 (ebk – ePUB)

Library of Congress Cataloging-in-Publication Data
Uhl, Axel.
  Business transformation management methodology / by Axel Uhl and Lars Alexander Gollenia.
      p. cm.
  Includes bibliographical references and index.
  ISBN 978-1-4094-4980-5 (hbk.) -- ISBN 978-1-4094-4981-2 (ebook)
  1. Reengineering (Management) 2. Organizational change--Management. 3. Management.
  I. Gollenia, Lars Alexander. II. Title.
  HD58.87.U45 2012
  658.4'06--dc23

                                                                                    2012022798

Printed in the United Kingdom by Henry Ling Limited,
at the Dorset Press, Dorchester, DT1 1HD

Contents

List of Figures

List of Tables

About the Editors

Prof. Dr Axel Uhl is the co-founder and Head of the Business Transformation Academy. He is also a member of the Business Transformation Services Leadership Team within the Services Division of SAP. Dr Uhl is a professor at the University of Applied Sciences and Arts Northwestern Switzerland. Prior to joining SAP, Prof. Uhl worked in senior management positions at Novartis, KPMG, DaimlerChrysler and Allianz. He holds a PhD in economics, and master degrees in business administration, educational sciences and information technology.

Lars Gollenia is Head of Business Transformation Services at SAP and a member of the SAP Services Delivery Executive team. Business Transformation Services is a global Line of Service with a local presence in all geographies. He is the founder and sponsor of the Business Transformation Academy, a global leadership network comprised of leading academics and selected executives of Fortune 2.000 companies. He has held a number of positions in the management consulting space. Prior to his current role he was responsible for Business Consulting in the EMEA region. Gollenia is a Graduate in Business Administration from the Friedrich-Schiller University of Jena, Germany and studied economics and international management at Harvard University in Boston, USA.

Notes on Contributors

Stephan Amling, Vice President, Global SAP Services Strategy, SAP AG
Stephan is Vice President Strategy and Execution for SAP's Global Services business unit. He joined SAP in May 2008 after more than 16 years in other business strategy and IT consulting organizations (e.g. Booz & Co., Accenture, IBM). He studied computer science and business administration at the Berufsakademie in Stuttgart, Germany, with a focus on research and solution development in the area of artificial intelligence and expert systems. He has a strong business and technology management background with personal experience in large-scale business transformation, IT strategy and complex IT solution development.

Contact: stephan.amling@sap.com

Dr Ernst Balla, Management Development, voestalpine AG
Dr Ernst Balla is responsible for Management Development at voestalpine which is a globally active group with 45,000 employees in 360 companies in 60 countries that produces, processes and further develops high-quality steel products. His biggest transformation project so far was the development and implementation of the new group-wide Management Development Program. Balla also teaches communication and team-development at the University of Applied Sciences in Linz.

Contact: ernst.balla@voestalpine.com

Prof. Dr Florian Blumer, Lecturer in Communication and Media Relations at the School of Business Basel, University of Applied Sciences and Arts Northwestern Switzerland
Florian Bulmer, a lecturer at the University of Applied Sciences and Arts Northwestern Switzerland, has 12 years of experience in consulting global companies in the fields of corporate and project communication, stakeholder management, innovation-management and open space-methodology. He has also worked as a consultant for companies from the financial industry as well as for SME and startups. Furthermore, he led the media department during the Bob World Championships in St Moritz (1997) and was a head coach of Swiss handball premium league teams.

Contact: florian.blumer@fhnw.ch

Michael Brandenburg, Director International Business Development, IESE Business School, University of Navarra
Michael Brandenburg leads the development of the international corporate business for IESE Business School, ranked since 2006 consistently as a global top-ten provider of

executive education. He received a Masters degree in engineering at Aachen University in 1983, his MBA at IESE in 1989 and an AMP in 2009. Michael has served as Manager at RWE, division head in SEAT-Volkswagen supply chain and as vice president in Capgemini Consulting. His major contributions are in the area of process improvement in the high-tech and automobile sectors and in the creation of high-performance management teams in international corporations.

Contact: mbrandenburg@iese.edu

Dr Andreas Elting, Principal Enterprise Architect, SAP AG

Andreas has more than 15 years' experiences in all phases of a typical business and IT project. In recent years he focused on leading initiatives on strategic level in SAP and non-SAP environments. Andreas was leading a global IT architecture community at SAP and contributed to EA service offerings and methods at SAP. He is also a major contributor to SAP EAF and TOGAF 9.0. Andreas is a speaker at exhibitions and conferences and published more than 30 papers in all major German IT newspapers. Andreas holds a diploma in Computer Sciences and a PhD in Psychology.

Contact: andreas.elting@sap.com

Prof. Dr Brent Furneaux, Assistant Professor in the Department of Accounting and Information Management, Maastricht University, School of Business and Economics

Brent Furneaux is an Assistant Professor in the department of Accounting and Information Management at Maastricht University. He is currently pursuing research that seeks to better understand information system (IS) decision-making processes such as those related to lifecycle planning, discontinuance and transformation. His research interests also include the nature, role, and significance of theory within IS research and the mechanisms by which information systems deliver value to organizations and individual users. Brent's research has been published in numerous conference proceedings, book chapters and journals including *MIS Quarterly*, *The DATA BASE for Advances in Information Systems* and *Information Technology and Management*. Prior to his academic career, Brent worked and consulted extensively within the pharmaceutical and hospitality industries.

Contact: b.furneaux@maastrichtuniversity.nl

Lars Alexander Gollenia, Head of SAP Business Transformation Services, SAP AG

Lars Alexander Gollenia is Head of Business Transformation Services at SAP and a member of the SAP Services Delivery Executive team. Business Transformation Services is a global line of service with a local presence in all geographies. He is the founder and sponsor of the Business Transformation Academy, a global leadership network comprised of leading academics and selected executives of Fortune 2000 companies. He has held a number of positions in the management consulting area. Prior to his current role he was responsible for business consulting in the EMEA region. Lars is a graduate in Business Administration from the Friedrich-Schiller University of Jena, Germany and studied economics and international management at Harvard University in Boston, USA.

Contact: lars.gollenia@sap.com

Thomas Gonser, Chief Enterprise Architect, SAP AG

With more than 25 years of professional experience, Thomas gained strong skills to bridge technology and business. Starting with software development including heading architecture and development at a small software provider and after several years as a middleware architect at Sybase, he joined SAP in the beginning of 2002 as head of the SAP NetWeaver Solution Center. In 2004 he became responsible for business and technology architecture within the Industry Business Unit (IBU) for communications. In 2008 he joined Business Transformation Consulting, Telecommunication and Utilities EMEA, where he successfully accomplished multiple architecture projects.

Contact: thomas.gonser@sap.com

Philipp Gubler, Research Assistant, Institute of Information Management, University of St Gallen

Philipp Gubler is research assistant and PhD student at the Institute of Information Management, University of St Gallen. He received a Master in Information, Media and Technology Management from the University of St Gallen.

Robert Günther, Head of Center of Expertise for Transformation Management EMEA, SAP AG

Robert Günther is a Managing Principal at SAP and leading the Center of Expertise for Transformation Management in EMEA with a focus on organizational change. Prior to SAP he was a Manager at IDS Scheer AG in Business- and Process Consulting where he overlooked numerous IT transformation projects in the automotive, consumer products and manufacturing industries. He has considerable international experience from working with major clients of SAP in the USA, the Middle East and Japan.

Contact: robert.guenther@sap.com

Dr Jürg Haefliger, Head Learning & Development, Sulzer Ltd.

Jürg Haefliger holds a PhD in Philosophy from the University of Basel and a Master degree in Strategic Human Resource Management from Bocconi University, Milan and Cornell University, Ithaca (NY). He is Head of Corporate Learning & Development at Sulzer Management AG (Switzerland). Before joining Sulzer, Jürg Haefliger held positions as Head Corporate Management Development & Corporate HRM Projects at Georg Fischer AG, as Partner with an international Consulting Company, and as Project Leader at the

Swiss National Science Foundation. He possesses in-depth knowledge in the field of learning and development in a global context.

Prof. Dominic Houlder, Adjunct Professor in Strategic and Entrepreneurial Management, London Business School

Prof. Dominic Houlder researches and advises major B2B service firms on developing C suite client relationships and more effective collaboration across lines of service, geographical boundaries and external partner organizations. He is currently working with PriceWaterhouseCoopers, G4S, Eversheds, SAP and Saatchi & Saatchi. He designed and led London Business School's new executive workout program for B2B service businesses, "Unlocking Your Client's Strategy".

Contact: dhoulder@london.edu

Tomasz Janasz, Research Associate at SAP Switzerland, SAP AG

Tomasz Janasz is a business administration graduate from the University of Hamburg. In 2008 he joined SAP as a business consultant with a main focus on project management, software implementation process, and quality assurance in major transformation initiatives. Since 2010, he has been a research associate at the Business Transformation Academy, where he has been given the responsibility for industry research and communication. He also co-developed the BTM². Currently Tomasz is pursuing his PhD at the University of Wuppertal (Germany) conducting research on the innovative concepts for sustainable urban transportation.

Contact: t.janasz@sap.com

Dr Roberto Klimmek, Director Finance & Controlling, Mercedes Benz Cars

Dr Roberto Klimmek has worked for Daimler AG since 1986 and has already held diverse positions within the company. Since 1994 he has been part of different executive boards of the company in Greece and Indonesia. From 2002 until 2005 he was the CFO of Smart. After that, he transferred to Mercedes-Benz, where he is now the Director of Purchasing, Insolvency/Risk-Management and Product Controlling.

Dr Oliver Kohnke, Chief Business Consultant, SAP AG

Oliver Kohnke is a Chief Business Consultant in SAP's Business Consulting. He received his Doctorate in Industrial and Organizational Psychology and Master of Computer Sciences and Business Administration from University of Mannheim. He has spent over 15 years supporting large-scale business transformations and IT system implementations at various international companies in a broad range of industries. His main areas of interest include organizational behavior, change management and technology acceptance. He is also author of several books and articles in international journals.

Contact: oliver.kohnke@sap.com

Ronald Marketsmueller, Business Transformation & Program Manager, SAP AG

Ronald is a graduate engineer (Ecole Polytechnique Fédérale de Lausanne) and has been active for over 20 years in consulting and global program management roles in many locations all over the world. Ronald's knowledge of English, French and German allows him to address multicultural challenges. Ronald was head of the program management Global Practice at SAP and co-developed the SAP BTM² and Program Management (PMI based) methodologies. Ronald's actual focus is on managing business transformation programs and he is actively involved in quality reviews of major customer programs.

Contact: ronald.marketsmueller@sap.com

Dr Martin Petry, Chief Information Officer, Hilti AG

Martin Petry became Hilti's CIO in 2005. He is responsible for a global team of 400 IT employees. Since 2009 he has also been in charge of Hilti's Business Excellence initiatives. Martin came to Hilti in 1993 and has held various leadership roles in Liechtenstein, Switzerland, Japan, Great Britain and on a global scale since then. Martin earned his PhD in applied mathematics from Georg-August University in Göttingen.

Christoph Pimmer, Research Associate, University of Applied Sciences and Arts Northwestern Switzerland

Christoph Pimmer is a research associate at the University of Applied Sciences Northwestern Switzerland (FHNW). He studied social and economic sciences. He worked on a number of transdisciplinary projects in Austria, Switzerland and Central America in the area of education, technology-enhanced mobile learning and information management in a university and corporate context. He published a number of articles in these areas and is a member of several international practical and scientific networks such as the London Mobile Learning Group. His current work and research activities focus on the area of mobile learning, work-based learning and medical learning.

Contact: christoph.pimmer@fhnw.ch

Prof. Dr Jan Recker, Queensland University of Technology

Jan is Professor for Information Systems and Woolworths Chair for Retail Innovation at Queensland University of Technology. His research focuses on process design practices, IT-enabled business transformations and organizational innovation. He has written over 100 books, journal articles and conference proceedings. He occupies editorial roles for several international journals and serves on the program committee of various conferences. He is Academic Director for Corporate Education and Consultancy at QUT and has provided consultancy and education services to over 30 Australian organizations.

Contact: j.recker@qut.edu.au

Prof. Dr B. Sebastian Reiche, Assistant Professor of Managing People in Organizations, IESE Business School

B. Sebastian Reiche is Assistant Professor in the Department of Managing People in Organizations at IESE Business School, Spain. He earned his PhD from the University of Melbourne, Australia. His research focuses on how actors access, maintain and leverage knowledge resources in multinational companies, and has appeared in scholarly journals such as the *Journal of International Business Studies* and *Human Resource Management*. Prof. Reiche teaches courses on human resource management, leadership and cross-cultural management in MBA and executive programs, and he maintains an extensive blog on topics related to expatriation (http://blog.iese.edu/expatriatus).

Contact: sreiche@iese.edu

Thomas Rennebaum has been working for Volkswagen Financial Services since 2003. After being involved with the Direktbank and with key accounts he is currently responsible for the marketing department. Before that he was working for Commerzbank and CortalConsors for several years where he had management functions in the areas of marketing and sales.

Prof. Dr Michael Rosemann, Director of the Information Systems Program, Queensland University of Technology

Dr Michael Rosemann is the author/editor of seven books, more than 200 refereed papers, editorial board member of ten international journals and co-inventor of two US patents. His research projects received funding from industry partners such as Accenture, Brisbane Airport, Infosys, Rio Tinto, Queensland Government, SAP and Woolworths. Dr Rosemann is a Visiting Professor at Viktoria Institute, Gothenburg, Sweden.

Contact: m.rosemann@qut.edu.au

Niz Safrudin, PhD Student, Queensland University of Technology

Niz is a PhD student within QUT's Information Systems School. Her research focuses on business transformation management and is funded by SAP BTA. She is currently investigating how services from various management disciplines are orchestrated in business transformations, inspired by (jazz) music orchestration. Prior to her PhD, Niz's background is in business process management, where her honours study on how novices model business processes won a best paper award at a BPM conference in the USA. Ms Safrudin is also an enthusiastic sessional academic who tutors corporate systems and business process modeling for both undergraduate and post-graduate students at QUT.

Contact: norizan.safrudin@qut.edu.au

Thomas Schild, Director Strategic Risk Management, SAP AG

Thomas is Director Strategic Risk Management within SAP's Global Governance, Risk and Compliance organization. He joined SAP in 1999 as marketing manager for Public Services. In 2004 he became business development manager for the Public Services Business Unit covering different roles and responsibilities including market strategy and portfolio planning and operations. Thomas has more than 20 years of business experience in product management, marketing, press and analyst relations, business development, operations, strategic planning and strategy development. Before joining SAP, Thomas had been working in the media and the IT sector in various positions. He holds a business and computer science degree from the University of Applied Sciences of Augsburg.

Contact: thomas.schild@sap.com

Daniel Schmid, Vice President, Head of Sustainability Operations, SAP AG

Daniel Schmid holds a degree in industrial engineering from the University of Kaiserslautern, Germany. He started his career in 1992 as a consultant at Kiefer & Veittinger, a company for customer relationship management that was acquired by SAP in 1997. From then on Schmid held various senior management positions within SAP Consulting. Since March 2009 he has managed Sustainability Operations at SAP on a global level.

Contact: daniel.schmid@sap.com

Werner Schultheis, Director of IT & Processes, Randstad Deutschland GmbH & Co. KG

Werner Schultheis is Director of IT & Processes at Randstad Germany and member of the supervisory board at VMS AG. After working five years as a project manager in the aerospace and automotive area at the Carl Schenck AG, he moved to Randstad sales management as a branch and afterwards district manager. Before he changed to IT & Processes, he was responsible for business development and product management. He holds a degree in engineering from the TU Darmstadt, Germany.

Contact: werner.schultheis@de.randstad.com

Prof. Dr Philip Stiles, Senior Lecturer in Organisational Behaviour, Cambridge Judge Business School

Philip is a faculty member at Cambridge Judge Business School, University of Cambridge, UK. Philip's research work focuses on transformation, high-performance organizations and human resource management. He works with a number of major companies worldwide and is currently Co-Director of the Centre for Internal Human Resource Management at the University of Cambridge.

Contact: p.stiles@jbs.cam.ac.uk

Paul Stratil, Vice President Corporate IT, SAS Autosystem Technik Verwaltungs GmbH

Paul Stratil, VP Corporate IT at SAS Autosystem Technik Verwaltungs GmbH, is heading the global IT organization. He has 25+ years' experience in the automotive sector with strong international experience at Daimler, Chrysler, Smart and the supplier industry. Based on his academic background as an engineer, he uses IT technology and organizational changes as facilitators for change management and business transformation, focused on innovations, efficiency, establishing strategic direction and shaping high-performance teams.

Contact: stratil@yahoo.com

Prof. Dr Axel Uhl, Head of Business Transformation Academy, SAP AG

Professor Dr Axel Uhl is head of the Business Transformation Academy at SAP. He has been a professor at the University of Applied Sciences and Arts Northwestern Switzerland (FHNW) since 2009. Uhl received his PhD in Economics and completed his Master in Business Information Systems. He started his career at Allianz and has worked for DaimlerChrysler IT Services, KPMG and Novartis. His main areas of research and interest are sustainability and IT, leadership and business transformation management.

Contact: a.uhl@sap.com

Prof. Dr Jan vom Brocke, Director of the Institute of Information Systems, Hilti Chair of Business Process Management, University of Liechtenstein

Professor Dr Jan vom Brocke is the Hilti Chair of Business Process Management at the University of Liechtenstein, Director of the Institute of Information Systems and President of the Liechtenstein Chapter of the Association for Information Systems. He has more than 15 years of experience in IT and BPM projects, and has published more than 170 peer-reviewed papers in the proceedings of internationally perceived conferences and renowned academic journals, including the *Business Process Management Journal* (BPMJ), *Business & Information Systems Engineering* (BISE) and *Management Information Systems Quarterly* (MISQ). He serves as a reviewer and editor for major IS conferences and journals including the *Journal of the Association for Information Systems* (JAIS) and the *Journal of Management Information Systems* (JMIS). He is author and co-editor of 16 books, including Springer's *International Handbook on Business Process Management* and the recently published Springer book *Green BPM – Towards the Sustainable Enterprise*. Apart from Liechtenstein, Jan teaches at a number of international universities including Addis Ababa University in Ethiopia and the University of St Gallen in Switzerland. He is an invited speaker and trusted adviser on IT and BPM around the globe.

Contact: jan.vom.brocke@uni.li

Dr Michael von der Horst, Managing Director Internet Solutions Group, Cisco Systems GmbH
Dr von der Horst is in charge of Cisco's eBusiness consulting unit for Financial Services in EMEAR. His team advises executives of Fortune 500 Financial Services Industry (FSI) customers on strategic business topics at the intersection of technology and business issues. Before joining Cisco in 1999, he was with the Boston Consulting Group for 10 years. He holds an MSc in computer sciences, a PhD in business administration from the Handelshochschule Leipzig and an MBA from INSEAD.

Contact: mvonderh@cisco.com

Prof. John Ward, Emeritus Professor, Cranfield University, School of Management
John was Professor of Strategic Information Systems and Director of the IS Research Centre at Cranfield prior to retiring in 2010. He is the co-author of the books *Strategic Planning for Information Systems* and *Benefits Management* and has published many papers in leading journals. John has a degree in Natural Sciences from Cambridge, is a Fellow of the Chartered Institute of Management Accountants and is a past-President of the UK Academy for Information Systems.

Contact: j.m.ward@cranfield.ac.uk

Prof. Dr Robert Winter, Professor and Director of the Institute of Information Management, University of St Gallen
Robert Winter is Full Professor of Information Management and Director of the Institute of Information Management, University of St Gallen (HSG). He is academic director of HSG's Executive Master of Business Engineering and HSG's PhD in Management programs. His research areas include situational method engineering, information logistics management, Enterprise Architecture management, integration management, healthcare network management and corporate controlling systems.

Contact: robert.winter@unisg.ch

Prof. Dr Felix Wortmann, Assistant Professor, University of St Gallen
Felix Wortmann is Assistant Professor at the Institute of Information Management, University of St Gallen. His research interests include business intelligence, big data and smart energy. From 2006 to 2009 he worked as an assistant to the executive board of SAP. He received a BScIS and MScIS from the University of Muenster and a PhD in Management from the University of St Gallen.

Acknowledgments

We gratefully acknowledge all the help and support we received, especially from the many business and IT managers, consultants and academics whose ideas and feedback enabled us to create this book. Their commitment and expertise did not only ensure that the methodology has been tried and tested in a wide area of business transformations initiatives, but also proved its relevance and value. For example the case study presented in chapter 11 is based on a real transformation initiative.

We would also like to thank the SAP organization and the University of Applied Sciences and Arts Northwestern Switzerland, especially Nicolas Steib and Prof. Dr Rolf Dornberger, for providing the necessary infrastructure..

Finally, we want to particularly thank Tomasz Janasz for preparing the manuscript as well as Dr Matthias Born and Dr Agnes Koschmider for their careful review and insightful comments which helped improving the quality of this work.

Preface

Companies across industries keep transforming their businesses to stay ahead of the game. There are many successful transformations to report: Apple, the former producer of computer hardware, is now the most expensively evaluated company at NYSE. The business model has changed dramatically from hardware-only to integrated consumer solutions. This led to an increase in net income from about US$1.3 billion in 2005 to almost US$26 billion in 2011.[1] Apple's success is not only a result of the perfectionism and the aura of its legendary leader Steve Jobs, but also based on its strong ability to understand customer needs and to transform along with the constant changes and advancements of today's markets.

Conversely, companies that do not transform their business fail. Recent studies show that companies that did not see the need or did not take successful actions to transform are no longer around. The comparison of the Fortune 100 list from 1966 with the one from 2006 compellingly demonstrates that as many as 66 of those companies don't exist any more. The rest of them have managed to survive but only 19 are still featured on the mentioned list.[2]

One recent example of such a failure is Kodak. A market leader in film-based business, Kodak at some point of time was not able to deal with the technological change from film-based business models to digital photography. In January 2012 the company eventually filed for bankruptcy. Ironically, Kodak even had invented the digital camera. However, the company was not able to tackle the challenges of this new technology and to transform its business model accordingly. Hence, the downturn of Kodak did not result from its incapability to innovate but from its fear of change and the consequences of a required transformation during a time when they were very successful.

The important question is: What makes one company succeed in their transformation and why do others fail?

SAP, the world-leader in ERP software solutions, is constantly supporting companies to become best-run businesses. In the past, SAP has helped many businesses around the world to transform from good to great companies. However, we recognize that not all companies have been completely successful in taking advantage of proven SAP software products. For example, we observed that out of five attempts to transform HR in global companies only one was totally successful, two were partly successful (delivering some but not all the benefits and taking longer than expected) and two were failures, abandoned before completion at enormous cost.

Overall we recognize that only every third business transformation project is completed on time, on budget and to expectations.[3] Furthermore we learn from our own

---

1   Statista (2011), Net income of Apple Inc. 2011: www.statista.com/statistics/155091/net-income-of-apple-inc-since-2005 (accessed April 2012).

2   Vermeulen, Freek (2010), *Business Exposed: The Naked Truth About What Really Goes on in the World of Business* (Harlow, New York: Financial Times/Prentice Hall).

3   The Standish Group, New Standish Group report shows more project failing and less successful projects: www.standishgroup.com/newsroom/chaos_2009.php (accessed May 2012).

research that 97 percent of all companies believe that they could derive even more value from their SAP investments.[4]

With this book, SAP is going beyond providing software and services, but providing the best-in-class methodology that needs to be applied for a successful business transformation. SAP has established the Business Transformation Academy, a global and interdisciplinary network of experts from science and practice. Under the leadership of the BTA, academia, representatives from our strategic clients and the most knowledgeable SAP business consultants have worked together in developing a holistic business transformation management methodology that combines and effectively integrates important individual disciplines such as Strategy Management, Business Process Management and Organizational Change Management to form a unified whole. This methodology is aimed primarily at management in business and IT organizations, providing practical support, forming a framework that reduces complexity, and helping to bring about the expected changes and added value of transformation. This book also discusses important findings from a variety of transformation projects and offers suggestions on how to increase the long-term transformational readiness of organizations. In doing so, we want to make another contribution to ensure a successful future for our customers and partners.

Lars Alexander Gollenia

---

4   SAP AG (2009), *Value Management: Driving Success Through Best Practices*: www.bta-online.com/kb/?p=141 (accessed May 2012).

CHAPTER 1
Introduction

AXEL UHL (SAP AG)

1.1 Overview

The ability to manage business transformation is vital for companies to stay competitive. Business transformation implies fundamental and complex organizational changes, not only within companies but also across the entire value chain. This can also radically change the relationship between a company and its wider economic and social environment. Typical examples of business transformations are outsourcing business processes, business model changes, mergers and acquisitions, or cross-functional and (inter- or intra-) organizational restructuring actions (Uhl and Pimmer, 2011).

Sustainable and successful companies react quickly to changing business environments and provide innovation in terms of client offerings and organizational structures. Furthermore, the ability to predict future demands and trends, or even to create new markets, relies on the capability to execute and implement a business transformation.

Only a minority of companies managed to transform themselves successfully. Various problems occur during the transformation process, including lack of top-level management support, poor implementation and execution of the transformation process, lack of skills and competences, resistance against changes, or conflicts of interests.

The transformation process is complex and time-consuming, and is influenced not only by all major core disciplines of an organization but also by its environment, such as customers, competitors, government and regulators, as well as investors. In other words, transformation always occurs within an entire ecosystem. In order to execute a successful transformation process, the management of a meta-routine is crucial.

BTM² provides a holistic and integrative perspective on the organization and the entire complexity of its ecosystem. It does not reinvent the individual management disciplines but rather provides a framework that integrates individual ones. The basis of the framework are the Meta Management disciplines, which provide the foundations for the success of other management disciplines including Strategy Management, Value Management, Process Management, Risk Management, Transformational IT Management, Competence and Training Management, and Program Management. Each individual discipline is well developed, including a large body of knowledge supporting them, and targets a specific group of professional people. Although, each group is very valuable for the organization, there exists a strong tendency for separation and a lack of integration between different departments. Many sources refer to this fragmentation of the organization as a major reason for failure during the transformation process and for the increased risk of resistance.

BTM² MOTIVATION:

1. Lack of a holistic, integrative, and scientifically proven business transformation management methodology (Lahrmann et al., 2011).
2. Low success rate of business transformation projects (less than 40 percent) (Isern et al., 2009).

This book presents BTM² as a new approach to business transformation management and provides a holistic and integrative methodology to address the difficulties in all kinds of transformation projects. Under the leadership of the Business Transformation Academy (BTA), an interdisciplinary team comprising 34 thought leaders from psychology, information technology, strategic management, process management and social sciences joined together to create a "360-degree" view of what business transformation means and how business transformation can be successfully executed by organizations. In general, one expert from SAP AG and one expert from SAP customers, as well as an academic expert, collaborated in each chapter.

OBJECTIVES OF THE BTM² HANDBOOK:

1. Provide guidance in planning and executing business transformation projects.
2. Provide a holistic, integrative, and generic approach.
3. Address different types of transformation projects.
4. Combine knowledge of all related organizational disciplines.

In contrast to existing literature, methodologies and procedures, the three distinctive areas of this book are:

1. *Providing a comprehensible, adaptable, holistic and integrative approach to business transformation.* Although it is commonly agreed that transformation is of strategic relevance, a conceptually robust and practical method to achieve this was missing. BTM² provides such a holistic and integrative methodology.
2. *Emphasizing the balance between rational and emotional aspects of transformation.* Many sources refer to business transformation as a technocratic exercise, where the success depends on an accurate diagnosis of need and an appropriate selection of communication means. Failure is justified by poor requirements analysis or insufficient communication. However, the emotional readiness of employees to absorb and accept transformation initiatives cannot be underestimated. This handbook specifically considers the rational and emotional aspects of business transformation.
3. *Providing an execution guide. This handbook discusses a wide range of theory and practice to understand the phenomenon of business transformation. However, it is primarily a practical work.* Often, managers in business transformation contexts know what to do, and yet they fail to execute. This phenomenon is an enduring feature of organizational life; in this book, highlighting how to close the knowing-doing gap is a major priority.

Within this handbook, we provide new content on key elements of business transformation management and new insights from case studies of recent business transformations, both successful and unsuccessful, which were used to develop and test the methodology. The book is intended for a wide audience: reflective managers, consultants, C-level executives and academics – indeed, everybody who is involved in business transformation.

BTM² VALUE PROPOSITION:
1. First integrative and holistic business transformation management methodology.
2. Provides a framework with clear phases, deliverables and corresponding methods.
3. Validated through leading universities and business schools.
4. Intensive research and case studies.
5. "Think tanks" for focus topics.
6. Provides best practice templates and accelerators.

1.2 Background on Business Transformation Management

Transformation is a common procedure for most, if not all, organizations. On the one hand, exogenous changes such as sustainability, technological innovations, globalization, economic conditions and the changing nature of the workforce have a profound impact on the way organizations execute business (Arthurs and Busenitz, 2006; Eisenhardt and Sull, 2001). On the other hand, endogenous changes such as product innovation, restructuring and new business model adoption also potentially result in large-scale transformation and consequently a disruption in the workplace (Donaldson, 1987; Eisenhardt and Bourgeois, 1988). Organizations require an excellent transformation process in order to sustain competitive advantage.

There exists a great body of literature designed to guide managers and their companies through the change process, and certainly there is an enormous amount of material, both in academic and practitioner literature, which provides solid prescriptions as to how transformations are executed and delivered (see, for example, Bogner and Barr, 2000; D'Aveni, 1994). From the practical point of view, awareness and understanding of the key concepts are well established, but the integration of these concepts and their execution within transformation programs is less well understood. From an academic point of view, theoretical work on transformation has coalesced around a series of frameworks that provide a reassuring abstraction but are largely silent on the practicalities of linking elements in a coherent and effective manner, particularly when this entails dealing with the complexity involved in most transformations.

Yet, despite the plethora of books, cases and how-to manuals, the transformation process remains a body of failure. One reason for failure in the transformation process is that it addresses the future. Therefore, transformation represents an experiment, which, due to different exigencies or unintended consequences, often turns out in different ways than originally anticipated. In addition, transformation always involves people, and so the issues of personality, attitude, capability to change and political behavior emerge, which are, by their nature, very difficult to predict and control. Considering the overall impact, the management of business transformation plays a critical role.

Business transformation management is the holistic management of extensive, complex changes on which the organization's future success strongly depends (FHNW, 2012).

Each transformation process is fragmented, consisting of various elements. However, the connections between these elements are either not developed or articulated, or they become fuzzy as the business transformation progresses, particularly to the people who are on the receiving end (Davenport, 1993; Galbraith, 1982). The problem of unconnected elements results from the assumption that change is linear and a unitary process or routine. Business transformation is not a unitary routine but a meta-routine, representing a set of routines which must be joined together in order to function properly (Feldman and Pentland, 2003). This is rooted in the idea of dynamic capabilities, the set of practices and processes that are required for the organization to recombine and revitalize itself (Teece, 2007; Helfat et al., 2007; Teece et al., 1997). As such, we clearly differentiate between traditional change management efforts and the management of business transformations. Change management focuses on behavioral changes and only considers a small set of clearly defined goals, whereas business transformation management provides a holistic view of the entire organization, considering complex changes to the business.

Nevertheless, the fundamentals of both are based on the same principles (Doz and Thanheiser, 1993). These have been developed over a long period of time and represent a solid conceptual and general knowledge of the entire change process. An important concept with respect to change management is called step models (Jick and Peiperl, 2002). These models identify a number of core activities and recommend an optimal execution route in order to maximize the success of the change process. The core of these models is a classic formulation of three phases: current state, future state and transition state, usually supported by a gap and force-field analysis (Kotter, 1990; Lewin, 1972). Step models are discussed in numerous change management literature and set the path for consultancy interventions in change management. An essential characteristic of the models is a combination of rational elements – for example, diagnosing need, shaping the vision and monitoring progress – and emotional elements – for example, mobilizing commitment, engaging with the vision, and building affinity and identity with the change.

Step models produced a wide variety of course books for managing change, concerning leadership, culture, influencing staff, and embedding change and maintaining momentum.

However, there are two major issues raised by the usage of step models. First, they imply a linear approach to change management, with each step leading to the next. Feedback loops are included generally, in the models, but essentially these are mechanistic approaches to change. Second, there is very little in the models to show the *nature of the linkage* between each step, so although each individual element of the model is outlined, how the overall change process is handled is less clear. This is problematic, both theoretically and practically. In theoretical terms, how change is managed as a collection of routines remains a missing piece in our understanding with step models, and though there have been calls to approach change from a holistic point of view, such calls have not been taken up in this tradition. In practical terms, how transformation is enacted not just in a piecemeal way but in an additive, synchronized manner has little by way of precedent in the extant literature.

For a meta-routine such as business transformation, the *coordination* between separate management disciplines is essential. It is vital to address the identified issues if business transformation management is to be effective. The first is that business transformation is a multilevel phenomenon. Behavior at the individual level will affect both group and organizational outcomes in terms of change. Similarly, change imposed from the top of the organization will have direct and indirect effects with levels lower down. Given the complexity of organizations, the interactions between levels will be complex and often non-linear.

1.3 Distinction to Other Frameworks and Methodologies

There are a number of approaches which do seek to take a holistic view; however, the existing approaches do not consider the key requirements to business transformation. In this section, we outline the differences and advantages of BTM² in comparison to traditional frameworks and methodologies.

ENTERPRISE ARCHITECTURE

Enterprise Architecture (EA) describes an approach to manage the rational efforts such as blueprint development or implementation with the aim to deliver a solution of the highest quality to the customer's satisfaction. It is an IT-driven framework and focuses on describing the architecture of an enterprise in order to improve the effectiveness and efficiency of the business. The foundation of Enterprise Architecture is to analyze the current business situation and to define relevant goals to be reached in the future.

EA management addresses big changes and small changes, whether in IT systems, business processes or data. It helps to understand what exists in the business now and what it will look like in future, where change takes place and happens, and to create artefacts that model these changes so everyone is clear. Despite ongoing efforts to further develop the business focus, value focus and/or strategy focus of EA frameworks, the main value proposition of EA management is to align IT solutions better with business needs. As a consequence, EA management would not be used, for example, to assess how much transformation an organization needs, how much transformation can be achieved in a certain time frame, whether an organizations culture needs to be (and can be) changed, whether political powers in an organization support or inhibit a certain transformation, just to name a few examples.

In contrast, BTM² intends to support the business in defining and implementing significant business transformation. As a consequence, it would not be used to manage a pure data migration or a technical upgrade where no business change is involved. It would also not be used to manage small, incremental change even if the business side is affected.

The addressed problems differ in their extent – while BTM² focuses on fundamental business change, EA management is applied for IT/business alignment, and to manage incremental changes as well. EA management specifies the "what" and therefore both the as-is state and the state that should be reached in order to achieve certain goals. BTM²'s primary object is the "how" process that focuses on the capabilities in the firm in order to ensure the best execution and situational adoption of this plan (e.g. in terms of ROI). In the end, both approaches aim for cost reduction and value creation. However, due to significant differences in users, goals, value creation logic, control, width, "deepness" mandatory skills and organization, EA management and BTM² should be regarded as different management approaches (Winter et al., 2012).

LEAN MANAGEMENT

Lean management is a longer-term process of continuous improvement. It takes time to develop the values and practices that this requires in all parties concerned. Adopting a holistic approach, targets, methods and tools are combined in such a way that, ultimately, an appropriate corporate culture is created in which everyone automatically asks themselves: "What can I do better today than I did yesterday?" So the employees themselves give the impulses for specific improvements (bottom-up), thereby generating a chain of many smaller changes. A lean transformation is not geared primarily towards cost reduction but towards the continuous quality and efficiency improvement of processes and products, with savings being a natural consequence. In order to implement lean management professionally, it is very helpful to establish a relevant organizational unit, which develops methods and qualifications. It has a considerable influence on the success of the transformation if managers lead by example, and practice the targets and principles of lean management themselves.

In contrast to lean management, business transformations are operated top-down, have a clear objective and define benefits to be achieved. The changes involved usually have a huge effect on the entire company. The key question here is about effectiveness: "Are we doing the right thing?" So the degree of change within a given period of time is correspondingly high and, therefore, also the risk of failing. The transformations referred to, and other practical experiences, have shown that a holistic approach is required to do full justice to the complex nature of business transformations. Since both the frequency and the ruthlessness of business transformations are on the increase, it makes a great deal of sense to establish the appropriate organizational and methodological competencies as fixed components in a company.

To manage the respective challenges correctly, one has to differentiate between a restructuring approach in the sense of business transformation, and the implementation of lean management. Bottom-up evolutionary change corresponds to lean transformation and, based on the same rationale, top-down revolutionary change corresponds to business transformation. The differences and similarities are summarized in Table 1.1.

Table 1.1   Comparison of lean transformation and business transformation

	Lean transformation	Business transformation
Transformation type	Continuous optimization	Major change
Timescale	Long term	Medium term
Transformation focus	Mainly efficiency	Mainly effectiveness
Transformation orientation	Bottom-up	Top-down
Role of managers	Important	Very important
Organizational anchor	Highly recommended	Highly recommended

MCKINSEY 7s FRAMEWORK

The McKinsey 7s framework is a management model to assess and monitor changes in the internal situation of an organization. The framework consists of seven core elements of an organization: structure, strategy, systems, skills, style, staff and shared values. An organization performs well under process of change if these elements are aligned and mutually reinforced (Peters and Waterman, 1984).

The approach describes diagnostic techniques rather than an analysis or implementation technique. Therefore, it is useful in analytics terms but does not consider specific aspects of the change elements or their linkages. BTM² provides this holistic and integrative methodology.

BALANCED SCORECARD

The balanced scorecard approach identifies a number of core areas, such as financial, customer, process and people (Kaplan and Norton, 2003). It provides a utility to define and cascade performance measures and targets (not necessarily economical ones), and develop a balanced target system. Furthermore, the balanced scorecard is used to control and measure the progress and achievement of the defined targets. This approach shows the inter-linkages between the various areas and is helpful in providing guidance to meta-management; however, it does not present a methodology for the process of transforming organizations.

1.4 Structure of the Book

This handbook is designed to address a fundamental need in our understanding of transformation. In the extensive transformation literature as well as in much company practice, there is a lack of a *holistic* and *integrative* business transformation management methodology. The aim of the handbook is to provide such a methodology. BTM² is generic enough to serve all different types of transformation programs but it is important to emphasize that the expertise and intuition of the transformation manager is needed to adjust the method to the specific context and requirements of the particular organization.

Business transformation ranges across the entire organization and implies changes in a variety of disciplines. This handbook describes each individual management discipline in detail and is organized in the following chapters:

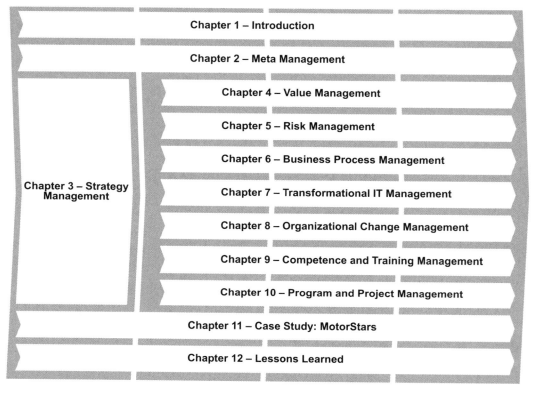

Figure 1.1   Structure of the handbook

Chapter 2: Meta Management provides the general framework to ensure the integration and success of the other management disciplines. In this chapter, we establish the general conditions of BTM² and provide guidance how to execute it.

Chapter 3: Strategy Management analyzes the needs and the causes for business transformation, as well as transformation readiness. In this chapter, we explain how to develop a successful transformation strategy, vision and roadmap. Strategy management assesses the organizational readiness and possible strategic risks, and outlines the expected results of business transformation.

Chapter 4: Value Management covers the objectives of business transformation and explains how key stakeholders can define business benefits and necessary changes in order to realize those objectives. The emphasis of this chapter lies in the creation of a clear understanding of the benefits to be achieved, the measurements, responsibilities and change needed.

Chapter 5: Risk Management elaborates on strategic and operational risks, which might jeopardize the success of the business transformation. The chapter develops approaches to mitigate and manage the identified risks along the enablement phase. In addition, risk management establishes emergency guides for upcoming or unidentified risks during the execution phase.

Chapter 6: Business Processes Management defines the scope of process changes and the expected improvements in performance. In this chapter, we explain how existing processes are discovered and (re)designed and new processes are introduced. Furthermore, the scope of discretion to change processes and align them to the local environment is discussed. The chapter also presents how process changes are implemented and their performance is evaluated.

Chapter 7: Transformational IT Management assesses to which extent IT changes are essential to enable a successful business transformation. The chapter provides a technology acquisition and deployment plan to create the new and necessary business information and systems architecture. Furthermore, we explain the required implementation and testing procedures of the new technologies and the development of the operational service(s) to ensure their effective utilization and performance.

Chapter 8: Organizational Change Management identifies the required types of changes and analyzes their impact on various parts of the organization, as well as the external ecosystem. The chapter explains how to select change approaches that handle the change types and respect the stakeholder interests during the business transformation. Furthermore, we describe how to produce a change plan in order to deliver the performance levels required without excessive business disruption. Finally, the chapter summarizes roles and responsibilities for carrying out the business transformation, and shows how to manage stakeholder relationships and establish mechanisms for monitoring the effectiveness of both implementation and subsequent organizational performance.

Chapter 9: Competence and Training Management focuses on the organizational competencies and individual skills as critical success factors of business transformation and future businesses. The chapter explains how to identify new or enhanced competences and skills, as well as roles and people, required during business transformation. Furthermore, we discuss necessary facilities and material in order to support staff and others, as well as provide estimations if they have been effectively deployed.

Chapter 10: Program and Project Management considers the program governance structure, roles and team structures, and reporting relationships to enable "best practice" program and project approaches and techniques to be deployed in executing the business transformation. The chapter determines how the overall program can be delivered through manageable combinations of projects that make the most effective use of available resources and how costs, quality and time will be monitored and controlled.

Chapter 11: Case Study: Motostars – Implementation of a Global HR System in an Automotive Company describes the protracted, challenging and costly attempts of a fictional automotive company to transform the strategic alignment of its HR department by implementing a shared service center and HR IT system. The chapter summarizes a number of characteristic elements executing business transformation.

Chapter 12: Lessons Learned from Business Transformation Case Studies presents the results of analyzing various business transformation projects, which were executed in large European corporations ranging across different industries including automotive, pharmaceuticals, construction, food, oil and chemicals, financial services, telecommunications and IT. The business transformations consider the development of

Orchestration of individual disciplines:
guidelines, leadership, culture, values and communication

Meta Management

Direction

Enablement

Strategy Management	Value Management	Risk Management	Business Process Management	Transformational IT Management	Organizational Change Management	Competence and Training Management	Program and Project Management
As-is data collection	Baseline analysis	360° strategic risk assessment	Determine scope of analysis	Business and IT capability assessment	Set-up and governance	Competence strategy	Program planning and governance
Analysis of needs and maturity level	Value estimation	Risk identification	From template to bespoke inventory	To-be analysis	Stakeholder management	Training need analysis	Program/project integration management
Design business vision	Detailed business case	Risk evaluation	Identify improvements/add attributes	Gap analysis	Change agent network	As-is analysis	Program/project scope management
Design business model	Agree ownership for realization	Define risk response plan	Map selected processes	IT roadmap plan	Communication management	Gap analysis	Program/project time and cost management
Integrated transformation plan	Plan benefit realization	Execute risk mitigation plan	Plan process implementation	Solution architecture design	Performance management – project team	Curriculum development	Program quality management
Business case	Execute benefit realization	Risk monitoring and reporting	Implement processes	IT deployment plan	Performance management – business	Training preparation	Program human resource management
Organizational model	Review and evaluate results	Risk management review	Evaluate processes	IT operations and service optimization	Change readiness assessment	Training	Program procurement management
Align with risk management	Establish potentials for further benefits	Risk management improvement	Establish improvement process	IT lifecycle management	Change monitoring	Evaluation and improvement	Program reporting

Figure 1.2   The BTM² – Big Picture

new products and services as well as the restructuring and reorganization of core business functions and introduction of global processes and systems.

The most important activities of each management disciplines are summarized in the BTM² Big Picture (see Figure 1.2). The boxes under each management discipline do not necessary represent the sequential order of the individual activities; instead, the authors included the major buzz words for each discipline.

BTM² is a generic framework which can be applied to different business transformation use cases, such as implementation of Enterprise Resource Planning systems, introduction of shared service centers, business process outsourcing or post-merger integration.

The methodology presented in this handbook is not meant to be a cookbook that describes the exact ingredients of a meal and the concrete procedure how to cook it. Instead, the goal is to outline and describe all relevant aspects of business transformation approaches, and to provide guidance in order to ensure that important aspects during business transformation are not neglected or forgotten. The handbook targets the management groups that focus and specialize in business transformation procedures. BTM² connects the leadership aspects with functional and subject-specific disciplines in order to provide a holistic approach and simultaneously reduce the irrational effort (see Figure 1.3) of a business transformation.

Irrational effort e.g.:
- fears because of e.g. mass layoffs
- personal ambitions and interests
- hidden agendas
- political behavior and actions.

Rational effort e.g.:
- technical implementation
- financial aspects
- human resources.

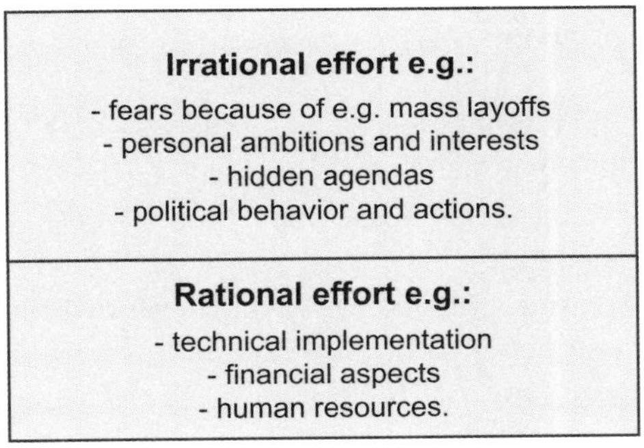

Figure 1.3   Irrational and rational efforts in business transformation

Bibliography

Arthurs, Jonathan D. and Busenitz, Lowell W. (2006), Dynamic capabilities and venture performance: the effects of venture capitalists, *Journal of Business Venturing* 21, no. 2, 195–215.

Bogner, William C. and Barr, Pamela S. (2000), Making sense in hypercompetitive environments: a cognitive explanation for the persistence of high velocity competition, *Organization Science* 11, no. 2, 212–26.

D'Aveni, Richard A. (1994), *Hypercompetition: Managing the Dynamics of Strategic Maneuvering* (New York: The Free Press).

Davenport, Thomas H. (1993), *Process Innovation: Reengineering Work Through Information Technology* (Boston, USA: Harvard Business School Press).

Donaldson, Lex (1987), Strategy and structural adjustment to regain fit and performance: in defence of contingency theory, *Journal of Management Studies* 24, no. 1, 1–24.

Doz, Yves L. and Thanheiser, Heinz (1993), Regaining competitiveness: a process of organisational renewal, in *Strategic Thinking: Leadership and the Management of Change*, edited by John Hendry, Gerry Johnson and Julia Newton (Chichester, New York: Wiley).

Eisenhardt, Kathleen M. and Bourgeois, L.J. (1988), Politics of strategic decision making in high-velocity environments: toward a midrange theory, *Academy of Management Journal* 31, no. 4, 737–70.

Eisenhardt, Kathleen M. and Sull, Donald N. (2001), Strategy as simple rules, *Harvard Business Review* 79, no. 1, 107–16.

Feldman, Martha S. and Pentland, Brian T. (2003), Reconceptualizing organizational routines as a source of flexibility and change, *Administrative Science Quarterly* 48, no. 1, 94–118.

FHNW (2012) Business transformation management, www.fhnw.ch/business/iwi/kompetenzschwerpunkte/business-transformation-management/business-transformation-management?set_language=en (accessed April 2012).

Galbraith, Jay R. (1982), Designing the innovating organization, *Organizational Dynamics* 10, no. 3, 5–25.

Helfat, Constance E., Finkelstein, Sydney, Peteraf, Will M.M., Singh, Harbir, Teece, David and Winter, Sidney (2007), *Dynamic Capabilities: Understanding Strategic Change in Organizations* (Malden, MA: Blackwell Pub.).

Isern, Josep, Meaney, Mary C. and Wilson, Sarah (2009), Corporate transformation under pressure, *McKinsey Quarterly* April (McKinsey & Company).

Jick, Todd D. and Peiperl, Maury A. (2002), *Managing Change: Cases and Concepts* (London: McGraw-Hill).

Kaplan, Robert S. and Norton, David P. (2003), Keeping your balance with customers, HBS Working Knowledge, http://hbswk.hbs.edu/item/3588.html (accessed March 2012).

Kotter, John P. (1990), *A Force for Change: How Leadership Differs from Management* (New York: Free Press, Collier Macmillan).

Lahrmann, Geritt, Winter, Robert and Uhl, Axel (2011), Transformation management survey: current state of development and potential of transformation management in practice, *360° – The Business Transformation Journal* June, no. 1, 29–37.

Lewin, Kurt (1972), Need, force and valence in psychological fields, in *Classic Contributions to Social Psychology*, edited by Edwin Paul Hollander and Raymond George Hunt (London: Oxford University Press).

Peters, Thomas J. and Waterman, Robert H. (1984), *In Search of Excellence: Lessons from America's Best-run Companies* (New York, NY: Warner Books).

Teece, David J. (2007), Explicating dynamic capabilities: the nature and microfoundations of (sustainable) enterprise performance, *Strategic Management Journal* 28, no. 13, 1319–50.

Teece, David J., Pisano, Gary and Shuen, Amy (1997), Dynamic capabilities and strategic management, *Strategic Management Journal* 18, no. 7, 509–33.

Uhl, Axel and Pimmer, Christoph (2011), Transdisciplinary knowledge for business transformation: the diverse potential of a global network of experts, *360° – The Business Transformation Journal* June, no. 1, 21–8.

Winter, Robert, Townson, Simon, Uhl, Axel, Labusch, Nils and Noack, Jörg (2012), Enterprise Architecture and Transformation: the difference and synergy potential, *360° – The Business Transformation Journal* forthcoming.

2 *Meta Management*

PHILIP STILES (Cambridge Judge Business School),
AXEL UHL (SAP AG) and PAUL STRATIL (SAS Autosystem
Technik Verwaltungs GmbH)

2.1 Overview

Every business transformation is different. The success depends on the complex interplay of actors in a multifaceted ecosystem. According to this understanding, the focus of meta management as the fundamental discipline in BTM^2 lies in providing a frame that helps to manage the complexity of business transformation.

This chapter presents Meta Management as a general discipline for business transformation, which is based on a *holistic* and *integrative* management approach. Meta Management is business-driven value-oriented, and integrates three pillars, namely: management disciplines, transformation lifecycle and leadership. A business transformation process is only successful if the leaders are aware of their roles and communication and have established a solid culture. These meta management principles are also sketched in this chapter since their implementation constitutes an important basis for the success of the overall BTM^2 framework.

In summary, the following (general) guidelines need to be considered to execute a successful business transformation project:

1. Orchestrate the individual management disciplines as an integrated and holistic approach.
2. Specify the cascade of the overall transformational goals for each management discipline and organizational member.
3. Install and establish the transformation lifecycle with the four phases: envision, engage, transform and optimize.
4. Assign roles and involve the business transformation manager in the process of transformation.
5. Create commitment across all involved parties and facilitate the buy-in from all important stakeholders and employees.
6. Cultural environment is set by skillful use of communication in order to provide a clear purpose and good understanding of transformation need, benefits, risks and change needed.

2.2 Pillars of Meta Management

Meta Management provides the overarching frame for different management disciplines (e.g. Strategy Management or Risk Management) and offers the linkages among the management disciplines, leadership, culture and communication which allows the transformation process to be effective. In summary, the method has the following advantages:

- It provides an iterative lifecycle model (envision, engage, transform, optimize), which allows understanding business transformation as a holistic process.
- It offers an overall business transformation structure, including management layers, formal and informal management roles.
- It focuses on the dimensions of the balanced scorecard for planning and controlling measures. Thus, meta management reuses a widely used performance management method.
- It delivers decision criteria for choosing the right leaders and promoters for key positions and facilitates transformational leadership.
- It helps to create culture and values on the basis of transformation principles and guidelines to internalize and institutionalize the transformation goals.
- It provides communication and engagement principles, and supports feedback loops.

This chapter does not provide a detailed cookbook. It is much more a coherent and consistent framework that reduces complexity, but which still must be adapted to the specific company by using the experience of involved individuals. Each company and each business transformation is different. Thus, simply copying "recipes for success" from one company can produce disastrous results at another.

2.2.1 BUSINESS TRANSFORMATION GOAL SETTING

The first important pillar of Meta Management is dealing with management disciplines, which are coherently integrated within this approach. BTM² includes several management disciplines: Strategy Management, Value Management, Risk Management, Business Process Management, Program and Project Management, Transformational IT Management, Organizational Change Management, as well as Competence and Training Management. Typically, each management discipline has a foundation set of knowledge, requirements and processes, which traditionally have their own set of assumptions, theory and terminology, rendering them largely opaque to colleagues in other disciplines. In turn, this can result in an unconnected overall process, which risks fragmentation and a lack of clarity and cohesion across the entire change chain. To overcome such risks, BTM² integrates and extends these disciplines, and provides a multidisciplinary view on business transformation.

The intention of Meta Management with respect to management disciplines is the orchestration of the overall set of these disciplines within change management, as set out in Figure 2.1.

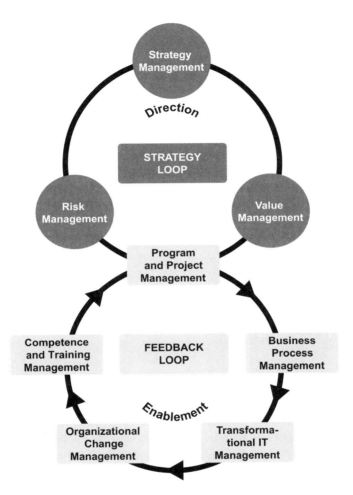

Figure 2.1   The Meta Management framework

The eight management disciplines are chosen in a logical way and are of two types.

1. Directional

The three disciplines of strategy management, value management and risk management can be referred to as the strategy loop of the BTM². Here, the transformation strategy is defined considering time and budget restrictions as well as associated risks. Moreover, the directional disciplines of BTM² create the case for action and vision of the future and set the direction for the transformation effort.

2. Enablement

It encompasses the management and synchronization of changes ranging from IT through process to organizational, plus the creation of new competencies through training and education, orchestrated through an organizational program management capability. The last of these is not about creating a "super-manager" but having people at all levels in the transformation who are well trained and knowledgeable about transformation. "Enablement" can also be referred to as the feedback loop of the BTM^2, where the strategy is being implemented and lessons learned. This learning feedback leads to the adjustment of the transformation strategy.

CHALLENGES CONCERNING THE MANAGEMENT DISCIPLINES:
1.   To understand interdependencies between management disciplines.
2.   To orchestrate the management disciplines efficiently.

KEY MESSAGE:
Business transformation has to balance economic, social and technical aspects. This requires the involvement of fields such as management, psychology and IT, which are mirrored in the nine management disciplines.

2.2.2 TRANSFORMATION LIFECYCLE

The second pillar of meta management is a transformation lifecycle, which provides an overall map of the change territory and allows understanding of the iterative nature of business transformation. Based upon the transformation lifecycle, the business transformation can be efficiently organized. The mistake that hampers a smooth business transformation is considering the transformation process as strictly linear; in essence, the transformation process is iterative and goes through different stages in recurring cycles. Therefore, a stage model with recurring phases is required. Figure 2.2 shows the four steps: envision, engage, transform and optimize. The management disciplines described in Section 2.2.1 are involved in all stages of the transformation lifecycle model since almost any aspect, from the transformation rationale to implementation options, may need to be revisited as the transformation and business context evolve. Inevitably, however, the emphasis will be more on the *directional* disciplines in the early stages and the *enablement* disciplines later.

In the following, we summarize the four phases of the transformation lifecycle and show the outcome and the requirements for each phase.

Envision

This phase embraces the "why" as well as the "how" question of change. "Why is business transformation needed and how capable is the organization to manage the transformation?" This phase diagnoses the need for business transformation. In addition,

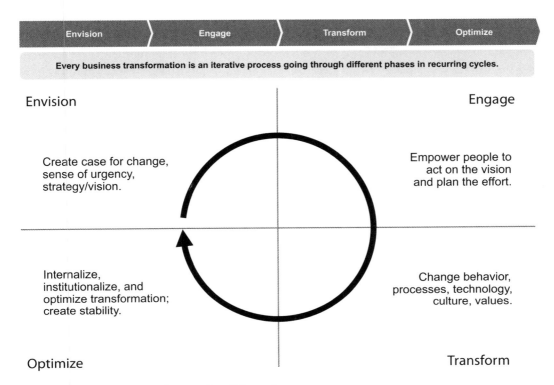

| Envision | Engage | Transform | Optimize |

Every business transformation is an iterative process going through different phases in recurring cycles.

Envision

Create case for change, sense of urgency, strategy/vision.

Engage

Empower people to act on the vision and plan the effort.

Internalize, institutionalize, and optimize transformation; create stability.

Change behavior, processes, technology, culture, values.

Optimize

Transform

Figure 2.2   The transformation lifecycle

the strategy and vision in dealing with the change need are developed. This step therefore combines both analytical capabilities with creativity and foresight. A further goal of the "Envision" phase is to create commitment to the developed strategy within the top management team. Vision is usually at the heart of the transitional process (Collins, 2003) but this does not necessarily mean grand vision – that is, the vision for the entire organization. On occasion, transformation may take place with a department or a business unit. Nor does it mean that business transformation requires visionary leaders (Goffee and Jones, 2000) if this is taken to mean charismatic, guru-like figures. It simply indicates that business transformation must have a clear focus and objective. A major question for managers is: "How capable are we as an organization to do this and to get a stakeholder agreement on the plan?"

Expected outcome:
1. Recognition of the need for business transformation
2. Identification of strategy and vision

Requirements:
1. Analytical capability
2. Creativity
3. Foresight

Engage

This phase represents the mobilizing of commitment in the organization. Involvement and communication are essential here, as well as the establishment of discrete projects to deliver change and drive momentum. Engagement would entail delivering both behavioral and attitudinal buy-in to the transformation. For that, transformation requires a clear understanding throughout the entire organization of what change is required, why it is required, how it is to be achieved and measured, and who is responsible. Detailed planning and continuous alignment with the business functions is required in order to gain commitment throughout the entire organization. The involvement within the middle management and employees especially is required to facilitate the transformation process.

Expected outcome:
1.   Communication of transformation
2.   Establishment of discrete projects

Requirements:
1.   Detailed planning
2.   Alignment with business functions

Transform

Transformation could include reorganization, new business processes and relationships, including creating new business entities, such as shared service centers, relocation and redeployment of staff, creating and utilizing new capabilities and enhancing employee competencies, and changing their behavior, attitudes and shared values. People need to understand the need for transformation and commit to a pace which is acceptable to them while enabling inhibiting walls between departments and businesses to be removed. The rational and the emotional elements have to be brought together to win hearts and minds.

   It also usually involves transformations to the organization's IT capabilities, operations, business processes, systems, technology and software. Changing the IT successfully at a speed which allows the organization to remain competitive is often the critical enabler of a transformation.

Expected outcome:
1.   New business units (e.g. service centers)
2.   New business processes
3.   New relationships

Requirements:
1.   People's understanding and commitment
2.   Changing the IT successfully

Optimize

Transformation must be embedded and internalized as the new "business as usual". The institutionalization of transformation – ensuring that quick wins are consolidated, processes and achievements are measured, and any laggard behavior is addressed – will create the conditions for effective business transformation and ensure that change capability is enhanced.

Expected outcome:	**Requirements:**
1. Measurement of processes and achievements	1. Internalize, institutionalize, and optimize transformation
2. Laggard behavior is eliminated	2. Create stability

Business transformation in practice is often messy and, to some employees engaged in it, unclear, as multiple activities vie for attention and the realities of dealing with obstacles confounds the best-laid plans. The iterative nature of change must therefore be encompassed. This is one of the most difficult management capabilities. The constant iteration and the preparedness to return to phases of the cycle to solve problems and reinforce messages is a key element of the transformation process.

CHALLENGES CONCERNING THE TRANSFORMATION LIFECYCLE:
1. The iterative nature of business transformation must be encompassed.
2. To deal with unintended consequences.
3. Effective and efficient change of IT.

KEY MESSAGE:
The constant iteration and the preparedness to return to phases of the cycle to solve problems and reinforce messages.

The ability of the transformation agent to move between the phases of the transformation lifecycle and to review the implications of change interventions and deal with unintended consequences is highly valuable and rare. Senge (2006) argued that change management has both theory in abstract and theory-in-use, the latter being the real enactment of the change process. Usually, theory-in-use represents a deep level of behavior and attitude, and reaching this level will not take just one meeting or one set of training activities.

This, of course, raises the question of who will be the transformation agent in such a holistic and iterative process. This topic will be addressed in the next paragraph.

2.2.3 MANAGEMENT ROLES INVOLVED IN META MANAGEMENT

The four phases of the transformation lifecycle are executed by several management roles.

In change management theory, an often neglected aspect of the process is the need to build a coalition (Jick and Peiperl, 2002). Though this appears implicitly in a number of change models, the dimensions of the team needed and their roles has been largely missing from major change conceptualizations. In the practical sphere, the composition of GE's transformation project teams in terms of a champion (high-level supporter of the change process), sponsor (responsible for operational accountability) and project manager (who oversees the day-to-day running of the business transformation) has been a strong pillar in terms of identifying the roles required. However, this approach has been light on detail over the particular accountabilities of each level, and also there is no real acknowledgment of the importance of the informal management roles required to make change happen. In the following we highlight a number of management roles, both at a formal and informal level, required in order to execute meta management (see Figure 2.3).

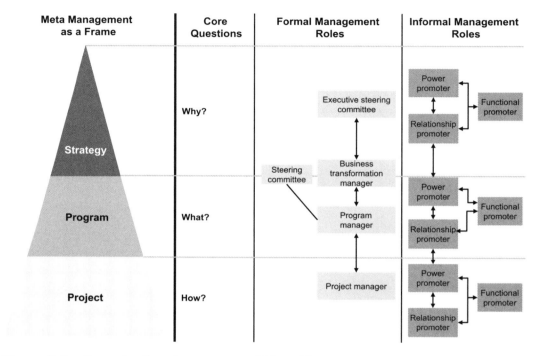

Figure 2.3   Organizational structure of Meta Management

Formal management roles

The formal management roles have a hierarchy reflecting both expertise and power. At the apex is the executive steering committee, which is responsible for the creation of the meta management framework and facilitating capability, culture and the environment for change.

The business transformation manager takes strategic decisions and manages the overall transformation program from beginning to end. He or she reports in the role of a key adviser to the executive steering committee and has a complete overview of all change programs, plans programs together with program managers, and considers dependencies between programs. His or her key interest is to make the overall transformation strategy happen and to realize the proposed business change and value. He or she stays in this role for the entire transformation roadmap, from the early planning (envisioning) phase until the optimization phase.

The program manager steers the individual programs in alignment with the business transformation goals and decides on policy, governance, reporting, document standards and program structures, and is accountable for finance, controlling and resource management of the program, as well as the benefit realization of his or her program. He or she also needs to break down this program into manageable projects, select the right project managers, coordinate the interdependencies of the projects, and build the bridge between project, program and over transformation strategy.

The project manager initiates, plans, executes and closes a project, and is accountable to the program manager for accomplishing the stated project objectives with respect to value, quality, cost, time and scope.

It is a central tenet of effective teams that clear roles, responsibilities and accountabilities are assigned (Katzenbach and Smith, 2005). This formal delineation of key management roles for transformation gives a more explicit characterization than current approaches, and the dual directional arrows stress that this is not a purely hierarchical approach but one which favors feedback loops at every touch-point. What is also important is the addition of the informal set of roles, which facilitates transformation within organizations. The informal side of organizations has long been recognized as having strong potential for either aiding or constraining transformation (Cooper and Argyris, 1998).

CHALLENGES CONCERNING FORMAL MANAGEMENT ROLES:

1.   To find people with domain knowledge and power.
2.   To assign roles, responsibilities and accountabilities appropriately.

KEY MESSAGE:

An organization with these particular management roles has clear roles and responsibilities that help to drive business transformation as an integrated program of manageable projects. This favors feedback loops.

Informal management roles

In the following, several informal roles are described which are empirically well founded, especially in the literature about innovation management (Gemünden et al., 2007).

The *power promoter* provides sponsorship at the highest level of leadership and the most powerful lever for transformation. He or she empowers the transformation program and project managers but does not mix sponsorship with project management. Power is used only exceptionally and where it is absolutely necessary to drive transformation forward. Misuse of power creates distrust and resistance.

The *relational promoter* delivers social competence, charisma and persuasive power, combining a strong network with a certain level of expert knowledge. With extensive relationships and a sound knowledge of internal matters, the relational promoter creates the willingness to change. This frequently requires the support of "opinion leaders" to implement transformation, and the relational promoter plays the role of intermediary due to his or her considerable social expertise and experience in situations of conflict. Usually people trust this person because of his or her personality and their long working time and commitment to the company.

The *functional provider* gives the transformation program a very high level of expert knowledge. He or she has considerable interest (and experience) in the topic of transformation and works in the line. This informal role is also very important because the functional promoter can answer specialist questions with expert know-how and has a good reputation as a specialist in the organization.

We find these informal management roles at all described levels of transformation: at the overall transformation level, the program level and the project level. In terms of content, the promoters differ in their degrees of specialist detail: strategic, tactical or operational.

The combination of these (informal) management roles in itself requires a great deal of coordination. For this to be ensured, the business transformation manager will be involved in the whole of the transformation process. This puts great demands on an individual since a transformation agent runs a number of risks, including isolation, being negatively perceived, unable to reintegrate back into the organization and being made a scapegoat in the event of poor execution (Beer and Nohria, 2000). So a good degree of courage, resilience and spirit are required on the part of the business transformation manager (Bossidy et al., 2002). In addition, of course, the skill and behavioral set for such an individual is unevenly distributed in the population – individuals who possess such a repertoire are highly sought after and valuable. Part of an organization's responsibility to ensure its sustained success is to develop and retain such individuals.

CHALLENGES CONCERNING INFORMAL MANAGEMENT ROLES:
1. To find people with sociality and perspicacity (in particular an appropriate business transformation manager).
2. Great deal of coordination.

2.3 Meta Management Principles

The transformation purpose and the highest transformation goals must be efficiently communicated, and guidelines to create cultural "ground" for transformation must be established.

Meta Management also provides guidelines to internalize and institutionalize the transformation purpose and goals. A successful business transformation is grounded on the following principles:

* Business transformation objective: define clear und comprehensible goals.
* Communication and coordination: communicate and "live" the vision.
* Leadership: "Walk the talk."
* Culture and value: define values and facilitate internalization.

These principles are explained in the next sections.

2.3.1 BUSINESS TRANSFORMATION OBJECTIVE

For a meta-routine such as business transformation, the coordination between separate management disciplines is essential. An approach that has gained broad acceptance is the balanced scorecard. As we stated earlier, although the balanced scorecard does not describe a change process, it nevertheless provides a valuable model by which different management disciplines can be integrated through the identification of mutually supporting goals.

The balanced scorecard is an ideal tool for a well-balanced goal definition within a business transformation project. Goals are operationalized through key performance indicators (KPIs) and serve as a basis for value management, evaluation and feedback. The recognition given to the different aspects of organizations is important. At a very broad level, change has been classified into economic aspects and organizational aspects (Beer and Nohria, 2000), with the economic aspects tending to dominate, primarily because of their greater capability to be measured and often the immediacy of their impact. However, the organizational aspects are no less important, given the need to build both employee and structural capability into the organization to ensure sustainable success. The dual requirement to build economic and organizational capability, highlighted by Beer and Nohria, is given a fine-grained working through, with the core financial and process metrics aligned with customer and people dimensions.

The other major benefit of the balanced scorecard is its relative simplicity in terms of breaking down the major aspects of the strategy and, for our purposes, the transformation goals, and enabling clear linkages between the core activities. Furthermore, it provides a clear rationale for the cascading of transformation goals through and across the levels of an organization. In this sense, the balanced scorecard provides strong support for the communicative aspect of the transition.

KEY MESSAGE:
The balanced scorecard is an ideal tool for a well-balanced goal definition within a business transformation project.

2.3.2 COMMUNICATION AND COORDINATION

For transformational efforts to be successful, the transformation agenda must be able to deal with *communication* within and between departments and businesses. However, what is often overlooked is the need to develop a common understanding of a transformation effort as a first principle. This essential first step – the Communication Principle – has often been an implicit ingredient in transformation efforts rather than an explicit one, but the whole change enterprise rests on this step. Without a compelling articulation of the need for transformation, the mobilization of commitment from the workforce will be not forthcoming. Communication involves:

- the communication of reasons for transformation ("why can't we stay the same") is needed – that is, its purpose and the main goals;
- establishing a common language to ensure unambiguous interpretation of key concepts – for example, through a glossary; and
- the communication of transformation values, principles and guidelines to create the cultural "ground" for transformation.

Specifically, this principle is not responsible for communication within and between individual disciplines. Though this activity is very important, it forms part of the regular communications process within organizations.

Difficulty with communication has long been viewed as a major contributing factor in the lack of transformational success. The importance of communication in change processes is undoubted and there are numerous models and practical prescriptions, highlighting communication intensity and channel choice (Garvin and Roberto, 2005). At the heart of communication approaches is a basic process framework which identifies:

1. the characteristics of the sender of the message;
2. the content of the message; and
3. the characteristics of the recipient.

Under the first dimension rests the credibility and trustworthiness of the sender. The second dimension addresses the issue of tailoring the message and the salience of its content. The third dimension identifies the capability of the receiver to understand the message (their absorptive capacity) and also the motivation of the receiver to act upon it.

The need to segment stakeholders to the transformation process is a requirement in order to gauge reaction to the change and the degree of acceptance and resistance that is encountered. The literature identified a number of typologies of stakeholder identification that address different tiers of business transformation:

- 1st tier: Those **imminently affected** by the business transformation – for example, people working in HR being relocated through the creation of a shared service center.
- 2nd tier: Those **directly affected** by business transformation – for example, people from the HR department affected through changed business processes.
- 3rd tier: Those **indirectly affected** by transformation – for example, internal and external customers of HR through an altered HR service delivery.

Naturally, each of these tiers may have different attitudes towards the transformation program, ranging on a broad continuum from highly accepting of the transformation to strongly resistant. Those on the first and second tiers who are positive about the transformation would become ambassadors for the program and would aid in spreading the benefits and the vision of the transformation. Persuading those indirectly affected is also important since though they may not be in the frontline of changes, their effect on organizational morale, should they distribute negative messages, is considerable (Hardy, 2009). Figure 2.4 shows the four dimensions of the balanced scorecard (customer, financial, process and people) in combination with the three tiers in order to address the specific communication needs within the organization.

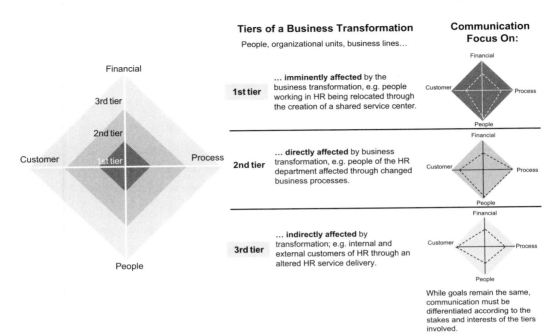

Figure 2.4   The dimensions of communication within BTM²

One fundamental enabler for an effective transformation process is the identification of a clear line of sight between the overarching organizational goals and the goals defined for the individual employee. This means that the cascade of overall transformational goals must be made specific for each management discipline and organizational member. Furthermore, the cascaded goals must be *meaningful* for the employee in terms of motivational content as well in relevant language that enables them to understand both "What's in it for me?" and "What am I supposed to do?". Though communication is important, obviously, for such a process to work, it is clear that acceptance of the transformation message is dependent not only on the message content but also on the credibility and trustworthiness of the leadership.

This means that "one message fits all" does not achieve the desired objective. Depending on the respective target groups' functional and hierarchical affiliation within the company, the communication must be individually adapted. Naturally, this does not mean that contradictory information should be provided; the communication of strategic objectives is standardized but it must be adapted for individual target groups in terms of its significance.

CHALLENGES CONCERNING THE COMMUNICATION PRINCIPLE:
1. Need to segment stakeholders to the business transformation process.
2. Identification of a clear line of sight (define transformational goals for each management discipline and organizational member).
3. Individually adopted communication principles.

2.3.3 LEADERSHIP

Once the transformation process is accepted, leaders need to help employees to interpret proposals for transformation (Garvin and Roberto, 2005). Skilled leaders use "frames" to provide context and shape perspective for new proposals and plans. Because transformation initiatives are open to numerous interpretations and filtering, it is important that employees are helped to gain a shared and consistent understanding of what the transformation requires. A prime mechanism is the establishment of a clear working language for the transformation process, in which all major concepts are defined – for instance, in a glossary – and measures are identified and understood. This shared language of transformation can be a constant reference point as the change moves into different areas of the organization, where different professional and technical languages can distort the meaning of the change concepts.

The basis for leadership is to build an organization that can effectively achieve its goals. There is a wide range of leadership theory, from instrumental approaches to inspirational ones (Bass and Avolio, 2012); all center on the nature of the relationship between the leader and the followers. In light of the arguments from the resource-based view of the firm that competitive advantage stems from valuable, rare and hard-to-imitate resources (Barney, 1991; Wright and McMahan, 1992), and the related literature on the importance of using talent for developing ideas and sustaining success, the emphasis on transformational leadership (Bass and Avolio, 2012) is not surprising. It is no coincidence that the transformational agenda in transformation management should mesh with the dominant view of transformational leadership. BTM² suggests a new leadership approach, which has the following characteristics:

- The role of the business transformation manager must allow for sufficient responsibilities and power to manage the overall transformation.
- The business transformation manager must have the respective competences and capabilities for such a complex task.

For the relationship between the leader and the follower, the dimensions include the following:

- Provide vision and sense of mission, gain respect and trust.
- Use symbols to focus efforts, express important purposes in simple ways.
- Promote intelligence, rationality and careful problem-solving.
- Give personal attention, treat each employee individually.
- Live the transformation: "Walk the talk."
- Be clear in what is accepted and what is not.
- In conflicts, find fair solutions and avoid winners and losers.

The link between transformational leadership and involvement is direct – transformational leadership embodies the idea of empowerment and involvement (Bass and Avolio, 2012). Furthermore, implicitly bound up with leadership style is the issue of organizational culture. Traditionally, leadership style has direct effects on the culture of an organization and vice versa, showing the example that others might imitate and also articulating the key values. All organizations have cultures of some kind, and there is huge variation, ranging broadly from integrated (unified culture) to differentiated (a set of subcultures with potential for either harmony or conflict) and fragmented (no clear coherence among sub-groups) (Conyon and Leech, 1994). These are not static descriptions but rather represent a dynamic, with organizations becoming more or less unified over time depending on changes both within and external to the firm.

CHALLENGES CONCERNING THE LEADERSHIP PRINCIPLE:
1.   Sufficient responsibilities and power to manage the overall business transformation.
2.   Respective competencies and capabilities for the transformation process.

KEY MESSAGE:
Intersection as wide as possible between the leadership role, his or her competencies and his or her responsibilities. Moreover, the position of a transformational leader must be seen as a position with high reputation: leaders need to be selected carefully, they need to have shown outstanding achievements in earlier change projects and their career path must be planned clearly.

2.3.4 CULTURE AND VALUE

In addition to the shared language, it is important that a cultural environment is set by skillful use of communication. For communication to work, there must be a cognitive element where employees understand what is being proposed and what it means for them. However, there must also be an emotional aspect to the communication, to ensure both yielding to the change message and commitment to it. Ensuring that the cultural ground is fertile is a major task of the communication principle. Employees need to feel that the organization has a purpose and that the change will contribute to their sense of what the organization stands for and is congruent with its core values.

To move towards the unified end of the continuum, the following three elements are required:

1.   the right people;
2.   leadership example; and
3.   socialization (Robbins and Judge, 2009).

Socialization involves the immersing of employees into the values and objectives of the transformation, and the internalization of these objectives and values (Schein, 1995). Central to this is the instilling of a sense of belonging, together with a non-coercive approach to the transformation, allowing autonomy for the employee. In essence, the journey between the axes (see Figure 2.5) finds resonance in the distinction between control and commitment (Walton, 1985). Control represents a strong behavioral focus on compliance enforced by appropriate incentives and sanctions, but commitment, at an affective level, entails the sense of identification with the business transformation and the belief in the overarching goals of the process (see Figure 2.5).

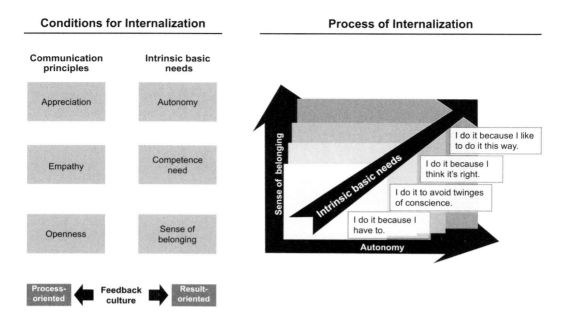

Figure 2.5   Core values and internalization as part of Meta Management

In Figure 2.5 the two key aspects are combined, namely communication principles and intrinsic basic needs. First, the communication principles cover partner-oriented or relationship-oriented approaches, comprising the aspects of appreciation, empathy and openness. Employees who are appreciated during the transformation process will have higher commitment and positive intent towards it. Empathy is important in understanding what people are going through as the business transformation affects their working lives and relationships, and openness is crucial in order to bring any constructive voices to the table or to surface conflict and resolve it.

Second, the intrinsic basic needs highlight the requirement to focus on motivation in the transformation process, rather than pure rewards and sanctions. Again, there are three fundamental elements. First, the transformation must be driven by *autonomy* – people must be given responsibility and freedom to enact the transformation process. The alternative is to get somebody to do something by using extrinsic motivation tools such as rewards or sanctions, but it is not possible to force people to like something. Second, the *competence need* highlights the importance of employees moving outside their comfort zone to embrace new practices and skills. Third, the *sense of belonging* identifies the need for individuals to belong to an attractive group or company, one that has clear identity, and whose transformation is sound and compelling.

Addressing both the communication principles and the intrinsic needs will increase the internalization of the business transformation objectives, leading to the greater likelihood of the effectiveness of transformation.

However, it is possible to internalize new forms of behavior, although this presupposes voluntariness, social integration and a feeling of doing the right thing.

CHALLENGES CONCERNING THE CULTURAL PRINCIPLES:
1. Define values and facilitate internalization.
2. Set up a cultural environment by skillful use of communication.

CHALLENGES CONCERNING THE META MANAGEMENT PRINCIPLES:
1. Overcoming the inertia of organizations.
2. Need to develop a common understanding of a transformation effort (meta-communication).
3. Find skilled leaders who provide context and shape perspective for new proposals and plans.
4. Clear working language.
5. Skillful use of communication.

KEY MESSAGE:
1. Communicate principles such as appreciation, empathy and openness.
2. Motivate intrinsic basic needs such as autonomy, competence needs and sense of belonging.
3. Addressing both the communication principles and the intrinsic needs will increase the internalization of the transformation, leading to the greater likelihood of its effectiveness.

2.4 Conclusion

The meta management chapter summarizes the guiding elements to create the right environment for successful business transformation. The chapter reflects leadership principles, core values and behaviors, and communication principles, as well as organizational structures that facilitate business transformation.

Business transformation is a complex and difficult process. The reason for that is the amount and diversity of stakeholders and interests, unclear expectations and responsibilities, and ineffective leadership and communication resulting in resistance, conflicts, anarchy and lack of support. Such complexity explains why many business transformation initiatives do not succeed, because there is no "meta management" of the overall process. This concept has rarely been discussed in the traditional change management literature. This chapter outlined some of the fundamentals of the meta management concept building on well-established principles, theories and experience from a number of disciplines, including stage models, stakeholder management, the balanced scorecard and transformational leadership.

One of the staples of change management research concerns the planned or emergent nature of change. In this chapter, transformation is conceptualized as a planned activity, but within meta management, there is flexibility to allow for changes in the environment and for fresh information to be factored into the overall process. In this way, Meta Management may be likened to a dynamic capability, bringing together different elements of change and allowing for their combination and recombination to ensure the sustained effectiveness of the organization. Large companies can suffer from sluggishness, inertia, bureaucracy, silo structures, poor communications, disenfranchised management and employees, and stifled entrepreneurial spirit, which, in combination, tend to inhibit or even prevent innovation, integration and learning. Understanding transformation from a holistic perspective is essential if the processes and relationships that regulate change are to be leveraged effectively. In the following chapters, we explore the various disciplines that make up organizational transformation.

Bibliography

Barney, J. (1991), Firm resources and sustained competitive advantage, *Journal of Management* 17, no. 1, 99–120.

Bass, Bernard M. and Avolio, Bruce J. (2012), Multifactor leadership questionnaire: the benchmark measure of transformational leadership, 2012: www.mindgarden.com/products/mlq.htm (accessed March 2012).

Beer, Michael and Nohria, Nitin (2000), Cracking the code of change, *Harvard Business Review* 78, no. 3, 133–41.

Bossidy, Larry, Charan, Ram and Burck, Charles (2002), *Execution: The Discipline of Getting Things Done*, 1st ed. (New York: Crown Business).

Collins, James C. (2003), *Der Weg zu den Besten: Die sieben Management-Prinzipien für dauerhaften Unternehmenserfolg* (München: Deutscher Taschenbuch-Verlag).

Conyon, Martin J. and Leech, Dennis (1994), Top pay, company performance and corporate governance, *Oxford Bulletin of Economics and Statistics* 56, no. 3, 229–47.

Cooper, Cary L. and Argyris, Chris (eds) (1998), *The Concise Blackwell Encyclopedia of Management* (Malden, Mass: Blackwell Business).

Garvin, David A. and Roberto, Michael A. (2005), Change through persuasion, *Harvard Business Review* 83, no. 2, 104–12.

Gemünden, Hans G., Salomo, Sören and Hölzle, Katharina (2007), Role models for radical innovations in times of open innovation, *Creativity and Innovation Management* 16, no. 4, 408–21.

Goffee, Robert and Jones, Gareth (2000), Why should anyone be led by you?, *Harvard Business Review* 78, no. 5, 62–70.

Hardy, Ben (2009), Morale: definitions, dimensions and measurement, unpublished PhD thesis (Judge Business School, University of Cambridge).

Jick, Todd D. and Peiperl, Maury A. (2002), *Managing Change: Cases and Concepts* (London: McGraw-Hill).

Katzenbach, Jon R. and Smith, Douglas K. (2005), *The Wisdom of Teams: Creating the High-Performance Organization* (London: McGraw-Hill).

Robbins, Stephen P. and Judge, Tim (2009), *Organizational Behavior*, 13th ed. (Upper Saddle River, NJ: Pearson Prentice Hall).

Schein, Edgar H. (1995), *Unternehmenskultur: Ein Handbuch für Führungskräfte* (Frankfurt: Campus Verlag).

Senge, Peter M. (2006), *The Fifth Discipline: The Art and Practice of the Learning Organization* (New York, London: Crown Business).

Walton, Richard E. (1985), From control to commitment in the workplace, *Harvard Business Review* 63, no. 2, 77–84.

Wright, Patrick M. and McMahan, Gary C. (1992), Theoretical perspectives for strategic human resource management, *Journal of Management* 18, no. 2, 295–320.

3 *Strategy Management*

AXEL UHL (SAP AG), DOMINIC HOULDER (London Business School), DANIEL SCHMID (SAP AG) and MICHAEL VON DER HORST (Cisco Systems GmbH)

3.1 Overview

This chapter presents how organizations or organizational units can successfully plan transformation alignments and implementations. A frequent cause of failure is an erroneous or inaccurate planning of a transformation strategy. This chapter systematically guides through the six major steps of developing a transformation strategy and explains the integration of essential aspects such as transformation need, transformation readiness, stakeholder management, options for action and the integration of a transformation plan.

Strategy management primarily addresses the "envision" phase of the transformation lifecycle, where a strategy is developed. Strategy development refers to the selection of appropriate team members, collection of data, analysis of transformation needs and readiness, design of a business vision and a business model, and the definition of an integrated transformation plan.

OBJECTIVES OF THIS CHAPTER:
1. Understand how to develop a business transformation strategy.
2. Familiarize with methods and tools for business transformation strategy development.
3. Learn how to analyze an organization's transformation readiness.
4. Learn how to develop a solid business transformation strategy.

3.2 Business Transformation Strategy

Successful business transformation depends on a well-defined strategy. The strategy definition phase of our methodology links the transformation program to the fundamental changes in the business' environment and corporate direction. These changes represent the triggers for transformation.

We believe that a business transformation must have robust strategic triggers if it is to succeed at all. These may relate to sustainability changes or new technologies, such as cloud computing or ubiquitous computing (Weiser, 1999), which are facilitating completely new business models and rendering existing ones obsolete. Intensifying global competitive pressures (Porter, 2004) (new competitors, buyers' bargaining power, suppliers' bargaining power, alternative products or services), demographic trends (growth in India, South America, India, and contraction in Europe, the USA and so on), and even failures within the enterprise can act as robust strategic triggers for transformation.

Sometimes the trigger for a business transformation is not strategic, but has more to do with the "ego" of the business leaders or key stakeholders. Ultimately, these transformations fail for lack of market acceptance or at an even earlier stage if not accepted by employees. In other cases, difficult personnel decisions were taken too late – for example, certain key persons were not replaced soon enough, even though, it was evident that they were opposed to the business transformation due to self-interest. As a result, the entire transformation process took longer than planned and the image of the program suffered long-term damage.

The step-by-step methodology described below for developing the business transformation strategy takes into account the complexity of the transformation itself. At the same time, it makes allowance for the fact that various management disciplines, such as Risk Management, Value Management, Business Process Management, Organizational Change Management, Transformational IT Management or Competence and Training Management, are required to elaborate the concepts involved.

The strategy method presented here is based on six logic steps and describes the first phase (envision) of the transformation lifecycle introduced in Chapter 2, Meta Management. Nevertheless, the strategy is subsequently being re-evaluated also in later phases, i.e. engage, transform and optimize (see Figure 3.1).

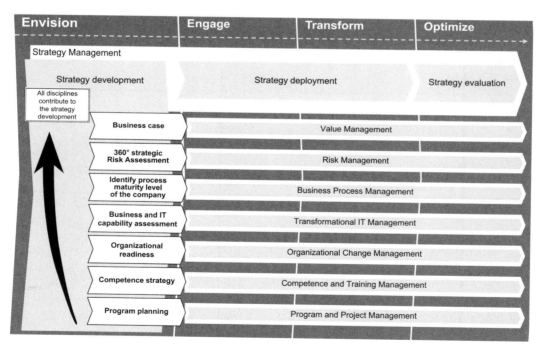

Figure 3.1   Strategy development as part of the envision phase in the transformation lifecycle

Developing the strategy provides answers to the following questions:

- What are the business transformation drivers and how do they affect the existing business model?
- What options does the enterprise have to act and what is the vision for the future enterprise? How should it position itself?
- What impact will the business transformation have on the value chain? Which parts of the value chain need to be optimized?
- What is our future competitive edge and what additional value can be realized by the business transformation?
- What are the strategic risks associated with the various transformation options?
- What are the technological requirements for the future business model? What adjustments need to be made?
- Which partners are required to realize the business model?
- How well is the enterprise organized and how experienced and motivated is the management?
- Does the enterprise have the experience required to adapt its processes and organization in line with new challenges? How loyal are the employees?
- How is the business transformation path structured?

3.3 Procedure for Developing the Business Transformation Strategy

The following methodological steps (see Figure 3.2) are intended to find the answers to these questions.

Each project starts by describing the subject matter and scope. In this phase, it is essential to select the right stakeholders and project members, and ensure that all of those involved have a common understanding of the project. A strategy phase predominantly, but not exclusively, involves the company's management. The next step entails clarifying the company's economic starting point – that is, its market position, competitors, product and service portfolio, key revenue and expenditure, as well as its strengths and weaknesses. The third step involves analyzing the acute transformation need and its causes as well as the organization's readiness to transform. Following this, the courses of action and future mission statement are developed. Step 5 contains a detailed description of the future business model including the production and product portfolio, as well as the future core processes, future organization and IT architecture to demonstrate the sustained success of the business model. Finally, a rough business transformation plan is elaborated that includes an estimate of the costs and benefits as well as the key steps required to conduct the business transformation. The six steps are explained in detail in the following sections.

3.3.1 STEP 1: PROJECT STARTUP

The importance of the Project Startup step is often underestimated, with most project sponsors attempting to shorten it significantly. It is often argued that the transformation strategy is important and that results are expected as quickly as possible. Yet, just as in

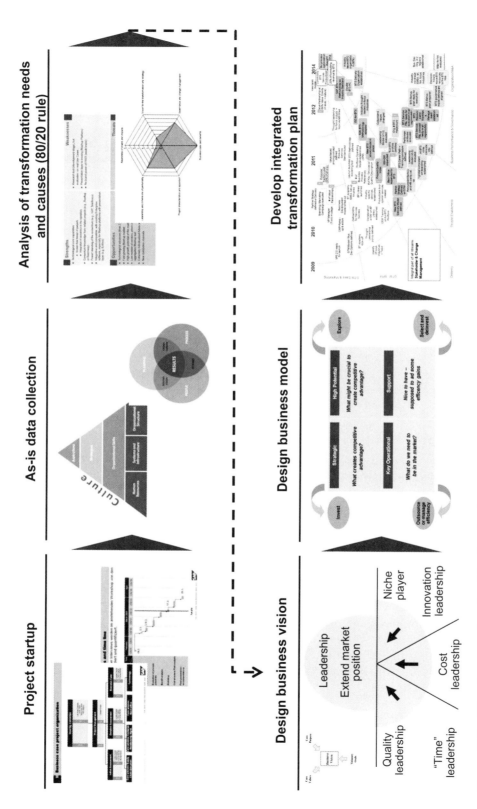

Figure 3.2   The six steps involved in developing a business transformation strategy

Project startup

As-is data collection

Analysis of transformation needs and causes (80/20 rule)

Design business vision

Design business model

Develop integrated transformation plan

other projects, neglecting certain initial aspects frequently has far-reaching consequences. Failure to include a key stakeholder or knowledge expert, for example, can have a profound negative impact. For this reason, the requirements and duties in the project startup step should be elaborated with the same due care as in the other steps within the project. Figure 3.3 summarizes the key characteristics of this step.

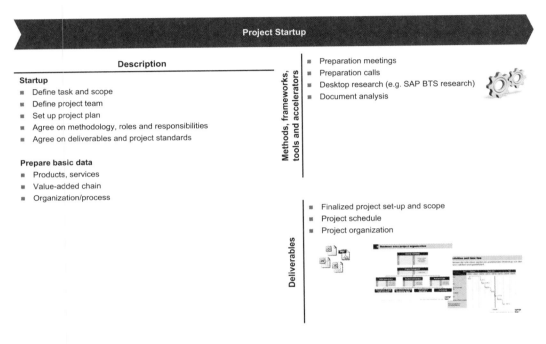

Figure 3.3   Project startup

3.3.2 STEP 2: AS-IS DATA COLLECTION

A record of the initial situation is an essential prerequisite for accurate business planning as the entire analysis is based on a systematic collection of the data related to the factors that shape the development of the company. This means that both the external and internal factors that will affect the future "transformed" company must be analyzed. The data required to do so must be of high quality; that is, it must be both conclusive and transparent. Among the key data that must form part of this analysis are external factors such as economic trends, the competitive environment, information about transformation drivers including globalization, demographic developments, sustainability aspects and technology drivers, as well as specific industry trends. In addition, the current mission statement must be scrutinized and critically assessed. This involves questions regarding the core mission and business and their contributions to earnings, as well as competition-related resources and capabilities: management, procurement, production, sales, technology, innovation and financing. This information is retrieved methodologically by analyzing data from accounting, interviews with managers and employees, examining business partners and competitors, and including research data. The result is a holistic picture of the enterprise. Figure 3.4 summarizes the key characteristics of this step.

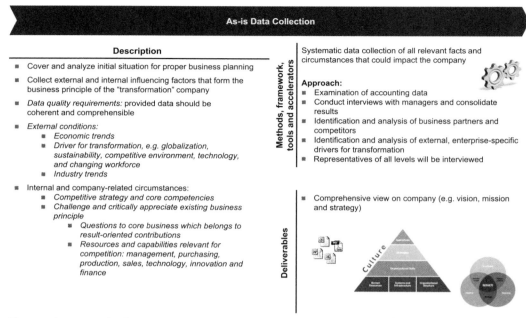

As-is Data Collection

Description

- Cover and analyze initial situation for proper business planning
- Collect external and internal influencing factors that form the business principle of the "transformation" company
- *Data quality requirements:* provided data should be coherent and comprehensible
- *External conditions:*
  - *Economic trends*
  - *Driver for transformation, e.g. globalization, sustainability, competitive environment, technology, and changing workforce*
  - *Industry trends*
- Internal and company-related circumstances:
  - *Competitive strategy and core competencies*
  - *Challenge and critically appreciate existing business principle*
    - *Questions to core business which belongs to result-oriented contributions*
    - *Resources and capabilities relevant for competition: management, purchasing, production, sales, technology, innovation and finance*

Methods, framework, tools and accelerators

Systematic data collection of all relevant facts and circumstances that could impact the company

Approach:
- Examination of accounting data
- Conduct interviews with managers and consolidate results
- Identification and analysis of business partners and competitors
- Identification and analysis of external, enterprise-specific drivers for transformation
- Representatives of all levels will be interviewed

Deliverables

- Comprehensive view on company (e.g. vision, mission and strategy)

Figure 3.4   As-is data collection

3.3.3 STEP 3: ANALYSIS OF TRANSFORMATION NEEDS AND CAUSES

This is one of the most important phases in the development of a business transformation strategy and is based on the experience that excessive business transformation pressure does not build up overnight but can peak across various phases. For this reason, the phase is divided into series of stages ("Lack of transformation awareness and transparency", "Lack of stakeholder commitment", "Lack of transformation strategy", "Lack of business success" and "Lack of liquidity") that a proactive and healthy enterprise passes through when it becomes "unhealthy" and insolvent.

The most effective solution is to take a proactive enterprise and perform a transformation analysis to investigate the effects that the transformation drivers have on the enterprise as well as the associated opportunities and risks. For companies in other stages, however, an analysis of the situation and crisis assessment is an integral part of the appraisal. It is important to understand that a sustainable transformation cannot be brought about without removing the causes of all crisis situations (Groß, 2009). Figure 3.5 outlines the different stages of the transformation need, which are explained in the following.

Case study example:

We were struck by an incident at a conference with the topic of business transformation. A delegate who was, to put it discreetly, rather stout of body rose up and said: "Transformation never really can work. Look at me: I am fat, but that is me, it is part of my identity, and I get along fine. There are always imperfections but we have to live with them."

In one sense, he has a point. All of us have imperfections and, as in the academic notion of path dependency, certain events and experiences have led us to where we are now. However, the reason why he is not willing to change is because the pressure is not high enough yet. But the rejection of change is foolhardy. The dangers of inertia are serious; from this individual's point of view, the onset of diabetes and then progressively worse symptoms. No doubt he feels that he will be the one exception to this decline, but we know without doubt that he will get progressively worse. And we know too that at some point, it will be too late for him to ever get back to full health – the chance will have been missed. At an organizational level, the complacency that sets in reduces information search, challenge withers away and there is a slowness to react to new circumstances. At some point, if business transformation is introduced (usually when a crisis occurs), it is too late to restore the health of the company fully.

Stage 0

Proactive – The company monitors the market developments, business environment, social and environmental changes, and adapts accordingly. In doing so, it has a high degree of flexibility in terms of the period and options available for readjustment.

Stage 1

A lack of awareness and transparency on the part of management with regard to transformation needs creates the basis for future problems such as a lack of stakeholder commitment during the transformation process. The difficulties, however, are not visible at this point in time.

Stage 2

The stakeholders are not in agreement about the future company orientation. There are personal conflicts at top management level. Key changes in direction are blocked. In many cases, decisions regarding personnel are not taken or the wrong personnel choices for key positions are made. The economic consequences, however, are not evident at this point in time.

Stages	Indicators and Consequences
Stage 0: (Pro-)active scanning and transformation according to external factors	▪ Observation and change in view of market trends, economic, societal and environmental developments ▪ High flexibility in terms of time and options as well as low pressure to company
Stage 1: Lack of transformation awareness and transparency	▪ Lack of knowledge and transparency for transformation need creates basis for future problems like a lack of stakeholder commitment ▪ However, negative impacts not visible yet
Stage 2: Lack of stakeholder commitment	▪ Stakeholders are not visible and lack of stakeholder commitment can result in wrong personnel choices for key positions ▪ Personal circumstances and conflicts at the management level can lead to the blockading of necessary transformation initiatives ▪ However, no business impact yet
Stage 3: Lack of transformation strategy	▪ Company starts losing customers due to lack of necessary transformation ▪ Decrease in turnover, increase in inventory and stocks ▪ Decomposition of overtime and short-time work ▪ High backlog for workforce or financial resources through failure to invest or false investments ▪ Dissatisfaction and loss of key employees can also be a result – loss of core know-how
Stage 4: Lack of business success	▪ Unclear operating results – total costs are not covered (still positive profit contribution) ▪ Ongoing lack of positive business results weakens execution power of leadership team ▪ Important problems are ignored or varnished
Stage 5: Lack of liquidity	▪ Capital consumption and negative cash flow ▪ Entrance to bankruptcy (variable costs are not covered – negative profit contribution) ▪ The company culture as an important system of common values often gets destroyed

Figure 3.5 Different stages of transformation and consequences

Stage 3

The company starts to lose key clients because it has not adapted to the change in requirements. It also experiences a decrease in sales and inventory stocks start to grow. The company responds by reducing overtime and introducing short-time work. It fails to make the necessary product developments and investments in human capital, or it makes the wrong investments. Growing dissatisfaction among management and employees can also give rise to a loss of core know-how. In turn, this can benefit competition and promote uncertainty among the workforce.

Stage 4

Operating results are no longer reliable. In addition, the absence of positive results is preventing the management team from implementing key projects. Key stakeholders no longer have confidence in management. Fundamental problems are ignored, glossed over or even concealed. Corporate culture represents a major business potential that encompasses the common values and conceptions. Any change processes involving corporate culture must be supported by the workforce. A continued or progressive crisis will harm a positive corporate culture and can significantly impede business potential.

Stage 5

This stage is characterized by capital consumption and a negative cash flow. The company loses credibility and experiences more and more difficulties in raising the capital it so urgently needs. In turn, this frequently leads to a later bankruptcy. The company culture is further damaged or even destroyed.

As the company's need to transform increases, so does the pressure to do so as quickly as possible. At the same time, its scope becomes more restricted as certain barriers arise (Groß, 1997). These become evident in Stage 4 at the latest – if not earlier– and are generally due to a loss in confidence on the part of key customers or suppliers, with the result that the company can no longer raise the financial resources it needs. These obstacles are also referred to as market exit barriers when the abandonment costs, for example, can no longer be funded, or also market entry barriers if the capital for a regional expansion, for example, is lacking. The term "employee and management barriers" (see Figure 3.6) is used to describe situations where the workforce's resistance to transformation is too high, and is primarily caused by communication that is unsatisfactory or too late. Resistance to transformation often stems from management level because the higher a person is in the company hierarchy, the more he or she has to lose and the greater the risk of image loss (Schein, 1995; Simon, 2007).

To obtain a reliable estimate of the business transformation need and elaborate sustained transformation concepts, a selection of the methods and tools (presented in Appendix A of this book) must be deployed.

Alongside the recognized analysis methods used in strategy development, which are mainly geared to market conditions, competitors and a company's core competencies,

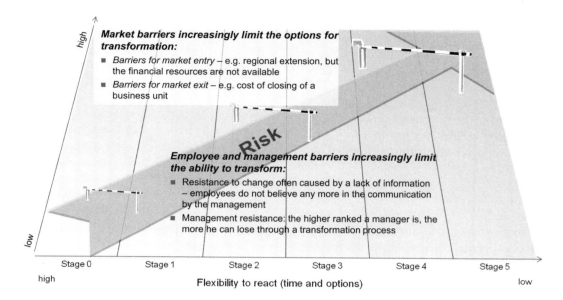

Figure 3.6   Transformation barriers

analyses that take a closer look at an organization's transformation readiness are becoming more and more important. These analyses are based on the observation that companies with similar strategies achieve completely different results even though the market conditions and their core competencies are similar. Consequently, it is important to know what factors affect the implementation of the business transformation. According to our research team, these are in particular: organizational readiness, process readiness and IT readiness. Even though it is difficult to make these "constructs" perceptible and thus measurable, we will attempt to establish an initial estimate here.

Organizational readiness

Normally, the people in an organization do not tend to change; without a willingness to change, however, the company cannot adapt quickly enough to new challenges. It goes without saying that the readiness to change of the workforce is directly linked to the process and IT readiness. It is unlikely that a company will have reached a high level of process or IT maturity and still have a limited organizational readiness. This may be the case, however, if corporate culture is destroyed as a result of mismanagement, for example, and employees consciously oppose change, as can actually occur in one of the later stages of the transformation need.

Generally, an organization's experience and willingness with regard to transformation can be measured by the level of collaboration throughout the company. Organizations with a lower transformation maturity frequently have predominantly local centers of power. In this case, change throughout the company is often hindered at a local level.

To promote collaboration in these decentralized structures, companies initially strive to establish a centralized organization, which, once empowered, aims to enforce central initiatives. The prescribed or forced changes, however, generally meet with relatively little acceptance and their success remains limited. This illustrates that leadership competence plays a key role in an organization's transformation readiness. If insufficient, conflicts are either sidestepped or tackled in a socially reduced manner.

In the first case, key decisions are frequently taken too late or not at all in order to conceal the conflict. The second case results in winners and losers – usually dictated by the balance of power. In turn, this creates a continuous cycle of conflict and often an increasing conflict escalation.

Enterprises that already demonstrate a high degree of collaboration in certain areas across the company have usually left these stages. They have established cross-company organizational units (such as shared services), which provide services for the company itself, its vendors or customers. Thinking in local or largely centralized structures has been replaced by a form of thinking that is geared more to the interests of the company as a whole. Collaboration itself is governed by uniform rules and values. At the highest level of maturity, collaboration between local and centralized structures is in a spirit of partnership where mutual respect is shown for all interests and decisions are based on the benefits to the entire company. Here, even employees question their own working practices independently and show a willingness to adapt to a shift in conditions. Such companies could also be described as learning organizations with a culture that essentially regards change as something positive and fosters mutual trust between the management and the workforce as well as between centralized and decentralized organizational units.

Process readiness

Transformations are generally associated with significant process changes – that is, changes to the way in which the company works. Experience of process management is extremely beneficial when it comes to changing and optimizing processes. The less process management experience a company has, the more complex and lengthy the transformation will be. Many locally different processes or many exceptions to the standard processes are an indication that a company has insufficient process management experience. In this case, generally no process owners have been defined that could configure cross-departmental processes. Other indications include excessive process loops, integration gaps, or undue control and approval steps. If a company has gained a certain level of process management expertise, it may have already standardized certain processes throughout its organization and defined initial responsibilities for process standardization. At the next maturity level, process owners have been defined for all cross-company processes and process know-how is well established throughout the company. If the entire organization thinks in processes, endeavors to improve these processes permanently and adapts itself flexibly to new requirements, it can be regarded as having a high level of process management maturity.

IT readiness

The ability to adapt processes flexibly to new requirements generally requires an appropriate IT infrastructure. Studies have shown, however, that companies differ considerably in terms of the state of development of their IT. Companies with a low state of development frequently have many heterogeneous IT solutions that are interlinked by a cumbersome set of interfaces. In most cases, accessing data is difficult, the systems are inflexible, there are many data silos and the quality of the data is poor. Generally, no global standards have been defined. Companies at a slightly higher level of development often have cross-company applications for some key processes and mission-critical data has been standardized throughout the organization. And yet there is no corporate-wide IT strategy and still many local and heterogeneous systems. Not until a company-wide IT strategy has been defined, standards for systems and data established, and local standalone systems systematically replaced (where expedient and feasible) can the IT infrastructure be regarded as mature. At an extremely high IT maturity level, however, the company has global and integrated IT-systems and uses state-of-the-art technologies efficiently in order to organize its IT operations in a flexible and cost-effective manner.

The transformation analysis results in a rating that can be used to assess potential transformation strategies (see Figure 3.7).

In summary, it can be held that a company's transformation readiness is extremely important for planning a transformation. In particular, it determines the radicalness with which a transformation can take place. In addition, the time available for the transformation plays a major role in this context. In general, a small interdisciplinary team is required for the analysis phase that applies the 80/20 rule to produce reliable results in a relatively short time and with reasonable effort.

CHALLENGES CONCERNING THE FIRST THREE STEPS: PROJECT STARTUP, AS-IS DATA COLLECTION AND ANALYSIS OF TRANSFORMATION NEEDS AND CAUSES:

1. Develop a common understanding of the project, create an efficient working environment and compose a "winning team" (including key stakeholders and knowledge experts).
2. Analyze the external (e.g. economic trends, the competitive environment) and internal factors that will affect the future "transformed" company.
3. Perform a transformation analysis to investigate the effects that the transformation drivers have on the enterprise as well as the associated opportunities and risks.
4. Measure the organization's willingness with regard to business transformation by the level of collaboration.

KEY MESSAGE:

Companies can gain an advantage (compared to companies with similar transformation strategies if they consider organizational readiness, process readiness and IT readiness during the implementation of the business transformation).

3.3.4 STEPS 4 AND 5: DESIGN BUSINESS VISION AND BUSINESS MODEL

The objective here is to develop a sustainable business model for the company. This entails investigating the core competencies of the company or performance potentials of

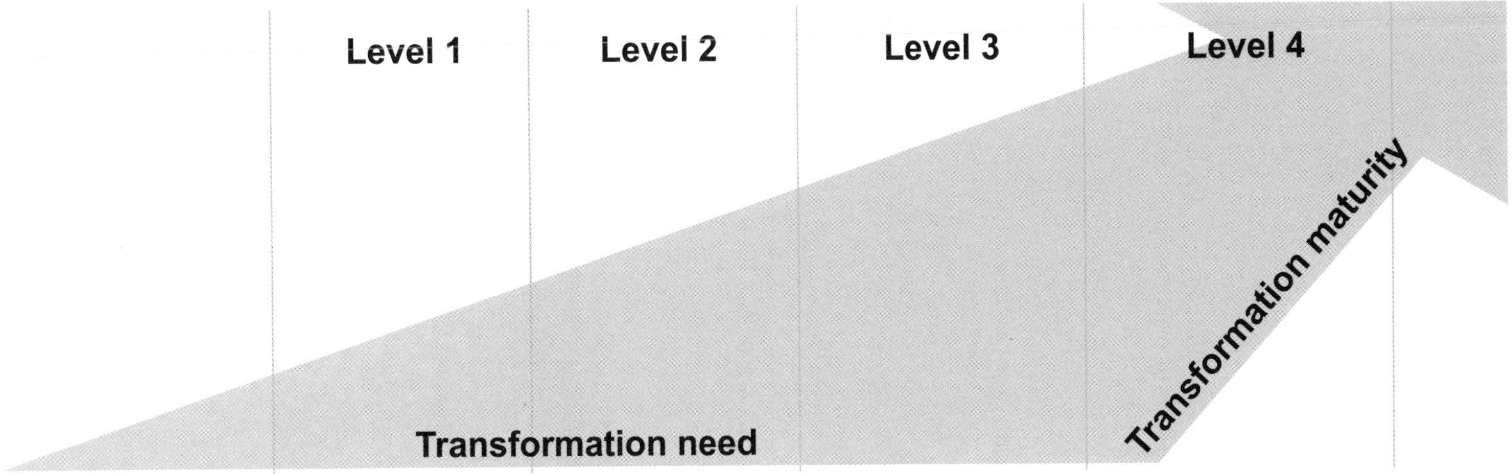

	Level 1	Level 2	Level 3	Level 4
IT readiness	Local IT applications, data not harmonized, different IT support concepts, lack of global strategy	Some global applications, first global reports and first data harmonized	Global IT strategy, local and global development, global support teams and processes, harmonized master data	Globally harmonized IT, global IT development, fully integrated IT systems, high reporting functionalities, outsourcing of less important tasks
Process readiness	Local processes, missing process standards, no process owners defined	Standards for a few global processes, first responsibilities for global processes defined	Global process owners, standards and tools, high process knowledge in organization	"Evergreen" processes for documentation and optimization, quick adaption to new market requirements
Organizational readiness	Lack of global policies, local "kingdoms", focus on local needs	First global concepts realized and global responsibilities, no global teams defined	Global teams instead of regional "kingdoms", well-defined local–global cooperation and policies	Flexible global organization, permanent improvement and innovation

Transformation maturity

Transformation need

Figure 3.7   Transformation readiness

certain individuals as well as developing new core competencies. Experience shows that companies with merely average competencies can "survive" at best. Those that perform below average are in a constant struggle for survival. According to Buzzell and Gale (1987), companies that have undergone a successful transformation generally improved their quality position, won market share, and/or cut production costs.

The aim of the business transformation is to increase the value of the company, which can be achieved through consolidation, risk reduction, or growth. The company's mission statement plays a key role here and should motivate employees to implement the goals of the transformation. This is extremely important because employees have to abandon their habits and learn new skills. It can also mean that some of the workforce will lose their jobs. The mission statement conveys a sense or orientation by giving employees an idea of how the company will look in the future and how it will prevail in the market.

The mission statement includes a description of the field of operations, the required resources and the value system of the company. The goal is to ensure that employees identify with the company's mission statement and this can only be achieved if the value systems do not contradict one another. The mission statement should also be described in a tangible manner that enables it to be applied to specific goals. In other words, it must provide the direction and level of difficulty for the key goals. As such, the mission statement plays a central role in coordinating resources in the context of a transformation.

A description of the mission statement, therefore, must encompass all of the key aspects of a company (see Figure 3.8). In addition to the business areas, production and sales program, the development of the value chain and manufacturing penetration, as well as the required resources and corporate values have to be described. Simon (2007) illustrates how important a mission statement can be. In his experience, the "hidden champions of the 21st century" – SMEs that have reached the leading position in their market – set themselves apart from their competitors primarily due to their strategic orientation.

Design Business Vision

- *Key objective:* **Sustainable business model**
- Focus on core competencies and human capital:
    - *average might means to keep the status and to survive*
    - *below average: permanent existence endangered*
- **Transformation value analysis**
  Potential value generation through consolidation, risk reduction and growth of the business
- **Importance of the business vision**
  Transformation process means significant changes to the company:
    - *employees have to change their working habits*
    - *new capabilities need to be learned*
    - *some employees might lose their job*
- **Transformation needs a clear vision,** so that the employees can get an understanding of how the company should look in the future and how it will succeed.
    - *description includes the:*
        - *business areas*
        - *resources*
        - *company values*
    - *the vision...*
        - *should provide the possibility to align the personal identity of the employees with the company identity*
        - *should be the basis for concrete objectives*
        - *becomes therefore an important means for coordination and alignment during the transformation*

Figure 3.8   Design business vision

A company's mission statement must be coherent and a successful strategy ensures that the key implementing measures are coordinated effectively. This requires a systematic consideration of the mutual dependencies involved. The mission statement is coherent if a company's strengths are developed and its weaknesses dismantled, and if strategy and organization are mutually compatible. Coherence also means, however, that the strategy and expectations of the enterprise environment fit.

Mission and strategy include (Doppler and Lauterburg, 1994):

- marketing and sales methodology;
- product and procurement processes;
- research and development projects;
- financing potential;
- workforce structures;
- supply of management and qualified personnel; and
- IT system.

The mission statement and strategy are geared towards four key efficiency criteria:

1. profitability;
2. sustainability;
3. market share;
4. risk.

The objective here is to identify permanent unique selling points that are perceived and valued by the customer. These can include cost leadership through economies of scale, efficient business processes and low-cost personnel structures.

Forming the mission statement initially entails deriving the strategic measures. A total of five basic strategies are available here:

1. Cost leadership: achieved by realizing economies of scale, reducing transaction costs and establishing low-cost structures in areas of fixed costs.
2. Quality leadership: differentiated by the benefits perceived by the customer.
3. Time leadership: a particular form of tangible customer benefit is punctuality, time savings, or the ability to develop products and bring them to the market and customer more quickly (time to customer, time to production, time to market).
4. Innovation leadership: the ability to develop new products and services through creativity and market knowledge, and thus always remain one step ahead of the competition.
5. Network and partner leadership: providing optimum coverage for and control of the value chain through an intelligent choice of the right partners.

Nowadays, however, it is not absolutely essential for companies to focus on exactly one of these strategies and then become leader. On the contrary, a better approach is to pursue several strategic options (see Figure 3.9) and combine the various strategies in such a way that this combination represents a unique selling point in itself. The initial situation and its analysis are important factors in the choice of strategy. Companies with a high need for transformation must determine their strategic direction and, above all,

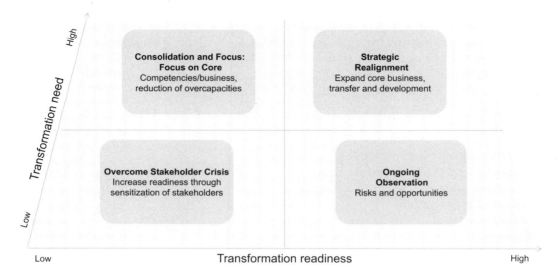

Figure 3.9   Strategic options

secure their survival in the short and medium term. In this context, the transformation readiness (see Figure 3.7) of the organization must be considered. In many cases, the transformation need is underestimated and the transformation readiness overestimated. As a result, either the transformation goals are too low or the organization is simply overburdened.

The development of an appropriate transformation strategy requires opposing transformation needs with transformation readiness. The combination of both facets leads to the definition of corresponding strategic options.

The following options for the transformation process arise from the initial situation:

Ongoing observation

If the pressure to transform is low and if the company has a high transformation readiness, it should continue to monitor its business environment and operate proactively.

Overcome stakeholder crisis (Groß, 2004)

If both the pressure to transform and the transformation readiness are low (for example, due to stakeholder conflicts), there is usually still enough time to pursue all options for action. First, however, the stakeholder crisis must be overcome. This is not always a simple undertaking – in some cases, the solution requires personnel changes. From a consultant's perspective, the situation is particularly difficult if the specific customer is the actual cause of the problem. Here, the solution requires particular sensitivity. The solution should also entail a rethink of corporate governance. By optimizing organizational structures, the company's ability to transform its business can be enhanced. In some cases, this can only be achieved by appointing the best people to key positions. Once these problems have been solved, the company can opt for consolidation or a strategic realignment.

Strategic realignment (Krüger, 2002)

If the pressure to transform its business is high and the company is also able to do so, a direct strategic realignment is also a feasible option and can be realized by initially strengthening its core business. Suitable measures here include brand profiling, closer positioning of core competencies in a niche market, building strengths and dismantling weaknesses, and leveraging environmental and market opportunities, as well as technological opportunities.

A further option is to extend the company's core business, for example, by offering complementary products and services or integrated solutions. The company could also attempt to transfer its products, brand, or other areas of expertise to new applications. This can be done, for example, by transferring core products to new customers or regions or resources and capabilities to new areas of business in order to leverage synergy effects.

Another option is to tap into new success potentials, for example, through developing innovative products or processes, ramping up core competencies, opening up to partnerships, or introducing dynamic network structures along the value chain.

Consolidation and focus (Hammer and Champy, 2006)

If the company, however, is under a significant pressure to act and has only limited transformation readiness, its only option for securing its survival is to overcome the product and sales crisis by consolidating and concentrating on its core business. This initially involves reducing overcapacities because the focus here is on cost efficiency. The company may also have to divest itself of certain divisions that are less efficient or sell

---

CHALLENGES CONCERNING THE DESIGN OF BUSINESS VISION AND MODEL:
1. Investigate the core competencies of the company or performance potentials of certain individuals as well as develop new core competencies.
2. Describe the mission statement in a tangible manner that enables it to be applied to specific goals. Provide the direction and level of difficulty for the key goals.
3. Consider the mutual dependencies of the key implementing measures.
4. Establish transformation strategy.

KEY MESSAGE:
Nowadays, it is not absolutely essential for companies to focus on exactly one of these strategies and then become a leader. On the contrary, a better approach is to pursue several strategic options and combine the various strategies in such a way that this combination represents a unique selling point in itself.

them. Outsourcing or offshoring certain areas or individual business processes too are potential initiatives if they produce cost savings.

Another option is to focus on the company's core competencies. This can mean concentrating on key basic requirements or focusing on selected products and markets where the prospects of success are good. However, it may also be expedient for the company to focus on those markets or products where its competitors are weak.

Once the company's mission statement and transformation strategy have been established, the next step is to describe its future business model. This entails the production and sales program, the sales and marketing plans, purchasing strategy, key research and development products, financing options, workforce planning and qualification planning, as well as the IT architecture and IT planning.

3.3.5 STEP 6: DEVELOP INTEGRATED TRANSFORMATION PLAN

Once the future business model has been developed, its implementation is planned before a final decision is taken by top management. Implementation planning contains a "high level" plan of all the necessary transformation steps, the associated expenditure, an estimate of the monetary and non-monetary benefits, and the strategic risks. At the same time, a rough description of the target organization and the organization model during the transformation is compiled. The transformation plan contains elements of all the management disciplines such as Program and Project Management, Business Process Management, Value Management, Transformational IT Management, Organizational Change Management, Risk Management, and Competence and Training Management. Success requires a close dovetailing of all these management disciplines and intensive dialogue between all of the experts involved in planning.

The business transformation plan begins with the design of the transformation framework (meta level). This requires an analysis of the necessary management and communication style as well as the values of the future company. If the company has enough time to complete the transformation, a participatory management style that promotes autonomy can bring about success. This also fosters identification with the company's future mission statement and ensures that its implementation is largely planned and designed by the employees themselves. In turn, it promotes motivation and entrepreneurial thinking within the company. The transformation plan should be tailored to open and objective communication. This means that the reasons for the transformation (case for action) are presented objectively and the pros and cons are discussed. The situation does not have to be exaggerated to conjure up a crisis situation if one does not actually exist.

If the company is under considerable pressure to complete its business transformation, it should nevertheless act with as much autonomy as possible and as much control as necessary. It goes without saying that the most important thing is to secure the company's survival, and the measures required to do this should also be implemented immediately. Nevertheless, it is precisely at this point that intensive communication regarding the reasons and the planned mission statement is essential to signal that this approach is only temporary while it is necessary to secure the survival of the organization.

It is also important to discuss and identify the key formal and informal roles for the transformation at an early stage. These include the top managers of the divisions that will be affected most by the transformation and that are crucial to the transformation. A decision should also be taken on the top sponsor (power promoter) of the transformation and who the business transformation managers will be. It is also advisable to decide on who will support the business transformation as the expert promoter and who can be relationship promoter. The steering committee for the transformation should also be appointed as the future decision-making body.

From a process management perspective, the key changes in the process organization that are required to describe the future business model should be determined. Starting from a rather abstract level, the processes that will change are identified and the target profile for these processes is described.

As a result, the need for change can be determined and the associated improvement potentials derived. In addition, the measures that are required to bring the company's process management maturity to the level necessary for the transformation should be planned.

Once the need for transformation has been determined, the necessary change management measures can be derived. Furthermore, an initial stakeholder matrix is compiled and an estimate is carried out for the key stakeholders as to what extent they will be affected directly or indirectly by the change and whether their attitude towards the business transformation is positive, negative or neutral. Following this, key change management measures are defined.

The benefits associated with the process changes are outlined in brief and – if possible – the monetary value is calculated. A monetary evaluation is not always possible, particularly if key strategic changes are involved. Value added can also be created that does not result directly from the process changes. Nevertheless, the objective is systematically and realistically to record and represent all of the key value-added aspects of the business transformation.

A further investigation should be carried out as to whether the job requirements associated with the process changes necessitate specialist or interdisciplinary employee

CHALLENGES CONCERNING THE DEVELOPMENT OF AN INTEGRATED TRANSFORMATION PLAN:

1. Analyze the necessary management and communication style as well as the values of the future company.
2. Tailor the communication plan in order to enable open and objective communication.
3. Discuss and identify the key formal and informal roles for the transformation at an early stage.
4. Determine the key changes in the process organization that are required to describe the future business model.
5. Analyze initially key qualification and training requirements.
6. Review the future IT architecture and compile an implementation plan.

KEY MESSAGE:

It is precisely at this point that intensive communication regarding the reasons and the planned mission statement is essential to signal that this approach is necessary to secure the survival of the organization.

qualifications. An initial analysis should indicate the key qualification and training requirements.

Changes to process flows usually also impact the company's IT. The future IT architecture has already been recorded as part of the IT maturity assessment. In addition, provisions must be made for adapting or implementing applications that are required as a result of the process changes. For this reason, the future IT architecture must be reviewed and an implementation plan compiled.

All of the measures are then subjected to a transformation risk assessment using the "360° Strategic Risk Assessment" approach (see Chapter 5, Risk Management). By applying this approach, information can be collected from a variety of perspectives – from managers, employees, partners, specialists and IT departments, as well as external experts. To provide greater transparency and a better overview, the connections between strategy, processes, need for change, training requirements, IT, benefits and risks are represented in a business transformation network.

3.4 Conclusion

Strategy management primarily addresses the envision phase of the transformation lifecycle and is concerned with strategy development. In this chapter an approach was presented to develop a strategy for business transformation by taking into account the complexity of the transformation itself. The approach is based on the following six steps:

1. Establish a "winning team" out of key stakeholders and develop a common understanding of the project.
2. Analyze the external and internal factors that will affect the future of a company to be transformed.
3. Investigate the effects that the transformation drivers have on the enterprise as well as the associated opportunities and risks.
4. Design a business vision.
5. Develop a sustainable business model for the company.
6. Implement the transformation plan.

To obtain a reliable estimate of the business transformation need and to elaborate sustained transformation concepts, a selection of appropriate methods and tools is presented briefly. Factors affecting the implementation of the business transformation are also summarized. According to our research team, these are in particular organizational readiness, process readiness and IT readiness.

It is worth mentioning that an integrated transformation plan considers all BTM² disciplines. Such a plan is necessary since the weakest element might determine the success or the failure respectively of the business transformation. Consequently, an interdisciplinary strategy team is also significant. Thus, a well-developed transformation plan and strategy strongly contribute to a successful business transformation.

ENVISIONING THE ORGANIZATION – AN EXCURSION BY DOMINIC HOULDER

Many transformation initiatives fail, or succeed only after a painful series of restarts and revisions. A typical dénouement, as our case studies show, is a "transformational" IT initiative running into the sand, over budget and with missing deliverables, in the wake of non-cooperation, rejection or even sabotage by key stakeholders in the organization. A key insight from our case studies is that the all the transformational initiatives need to follow, not lead, a vision of the organization. A major source of transformational failure is allowing organization design to become a consequence of the transformation process, rather than its guiding principle.

Envisioning the desired organization at the start of the transformation process most obviously helps to ensure buy-in from its stakeholders and eases the subsequent task of change management. But it is crucial for a more fundamental set of reasons that relate to the drivers of transformed company performance.

Maximizing shareholder value is a central performance objective for most companies, and finance theory shows that this depends on achieving sustainable, profitable growth. In general, the triggers for transformation are concerns about untapped opportunities for profitable growth that the company is unable to realize, or even concerns about the drivers of profitable growth tipping into reverse. Profitable growth depends on competitive advantage in exploring and exploiting opportunities, which – as the strategy literature shows – in turn hinges on the possession of "strategic resources" that are the building blocks for creating customer value, and which are also scarce, and hard to imitate or substitute.

What exactly are these resources? In a world of increasingly knowledge-intensive businesses these strategic resources, in plain terms, are people. To transform performance, we need, in the end, to transform people – that is, to free individuals to unleash their own personal competitive advantages, to do their tasks of value creation superbly, collaborating effectively with others. The cradle for this is what we describe as the "organization": the structures, processes, systems, culture and policies that when transformed will enable people to accomplish great things, realizing opportunities and removing obstructions.

Transformational aspirations are often couched in terms that are familiar and meaningful to those at the top of companies and those who advise them – shareholder value, market position, value chains, ecosystems, processes and the like. But to ensure success, the envisioning phase of a transformation must ensure that all of these can be translated into what the transformational change means for individuals and their jobs, and are embedded in the definition of the target organization that will make individual transformation possible.

In addition to defining the target organization – the people, processes and purpose of the future – the envisioning phase needs to include a definition of the enabling organization that will work within the organization as a whole to bring about the transformational change.

The Target Organization

Our case studies of global businesses show a shared pattern of transformation. In the latest, most successful phases of transformation, these companies are leading the process with a vision of people, their jobs and organization design. But to get to that point has, in all cases, been a struggle. The companies in our case studies have learned the hard way that definition of the target organization is key to transformational success.

In their early years, like many global leaders these companies were centralized around their home countries or core businesses, where, typically, key customers, partners, efficient capacity and expertise were all co-located. As they developed a global footprint, the early organization model was one of core and periphery: the core being the home country or primary activity, and the periphery arising from emerging opportunities in more remote geographies or product markets. Power was typically concentrated at the center, often expressed through strategic plans tightly governing activities through a hierarchy.

In a first phase of transformation, all of these companies decentralized with increasing vigor during the 1990s. In some cases this mirrored the growing importance of markets and supply sources beyond the traditional heartland, and the rise to power of country managers who demanded autonomy commensurate with the size of their budgets. In another case, decentralization mirrored the diversification of the group across three distinct industries and 130 operating companies, leaving little scope for the center to act other than as a holding company. Another company in our set of case studies decentralized under the culture shock of merger: only a loose combination of two very different organizations – one a trusted, high-quality provider, the other a low-end producer in the same sector – was possible given the different histories, values and market positions. Our case studies included a new corporate venture which was conceived in the late 1990s as a business organizationally separate from its parent: an island of technology, with its own partner ecosystem, product strategy and route to market, without any connection to the parent company's IT architecture, business processes or systems.

Allied to these company-specific factors was the rise, during the 1990s, of management theories celebrating the virtues of autonomy and accountability so as to enable fast responses to local opportunities and laser-like focus on local performance. The corporate parenting role, in many cases, became one of financial control – focused on outputs – rather than strategic planning. At local level, heterogeneous processes, policies and systems tended to proliferate in this period, in all the cases that we studied. Centralization was out of fashion: IBM, Japan and the Soviet Union had all gone wrong simultaneously. This first phase of transformation had an organizational vision at its core: setting people free from bureaucracy. But freedom came at a price.

Despite the virtues of local autonomy, the companies in our sample found that decentralization brought with it mounting disadvantages, which – after 2000 – gave rise to efforts to reverse the trend to varying degrees. From a global perspective, there were increasing opportunities for labor cost arbitrage: consolidating activities into low-cost locations. Consolidating hitherto local activities provided benefits that went beyond cost savings: knowledge-intensive activities could be aggregated into global hubs, bringing centers of expertise up to the level needed for sustainable world-class excellence. Moreover, the fragmentation associated with decentralized organizations meant that opportunities for synergy and knowledge transfer could be missed. All of these factors could tip the balance of competitive advantage or disadvantage at the business level. At the level of the corporation as a whole, it was becoming apparent that the decentralized model could not be controlled, other than through high-level and usually historic financial data, and this had become less acceptable in an era of greater risk. Corporate leaders saw a greater need to move the global enterprise more swiftly as new opportunities and threats emerged. As well as slowing down responsiveness at a global level, the complexity of different local processes, systems and policies created gave rise to costs that needed to be addressed through simplification and a measure of recentralization.

This was the backdrop to the more recent phases of transformation seen in our case studies from 2000 to 2010. But despite the obvious economic benefits to be gained through recentralization, in all the cases that we studied the transformation initiatives encountered varying degrees of organizational obstruction. Local autonomy had been a hard-won prize for many senior managers. This would not be given up without a compelling argument that went beyond the projections of cost savings that were typical of business cases made at the time. The winning arguments were those that defined an organizational vision that would enable key stakeholders to do their jobs excellently.

In two of our case studies, for example, success in HR transformation initiatives after 2005 depended on the core proposition that – far from undermining the autonomy of HR directors and their business partners – more effective global collaboration and support would empower them to perform their local roles far more effectively. The creation of global hubs as centers of excellence in learning and development, for example, gave in-country HR directors access to world-class resources that could not be matched locally. The global standardization of policies and the centralization of administration in global delivery centers reduced complexity and saved costs. But more vitally it freed HR directors to concentrate on the core of their task – supporting the business partner with excellent HR advice. Here, the organizational vision was one of connectivity: localizing where autonomy was critical to value creation, and globalizing where scale was critical to supporting value creating activities at a world-class level.

The first, decentralizing phase of transformation in the organizations we studied aimed to release individuals from the old bureaucratic constraints. But over time this turned out to be insufficient: the more recent phases of transformation have focused on restoring connectivity where this adds value to people's jobs, creating connected global powerhouses rather than fragmented islands of activity. In this new phase of transformation, defining the target organization – how connectivity will help individuals rather than constrain them in old bureaucratic ways – is key to success, as key stakeholders will recognize that the move away from decentralization entails a loss of freedom. The corresponding gain needs to be clearly spelled out.

The Enabling Organization

Transformation inevitably entails conflict: between old and new and – vitally, between those whose task is to enable change, and those whose task is to run the existing business. Indeed, conflict drives transformation as we have seen in the dialectical process of change from centralized through decentralized to connected organizations in our case studies. To ensure that conflict does not derail the transformation, defining and safeguarding the enabling organization is critical.

The enabling organization is comprised of the people and processes that make transformational change happen. It is much more than a project team: it owns the transformation strategy; it may often be permanent, charged with enabling successive waves of transformation across functions, geographies and time. Because it is a distinct organization within the company, the boundaries around it allow the existing businesses to continue running effectively with minimum disturbance and distraction while the transformation is in progress. Because managing conflict is a central role for the enabling organization, its definition during the envisioning phase needs to show how conflict will be managed.

Here are Four Key Principles

The first is to ensure that the enabling organization is given power and protection from the top of the company. In our most successful case studies, the enabling organization was directly championed by the CEO or board-level function head (in the case of the HR transformations we studied), and those leading it reported directly to the C-Suite. Championship entails commitment: again, in the successful case studies we explored, the CEO or function head had identified their own, personal success or failure with the transformation agenda. This meant "burning bridges" through public statements of objectives, so that yielding to pressures for delay or reversal from opposed stakeholders would carry too humiliating a personal price.

The second is to bring the conflicts within the boundaries of the enabling organization. The full range of stakeholders needs to be given a voice: not just for the sake of buy-in but because they will represent the reality test for the definition of the target organization and implementation pathway. The conflicts in our case studies were rich sources of learning, leading to valuable breakthroughs in the context of a clear commitment to change.

The third is to make the definition of the enabling organization personal. Organizations are people, connected through processes by a purpose. Individuals will need to see their role in the enabling organization defined in terms of their personal task and career. This matters, because in too many cases being part of a transformation project has meant career death for talented, high-potential people: because of enmities aroused by conflict, the absence of familiar performance metrics enshrining success or simply too much time spent away from running the businesses, which are usually the source of recognition and power. It matters all the more because the enabling organization will need to include some of the company's best people who cannot be squandered and who will need to be convinced about their future prospects. In effect the enabling organization needs to be defined as a positive top talent career track, with well-envisioned selection criteria, metrics, development and exit paths.

The fourth is to ensure that the enabling organization becomes the source of key appointments in the target organization. If those running the businesses have had experience of the transformational task, they are more likely to understand the meaning of further phases and make conflict between old and new fruitful rather than destructive. And, as we found in our case studies, where transformation is becoming continuous, this provides the basis for a confident transformational culture to permeate the target organization as it takes shape.

Bibliography

Buzzell, Robert D. and Gale, Bradley T. (1987), *The PIMS Principles: Linking Strategy to Performance* (New York, London: The Free Press).

Doppler, Klaus and Lauterburg, Christoph (1994), *Change-Management: Den Unternehmenswandel Gestalten* (Frankfurt/Main, New York: Campus).

Groß, Paul J. (1997), Die Prüfung der Sanierungsfähigkeit im Rahmen der Insolvenzordnung, *Wirtschaftsprüfer Kammer Mitteilungen* (WPK-Sonderheft), Dezember, 4–20.

Groß, Paul J. (2004), Die Wahrung, Einschätzung und Beurteilung des „Going-Concern" in den Pflichten- und Verantwortungsrahmen von Unterneh-mensführung und Abschlussprüfung (Teil 2), *WPg – Die Wirtschaftsprüfung* 57, no. 24, 1433–50.

Groß, Paul J. (2009), Wesentliche Gesichtspunkte der Erarbeitung von IDW ES 6: zu den Hintergründen und Neuerungen des IDW Standards: Anforderungen an die Erstellung von Sanierungskonzepten, *WPg – Die Wirtschaftsprüfung* 62, no. 5, 231–45.

Hammer, Michael and Champy, James (2006), *Reengineering the Corporation: A Manifesto for Business Revolution* (New York: Harper Collins).

Krüger, Wilfried (2002), *Excellence in Change: Wege zur Strategischen Erneuerung*, 2nd ed. (Wiesbaden: Gabler).

Porter, Michael E. (2004), Wie die Kräfte des Wettbewerbs Strategien beeinflussen, *Harvard Business Manager*, no. 10, 49–61.

Schein, Edgar H. (1995), *Unternehmenskultur: Ein Handbuch für Führungskräfte* (Frankfurt: Campus Verlag).

Simon, Hermann (2007), *Hidden Champions des 21. Jahrhunderts: Die Erfolgsstrategien Unbekannter Weltmarktführer* (Frankfurt/Main: Campus).

Weiser, Mark (1999), The computer for the 21st century, *ACM SIGMOBILE Mobile Computing and Communications Review* 3, no. 3, 3–11.

4 *Value Management*

JOHN WARD (Cranfield University, School of
Management), THOMAS RENNEBAUM (Volkswagen
Financial Services AG) and STEPHAN AMLING (SAP AG)

4.1 Overview

This chapter describes an approach and a set of tools and techniques that organizations can use: a) to identify the potential business value of a transformation, b) to decide whether the investment is both worthwhile and achievable, and then c) to manage the elements of value through to successful delivery. The value management approach outlined here is based on proven techniques for identifying, planning, managing and evaluating the benefits of a business transformation. It depends on the engagement of stakeholders in the preparation of the business case and benefits plan to create the knowledge and commitment required to realize the benefits.

OBJECTIVES OF THIS CHAPTER:

1. Develop an understanding of what is meant by *value* and *benefit* in the context of business transformation.
2. Demonstrate why Value Management is an essential and continuing activity throughout the transformation lifecycle.
3. Understand how to use the key tools and techniques of Value Management within the four phases of envision, engage, transform and optimize.

4.2 Value Management in Business Transformation

The management of IT payoffs begins prior to the investment and continues through post implementation.

(Kohli and Devaraj, 2004)

The same is true of Value Management in all business transformations, whether or not they are enabled by IT. It is an essential activity at all stages of the transformation lifecycle, if the maximum value is to be gained from the changes.

Value does not just mean the financial benefits expected to be gained from the business transformation; it includes all the improvements that are perceived as beneficial by the organization's internal and external stakeholders. These can range from measurable performance improvements to opinions about the organization, how it conducts itself and the image it presents to the world.

Value Management is one of the three *directional* management disciplines along with Strategy Management and Risk Management. Together these provide the rationale for the business transformation and establish a realistic understanding of what can be achieved and the main factors affecting success. The evidence from the transformation case studies shows that if any of these three disciplines is overlooked or done poorly, the transformation will deliver fewer benefits than anticipated or may not even be completed.

In business transformations over an extended period, it is likely that many aspects of the value expected will be uncertain, as will be the resources and costs required to complete the later phases of work. Hence it may not be possible to produce a reliable business case that can enable the approval and allocation of all the funds required at the start of the transformation. Organizations deal with this in a number of ways, including:

- authorize all the funding based on the initial estimate of value, but require regular reappraisal of the expected value through interim reviews or "health-checks" during implementation;
- accept the initial estimates, but only authorize expenditure for transformation component projects which can be clearly justified, while reserving funds for later allocation, when the further phases of work and the benefits become more obvious. This implies that each component project may require a separate business case; and
- link approvals to the annual budget cycle, only authorizing expenditure for the parts of the program to be undertaken in the current financial year, but including estimates for the later work in future year financial forecasts.

Which of these or other options is chosen will largely depend on the financial control and investment policies of the organization, but will also be influenced by the predictability of economic and business conditions during the transformation period. The approach to value management described in this chapter can be adapted to accommodate these and other alternative ways of managing the financial risks associated with extensive and extended transformation programs. The transformation lifecycle is also designed to allow for these different ways of dealing with the uncertainties involved.

In the envision phase the emphasis is on determining what new or additional value the business transformation could create for the organization in relation to its business strategy and factors that determine success in the industry.

During the engage phase that strategic value is translated into specific benefits that should accrue to the organization, its customers, trading partners and all internal stakeholders if the changes proposed can be achieved successfully.

As the transform phase evolves each of those benefits, now owned by specific stakeholders, is tracked and reviewed to ensure that it is still achievable. Benefits may increase in value as the effects of the changes are better understood or decrease if changes prove difficult to accomplish completely and successfully. Iterations in the overall transformation process should be, at least in part, driven by the increased knowledge of the actual value that the changes can deliver. Ensuring that the value expected is still achievable if the business context or priorities change significantly, may even require re-envisioning the whole transformation and redefining the overall value it is trying to achieve.

Reviewing what has been achieved and ensuring the new value can be sustained or even enhanced as the changes become *business as usual* is a key aspect of the optimize phase. This should also include an assessment of further potential benefits that could now be achieved, but were not apparent before the changes had actually been made, as well as actions to recover any benefits that have not as yet been realized but still can be.

The value management approach described in this chapter is mainly derived from the benefits management process and toolkit (Ward and Daniel, 2006) which is already in use in many organizations around the world. In this context the definition of benefits management can be adapted to be:

"The process of organizing and managing so that the potential value from a business transformation is actually realized."

A benefit is defined as an advantage provided to specific groups or individuals. A key premise of benefits management is that benefits only arise from changes made by individuals or groups, and these changes must be identified and managed successfully. *"Benefits* realization" and "change *management"* are therefore inextricably linked. Its origins are in improving the business value delivered from IT-enabled transformation programs and projects, but organizations are now using it for a wide range of large business change programs, since many of the issues are the same, with or without IT. Like the meta management model, it is an iterative process and there is a close alignment between the components of both.

Figure 4.1 shows the overall Value Management process and how the activities relate to the four phases of the transformation lifecycle.

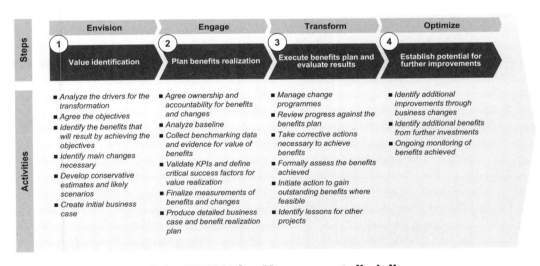

Figure 4.1   Phases of the BTM² Value Management discipline

Our research surveys (see Ward et al., 2007, and Ward and Daniel, 2008) have shown that although organizations recognize the importance of these activities the majority do not believe they carry them out very successfully and this may explain why the majority of change programs fail to deliver all the value expected. Table 4.1 summarizes the findings from over 200 international organizations. The results show there is much that organizations can gain from a comprehensive value management approach applied throughout the transformation lifecycle.

Table 4.1   Levels of satisfaction with key Value Management activities

	Not satisfied with their current approach
Identifying value and benefits	68%
Investment business cases and benefit plans	69%
Managing the delivery of benefits	75%
Evaluation and review of value realized	81%

4.3 Value Identification

In the envision phase of a new business transformation initiative it is essential to identify and agree the underlying reasons why change is necessary and why the status quo is no longer a viable option. This requires an analysis of the external and internal drivers affecting the organization's current and future performance or even its survival. This analysis is discussed in Chapter 3, Strategy Management, and it is important that the resulting drivers are specific to the organization and its situation and they capture both the need for transformation and the timescale within which it has to be accomplished.

The business transformation should be a response to one or more drivers, normally formulated in outline by the executive team during development of the business strategy, but in defining the objectives and overall scope of the transformation the drivers need to be verified and made explicit: "Why do we need to change and why now?" The drivers also need to express the expected consequences of not changing and should help define the aspects of the business that need to change.

For example, an external driver could be:

> *We are losing too many customers due to our inconsistent service levels and increased consumer expectations which our main competitors can now achieve 90 percent of the time.*

Or an internal driver:

> *Our rate of new product introductions is below the level required to replace the profits from obsolescent products in the next three years.*

4.3.1 THE BUSINESS TRANSFORMATION PORTFOLIO

Based on the drivers, the business transformation can be classified according to the overall business impact expected and the nature of the business and organizational changes that will be required in terms of the balance of:

a)   changes to remove problems or overcome constraints, relative to
b)   innovations to create and exploit new capabilities or opportunities.

The different types of transformations can be classified using the portfolio matrix shown in Figure 4.2. In this context, most transformations will be either *strategic*, involving innovations, or *key operational*, removing constraints to remaining competitive, or a combination of both. *Strategic* transformations may also have *high potential* components – new options to be evaluated – and aspects of *key operational* transformations may include elements that are clearly *support* – removing or replacing inefficient or costly processes. Some transformations will include elements of all four types. In general, success depends on first removing the problems and constraints, after which required innovations become easier to accomplish and also further opportunities emerge (Peppard and Ward, 2005).

If the initiative is entirely *support* or *high potential* in nature it should be managed as a discrete project, not a transformation. From experience it is important to make this distinction to prevent escalation of non-critical initiatives to become major organizational change programs. Evidence from some of our cases, especially in the HR area, shows how easily this can happen, when the main benefits result from procedural efficiencies, but achieving them somehow requires the implementation of global HR data bases.

Figure 4.2   The transformation portfolio matrix

By considering all the current and planned transformation initiatives as an investment and change portfolio, management can begin to assess the implications of the overall extent of the changes it is expecting to happen, the resource commitments that implies and also potential risks that may be created. It also enables priorities to be set and the relationships among the programs to be explored to optimize schedules, reconcile contention for key resources, avoid "digging up the road too often" and mitigate the potential effects of organizational "change fatigue".

4.3.2 SETTING OBJECTIVES FOR BUSINESS TRANSFORMATION

The objectives for any transformation or project should "paint a picture" of what the world is expected to look like if it is completed successfully, expressed in a few, preferably no more than five, concise statements that everyone involved can understand. They should be quite specific, defining the transformation so that it cannot be confused with any other initiative or project. Each objective should have an explicit link to one or more of the strategic drivers to demonstrate why achieving it matters.

They should also, as far as possible, comply with the concept of SMART objectives: Specific, Measurable, Achievable, Relevant and Time-bound, but equally importantly they should "tell a story" that makes sense to all the key stakeholders, such that they want to contribute their knowledge and time. That often implies that they can see benefits for themselves in the achievement of one or more of the objectives. From experience, the sequence of expressing the benefits also matters for three main reasons:

1. Externally facing objectives that will benefit customers will have broader organizational acceptance than objectives that suggest benefits to particular internal groups.
2. Positive, creative objectives about new or better things that will happen should come first, since they are more likely to encourage action than negative or reductionist objectives.
3. The story being told should be memorable, if the transformation is truly worthwhile. And having more than five objectives makes the story too difficult for most people to remember.

For example, in the UK NHS Long Term Conditions (e.g. diabetes) Program, restructuring the objectives to:

- first describe how patients' health and quality of life would improve;
- then how services would be better organized to reduce clinical risks and be less stressed by emergencies;
- next how staff would have their professional skills and discretion increased; and
- finally how efficiencies would be achieved to reduce waste and cope with increased patient volumes,

led not only to more buy-in to the changes from clinicians, but also enabled more pragmatic and acceptable approaches to achieving the changes to be identified.

Although the initial business transformation objectives should be set in the envision phase, by the executive management team, they frequently require some revision during the engage phase, when both the specific benefits that can be realized are clearer and the potential changes are understood in more detail. If the objectives are modified, the new ones must be agreed by all the main stakeholders and endorsed at executive level. Setting the initial objectives also often helps identify who the key stakeholders are and who at the executive level would be the most effective transformation sponsor.

In many transformations these activities are rushed through, since it is not always appreciated that in being precise and rigorous about the objectives, shared assumptions are being explored and agreement reached concerning what the transformation *is not about*, as well as what it is expected to achieve. This helps prevent later breakdown into disconnected streams of activity as some stakeholders selfishly pursue or protect their own interests, with disregard for, or even at the expense of achieving the overall value expected – this is known as "segmented institutionalism" (Kumar et al., 1998), a very destructive force which explains the underachievement of many change programs, including some of our case studies. Vagueness or ambiguity at the start leaves considerable scope for misunderstanding and divergence later.

4.3.3 FROM OBJECTIVES TO BENEFITS

As mentioned above, the benefits management rationale is that benefits and changes are inextricably linked and have to be considered at the same time, rather than creating a list of benefits and later working out how to achieve them. The business case should not only explain the value to be delivered from the investment, but also provide adequate evidence that the value can actually be achieved.

For *strategic* transformations the value will result mainly from innovating in the products or services the organization provides, or the markets and customers it serves or by conducting business in new ways or a combination of these. In the case of SMART, the transformation was intended to deliver all of these: a new product for a new customer segment to be manufactured and sold through a new business model.

Key operational transformations on the other hand tend to deliver value associated with rationalizing or redesigning existing processes, relationships and structures to improve aspects of performance, for example, through greater consistency, reliability, efficiency and faster response times. These in turn should result in meeting customer expectations, achieving required margins and making more effective use of organizational resources and capabilities.

Before a robust business case can be produced, a number of questions need to be considered. The answers are used to help develop the investment case and also a viable change management plan to deliver the benefits.

1. What specific benefits will be realized by particular stakeholders if each of the investment objectives is achieved?
2. How will each benefit be measured?
3. Who "owns" each benefit and will be accountable for its delivery?
4. What changes are needed to achieve each benefit?
5. Who will be responsible for ensuring that each change is successfully made?
6. How and when can the identified changes be made?

The knowledge required to address these questions is unlikely to be found in any one individual, but will be distributed across a number of people, who must be brought together normally in a workshop mode to provide the answers. A technique to both facilitate this process and document the results is the benefits dependency network, a template for which is shown in Figure 4.3.

4.3.4 THE BENEFITS DEPENDENCY NETWORK

Each transformation objective is examined from the perspective of different groups of stakeholders to identify the benefits they will gain when the objective is achieved. This should be done preferably by the representatives of the group, but in some cases it will have to be on their behalf (e.g. for customers) at the workshop. But any *proxy* benefits should be validated with the stakeholders themselves later.

Investment objectives and benefits differ in the following way: the objectives are the overall goals or aims of the transformation, which are agreed by all relevant stakeholders. In contrast, benefits are advantages provided to specific groups or individuals as a result of meeting the overall objectives. Provided the benefits to different parties do not give rise to conflict, there is no need for all stakeholders to agree each benefit. For most transformations meeting each of the objectives will provide benefits to a number of different stakeholders, so while an investment may have only three or four objectives, it may well produce a large number of benefits.

This definition of benefits also implies two things: if no-one wants the benefit, it does not exist and the benefit is defined by the stakeholder(s) concerned. Initially it is important to capture the benefit in the words that the stakeholder uses, rather than in generic terms, both to gain the commitment to achieving it and ensure its meaning is fully understood. For example, a busy hospital nurse would see the benefit of a reduction of time spent on paper work as being able to spend more time on patient care. If this is expressed by management as "increased nursing efficiency", it fails to capture the main purpose of nursing, which is to provide high-quality care.

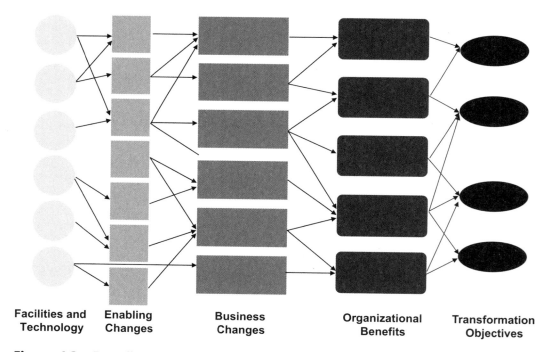

| Facilities and Technology | Enabling Changes | Business Changes | Organizational Benefits | Transformation Objectives |

Figure 4.3   Benefits dependency or business transformation value network

Source: Reproduced with permission from Ward, John and Daniel, Elizabeth (2006), *Benefits Management: Delivering Value from IS & IT Investments* (Chichester: Wiley).

For each benefit expressed the first test is "How will we know it has been achieved?" or "Can it be measured?" Measures can be subjective opinions and in some cases have to be, but it is preferable if a more objective measure can be identified. For benefits that survive this test the next stage is to identify the changes that will have to be made if the benefit is to be realized. Changes can be categorized into three types: business changes, enabling changes, and facilities and technology (see Figure 4.3):

Business changes are permanent changes to working practices, processes, structures or relationships that are required to be implemented and sustained to deliver the benefits.

Enabling changes are typically "one-off" changes which are prerequisites for making the business changes or to bring the new technology or facilities into effective operation. Enabling changes involve such tasks as defining and agreeing new job roles and responsibilities, redesigning processes, establishing new performance management systems and training in new business skills. One enabling change that is often overlooked is "decommissioning" the old processes and ensuring obsolete practices are actually stopped. Designing a new process or business model is an enabling change, whereas carrying it out to meet performance expectations is a business change. There is also often some confusion between benefits and changes: for example, "standardized or consistent processes" are often quoted as a benefit, but in reality are just changes; the benefit could be, for example: "reduced loss of orders due to unpredictable service levels" or "reduced staff training costs".

Facilities and technology, including IT applications and infrastructure, are also enablers and are often the "active ingredient" that makes the transformation possible, but normally need to be connected through other enabling or business changes to deliver business benefits.

The network is created by working from back from the objectives through benefits that should be gained, to the changes and new capabilities required to produce the benefits. It is then "joined up" from left to right to assess whether the combinations of changes are sufficient to deliver the benefits and in turn the transformation objectives. It should clearly show the combinations of changes needed to deliver each benefit and also all the benefits that should result from a particular change or set of changes.

Reviewing the network may reveal further changes that are needed, or additional benefits that could result from the changes proposed. Equally, some of the benefits may prove not worthwhile when the changes needed to achieve them are too difficult, costly or risky. If it appears that a large number of the benefits depend on very challenging or high risk changes the network should be explored to find ways of phasing or breaking down the changes to be more manageable or trading off some of the benefits to reduce the risks of not achieving others.

4.3.5 THE INITIAL BUSINESS CASE

Once the network is believed to represent the main elements of the business transformation and it appears to be feasible, a first-cut business case assessment can be prepared by making an overall "order of magnitude" estimate of the likely costs of the changes and giving executive management the opportunity to decide if it is an investment they are willing to make to achieve the objectives. A thorough financial evaluation of the benefits will be made before the final business case is prepared, as will be discussed later in the chapter, but at this stage the decision is whether to proceed further into the engage phase, not to implement. Issues of ownership and measurement are also discussed in more detail later.

Figure 4.4 shows an example part of a network for a transformation of the European marketing and sales activities in a paper manufacturer, associated with the implementation of a new Customer Relationship Management (CRM) system.

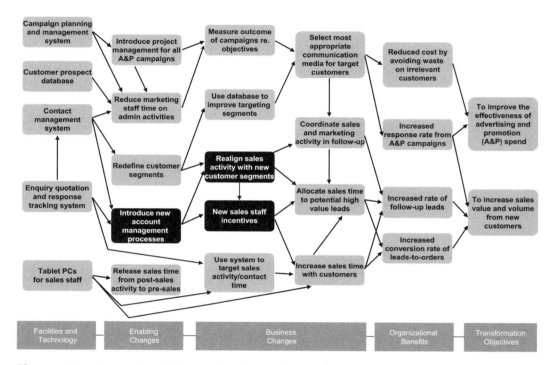

Figure 4.4   Part of a CRM-enabled transformation network

Source: Reproduced with permission from Peppard, Joe, Ward, John and Daniel, Elizabeth (2007), Managing the realization of business benefits from IT investments, *MIS Quarterly Executive* 6, no. 1, 15–25.

4.3.6 THE PROCESS IS AS IMPORTANT AS THE PRODUCT

Problems are often the result of either a lack of common understanding of the purposes of changes or different perspectives on how to achieve them successfully.

(Ramiller and Swanson, 2003)

The process of developing the network through the involvement of the main stakeholders in the transformation is an effective way of both gaining acceptance of the need for change and also achieving a consensus on how the changes can be accomplished. Even though the network will be revised as more detail is added regarding the changes as the transformation proceeds, it is an effective way of communicating what it is expected to involve, along with the argument as to why it is needed, the objectives and the overall value expected to be realized.

CHALLENGES CONCERNING THE VALUE IDENTIFICATION:
1.   Identify strategic drivers and establish the initial business transformation objectives.
2.   Classify the business transformation based on the strategic drivers according to the overall business impact and contribution expected.
3.   Identify the potential benefits and main changes needed to achieve them.
4.   Make an initial assessment of the transformation business case based on the potential benefits and an estimate of the likely costs.

KEY MESSAGE:
If it appears that a large number of the benefits depend on very challenging or high risk changes, the benefits dependency network should be examined to find ways of phasing or breaking down the changes to be more manageable, or trading off some of the less important benefits to reduce the risks of not achieving others.

4.4 Plan Benefit Realization

Identifying *"owners"* for both the benefits and changes is an essential aspect of the engage phase and should be done before the final business case is prepared, to increase the commitment of the main stakeholders to its contents (see Section 4.4.1). In addition, a baseline analysis is required to establish current performance levels for each of the main benefits, so that the estimated improvement is realistic (see Section 4.4.2). Based on these results, the final business case is prepared (see Section 4.4.3) and a benefit realization plan is created, which not only explains the required steps and responsibilities, but also the dependencies between changes and benefits (see Section 4.4.4).

4.4.1 AGREEING OWNERSHIP OF THE BENEFITS AND CHANGES

Identifying *"owners"* for both the benefits and changes is an essential aspect of the engage phase and should be done before the final business case is prepared, to increase the commitment of the main stakeholders to its contents. "Owners" are those named individuals or job role holders who accept responsibility for doing all they can to make the changes happen successfully, or to work with those making changes to ensure that the benefits are achieved. Each change "box" and benefit on the network needs to have an owner or in some cases joint owners. This makes clear the roles, responsibilities and accountability of managers and other stakeholders in the transform phase. The network shows how those roles and responsibilities are related among stakeholder groups: who depends on whom. The boxes highlighted in Figure 4.4 show three significant changes that were combined as one project, within the transformation program, for which the sales director took personal responsibility.

It is also the role of the benefit owners to describe the benefit in the business case, how it will be measured, define the current baseline and decide whether it can be quantified and valued in advance, as described later. Equally it will be the owners' task to measure the extent to which it has been achieved after implementation of the relevant changes.

4.4.2 BASELINE ANALYSIS

Having prepared an outline business case that argues that overall the business transformation can deliver the required contribution to the business strategy at an acceptable cost, further work is needed to refine the business case, not just to obtain funding but as a way of gaining organizational commitment to carry out the changes. Included in that is a baseline analysis for each of the main benefits to establish current performance levels, so that the level of potential improvement is realistic and can be quantified as far as possible.

This involves two main steps.

1. To establish whether there are current measures in place which provide the data and if not, if they can be established at an acceptable cost to define the current position.
2. The organization can use benchmarking or other data to compare its level of performance with others to understand the degree of improvement that can reasonably be achieved and then whether the changes proposed will be likely to deliver that improvement. There is normally a wealth of benchmarking data available within an industry for established processes and practices, but if the changes are innovative or radical, it will be necessary to look at other industries or carry out some form of prototype, pilot or experiment to explore and evaluate the potential for improvement.

It is important to establish "where we are now" in relation to each of the benefits to help build as robust and accurate business case against which success will eventually be measured. But also an accurate assessment of the current situation will normally reveal priority areas for improvement within the transformation and help schedule the changes to deliver some "quick wins". For example in the CRM network above, it was soon clear that as many as 70 percent of the A&P campaigns ran behind schedule, mainly due to over-estimating resource availability. The introduction of project planning tools quickly improved the accuracy of the schedules and reduced the problems, the delays and uncertainties were causing in both marketing and sales.

An accurate baseline also increases the credibility of the transformation for many stakeholders, leading to greater commitment and involvement in improving the situation. Often (and some of the case studies showed this), management ambitions for the transformation may not have much relationship to the current situation in many parts of the organization. For example in some of the global HR programs, the value of "transparency" to make better use of organizational resources and skills did not fit with the reality of the very limited movement of staff across different business units or countries and the existing programs for staff development within each unit. The baseline analysis will also help gain stakeholder buy-in during the engage phase, if they believe the improvements are both worthwhile and achievable, given the current situation. This can help overcome a major issue that has caused many business transformations to fail, and could be observed in some of our case studies:

There may be a major disconnect between the strategic intent of a decision to implement a system and the resulting actions that must be completed.

(Bancroft et al., 1998)

4.4.3 DETAILED BUSINESS CASE

In our surveys it was somewhat disturbing to find that although most organizations require business cases to be produced for most projects and programs, especially when IT expenditure is involved, many were less than satisfied that the business cases had a significant influence on the success of the investment. We found that although 96 percent of organizations develop business cases for most project investments, 69 percent are not satisfied with the quality or usefulness of those business cases. Motives for developing business cases and levels of satisfaction were expressed as:

1. To secure the investment budget: 93 percent (*63 percent were satisfied*).
2. To identify all the potential benefits: 76 percent (*46 percent were satisfied*).
3. To secure business commitment to implementation: 79 percent (*37 percent were satisfied*).
4. As a basis for reviewing the success of the investment: 78 percent (*38 percent were satisfied*).

This suggests that the main purpose of the business case is to obtain funding and they generally achieve that – it's only after that the problems arise. The ultimate purpose of a business case is to commit the organization to achieving the benefits expressed in it and this does not appear to happen often enough. Other studies have produced similar conclusions (Ross and Beath, 2002). Part of the reason is the continued insistence in many organizations on a mainly or even exclusively financial case. While the aim of any business case is to express as many of the benefits as possible in financial terms, an exclusive focus on such benefits can result in a number of issues, for example:

- encouraging "creative" calculations of financial benefits based on inadequate evidence;
- making unrealistic assumptions to claim sufficient financial benefits to provide the necessary return in relation to the costs;
- discouraging innovative projects since the financial benefits of innovation may be less certain;
- focusing on purely efficiency gains from improved individual processes, but often at the expense of overall organizational effectiveness; and
- understating the organizational costs of implementation, such as process redesign, restructuring and training.

The results of our surveys confirm that the more successful organizations include a wider range of benefits in their business cases than the less successful, especially benefits associated with innovation and improved co-operation, both internally and with trading partners. Although these benefits are more difficult, but not impossible, to quantify they provide a more complete view of the business value that many transformations produce. The less successful organizations tend to limit the benefits included to those associated with efficiency improvements and cost savings. While some senior managers are primarily interested in the financial benefits, many other stakeholders, such as customers and employees can be more interested in the "softer" or more subjective benefits. It is these benefits, rather than the financial ones that are likely to lead to greater commitment from those stakeholders to making the investment successful.

> Business benefits realized depend on achieving a fair balance of benefits between the organization and its stakeholders. The issue of gain sharing is of critical importance ... with no apparent benefits to them, stakeholders are likely to resist the system.
>
> (Jurison, 1996)

Having identified the potential benefits from the transformation they can be analyzed and reviewed in terms of their nature and value using a structuring approach, whereby each benefit is described in the model shown in Figure 4.5.

Degree of Explicitness	Do New Things	Do Things Better	Stop Doing Things
Financial benefits	By applying a cost/price or other valid financial formula to a quantifiable benefit, a financial value can be calculated.		
Quantifiable benefits	Sufficient evidence exists to forecast how much improvement/value should result from the change.		
Measurable benefits	This aspect of performance is currently being measured or an appropriate measure could be implemented. But it is not possible to estimate by how much performance will improve when the changes are complete.		
Observable benefits	By use of agreed criteria, specific individuals/groups will decide, based on their experience or judgment, to what extent the benefit has been realized.		

Figure 4.5   Framework for structuring the benefits and building the business case

Source: Reproduced with permission from Ward, John and Daniel, Elizabeth (2006), *Benefits Management: Delivering Value from IS & IT Investments* (Chichester: Wiley).

This framework classifies or structures the benefits according to two factors: the type of change that gives rise to the benefit and how much is already known or can be determined about the benefit before the investment is made – the *degree of explicitness*. Each of the benefits expected is placed within one column and one row of the framework. This clearly shows the mix of financial as well as more subjective benefits and the types of business changes necessary to deliver them. This activity of structuring or analyzing the benefits, rather than simply compiling a list of benefits, as found in most business cases, encourages greater discussion and evidence gathering about the expected benefits and helps to produce a more robust and deliverable business case.

The first stage of using the framework is to classify each expected benefit according to the main type of change needed to realize it, as shown in the columns in Figure 4.5. It may seem simplistic to relate each benefit to one of only three causes, but benefits arise because:

1. the organization, its staff or trading partners can *do new things*, or do things in new ways, that prior to this transformation were not possible; or
2. the organization can improve the performance of activities it must continue to do, i.e. *do things better*; or
3. the organization can *stop doing things* that are no longer needed to operate the business successfully.

Senior management is often more interested in the benefits which enable new activities or innovations or that stop waste, rather than merely *doing things better* and the purpose of most transformations should include creating new and removing old practices.

Having placed each benefit in a column, the next step is to assign each benefit to a row of the framework. An important feature of locating benefits in the rows is the provision of evidence. Any benefit can be initially allocated to the *observable benefits* row. Evidence must then be provided, by the benefit owner, to move it to the rows above, which represent increasing levels of explicitness and knowledge about the value of the benefit.

Observable benefits

Some benefits can only be "measured" by opinion or judgment and they are often described as intangible, soft or qualitative. While subjective judgments are acceptable a clear statement of the criteria to be used to assess achievement and also who is appropriate to make that judgment needs to be agreed. Assessment by qualified people is often the only way of determining whether some benefits, such as improved staff morale or customer satisfaction, have been realized. However, if these have been tracked for a period of time through surveys, it may be possible actually to measure, rather than merely judge the benefit. While "soft" benefits, even in total, are unlikely to be sufficient to justify the changes, they must not be ignored or trivialized. They may accrue to large numbers of stakeholders, whose changes in behavior are essential to the realization of the more substantial organizational benefits.

Measurable benefits

These are benefits where there is already an identified measure in use or where one can be easily put in place. However, importantly, it is not possible to estimate in advance how much performance will improve when the transformation is completed. Wherever possible, existing measures, particularly if they are part of the organizational performance measurement system or its KPIs (key performance indicators) should be used, to ensure that achieving the benefit is seen as integral to delivering the business strategy. As above, it will also mean that the current baseline is already known. If there is no existing measure or it is deemed too difficult or expensive to set one up, then the benefit is "relegated" to observable and suitable subjective criteria for evaluation identified.

Quantifiable benefits

In addition to being able to measure performance before and after the investment, quantifiable benefits are those where the expected size or magnitude of the improvement can also be reliably estimated. As quantifying benefits inevitably involves forecasting the future, the challenge is to find ways of doing this that are as accurate and robust as possible. A number of approaches to overcoming this quantification problem are discussed briefly below. From our research, one of the common weaknesses of many investment cases is the lack of evidence provided to substantiate any assumptions made in quantifying the benefits. Without legitimate quantification, it will be difficult, if not impossible to calculate a realistic financial value. Hence the step between measurable and quantifiable is the most critical in converting a qualitative argument to a sound economic case for investment.

Financial benefits

These are benefits that can be expressed in financial terms, based on sufficient evidence that shows that the stated value is likely to be achieved. Hence all financial benefits are the result of applying a financial value or formula to a "proven" quantifiable benefit, i.e. one supported by credible evidence. The financial benefits can then be combined to calculate an overall estimated economic value of the transformation, and in combination with the expected costs, the rate of return or payback. While these financial evaluation techniques are well known and often used, there is only value in them if the underlying data on which the financial calculations are based are reliable and can be verified. Even those organizations which apply financial appraisal techniques rigorously appreciate that basing decisions solely on estimated financial values will limit the types of business investments it makes (Kohli and Devaraj, 2004).

The analysis of the BTM^2 case studies showed that many of the business cases were quite vague, based on a benefits vision, rather than an evidence-based set of benefits and an understanding of how they could be realized. There was a clear relationship between successful completion of the business transformation and the development of a comprehensive and rigorous investment case which demonstrated that the value expected was achievable.

Historical data and modeling or simulation

If a benefit results from stopping doing something, then the size of the expected benefit can usually be estimated from existing internal historical data. It is often important to establish evidence over a relevant time period, such as a year or through a peak in the trading cycle. However, it may only be necessary to sample the data to find sufficient representative evidence from which the overall value can be extrapolated.

This may not be enough to determine how performance will improve when the new capability and associated changes have been implemented. In such cases, modeling or simulation can be useful. For example, a police force was interested in introducing a new crime and incident recording bureau through which both the public and police officers would report crimes and incidents, ensuring a single source of complete information to reduce delays and costs in subsequent activities, such as investigation, reporting and even prosecution. However, while they had existing data about crime and incident patterns, they did not know how this would translate into calls to the new bureau. Simulation software provided by the vendor of the call center system allowed them to model likely call patterns based upon their existing knowledge of crime and incident occurrences. Combined with case history data, the costs that could be avoided were estimated.

Benchmarking and reference sites

Benchmarking is commonly used in a number of industries as the starting point for improvement programs and can be a valuable approach to quantifying benefits, in relation to "best practices" in the industry, or in comparable processes in other industries. Some examples of benchmarking approaches are shown in Figure 4.6. Although benchmarking is helpful for identifying potential improvements to established processes and practices for obvious reasons, it is less useful when trying to quantify the benefits from innovations. Unless the innovation is the first of its kind in the industry, there will be some "reference" or exemplar sites where similar changes have been made. Assuming information can

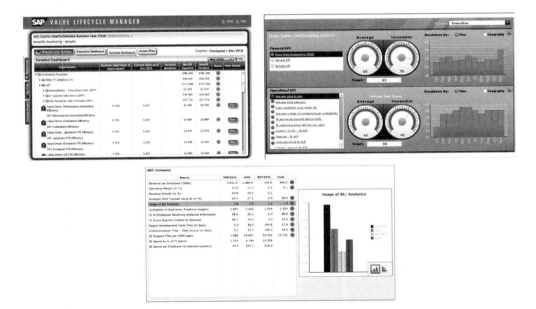

Figure 4.6   Some examples of using benchmarking to establish potential benefit values

be obtained (legally!), it is also important to understand where the organization started from, in performance terms, in order to assess how much of the improvement they have achieved is relevant and feasible. Of course, where organizations believe they are achieving an advantage from an innovation, it is unlikely that they will be willing to share all the secrets of their success, so the information gained from or about them has to be treated with a degree of caution.

Pilot projects

Pilot projects may be necessary to identify, confirm and evaluate the benefits that can be achieved from new business models and ways of working. To provide convincing evidence requires studying a comparable control group still working in the old way. In the CRM example shown above, the new processes for campaign management and sales follow up were trialed on a campaign in one market, while the same campaign was run traditionally in another, similar sized market. The new processes delivered nearly 50 percent higher sales, which, even allowing for the additional enthusiasm in the trial site (known as the "Hawthorne effect") indicated that a 20–30 percent increase would be achievable for most campaigns.

In addition to the benefits, a full business case must obviously include all costs and an assessment of the associated risks. It is important to include recurring costs associated with the outcome of the transformation as well as the one-off costs associated with new technology and achieving the changes. Generally the majority of technology and facilities costs are relatively easy to estimate, even if sometimes difficult to control during implementation. However, the costs associated with making business and organizational changes are less predictable and are often either underestimated or not included at all. From our evidence, it is the cost of these changes, particularly when they affect a wide range of stakeholders that leads to the significant cost overruns often reported for large transformations, even though nearly 60 percent of our survey respondents believed they were generally good at estimating costs.

In terms of assessing the investment risks, there are well-established ways of estimating financial and technical risks. However, it is often the willingness or ability of the staff within the organization to make the business or organizational changes that prevents the benefits from being achieved. This is where the development of the benefits dependency network provides a means of assessing not just overall project risk but risk in relation to each benefit. By considering the difficulty of making each change required to deliver a particular benefit, the risks of not achieving the business case can be assessed. The value of the particular benefit at risk will then suggest the importance of taking action to avoid or mitigate the risk. Risk management is discussed in depth in the next chapter.

Overall the business case should "tell a story" of what is expected to happen and why, starting with the strategic drivers, leading to the transformation objectives, then the detailed benefits, the major changes involved and expected costs, plus an understanding of the risks which need to be managed to avoid the transformation delivering less than expected or even fail altogether.

4.4.4 PLANNING BENEFIT REALIZATION

The final business case should be supported by a benefit realization plan which explains not only the activities, responsibilities, timescales and resources needed, but also the relationships and dependencies between the changes and benefits. It should contain:

- a full description of each of the benefits and changes, with responsibility and actions needed for delivery clearly defined and agreed;
- measures for all the benefits and, where appropriate, estimates of the expected *value* of each benefit at the end of the transformation and when the benefit should be realized;
- measurements to establish the current *baseline* at the start of the investment;
- agreed ownership of all the changes and actions in place to address all the stakeholder issues that may affect the achievement of the changes (the management of stakeholder interests and issues is discussed in Chapter 8, Organizational Change Management);
- the evidence or criteria to be used to assess whether each change has been successfully carried out; and
- a complete and fully documented benefits dependency network to show all the benefit and change relationships.

The plan is produced by analyzing the benefits dependency network – almost all the information needed is on the network. As well as describing the activities on the network and their relationships, it is valuable to look at the *benefit streams*: sets of changes and benefits that can be planned and executed without depending on other changes, so that early benefits or "quick wins" can be achieved. Optimizing this may mean breaking down some of the larger changes to create opportunities for earlier realization of some benefits. These sets of related changes and benefits can become either discrete phases or even sub-projects within the transformation.

Examples of benefit and change templates used by one organization, that has adopted the benefits management approach can be found in Appendix B of the handbook. They also include columns to accommodate revisions as the transformation proceeds. Further columns can be added for recording the actual achievements. These will later be input to the benefit review process described in Section 4.5.2.

The contents of the benefits realization plans are normally developed and finalized during the engage phase, in a series of workshops attended by those responsible for related changes and benefits. Measurements and success criteria will be also agreed, along with resources required and working arrangements among the stakeholders involved and also technical professionals and other experts and specialists, such as HR managers, who can undertake some of the change activities.

Each change or benefit item in the plan should also identify if there are any key milestones when its achievability needs to be reviewed, either due to the need to validate assumptions or test whether intended changes can actually be made successfully. Also, if any events or issues external to the program are likely to affect the outcome – for example, reorganizations or acquisitions – changes in the market conditions or the consequences of other change initiatives become known. Some of the changes will probably be major projects in themselves which deliver some of the benefits much earlier than the overall transformation. Achievement of these may suggest better ways of making subsequent changes and could either increase or decrease the potential value of later benefits.

In cases of extensive but similar changes across a number of business units or locations, the plan could include one or more pilot implementations to test whether the changes actually work *and* deliver the expected benefits. In a number of our case studies this happened, but in some the selected pilots were not representative of the overall organization and the results were not convincing, leading to reduced commitment elsewhere. This was particularly the case when the pilot was in a small unit or one where the changes were simpler and benefits more limited than in a larger more complex business unit.

However, in the Hilti case (vom Brocke, Petry and Schmiede, 2011) the piloting not only showed how the changes and most of the benefits could be achieved, but also enabled an improved implementation plan for the roll-out across the organization, to deliver more customer benefits than originally anticipated.

CHALLENGES CONCERNING THE PLANNING BENEFIT REALIZATION:

1. Assigning ownership to each change and benefit on the benefits dependency network.
2. Agree to measurements and success criteria for all benefits and changes and actions and resources required to implement them.
3. Base the quantification and value of benefits on an accurate current baseline and evidence from sources such as historical data, benchmarking or reference sites.
4. Consider a pilot implementation to test whether the changes actually work and deliver the benefits (optional).
5. Identify all costs and risks and prepare a rigorous, detailed business case, supported by a benefit realization plan, to which the main stakeholders have signed up.

KEY MESSAGE:

Some of the changes will probably be major projects in themselves which deliver some of the benefits much earlier than the overall business transformation. Achievement of these may suggest better ways of making subsequent changes and could either increase or decrease the potential value of later benefits.

4.5 Executing the Benefits Plan and Evaluating Results

The benefits plan is a component of the overall program plan for the business transformation. During the *Transform* phase, the benefits plan is executed and monitored (Section 4.5.1) and the achievement or otherwise of the benefits reviewed (Section 4.5.2) by the program manager and managers of the component projects, lead stakeholders and the governance group.[1]

---

1   Management and governance of the transformation program is discussed in depth in Chapter 10, Program and Project Management.

4.5.1 EXECUTING THE BENEFITS PLAN

The benefits plan should be maintained and updated as an integral part of the transformation plan. Both the benefits dependency network and the detail in the benefits and change templates should reflect the current expectations of the program.

As the transformation evolves, inevitably the plans will have to change, due to changes in resources and personnel plus unexpected events or problems that have to be assessed and dealt with. Therefore it is wise to plan for one or more "value reviews" or "health-checks" to revalidate the transformation business case, once some of the more important changes have be carried out or if the business case has become less valid, in some aspects, due to issues or developments elsewhere. The starting point for any interim review should be the existing benefits plan and ask: "What is the effect on the benefits and our ability to achieve them?" This should ensure that actions taken are appropriate to the overall transformation objectives, rather than just the immediate management or business problem and that all the relevant stakeholders understand the implications and are involved in decisions to change the plan.

A major pharmaceutical company introduced "benefit health-checks" in 2008 for all major IT-enabled change projects in the R&D function. On average this increased the benefits achieved, from new knowledge gained from the early changes, and also reduced timescales and costs for delivering other benefits through revisions to the change plans. The process also uncovered problems in some projects which resulted in scope reduction and even abandonment, when it was clear few, if any benefits would now be obtained.

While it is desirable to check the progress of activities affecting all the benefits, it is essential to understand whether the key or headline benefits – those few, maybe 3–6, against which the success of the transformation will eventually be judged, are still achievable. Some should be the main financial benefits, but others that affect the organization's KPIs are often equally important and a balanced scorecard approach or dashboard is usually helpful in tracking overall progress against the value expected. Costs will normally be tracked carefully, but parallel tracking of the benefits provides executive management with a holistic, balanced view of the transformation's progress, so that they can decide to intervene if the pattern is causing concern.

4.5.2 REVIEWING AND EVALUATING THE RESULTS

When the main benefits and value from the business transformation will be reviewed should be explicit dates in the transformation plan. In a large transformation project several evaluation reviews will be necessary, as significant benefits should accrue long before it is completed. In one case we studied, the second and third phases of a major transformation were dependent for funding on savings made in the first phase (Rayner et al., 2001). One of the factors that differentiates successful from less successful companies in their programs and projects is the management resolve to evaluate them *after* completion. As shown in Table 4.1, most organizations we surveyed considered this a weakness, but over 70 percent of the more successful at least carried out reviews, compared with under 40 percent of the less successful. Given that nearly 60 percent of the less successful ones admitted overstating the benefits to gain investment approval, these variations are not really surprising.

Once sets of related technology or facilities have been established and the enabling and business changes implemented, there should be a formal review of what has and has not been achieved. This is aimed at maximizing the benefits gained from the particular investment *and* increasing the benefits from future investments. As suggested earlier interim reviews should be carried out at key points during the program, to help steer it towards success, but also because waiting until the end reduces the scope for learning how to improve the implementation. The purposes of evaluation reviews involve both assessment of the results of the transformation itself and organizational learning as shown in Figure 4.7.

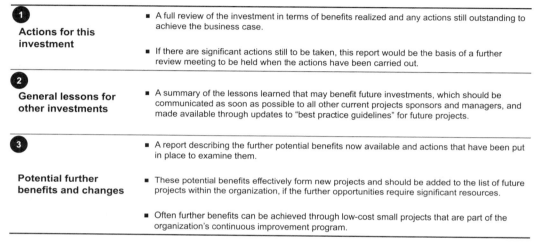

Figure 4.7   Key elements of the review process

Source: Adapted with permission from Ward, John, and Daniel, Elizabeth (2006), *Benefits Management: Delivering Value from IS & IT Investments* (Chichester: Wiley).

The evaluation should involve all key stakeholders and focus on what has been achieved, what has not (or not yet) been achieved and why, and identify further action needed to deliver outstanding benefits, if possible. The reasons for lack of benefit delivery may be due to misjudgments or lack of knowledge in preparing the benefits plan or problems during its execution. Another aspect of this review is to identify any unexpected benefits that have arisen and understand how they came about. This again may prove valuable input to improve the early stages of future projects. Equally any "disbenefits" or negative consequences that resulted should be understood in order take action to overcome them, if that is possible, and to avoid them in future projects. A structure for such a review meeting and the main deliverables is suggested in Figure 4.8.

It is worth stating that any post-implementation review should not become a "witchhunt"; it must be an objective process with future improvements in mind, not a way of allocating blame for past failures. If it is seen as a negative process, honest appraisal and a constructive critique of what has happened become impossible and the whole process falls into disrepute or is not carried out.

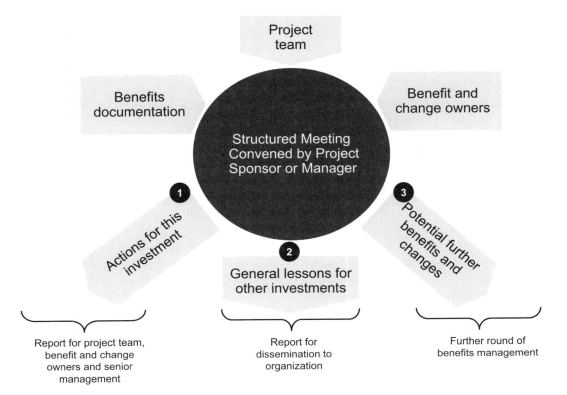

Figure 4.8   Model of the review process inputs and outputs

Source: Reproduced with permission from Ward, John and Daniel, Elizabeth (2006), *Benefits Management: Delivering Value from IS & IT Investments* (Chichester: Wiley).

CHALLENGES CONCERNING EXECUTING THE BENEFIT REALIZATION AS WELL AS REVIEWING AND EVALUATING THE RESULTS:

1. Carry out interim reviews or health-checks to ensure activities affecting benefits achievement are progressing satisfactorily.
2. Check if the key or headline benefits are still achievable or have increased or decreased as the transformation has evolved.
3. Review the transformation business case if significant changes to the benefits, risks or costs invalidate the existing investment justification.
4. Identify any unexpected benefits that have arisen and understand how they came about and also the reasons for any expected benefits not being achieved.

KEY MESSAGE:

The reasons for lack of benefit delivery may be due to misjudgments or lack of knowledge in preparing the benefits plan, problems during its execution or changes outside the transformation that made them unachievable.

4.6 Establishing the Potential for Further Benefits

Having reviewed what has happened, it is equally important to consider if further improvements are now possible following the completion of the business transformation (or major part of it), in the light of the new levels of business performance that have been achieved (Section 4.6.1) and ensure that benefits achieved are sustained over time (Section 4.6.2).

4.6.1 IDENTIFYING FURTHER BENEFITS

This should be a creative process involving the main stakeholders and any others who may be able to contribute, using the increased knowledge now available to identify new opportunities and the benefits they offer. These benefits may be achievable through additional business changes alone or may require more technology investment. Any worthwhile benefit opportunities should result in actions to considering whether there is a business case for further investment. Alternatively further benefits can often be achieved by tuning processes, adjusting how activities are performed or additional training and can be considered as *business as usual*.

If this is not done, many available benefits may be overlooked. For maximum value to be gained from the transformation, benefit identification should be a continuing process from which other beneficial change projects may be defined. As suggested in Figures 4.7 and 4.8, this exploration should initially be part of the review process, since the knowledgeable stakeholders are together and it encourages forward thinking rather than merely contemplating the past.

4.6.2 ONGOING MONITORING OF THE BENEFITS

In most cases the review and assessment of potential further benefits is not just a one-off process, since it results in actions to recover benefits or realize new ones and this may take some months after implementation to complete. Equally some benefits can decay after implementation, especially if, over time, old practices creep back in or new problems emerge. Ensuring they are sustained is part of the optimize phase and monitoring the ongoing performance levels is necessary, for up to 12 months in some cases.

In a multi-year transformation, some aspects will be in the optimize phase while others are still being implemented, and benefits in some areas will be cumulative or additive as further changes are completed. At the same time some changes may not produce the benefits expected, for explicable reasons. For a large transformation it is advisable to describe the annual values of benefits expected and then review the actual benefits delivered in that year. This can be particularly important for financial benefits that have been included in future years' budgets. In some organizations this is done at the project or program portfolio level to assess how well both decision making and implementation are being accomplished.

Figure 4.9 combines the main rationales for the stages and types of reviews often needed to monitor overall performance.

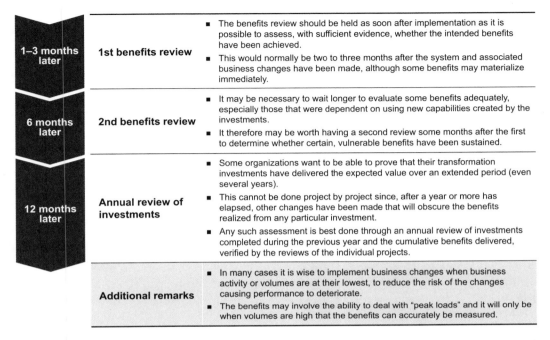

Figure 4.9   Ongoing reviews of value delivered

Source: Adapted with permission from Ward, John and Daniel, Elizabeth (2006), *Benefits Management: Delivering Value from IS & IT Investments* (Chichester: Wiley).

CHALLENGES CONCERNING THE ESTABLISHMENT OF POTENTIAL FOR FURTHER BENEFITS:

1.   Identify the further improvements now possible in the light of the new levels of business performance that have been achieved.
2.   Continue to monitor the benefits achieved to ensure they are sustained over time.

KEY MESSAGE:

For a large transformation it may be advisable to describe the annual values of benefits expected and then review the actual benefits delivered in that year.

4.7 Conclusion

Value management is a continuous activity throughout the transformation lifecycle, not just something which is done to develop the business case or justify the investment costs. Our research and working with organizations over the last 15 years has shown that success in delivering value from projects and transformations can be increased by:

- having comprehensive and rigorous business cases;
- adopting a value management process which includes benefit realization plans;

- linking the benefits to the specific changes needed to deliver them;
- agreeing ownership of the benefits and changes; and
- carrying out post-implementation reviews of benefits achieved.

The credibility of the story that the business case tells about why change is needed, the benefits the organization and each stakeholder will gain and how those can be realized, will influence the level of commitment of those involved. The case studies also show the clarity of the objectives and benefits that are expected has a significant influence on the success of the business transformation and even on whether it will be completed. In a number of the cases the value was vague, often rather generic and not specific to the situation of the organization, leading to a lack of credibility in the arguments for change or lack of interest and engagement by some important stakeholders. In some of the cases, although the business case was attractive, there was little evidence presented to demonstrate how the benefits described could be achieved.

Value does not imply financial value alone; it includes all the improvements that are perceived as beneficial by both internal and external stakeholders. Some are able to be estimated in advance in terms of the level of improvement that can be achieved from the intended changes. That relies on having a known baseline at the start of the transformation plus evidence that justifies the estimate of the future level of achievement. Other cannot be forecast, but it is still important to measure them after the changes have been made. In fact, the certainty of post implementation review of the value eventually achieved is an organizational discipline that encourages rigor in formulating and implementing the benefits realization plan.

Bibliography

Bancroft, Nancy H., Seip, Henning and Sprengel, Andrea (1998), *Implementing SAP R/3: How to Introduce a Large System into a Large Organization*, 2nd ed. (Greenwich, CT, USA: Manning Publications).

Jurison, Jaak (1996), Toward more effective management of information technology benefits, *The Journal of Strategic Information Systems* 5, no. 4, 263–74.

Kohli, Rajiv and Devaraj, Sarv (2004), Realizing business value of information technology investments: an organizational process, *MIS Quarterly Executive* 3, no. 1, 55–70.

Kumar, Kuldeep, van Dissel, Han G. and Bielli, Paola (1998), The Merchant of Prato revisited: toward a third rationality of information systems, *MIS Quarterly* 22, no. 2, 199–226.

Peppard, Joe and Ward, John (2005), Unlocking sustained business value from IT investments, *California Management Review* 48, no. 1, 52–70.

Peppard, Joe, Ward, John and Daniel, Elizabeth (2007), Managing the realization of business benefits from IT investments, *MIS Quarterly Executive* 6, no. 1, 15–25.

Ramiller, Neil C. and Swanson, E. Burton (2003), Whether, when, and how to innovate with information technology: what do empirical studies tell us?, Information Systems Working Paper, The Anderson School at UCLA.

Rayner, Paul, Ward, John and Franken, Arnoud (2011), Project portfolio management in the IT industry: how an IT company successfully took its own medicine, Cranfield University, School of Management.

Ross, Jeanne W. and Beath, Cynthia M. (2002), Beyond the business case: new approaches to IT investment (2002), *MIT Sloan Management Review* 43, no. 2, 51–9.

vom Brocke, Jan, Petry, Martin, Schmiede, Theresa (2011), How Hilti Masters Transformation, *360° – The Business Transformation Journal June*, no. 1, 38–51. Ward, John and Daniel, Elizabeth (2006), *Benefits Management: Delivering Value from IS & IT Investments* (Chichester: Wiley).

Ward, John and Daniel, Elizabeth (2008), Increasing your odds: creating better business cases, *Cutter Benchmarking Review* 18, no. 1.

Ward, John, Hertogh, Steven and Viaene, Stijn (2007), Managing benefits from IS/IT investments: an empirical investigation into current practice, in *40th Annual Hawaii International Conference on System Sciences (HICSS'07)*: 206a.

CHAPTER 5 *Risk Management*

BRENT FURNEAUX (Maastricht University, School of
Business and Economics), TOMASZ JANASZ (SAP AG),
THOMAS SCHILD (SAP AG) and ROBERTO KLIMMEK
(Mercedez Benz Cars)

5.1 Overview

Risk Management provides fundamental guidance to the planning, development and effective execution of a business transformation. Hence, it is essential that business transformation managers seek to manage those risks that relate to the process of transforming an organization towards a desired future state and those risks that relate more to the possibility that this desired state becomes either obsolete or sub-optimal. In other words, effective risk management is needed to minimize the unpredictability associated with transformation related initiatives. Moreover, successful business transformation requires that sufficient attention be directed towards managing different categories of risks at both the strategic and operational levels.

Organizations need to go beyond simply addressing risks that are inherent to an individual business transformation since, in isolation, such aggregation provides only limited guidance to those seeking to understand and manage the complex interdependencies that surround strategic risks. Such risks have been found to represent some of the largest threats to successful business transformation. Consequently, effectively managing strategic risks supports successful business transformation.

Risk management within BTM^2 involves the following steps:

1. Envision: 360° strategic risk assessment addresses the identification and assessment of strategic risks. Risks can be identified using such tools as scenario planning. The outcome of this step is a strategic risk map with a consistent and aligned 360° view on key strategic risks for the business transformation.
2. Engage: Risk analysis and Risk response plan involves the assessment of underlying business cases of proposed transformations in light of potential risks. Generally speaking, the impact of risks is assessed based on cost, schedule and deliverables.
3. Transform: Execute risk response plan and monitor risks refer to the monitoring of the emergence of risk events or execution of planned responses. During this step a status report of risks is provided to the steering committee of the transformation program and program reviews are conducted at set milestones.
4. Optimize: Review and evaluate risks encompasses inspection and improvement of risks and opportunity identification. This step is most likely to be successful if an open risk dialogue is created between management and the board and critical alignments of strategy development and execution are monitored.

5.2 Risk Management in Business Transformation

Risk can be defined as any uncertainty surrounding future outcomes that might have positive or negative implications for these outcomes (see, for example, International Standards Organization, 2009, or Project Management Institute, 2004). As such, risks can simultaneously represent a threat to the success of a business transformation and an opportunity to enhance or extend the value of such a transformation. Given that risks arise when uncertainty is present, risks are both widespread and of fundamental importance to organizational efforts. Varying degrees of risks are encountered in almost every initiative that an organization might undertake. Effective risk management is, therefore, essential to the success of these initiatives, particularly when they are as broad and complex in their scope as business transformation.

5.2.1 CLASSIFICATION OF RISKS

Risks can be classified as *strategic or operational*. Effectively managing strategic and operational risks require that the differences between the two categories is clearly understood. Examples for each of these two risk categories are provided in Table 5.1.

The first category, *strategic risk*, is represented by those risks that are inherent to an organization's strategy formulation and execution. These risks typically relate to assumptions and decisions that have been made concerning markets, customers, products, mergers, acquisitions and other top-line management activities. Strategic risks include external risk drivers, such as technology shifts, changes in customer behavior, competitive moves that could impact, either negatively or positively, the ability of a company to achieve strategic objectives on a two- to five-year horizon.

Strategic risk can be further divided into *internal* and *external* risks. Internal risks are inherent to a company's strategy formulation and execution and they thus relate to decisions about markets, customers, products, M&A activity and other top-line business decisions. External risks lie outside of "normal" expectations and thus appear rapidly and with little warning. The relevance of an external risk to a business transformation is dependent on the extent to which it will impact the likely future assumed in the planning and development of the business transformation. Thus, for example, the appearance of a disruptive technology might only be considered a relevant risk if the benefits of a business transformation are dependent on the continued dominance of an alternative to this technology. Although the impact of an external risk and the likelihood that it will occur can be extremely difficult to quantify, in practical terms the extent to which

Table 5.1   Examples of different strategic and operational risks

Strategic risks	Operational risks
• Market risk drivers • Technology risk drivers • Regulatory and compliance risk drivers • Macro economic risk drivers • Social risk drivers • Environmental risk drivers • Geopolitical risk drivers	• Financial risks related to the financial returns that a project ultimately delivers • Technology risks related to the specific technologies being implemented • Security risks related to unauthorized system access and use • Information risks related to such things as the accuracy and availability of the information provided by a system • People risks related to the people charged with implementing and using a system • Business process risks related to the processes that a system must support

risks can be quantified falls on a continuum that ranges from wholly unquantifiable to wholly quantifiable. External risks can then be understood as those risks such as economic turmoil and the breakdown of entrenched political regimes that fall toward the less quantifiable end of this continuum.

The second category, operational risk, focuses primarily on risks that have the potential to impede the extent to which a specific business transformation achieves its stated objectives. On the operational level, risk management helps to ensure that a particular business transformation initiative takes an organization to where it had planned to be. Operational risk management aims to provide direct, ongoing support to the routine execution of business transformation initiatives rather than providing guidance to their overall direction. Operational risks can thus be more narrowly understood as any uncertainty that could impact the likelihood that a specific business transformation will be successful.

In many ways, the difference between strategic and operational risk relates to a distinction that is widely made between business and project risk (Office of Government Commerce, 2009). While strategic risks are primarily related to business risk, risks on the operational level more typically relate to risks that are inherent to specific business transformations. Despite the somewhat narrower perspective associated with operational, it should be clear that strategic and operational risks are closely linked and, as a result, share many of the same processes.

Given the narrower focus of operational risks, it becomes clear why efforts to manage such risk tend to focus more on minimizing unwanted outcomes over identifying and pursuing opportunities. At the project or program level it is usually far more important to deliver on specific objectives than it is to pursue enhancements and extensions to these objectives. Project and program managers will, for the most part, be primarily concerned with risks at the operational level while business transformation managers will need to maintain a much broader focus on risks that encompasses strategic and operational risks.

Strategic risks:	Operational risks:
• impact, either negatively or positively, the ability of a company to achieve strategic objectives.	• impede the extent to which a specific business transformation achieves its stated objectives.
→ This category of risk concerns business risks and business decisions.	→ This category of risk addresses risks of a specific business transformation.

5.2.2 EVOLUTION OF RISK MANAGEMENT

Businesses operate in a highly interconnected environment that is regularly subject to rapid, unexpected change. Major events that were once thought to be highly unlikely or relatively isolated in their impact have now been observed to occur with some degree of frequency and to have globally significant consequences. This has challenged organizations to manage risk more effectively, particularly at the strategic level. Effectively managing business transformation now requires an organization to go beyond simply aggregating the operational risks of individual business transformation programs. In isolation, such aggregation provides only limited guidance to those seeking to understand and manage the complex interdependencies that surround strategic risks. Given that these risks have been found to represent some of the largest threats to successful business transformation, the past decade has witnessed a fundamental shift in our understanding of business transformation risk and how this risk should be managed. In particular, there has been a shift away from an operationally-oriented focus (representing traditional risk management) toward an understanding that more fully encompasses operational and strategic perspectives (see Figure 5.1).

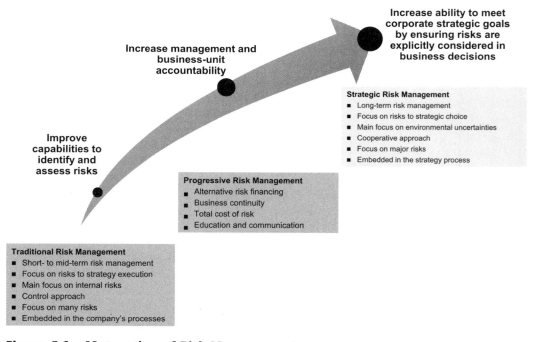

Figure 5.1   Maturation of Risk Management

Strategic risk management provides a comprehensive risk management framework that extends from the initial conceptualization of a business transformation through to the program that is developed to deliver planned benefits and the individual projects created to implement this program. A key advantage of strategic risk management is the ability to discover important risks that can impede an organization's efforts to fulfill short- and long-term strategies.

5.2.3 THE RISK MANAGEMENT PROCESS

Over the past several decades numerous processes for managing risks have been developed and used to support the management of almost every conceivable form of organizational initiative. This has resulted in the incorporation of best practice risk management processes into several widely accepted international standards and bodies of knowledge.[1] Despite the diversity of perspectives that have been offered and irrespective of whether the emphasis is on strategic or operational risk, risk management consists, in essence, of four key steps: the identification of relevant risks, analysis and evaluation of relevant risks to determine their significance, development of a plan to respond to those risks considered particularly significant, and ongoing monitoring and reporting of risk-related issues (see Figure 5.2).

These four steps are supported by an overarching risk management plan or framework and by efforts to review and improve the risk management process on an ongoing basis. A risk management plan or policy provides the overarching organizational framework for conducting risk management. This framework helps to establish such things as an organization's approach to managing risk, its tolerance for risk, the scope of contingency planning, how much contingency will be allocated to address risks, how contingency resources are allocated, the requisite reporting and monitoring of risk, and the relative importance of parameters such as risk impact and probability of occurrence. An effective risk management framework offers an organization a number of important benefits including greater transparency surrounding the risks that are being faced, opportunities to adapt quickly to changing circumstances, improved decision making and greater consistency across business transformation initiatives that helps to facilitate rapid redeployment of organizational talent.

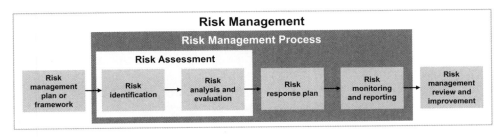

Figure 5.2   The Risk Management process

---

1   Among the more salient of these are the PRINCE2 method offered by the UK Office of Government Commerce (OGC), the Project Management Body of Knowledge (PMBoK) from the Project Management Institute (PMI), ISO31000 from the International Standards Organization (ISO) and the integrated framework for enterprise risk management from the Committee of Sponsoring Organizations (COSO) of the Treadway Commission.

5.3 Risk Management in BTM²

Economic theory argues that risk or uncertainty must be present in order to achieve positive value and that the amount of value extracted is proportional to the level of risk that is present. Risk management as part of BTM² seeks to take advantage of this principle by systematically identifying, assessing, responding to and monitoring the threats and opportunities that surround business transformation initiatives. Emphasis centers primarily on those external risks and opportunities that can impact the mid- to long-term business value that business transformations yield. Unlike traditional risk management approaches, the focus of the strategic perspective within BTM² risk management is of particular importance and distinguishes the BTM² approach from other methodologies. Risk Management in BTM² offers a wider focus than traditional risk management as it tries to manage risks enterprise wide in an integrated and collaborative fashion, taking into account the basic idea that many risks are connected within and sometimes beyond the borders of an enterprise.

5.3.1 IMPORTANCE OF A STRATEGIC PERSPECTIVE IN RISK MANAGEMENT

Effective strategy execution has remained a top priority for senior management even after the recent financial crisis and economic downturn. However, while organizations may have had risk management processes, they did not always adjust strategies when new risks emerged or risk levels changed. In addition, not all organizations included the consideration of risks and how they would be managed in setting strategic and operating plans. To overcome these traditional barriers, organizations need to ensure that Strategy Management and Risk Management operate hand in hand. Without aligning the two, businesses are limiting the full potential of their strategies as they are executing without any knowledge of potential threats that could inhibit their success. A strategy developed and executed without understanding the associated risks is inherently flawed. To combine strategy and risk, to have a truly risk-intelligent business strategy, organizations must clearly understand their exposure to both strategic risk and execution risk. BTM², as a holistic and integrative methodology, provides this connection between the risk management discipline and the strategic perspective.

Within the context of BTM², strategic risk management is primarily concerned with identifying broad-based, externally-driven risks and exploring the implications that these risks have for the suitability of business transformation plans. The process of strategic risk management thus helps to ensure that transformation initiatives are pursued in alignment with business objectives while still considering the possibility that chosen transformations may prove ill-suited to future needs. In essence, strategic risk management in BTM² focuses on evaluating whether an organization is pursuing business transformations that move it in directions that will be appropriate to the future.

5.3.2 MANIFESTATION OF RISK MANAGEMENT IN BTM²

In the business transformation approach, risk management is tightly integrated with the other management disciplines of BTM². Risks need to be identified for every individual management discipline (see Figure 5.3). The responsibility of risk management is to ensure that all disciplines are executed and implemented as anticipated. For example, the

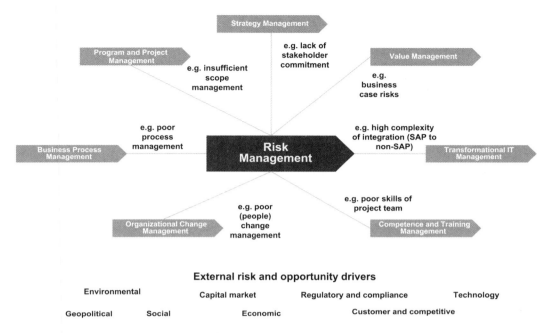

Figure 5.3   Manifestation of Risk Management in BTM²

discipline of Competence and Training Management has to ensure an appropriate skill set within the project team.

Risk management within BTM² can be seen as providing overarching guidance to business transformation by steering it towards opportunities and away from some of the many pitfalls that could be overlooked by considering only impediments to the execution of specific business transformations.

The importance of risk management to both the planning and execution of business transformation places it as one of the three management disciplines of the *directional* type while simultaneously extending across all of the BTM² disciplines of the *enablement* type (see Figure 5.4). Hence, it is the integration of Risk Management with Strategy Management and Value Management that provides overall direction to business transformation. Strategy management, value management and risk management serve, respectively, to identify the need for business transformation, establish the value that planned business transformation initiatives hold for an organization and highlight the ways in which this value can be maximized.

Achieving this level of sophistication means that strategic and operational risk management must be tightly integrated into the development of an overall transformation strategy and into the risk management processes that surround the execution of business transformation. Such integration helps to ensure that business transformation programs are appropriate to both current and future business needs. It also permits those involved in the execution of a transformation to identify when the potential to take advantage of a specific opportunity arises and to flag this potential to those in a position to act upon it. By incorporating the capacity to respond rapidly to emerging threats and opportunities in this way, transformation programs can be both radical in scope and dynamic in character.

Figure 5.4   Directional BTM² disciplines

As a result, organizations will be less likely to persist with business transformations that were intended to respond to future scenarios that have become much less likely.

However, as an organization moves from the envisioning phase towards the phases of engagement and transformation, the nature of the risks that are of primary concern shifts toward those risks that are specifically related to the execution of a particular initiative. In other words, emphasis shifts away from viewing risk as a driver of change and toward viewing risk as a threat to the successful execution of a transformation project or program.[2]

CHALLENGES CONCERNING THE BTM² RISK MANAGEMENT:
1.   Understand that risks are associated with strategy.
2.   Provide guidance for risks of all management disciplines.
3.   Evaluate appropriate pursuit of business transformation with future plans.

5.3.3 BUSINESS TRANSFORMATION RISK MANAGEMENT PROCESS

The standard risk management process can be mapped to the BTM² Risk Management discipline. Therefore, we consider the four stages of the transformation lifecycle: envision, engage, transform and optimize (see Figure 5.5).

---

2   See Chapter 3, Strategy Management, for further discussion surrounding the role of risk in driving business transformation.

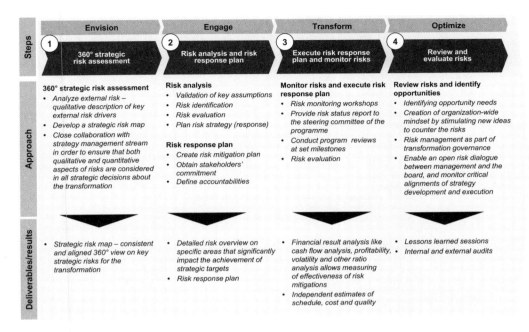

Figure 5.5 Phases of BTM² Risk Management

The first phase, envision, focuses on the strategic perspective of risk management, where the aim is to identify risks before they lead to a crisis. In addition, the first phase analyzes the strategic course of actions and focuses on transformation risks. During the second phase, engage, risks are analyzed in detail and response plans are created. The third phase, transform, actively manages the different risks by executing risk response plans. Finally, the risks are evaluated and reviewed in phase four, optimize. The particular phases and their activities are explained in detail in the next four sections.

5.4 360° Strategic Risk Assessment

As we highlighted in Section 5.3.1, the strategic perspective is an integral part of BTM² risk management. It is used to identify a comprehensive set of possible events and scenarios that could compromise an organization's ability to achieve its strategic objectives and could threaten commercial interests or intangible values such as reputation and brand image. It is the scope of the potential threats and the focus on external factors and organizational growth that differentiates "strategic risk management" from "operational risk management" with the latter being more focused on preserving value.

While operational risk management often applies a "bottom-up" approach, employing risk registers and sophisticated software packages, strategic risk management often adopts more of a "top-down" approach (see Figure 5.6).

The identification and assessment of strategic risks is performed in the envision phase. In the following, we explain the relevant activities in more detail.

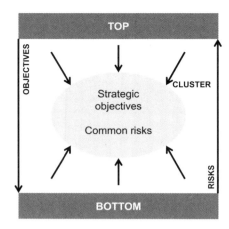

Figure 5.6   Top-down and bottom-up risk assessment

5.4.1 DISCOVERING STRATEGIC RISKS

External risk drivers encompass technology shifts, changes in customer behavior, and competitive moves that could impact, either negatively or positively, the ability to achieve business transformation objectives. Broadly speaking, such risks can be categorized as being related to customers, competitors, social and geopolitical factors, capital markets, economic conditions, technology, environment, regulations and compliance. In contrast to external risks, internal risks typically relate to people, processes and products. Given the importance of external risks to risk management, the process of identifying risks needs to incorporate an outside-in view from external analysts and experts.

Strategic risks and their drivers are tightly woven within a context of ever-changing market dynamics. As a result, effective risk management requires thorough monitoring of changing conditions in the external environment and comprehensive assessment of the impact of the underlying risks. The process of risk management thus becomes an iterative one in which risk drivers can be seen as driving the strategic environment toward one of many possible futures. By linking risks to risk drivers and future scenarios in this way, risk management permits an organization to identify and implement the transformation programs needed to face the most likely future scenarios. Implementation of these transformations contributes, over time, to a new market dynamic.

5.4.2 STRATEGIC RISK MAP

Early identification of strategic risk can be supported through the establishment of a risk radar that directs attention to the most salient risks while maintaining an ability to monitor for the appearance of newly salient risks. The notion of risk radar can best be understood in relationship to the notion of a strategic risk map (see Figure 5.7).

While a strategic risk map provides a comprehensive overview of all potential risks facing an organization, the process of strategic risk assessment narrows attention to those points on this map that are particularly relevant to an organization and its transformation plans. Assessing strategic risk can be a difficult and time consuming effort. Although a number

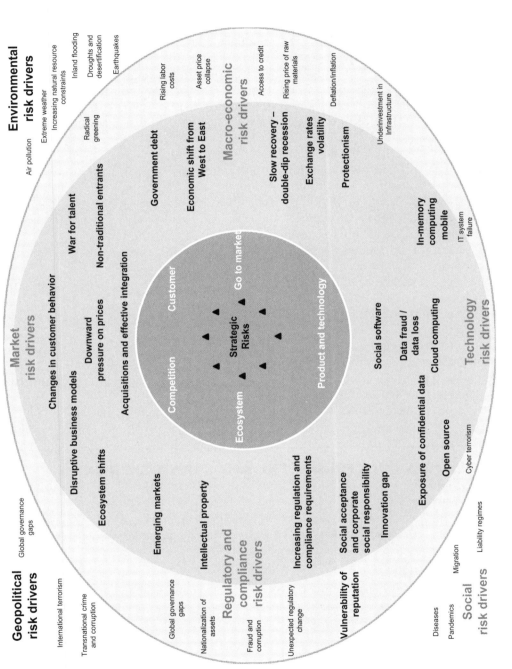

Geopolitical risk drivers

Global governance gaps

International terrorism

Transnational crime and corruption

Environmental risk drivers

Air pollution

Extreme weather

Increasing natural resource constraints

Radical greening

Inland flooding

Droughts and desertification

Earthquakes

Market risk drivers

Changes in customer behavior

Disruptive business models

War for talent

Ecosystem shifts

Non-traditional entrants

Downward pressure on prices

Acquisitions and effective integration

Emerging markets

Intellectual property

Government debt

Economic shift from West to East

Macro-economic risk drivers

Rising labor costs

Asset price collapse

Access to credit

Rising price of raw materials

Slow recovery – double-dip recession

Exchange rates volatility

Protectionism

Deflation/inflation

Underinvestment in infrastructure

Customer

Go to market

Competition

Strategic Risks

Ecosystem

Product and technology

In-memory computing mobile

IT system failure

Social software

Data fraud / data loss

Cloud computing

Technology risk drivers

Regulatory and compliance risk drivers

Global governance gaps

Nationalization of assets

Fraud and corruption

Unexpected regulatory change

Increasing regulation and compliance requirements

Social acceptance and corporate social responsibility

Innovation gap

Vulnerability of reputation

Exposure of confidential data

Open source

Cyber terrorism

Social risk drivers

Diseases

Pandemics

Migration

Liability regimes

Figure 5.7   A strategic risk map with external drivers

of tools and techniques are available (see Appendix C), one particularly useful approach relies on rigorous, integrative use of scenario planning techniques (Schoemaker, 1995) and formal statistical methods such as cluster analysis. While scenario planning techniques can be applied to strategic risk assessment without the use of formal statistical methods, these formal methods greatly facilitate the process of data analysis and improve the rigor of the assessment. This is particularly important given the large number of parameters involved and the considerable degree of interdependency among these parameters.

The process of scenario planning requires that an organization identify its current market context and likely future scenarios based on key risk drivers and their interdependencies. These future scenarios are then considered in relation to business objectives and planned transformation initiatives to understand how risk drivers might impact the extent to which the direction that an organization is taking will correspond to possible futures. This assessment can thus serve to identify the key risk drivers that threaten to steer a business environment toward less desirable futures. As such, it underscores the most important risk drivers on a strategic risk map and fosters the formulation of suitable Key Risk Indicators (KRIs) that can be used to monitor and predict those internal and external events that are most likely to threaten a business transformation.

Undertaking a thorough assessment of transformation business cases in light of potential risks offers a number of benefits to organizations. In addition to providing an unbiased view on transformation risk, it also supports:

- better validation of the financial analysis that supports a business case and its key assumptions;
- quantification of risks in a manner that takes uncertainties into account based on input from key stakeholders and external experts;
- preparation of an overview of major risks and proposed response strategies to better support the decision making process; and
- better management of risks in the execution phase of the transformation.

CHALLENGES CONCERNING THE 360° STRATEGIC RISK ASSESSMENT:
1. Define a strategic risk map.
2. Assess the underlying business case of any proposed transformation.
3. Consider risk interdependencies as well as qualitative and quantitative aspects of risks.

KEY MESSAGE:
Underscores the most important risk drivers on a strategic risk map and ensures that risk interdependencies as well as qualitative and quantitative aspects of risks are considered before a board decision is made.

To summarize, strategic risk identification should aim to:

- identify key interdependencies among both internal and external risks drivers that could affect multiple transformation initiatives and might hinder the overall execution of the business transformation;
- identify potentially disruptive factors from external risk drivers; and
- provide a broader view on uncertainties.

5.5 Risk Analysis and Risk Response Plan

Once the action for transformation has been identified based on scenario planning and other techniques, it becomes necessary to assess the underlying business case of any proposed transformation in the engage phase. Assessment of a transformation business case involves undertaking deep dives into those risk areas identified during the envision phase as well as the identification of specific operational risks. These deep dives provide an unbiased view on every transformation initiative. It gives transparency to the top risks associated with individual initiatives and offers a detailed overview of specific risk areas that have the potential to significantly impact the achievement of a successful business transformation.

5.5.1 RISK IDENTIFICATION

Given the complexity of transformation projects, their inherent novelty and the large number of risks that are typically present, it can be extremely difficult to effectively identify and categorize all significant risks. It is for this reason that the risk identification effort should aim to incorporate a diversity of perspectives and focus almost exclusively on risk identification. Ideally, risk analysis, evaluation and the development of risk responses should be deferred at this stage in order to ensure focus and avoid expending needless effort developing responses to risks that are ultimately deemed unimportant. Nonetheless, it may be necessary to integrate risk identification, risk analysis and risk evaluation into a single risk assessment effort if availability of key participants is limited. While this can create some challenges, considerable preliminary guidance is available both in relation to the categories of risks that may be salient and in relation to techniques that can be used to facilitate the process (see Appendix C).

The significance of each risk can be assessed by understanding its implications for each of the key benefits of the transformation as identified during the process of value management. Linking risks to benefits in this way helps to ensure that identified risks are truly significant to the business transformation and that all of the key risks that might impact expected benefits have been identified. An important consideration during the assessment of transformation business cases is ensuring that risk interdependencies as well as qualitative and quantitative aspects of risks are considered before a board decision is made. Notable interdependencies among risks can significantly increase the overall threat that is being faced.

Risk identification is not a solitary effort and its effectiveness can be enhanced considerably through the designation of transformation risk champions. Transformation risk champions are, in essence, functional area specialists who are working on a transformation initiative. Such individuals offer a unique perspective in that they are closely involved in the business transformation and are thus quite familiar with its objectives. At the same time, they offer a business perspective based on their specific functional expertise and they understand the transformation's risk drivers and how these influence the business (see Figure 5.8). For example, a purchasing manager involved in a transformation deals regularly with supply chain risk as part of his or her job function. Since this makes such individuals inherently sensitive to supply chain risk, they are well situated to serve as effective champions for supply chain risks related to a transformation.

In addition to drawing on the expertise of risk champions, the process of risk identification can be further optimized and simultaneously made more dynamic by relying on an iterative process that repeatedly cycles between top-down and bottom-up perspectives (see Figure 5.6).

Extensive research and practical experience with risk identification has led to the formulation of a wide range of risk categorization frameworks or breakdown structures that can be especially useful in identifying operational risks. Since operational risks are typically of a more routine character, these frameworks help to ensure that thorough consideration is given to all of the risks that a transformation project might face (see, for example, Jourda and Michaelson, 2009). As such, a risk breakdown structure represents the operational equivalent of a strategic risk map (see Figure 5.7). There is, in fact, some degree of overlap in the categories of risk suggested by many risk breakdown structures and those suggested by strategic risk maps. The following categories of IT project risk are, for example, identified by McKeen and Smith, 2004:

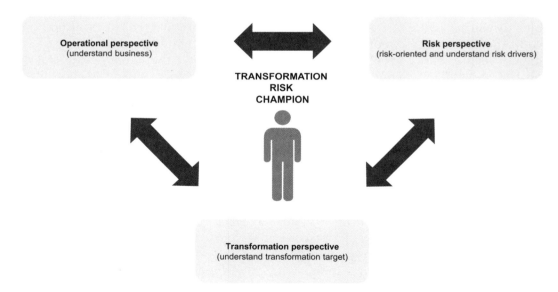

Figure 5.8   Transformation risk champions

- financial – risks related to the financial returns that a project ultimately delivers:
  - low or excessively conservative estimates of costs and benefits;
  - incorrect assumptions concerning foreign exchange rates;

- technology – risks related to the specific technologies being implemented:
  - performance limitations;
  - scalability problems (too much success);
  - inadequate reliability;
  - obsolescence;
  - rapid or delayed adoption by competitors;
- security – risks related to unauthorized system access and use:
  - user authentication difficulties;
  - weak control and authorization;
- information – risks related to such things as the accuracy and availability of the information provided by a system:
  - privacy impediments;
  - decision errors due to missing or incorrect information;
  - unexpected availability of a data conversion tool;
- people – risks related to the people charged with implementing and using a system:
  - competence shortcomings and discovery of unexpected competencies;
  - burn-out;
  - conflict;
  - inadequate or superior change readiness;
- business process – risks related to the processes that a system must support:
  - changing business needs;
  - discovery of additional opportunities to rationalize processes;
- management – risks related to management support and oversight of a project:
  - management turnover;
  - shifting attention.

Risk breakdown structures or categorization frameworks can be used in two key ways. They can be used either as a starting point in the risk identification effort or subsequent to other risk identification efforts as a means of verifying that important categories of risk have not been overlooked. In identifying risks on the operational level, it is important to recognize that these risks can extend beyond the transformation project itself to include such issues as operational failures, economic shocks and natural disasters such as the Fukushima Daiichi nuclear disaster in 2011. Similarly, the impact of risk events can readily extend beyond the scope of the transformation effort to include such things as damage to corporate or brand reputation and an inability to produce key products with one example being the Deepwater Horizon oil spill in 2010. Thus, irrespective of the particular merits of a specific categorization framework, it is important to go beyond the use of such frameworks to ensure that risks have been thoroughly identified.

A number of formal techniques and data sources are available to assist with this effort. Salient among these is the Delphi method (see Appendix C). Variants of this method have been widely used to elicit consensus among groups of relevant experts concerning key project risks (Schmidt et al., 2001). Similarly, an essential element of the Risk Diagnosing Method (RDM) is a procedure for ensuring that project stakeholders put forth important risks irrespective of the implications that these risks might have for the initiative or for an organization's political dynamics (Keizera et al., 2002). Although the RDM was originally developed for use in product development projects, it can be used to elicit the risks of transformation projects and programs. RDM may be particularly valuable in organizational cultures that are less open to public debate and criticism. Other tools and techniques for identifying strategic and/or operational risks are summarized in Appendix C.

5.5.2 RISK EVALUATION

While it is possible for risks to be identified by a wide range of individuals and groups working either within or outside of an organization, analysis and evaluation of these risks is best performed by individuals with suitable expertise. Risk analysis and evaluation may, however, be integrated into a single risk assessment process depending on organizational circumstances. Irrespective of the approach taken, the purpose of risk analysis and evaluation is to understand the relative significance of identified risks. In the context of strategic risk management this effort serves to highlight the most needed transformations and to establish the extent to which planned transformations will be suited to future circumstances. In the context of operational risk management, the process of risk analysis and evaluation serves to highlight those risks that are in need of risk response planning. Thus, while strategic and operational level assessments create a need for specific responses, the nature and scope of the responses that result will differ considerably.

Risk evaluation is essentially a two-stage process that involves first determining the likelihood that risk events will occur and then evaluating their potential impact. However, more sophisticated approaches tend to incorporate some consideration for issues such as risk appetite, the speed of risk onset and risk ownership to provide a more comprehensive overview of risk. In determining risk likelihood and impact it is possible to use both qualitative and quantitative techniques. Qualitative techniques assess likelihood and impact using categorical values such as low, medium and high. Although this approach is quite common, it is also common for quantitative values to underlie these categorical values. For example, an impact estimated at less than 1 percent of total budget might be considered a low-impact risk while an impact of greater than 10 percent might be considered high impact. Irrespective of the approach taken, it is essential that all such scales be clearly defined in the risk management framework. This ensures that they are understood and used consistently by all stakeholders throughout the course of a transformation initiative as well as across initiatives.

Although the occurrence of a risk event can have implications for many aspects of a business transformation, it is particularly important to consider its implications for the transformation's cost, schedule and deliverables. Assessing the impact of risks on these dimensions makes it possible to direct particular attention to those risks having significant implications for the dimension or dimensions deemed most important to the success of a transformation. For example, it may be particularly important to benefit achievement that a certain stage of a transformation be completed within a specified time frame and, as a result, schedule-related risks would be regarded as being especially important during that stage. Incorporating such considerations requires, however, that the basis for a transformation's benefits be established in advance and clearly linked to specific changes through the application of sound value management practices.

Once all risks have been assessed for their impact and likelihood, they can be prioritized by placing them on a matrix such as that shown in Figure 5.9. Risks falling in the "dark" regions (usually illustrated in red color) of this matrix are of greater significance and should therefore receive greater attention in the risk response planning effort as well as during risk monitoring and reporting. Note, however, that maintaining separate

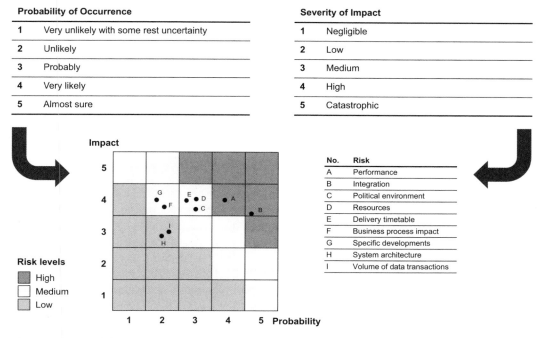

Probability of Occurrence

1	Very unlikely with some rest uncertainty
2	Unlikely
3	Probably
4	Very likely
5	Almost sure

Severity of Impact

1	Negligible
2	Low
3	Medium
4	High
5	Catastrophic

No.	Risk
A	Performance
B	Integration
C	Political environment
D	Resources
E	Delivery timetable
F	Business process impact
G	Specific developments
H	System architecture
I	Volume of data transactions

Risk levels: High, Medium, Low

Figure 5.9   Risk portfolio

assessments of the impact of risk on dimensions such as cost, schedule and deliverables necessitates the development of risk matrices for each of these dimensions unless impacts are first converted to a common unit. Thus, it is often preferable to express all risk impacts in monetary terms. It can, for example, be difficult to determine whether a schedule delay of three months represents a larger impact than a 5 percent cost increase or a modest scope reduction unless all of these potential impacts are expressed using a common currency. Doing so does, however, require that effort be expended to understand the costs associated with a three month delay and the costs of the specific scope reductions that might be necessary. Depending on the circumstances being faced, a three-month delay may result in such things as additional costs to continue operating a legacy system, lost revenues and increased labor costs. Similarly, the impact of benefits stemming from an opportunity to complete a business transformation three months early should also be expressed in monetary terms in order to clearly identify and capitalize on those upside risks with the greatest potential.

Efforts to establish the impact of risk events must aim to be broadly inclusive. For example, in evaluating opportunities it is important to recognize that the "impact" of an opportunity actually represents its value and this value can come in many forms and arise from a wide range of sources. Value might, for example, be found in increasing employee satisfaction, fostering positive relations with a local community or enhancing brand reputation.

An important aspect of transformation risk assessment is the need to aggregate the preceding analysis to understand the overall risk of a transformation initiative and to fully assess interdependencies among all risk events. Overall risk can be evaluated by, for example, placing upper and lower bounds on transformation initiative estimates to reflect all identified risks. Such bounds on individual estimates can then be aggregated to determine upper and lower bounds on overall estimates. In addition to this relatively simple approach, more advanced techniques such as Monte Carlo simulation (see Appendix C) make it possible to establish statistically based confidence intervals on estimates and to evaluate the implications of interdependencies. Real options techniques and the use of risk option mappings can also be helpful (see, for example, Benaroch et al., 2007). Appendix C offers a brief overview of these and other tools that are available to assist with the process of risk assessment.

5.5.3 DEFINE RISK RESPONSE PLAN

Risk responses are developed in accordance with risk management policy for those risks that have been assessed as significant. The risk response plan or risk register describes specific risks, notes the likelihood that each will occur, establishes who is accountable for monitoring and responding to each risk event, and outlines suitable responses to these risk events. The development and implementation of an effective risk response plan requires the commitment of key stakeholders in order to ensure that timely action is taken should a risk event occur and to ensure that needed resources are available to support any required action. Having a plan to address a critical issue such as an unexpected lack of change readiness is likely to be of little value if management is unwilling to fund the actions that the plan calls for or if the plan requires too long to initiate.

Once all identified risks have been evaluated and prioritized, plans can be developed to respond to those strategic risks that fall on the risk radar and those operational risks that have been assigned the highest priorities. It is important to recognize that the purpose of risk response development is not to entirely eliminate risk since this is clearly impossible. Rather, its purpose is to prepare for the most significant risks faced by a transformation project and to effectively address those risks that are actually encountered. Thus, prior to developing responses, the minimum risk priority level warranting the development of a response must be determined. This cut-off point will clearly be impacted by the risk tolerance of the organization and key project stakeholders. While cut-offs should generally be part of the risk management framework, in some cases it may be necessary to direct explicit effort to better understanding the risk tolerance of key stakeholders so that risk response efforts are seen as appropriate to the specific transformation being undertaken.

In the case of strategic risks where it may be difficult to assess the likelihood of occurrence, efforts to increase preparedness may be the most appropriate response. Under most other circumstances, there are four general approaches that can be used to address or respond to risks (Project Management Institute, 2004). These are risk prevention, risk transfer, risk reduction (mitigation) and risk acceptance.

Risk prevention (avoidance)

Risk prevention encompasses any action that aims to eliminate something that is presenting a risk. Avoiding risks altogether may appear to be the preferred response to high-priority risks though avoiding such risks can prove very difficult to accomplish in practice. Nonetheless, it may, for example, be possible to change the scope of a business transformation project to eliminate the use of unproven technology in favor of more established technology. Caution is, however, warranted since these kinds of actions can introduce entirely new set of risks and might also undermine a significant portion of the value of the undertaking. For example, not entering a business to avoid the risk of loss also precludes the possibility of earning profits. Examples of risk responses that rely on risk prevention include not buying a property or business in order to avoid legal liability or using open standards to avoid the risks of proprietary lock-in.

Risk transfer

Risk transfer involves the transfer of responsibility for the impact of a risk event to an outside party. Transferring risk is, in many cases, an expensive way to address risk since it frequently involves the purchase of insurance or the need to insist on robust warranty clauses that can drive up costs. In addition, for many risks it is simply not possible to transfer risk. Examples of risk transfer include the purchase of liability insurance to protect an initiative against unexpected legal threats or the use of a fixed price contract to transfer risks associated with technical complexity.

Risk reduction (mitigation)

Risk reduction or mitigation involves manipulating the significance of a risk event for a transformation initiative. Risk reduction is often the preferred method for addressing notable risks that cannot be avoided. Efforts to reduce risk can include changing the likelihood of a risk event, altering its impact and/or increasing the chances that its occurrence will be detected before it poses a serious threat. For example, concerns that employee dissatisfaction will undermine commitment can be mitigated by routinely evaluating satisfaction to ensure that it does not fall to a problematic level. Other examples of risk reduction include outsourcing of technical work to reduce the technical risk faced by an organization that has limited in-house expertise.

Risk acceptance

Risk acceptance involves accepting the loss or benefit that would arise should a risk event occur. The risk that important team members might leave an organization before completing their work on a transformation may, for example, be accepted if it is believed that the likelihood of this happening is relatively low. Since it is never possible to eliminate all risk, accepted risk will likely be quite significant in a large transformation project even if none of the accepted risks are significant on their own. Although this might seem to be undesirable, sometimes it is enough to simply heighten awareness of risks so that those involved in a transformation can be mindful of signs that they might arise and take pre-emptive action. As noted previously, accepting risk also presents the potential to take advantage of opportunities.

Contingency plans need to be developed for particularly significant risks before accepting them is warranted. For example, accepting the risk that organizational change readiness differs considerably from what was anticipated may involve planning for how the pace of change can be slowed or redistributed if readiness is too low as well as identifying additional opportunities that could be captured if readiness proves higher than expected.

Risk response planning does not end with the development of risk response plans. An important aspect of the planning process is to ensure that ownership of risks is assigned to specific individuals. Accountability for the most significant risks will generally be assigned to higher levels of authority within the organization given the typically higher value at risk and wider scope of resources that will be required to respond (see Figure 5.10 and Figure 5.11). Prior to proceeding it is also necessary to evaluate response plans to ensure that they are technically feasible, financially justified in light of the expected benefits of the transformation and can be implemented under the circumstances in which they will be implemented. It is, for example, essential that sufficient time is available to implement response plans. This can be supported by establishing, in advance, the time that is likely to be available between when the occurrence of a risk event is detected and when the implementation of a response must be completed.

Evaluation of risk response plans can be supported through the use of cost-benefit analysis to determine the suitability of plans in relation to the magnitude of the threats that are posed. In extreme cases this analysis may even suggest that an initiative be abandoned if, for example, a cost effective response cannot be devised for a high-likelihood, high-impact threat. Risk response planning and execution must also remain cognizant of the business value of the transformation to ensure that this value is not undermined by the risk response effort. Appendix C summarizes a number of other tools such as scenario planning and stakeholder analysis that can be useful in developing and evaluating risk response plans.

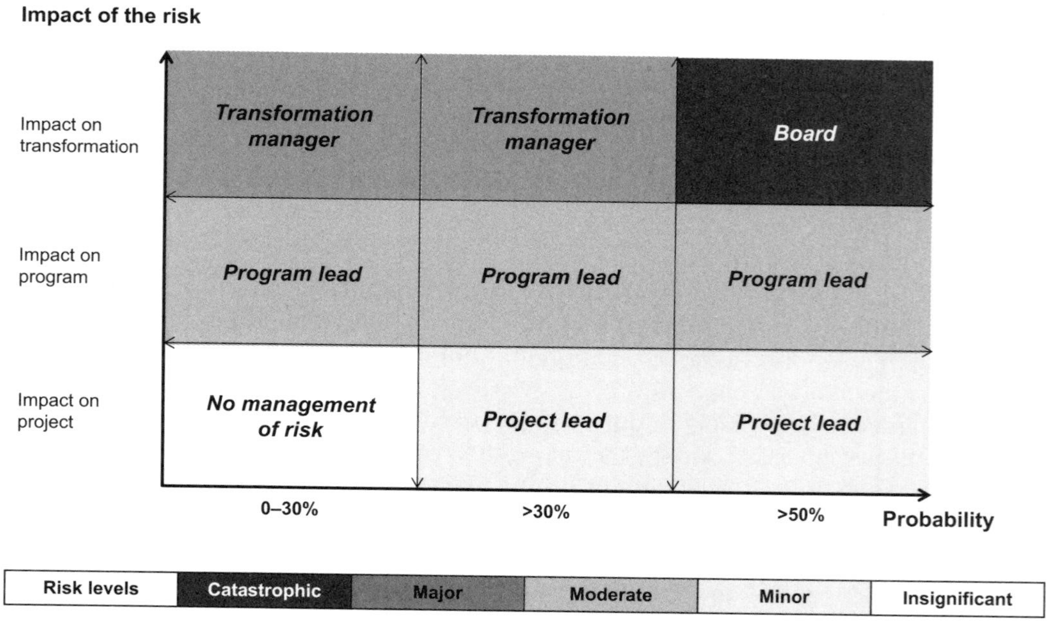

Impact of the risk

Impact on transformation	*Transformation manager*	*Transformation manager*	*Board*
Impact on program	*Program lead*	*Program lead*	*Program lead*
Impact on project	*No management of risk*	*Project lead*	*Project lead*

| | 0–30% | >30% | >50% | Probability |

| Risk levels | Catastrophic | Major | Moderate | Minor | Insignificant |

Figure 5.10 Determining risk accountability

Risk Number and Risk Level	Risk Description	Risk Owner	Accountability
1: Moderate	Workers' compensation	Program lead	HR
2: Major	IT integration	Business transformation manager	CIO
3: Moderate	Brand/reputation	Program lead	Marketing
4: Major	Property rights and general liability	Business transformation manager	Legal
5: Minor	Resources	Project lead	Purchasing dept.

Figure 5.11 Risk accountabilities

CHALLENGES CONCERNING THE RISK ANALYSIS AND THE RISK RESPONSE PLAN:
- Find appropriate transformation risk champions.
- Apply risk categorization frameworks or breakdown structures that can be especially useful in identifying operational risks.
- Prioritize risks by placing them on a matrix with the dimensions cost, schedule and deliverables.
- Determine the minimum risk priority level.
- Gain commitment of key stakeholders to ensure that needed resources are available to support any required action.

KEY MESSAGE:
An important aspect of transformation risk assessment is the need to aggregate all related analysis to understand the overall risk of a business transformation and to fully assess interdependencies among all risk events.

5.6 Execute Risk Response Plan and Monitor Risks

A significant portion of the value of the risk management effort is extracted during the execution of a transformation. Development of a comprehensive risk register with thorough response planning is of limited value if little effort is made to monitor the emergence of risk events or execute planned responses in a timely manner. Hence, it is essential that criteria are in place to determine when a risk has been actualized. These criteria or KRIs must be monitored on a regular basis to ensure that escalation and response plans are triggered when needed. When used with escalation criteria, KRIs help to keep management informed of emerging strategic and operational risk. The response plan and monitoring of risks is executed in the transform phase.

Throughout business transformation it is essential that regular risk review meetings take place to monitor the occurrence of risk events, close risks that are no longer relevant, identify potential new risks and opportunities, and assess the progress and effectiveness of risk responses that have been initiated. Conducting a sound risk review meeting requires that the risk management plan be kept current and that it incorporates all feedback obtained in relation to the risks surrounding a transformation initiative. Since this is an ongoing process, it facilitates observation of changes in risks and the identification of new opportunities that result from changes in business imperative or methodology. A summary of risk review meetings should be provided as a status report to the program steering committee. This summary also provides a convenient communication mechanism that can help link risks on the operational level to risks on the strategic level.

The use of leading KRIs with good predictive capabilities is critical to the successful management of transformation risks. As such, the identification of effective KRIs should be based on a structured design approach. Given the nature of risk, some of the same tools used to monitor the progress of a transformation project can also be used to monitor risk. For example, unfavorable cost and schedule variances might suggest that a transformation effort is not going as planned and may be experiencing certain risks. Further to this, tools such as root cause analysis and cost-benefit analysis can be used to evaluate the occurrence of a risk event to ensure that the planned response remains appropriate in light of what led its occurrence. Appendix C identifies a number of other tools that are of potential value in supporting the process of risk monitoring and reporting.

An important benefit of ongoing risk monitoring and reporting throughout the course of a business transformation is the potential it creates to rapidly identify and leverage opportunities as these arise. This helps to avoid being caught in the pursuit of obsolete objectives and ensures that ongoing action remains appropriate to the strategic risk environment in which an organization operates. As such, the process of risk monitoring and reporting serves as a form of "health check" on the transformation program as well as its supporting projects. Both the progress and viability of the transformation can be reviewed and revised based on the emerging risk environment highlighted during this check. However, the dynamic change that the monitoring and review effort can trigger serves to highlight the importance of linking both strategic and operational risk to the processes of Organizational Change Management and Competence and Training Management. Responding to a particular risk might, for example, require distinct skills

CHALLENGES CONCERNING THE RISK RESPONSE PLAN AND RISK MONITORING:

1. Changing the likelihood of a risk event before it poses a serious threat.
2. Identify Key Risk Indicators (KRIs) to determine when a risk has been actualized.
3. Conduct sound risk review meetings.

KEY MESSAGE:

Important benefits of ongoing risk monitoring and reporting throughout the course of a business transformation are keeping risks updated, obtaining ongoing feedback and the potential it creates to rapidly identify and leverage opportunities as these arise.

and competencies. Business transformation managers must, therefore, remain ever mindful of the implications that risks at every level have for all aspects of the *direction* and *enablement* types of business transformation.

5.7 Review and Evaluate Risks

The final stage of the risk management framework is to review and improve risk management efforts and identify opportunities. This step is performed in the optimize phase. Reviewing risks is an ongoing process in order to determine change in risks and also to identify new opportunities resulting in change in business imperative or methodology. Identifying opportunities requires the creation of an organization wide mindset aimed at stimulating new ideas to counter risk.

The following processes facilitate the risk review process:

a) Lessons learned sessions: Lessons learned at the end of each lifecycle provide data points needed for risk reviews.
b) Financial results: Financial result analysis like cash flow analysis, profitability, volatility and other ratio analysis helps to evaluate the effectiveness of risk responses.
c) Audits: Internal and external audits strengthen risk management processes and ensure minimization of exposure.
d) Independent estimates: Independent estimates of schedule, cost and quality can provide comparison data points for planned deviations from a transformation program.
e) Executive commitment: Commitment from executives is an important aspect of the review process.

CHALLENGES:
1. Identify new opportunities resulting in changes in business imperatives or methodologies.
2. Create organization-wide mindset.

KEY MESSAGE:
Reviewing and evaluating risks is an iterative and ongoing process.

5.8 Conclusion

Risk management helps an organization to recognize when it needs to change while simultaneously permitting it to recognize the opportunities that risks present. Given these insights, managers are better equipped to select the right transformation initiatives and to pursue these initiatives most effectively. Effective management of risk at both the strategic and operational levels is essential to transformation success given the considerable uncertainty involved and the magnitude of the risks that are present.

Acknowledgment – This chapter was delivered in cooperation with the office of Global Strategic and Product Risk Management of SAP AG.

Bibliography

Benaroch, Michel, Jeffery, Mark, Kauffman, Robert and Shah, Sandeep (2007), Option-based risk management: a field study of sequential information technology investment decisions, *Journal of Management Information Systems* 24, no. 2, 103–40.

International Standards Organization (2009), *Risk Management – Principles and Guidelines,* ISO 31000:2009: www.iso.org/iso/catalogue_detail?csnumber=43170 (accessed March 2012).

Jourda, Catherine and Michaelson, Christopher (2009), Exploring emerging risks: extending Enterprise Risk Management (ERM) to address emerging risks, PricewaterhouseCoopers.

Keizera, Jimme A., Halman, Johannes I.M. and Song, Michael (2002), From experience: applying the risk diagnosing methodology, *Journal of Product Innovation Management* 19, no. 3, 213–32.

McKeen, James D. and Smith, Heathe A. (2004), *Making IT Happen: Critical Issues in IT Management,* 2nd ed. (Chichester: Wiley).

Office of Government Commerce (2009), *Managing Successful Projects with PRINCE2,* 5th ed. (London: The Stationary Office).

Project Management Institute (2004), *A Guide to the Project Management Body of Knowledge: Third Edition (PMBOK Guides),* 3rd ed. (Newtown Square, PA: Project Management Institute).

Schmidt, Roy, Lyytinen, Kalle, Keil, Mark and Cule, Paul (2001), Identifying software project risks: an international Delphi study, *Journal of Management Information Systems* 17, no. 4, 5–36.

Schoemaker, Paul J. (1995), Scenario planning: a tool for strategic thinking, *Sloan Management Review* 36, no. 2, 25–40.

6 *Business Process Management*

JAN VOM BROCKE (University of Liechtenstein), MARTIN
PETRY (Hilti AG) and THOMAS GONSER (SAP AG)

6.1 Overview

Business Process Management (BPM) has evolved as one of the most important
management capabilities today. Also in BTM² it plays an essential role as an enabling
factor for successful business transformations. Where does this importance come from?
The answer is fairly simple: Since "processes" essentially are "what organizations do",
transforming organizations essentially means changing an organization's processes.
Therefore, the body of knowledge on contemporary Business Process Management can
contribute a lot to BTM².

The specific focus of BPM within BTM² essentially lies on the design of new processes
implementing new business practices. In particular, BPM within BTM² addresses the following
steps (referring to the transformation lifecycle) for business transformation success:

- Envision: create the *big picture* of process management. Essential steps comprise both
  designing an enterprise process framework and assessing the organizations process
  maturity.
- Engage: conduct specific action in order to perform process-related work. Most
  significantly, this involves both analyzing as-is processes and innovating to-be
  processes. In addition, a governance structure needs to be put in place to frame the
  implementation of new processes.
- Transform: conduct work aiming at implementing the new processes according to the
  to-be processes. This relates to technical implementations but also to organizational
  implementations comprising the definition of performance indicators as part of the
  process controlling.
- Optimize: carry out continuous monitoring in order to find ideas for continuous
  improvement of the processes.

OBJECTIVES OF THIS CHAPTER:
1. Understand how to implement a transformation strategy in operational business.
2. Learn different methods and languages for business process design.
3. Learn that process management does not equal process modeling, but rather requires
   a careful consideration and mediation between IT, business and people-related tasks.
4. Understand how to use BPM in the transformation lifecycle.

6.2 What is BPM?

The relevance of BPM is widely recognized in both industry and academia. The Gartner Group (McDonald and Aron, 2010), for example, identified the improvement of business processes as a top issue on the CIO's agenda for the sixth year in a row. At the same time, BPM has emerged as an important field of research (Rosemann et al., 2008; van der Aalst and ter Hofstede, 2005; vom Brocke et al., 2011; zur Muehlen and Indulska, 2010). With its roots in a number of well-known approaches such as workflow management, business process re-engineering and total quality management (Harmon, 2010), BPM to date stands for an integrated management approach (Rosemann and vom Brocke, 2010). As such BPM seeks to develop organizational capabilities facilitating excellence and innovation in business addressing a wide range of applications (Hammer, 2010; Zairi, 1997).

Why are business processes so important and why is Business Process Management a top issue on the CIO's agenda? The relevance of BPM essentially originates from the nature of process. In fact, all operations in a company – or any other type of organization – are performed by processes. In this regard, *process* means *what companies actually do*. In other words, process is *how* work is done. So, no wonder that processes are everywhere and that processes are vital for economic success in all kinds of business. Very naturally, this also holds true for business transformation. In fact, business transformation can be perceived as changing processes. There are running processes in place, we invent new processes and this all means changing and replacing processes and also communicating and learning process change.

What then is the nature of process? According to Hammer and Champy a process simply is "a set of activities that put together produce a value to a customer" (Hammer and Champy, 1993). Thus, focusing on customers as well as thinking in activities are indeed two major characteristics of process-orientation. When engineering processes, further details are considered in order to analyze processes such as the "self-contained, temporal and logical order of those activities" (Becker and Kahn, 2011) as well as the characteristic of business processes to "realize an organizational objective or policy goal" within a given "set of conditions" (van der Aalst and van Hee, 2002). The most essential characteristics of processes are displayed in Figure 6.1.

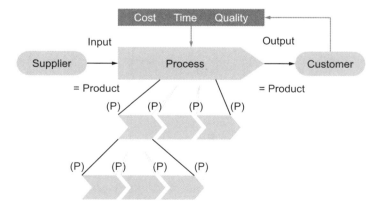

Figure 6.1   Characteristics of process

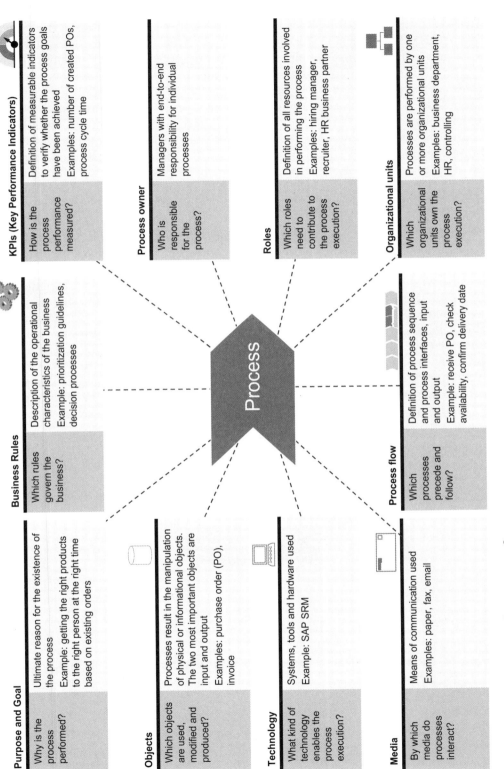

Purpose and Goal

Why is the process performed?

Ultimate reason for the existence of the process
Example: getting the right products to the right person at the right time based on existing orders

Objects

Which objects are used, modified and produced?

Processes result in the manipulation of physical or informational objects. The two most important objects are input and output
Examples: purchase order (PO), invoice

Technology

What kind of technology enables the process execution?

Systems, tools and hardware used
Example: SAP SRM

Media

By which media do processes interact?

Means of communication used
Examples: paper, fax, email

Business Rules

Which rules govern the business?

Description of the operational characteristics of the business
Example: prioritization guidelines, decision processes

Process flow

Which processes precede and follow?

Definition of process sequence and process interfaces, input and output
Example: receive PO, check availability, confirm delivery date

KPIs (Key Performance Indicators)

How is the process performance measured?

Definition of measurable indicators to verify whether the process goals have been achieved
Examples: number of created POs, process cycle time

Process owner

Who is responsible for the process?

Managers with end-to-end responsibility for individual processes

Roles

Which roles need to contribute to the process execution?

Definition of all resources involved in performing the process
Examples: hiring manager, recruiter, HR business partner

Organizational units

Which organizational units own the process execution?

Processes are performed by one or more organizational units
Examples: business department, HR, controlling

Process

Figure 6.2   The integrative power of process

Given this understanding of process, what is so special about process thinking in management? In fact analyzing workflows in organizations has already been part of the genes in early contributions on management (Taylor, 2006) and organizational design (Nordsieck, 1955; Kosiol, 1976). A major reason is the integrative power of processes. Since processes are the place where work actually occurs, all elements relevant for managing work somehow relate to process. Therefore, taking a process-oriented perspective helps to align various elements, most notably related to: task, technology and people (Kosiol, 1976). In Figure 6.2, we give an example of different aspects typically to be aligned following the notion of process. The various aspects nicely illustrate the integrating nature of process: that focusing on processes greatly helps coordinating diverse aspects relevant implementing and managing operations in an organization.

With the ability to integrate, process-thinking contributes to a major challenge in today's business, namely *IT business alignment* (Henderson and Venkatraman, 1993; Luftman, 2005). Processes provide a linking bridge between *IT* and *business* (vom Brocke, 2011), since they operationalize business needs and can, thus, serve as a blueprint for technical implementations. At the same time, new technology may inspire new ways of doing business that can be evaluated according to their impact on processes generating business value. Hence, while structure may follow strategy (Chandler, 1962) or vice versa, process thinking is a good lens to align both strategic and structural considerations. Vital to value generation is also the role of people. In most cases the alignment of *IT* and *business* essentially works through people who understand business-related tasks and are capable of leveraging modern IT to fulfill these tasks (vom Brocke et al., 2011). In this regard human resource management is important in BPM as it provides for developing the right competences to perform processes most efficiently. The interplay of tasks, people and IT jointly creating value through processes is summarized in Figure 6.3.

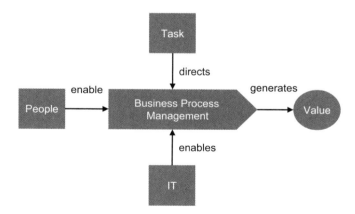

Figure 6.3   BPM driving value through an alignment of task, technology and people

In order to master the alignment of IT and business more specifically, process models are designed. These models are representations of processes that can be specified on various levels of abstraction and from different angles. The business process pyramid by

Harmon (2004) may serve as an example to further illustrate the role of process models in the wider Enterprise Architecture (see Figure 6.4).

The process pyramid by Harmon (2010) describes corporate business process and change efforts in terms of levels that, ideally, should be considered simultaneously. At the enterprise level, organizations coordinate their processes across the entire enterprise. This comprises aligning processes with strategies and defining BPM governance and measurement systems for the entire organization. At the business process level, organizations are exploring a wide variety of new approaches to process analysis and redesign that intend to support the enterprise wide strategy leveraging both technical and human resources on the implementation level to support process work.

Talking about process *models*, a sharp value-focus needs to be taken. We have witnessed decades of extensive process modeling initiative that has but delivered little to no value. Hence, finding both the right level of detail and the right extent of modeling activities is crucial to the success of BPM. We thus call for a value-oriented approach to process management that reflects both economic consequences of single actions and aims to assure a positive return on investment in process transformation (vom Brocke et al., 2010; vom Brocke and Grob, 2011). One powerful means to improve the efficiency and effectiveness of process modeling is reusing conceptual models that have proven successful in certain organizational context. Hence, reference models play an essential role in value generating modeling activities (vom Brocke, 2006).

While process modeling is a strong element of a BPM methodology, the management of business processes needs to be addressed from an organizational wide perspective. Recent studies suggest that actually six core elements of contemporary BPM need to be considered, namely: methods, IT, governance, strategic alignment, people and culture (Rosemann and vom Brocke, 2010). These elements are derived from research on BPM

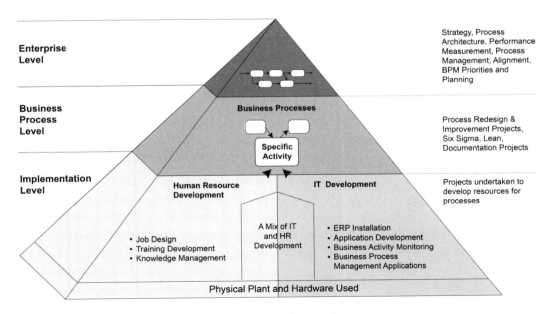

Figure 6.4 The role of process in Enterprise Architecture

Source: Harmon, 2010)

maturity models (de Bruin, 2007; Harmon, 2004, 2007). They can be used in order to assess the current maturity level of an organization (SEI, 2006) and to develop strategies to further develop its BPM maturity according to the specific context factors relevant for one organization.

It is important to consider that – while this chapter takes a focus on methodological issues of BPM complementing BTM² – a successful BPM initiative needs to take into account all six factors mentioned above. In fact, most BPM initiatives that failed did actually overemphasize the modeling part of processes, as mentioned above. To our experience it is essential to learn using BPM methods and technology as a tool but at the same time to carefully consider strategic alignment governance, people and culture in BPM. Successful companies manage to systematically build capabilities in all of the six BPM core elements.

While these six core elements characterize contemporary BPM in general, there is a special focus on BPM as part of BTM². This is because BTM is a holistic management approach itself that considers dedicated aspects of transformation also relating to strategic alignment, governance, methods, IT, people and culture itself. In the next section, we, therefore, present the specific contribution BPM can make for BTM² in more detail. We identify dedicated phases comprising major BPM activities that interact with the other BTM² related management disciplines presented in this book.

CHALLENGES CONCERNING BPM:
1. Build the right competencies to perform processes most efficiently.
2. Describe corporate business process and change efforts in terms of levels considering different factors that, ideally, should be considered simultaneously.
3. Consider a value-oriented approach to process management that reflects both economic consequences of single actions and aims to assure a positive return on investment in business transformation.

KEY MESSAGE:
Recent studies suggest that actually six core elements of contemporary BPM need to be considered, namely: methods, IT, governance, strategic alignment, people and culture. Successful companies manage to systematically build capabilities in all of the six BPM core elements (Rosemann and vom Brocke, 2010).

6.3 Business Process Management in Business Transformation

As part of the BTM², BPM serves as the *enablement* type of Meta Management. Hence, results from Strategy Management, Value Management and Risk Management set the scene and give direction, while other management disciplines such as Program and Project Management, Transformational IT Management, Organizational Change Management, and competence and Training Management and support the BPM-related activities.

The specific focus of BPM within BTM² essentially lies on the design of new processes implementing new business practices. For that purpose BPM offers a wide range of knowledge that can be leveraged. That said, it is obvious that BPM in this sense focuses on methodological issues in particular while other elements of contemporary BPM are partly covered in other chapters of BTM². This particularly becomes apparent considering the implementation of business transformation, which is described in more detail in the chapters on Transformational IT Management, Organizational Change Management, and Competence and Training Management. Hence, BPM in BTM² mainly contributes to envision new processes derived from strategy. It operationalizes them to an extent they can be implemented regarding given organizational, technological and people-related conditions.

Introducing BPM as part of BTM², we take a procedural perspective, in order to capture major work steps related to the redesign of processes. With this, we follow up on former contributions in the field, most notably (Becker et al., 2011; Harmon, 2007; vom Brocke and Rosemann, 2010b, 2010a). While we are in line with these former contributions, our approach is specifically characterized by three aspects:

1. The approach is embedded in BTM². With this, we do not present a standalone BPM approach but rather essential steps where the BPM body of knowledge can specifically add BTM². In this regard, we particularly refer to the other chapters of this book in order to complete the picture (see Figure 6.6).
2. The approach considers an ERP environment, most notably the SAP body of knowledge on systems implementation (Snabe et al., 2009). While it also comprises general aspects of process design, it particularly considers the context of SAP systems and methods for process implementation.
3. The presentation of the approach given in this chapter can only serve as a rough guideline.

There are more detailed contributions on the various aspects covered, so we recommend further reading. While the description cannot be complete, we do hope, however, to capture most important issues for practice that may also stimulate further exploitation.

Figure 6.5 shows how the transformation lifecycle is mapped to various activities related to BPM.

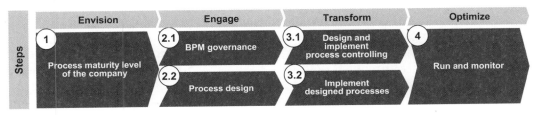

Figure 6.5   Phases of BPM in BTM²

The transformation lifecycle shows the typical phases to run through in a business process redesign project. Given BTM², BPM has various interfaces to the other disciplines as displayed in Figure 6.6.

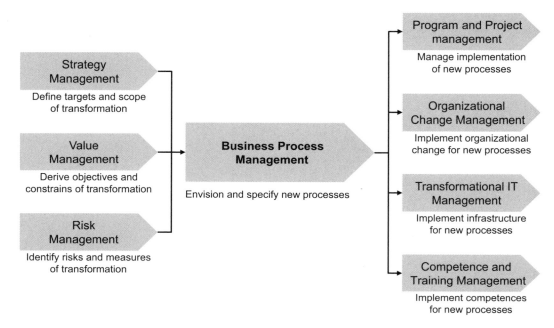

Figure 6.6   BPM interfaces to other management disciplines of BTM²

BPM receives diverse input from the disciplines giving direction in BPM, namely Strategic Management, Value Management and Risk Management:

- Strategy Management: provides the overall direction for the BPM activities in BTM². Both business vision and business model give an orientation where to the transformation should lead. In addition, the business transformation plan provides further detailed information as to timeline and budget of the transformation.
- Value Management: provides an orientation on major value drivers of the process area subject to business transformation. In addition, results from benchmarking and value scenario planning serve to provide a frame and thus operationalize targets for the to-be processes. Both the performance evaluation of alternative process designs and the process controlling related activities directly make use of value management results.
- Risk Management: provides a picture of various risks related to business transformation. The knowledge risks are vital to BPM since processes have to be designed to manage these risks. Therefore, the results from both 360° strategic risk assessment and plan risk strategy are important to design processes that meet strategic objectives, generate preferable value and also make sure risks are considered and managed properly.

Building on the direction for business transformation, BPM envisions and specifies processes that actually prove to operate the to-be state of business. Since BPM only provides the blueprint for new processes, further activities are needed to actually implement processes according to this blueprint. For this purpose, BPM has the four following interfaces of enabling BTM^2 management disciplines:

1. Program and Project Management: serves to manage transformation projects and programs related to the implementation of the new processes. The discipline essentially receives the to-be models from the BPM discipline together with specifications related to governance structures, controlling measures, implementation plans and constraints for the run and monitor phase. It serves to coordinate the activities related to the implementation of the new processes, particularly dealing with Transformational IT Management, Organizational Change Management, and Competence and Training Management.

2. Transformational IT Management: serves to develop the IT infrastructure needed in order to run the new processes. The discipline receives the to-be processes along with corresponding specification of the implementation process and develops the IT infrastructure accordingly. In addition, also IT innovation may enable new processes and, thus, in turn, may also generate new strategic options.

3. Organizational Change Management: serves to provide the organizational frame needed to bring the new processes to life in the organization. The phase particularly receives the to-be models together with the governance structures, the controlling measures and the considerations for the run and monitor phase. Organizational change management makes sure that business transformation is managed smoothly and that the new processes are supported in operational business.

4. Competence and Training Management: serves to make sure that people's competences are developed well enough to perform the new processes at best performance. The discipline receives the to-be-models, governance structure, controlling measures and expectations for the run and monitor phase. It steers diverse HR processes providing the required competences through trainings and recruiting initiatives.

In the remainder of this chapter, we will present the phases of BPM in BTM^2 in more detail, illustrating major tasks and methods for business process redesign. We also make references to other management disciplines of BTM^2.

6.4 Process Maturity Level of the Company (Envisioning)

It is essential to first provide a good orientation before going into detail on special issues of selected processes. A lot of process management initiatives get lost in detail and, thus, miss focus and fail to contribute value. In order to set focus and direction, two elements are particularly relevant: the process framework and the process maturity assessment. The process framework serves to come up with a first orientation of the process landscape relevant in a certain business transformation. Successful process-oriented companies do have an enterprise process framework, for instance. But also for selective areas process frameworks can be designed before going into more detail. Ideally, these frameworks fit on one page and are easy to remember and communicate. On such a basis, the maturity of processes within this framework needs to be assessed. Processes can either be very emerging or highly routinized to give an example. This has a strong impact on subsequent management decisions and transformation tasks. Both elements, the process framework and the process maturity assessment will be further described in the following sections.

6.4.1 PROCESS FRAMEWORK

A process framework serves as *map* and, thus, helps to coordinate BPM activities. The idea is to identify and allocate major building blocks of a business environment and to relate these blocks to one another. This helps to focus on relevant areas and also to master the interdependencies between different areas. There are several options for designing process frameworks (e.g. Becker et al., 2011), the easiest being a straight forward drawing of a picture meaningful for the people involved in the project. The more initiatives launched in an organization the more standardized these maps may be designed. One approach that has proven successful in a number of projects is to structure a process framework on three layers. This approach is illustrated in Figure 6.7.

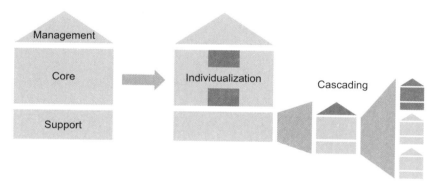

Figure 6.7   Designing process frameworks on three layers

In line with the literature (Hammer, 2010; Becker et al., 2011) process frameworks can be built distinguishing core processes, support processes and management processes:

- Core process: What is the system actually in place for? What value does it deliver for its customers?
- Support process: What resources and services are needed to make the core processes work?
- Management processes: What is needed to give the system the right direction, evaluate current performance and initiate interventions?

The approach presented here suggests a general grouping of processes according to these three categories: Within each category, the project team is free to position their processes in a way it is meaningful for all stakeholders. Particularly within the core-process area, structures have often been designed by project teams that have a symbolic meaning. Examples are a wide range of *letter-shaped* frameworks, such as the retail H, the consulting C or the university U (Becker et al., 2011). In this regard, the process framework has a strong symbolic power. It is an important element for the identification of the team and serves as a powerful means for communication.

Another advantage of the process framework presented here is its applicability in various business units and on different levels of abstraction. For instance, a process area classified as a support process on a corporate scale (e.g. human resource management) may well be further analyzed in more detail, while using cascading (see Figure 6.7). Applying the three-staged framework, again, this support process can be analyzed unfolding a core, support and management process area itself (e.g. core, support and management related to human resource management). By means of this, the approach is therefore suitable for both standardizing framework design on a corporate scale and offering flexibility to analyze specific business areas more specifically.

CHALLENGES CONCERNING THE PROCESS FRAMEWORK:

1. Identify and allocate major building blocks of a business environment and relate these blocks to one another.
2. Create a process framework distinguishing core processes, support processes and management processes.

KEY MESSAGE:

A lot of BPM initiatives get lost in detail and, thus, miss focus and fail to contribute value. Hence, process design in BTM² should start making sure that focus and direction are set right for future phases.

6.4.2 PROCESS MATURITY MODEL

In addition to capturing the operational environment of process areas it is vital to understand the maturity level of processes – and process management capabilities – in these areas of interest. Most of today's maturity models go back to the Capability Maturity Model (CMM) developed by the Software Engineering Institute at Carnegie Mellon University, Pittsburgh, PA. This model was originally developed in order to assess the maturity of software development processes. The basis for applying the model is confirmed by Paulk et al. (1993) who stated that improved maturity results "in an increase in the process capability of the organization". CMM introduces the concept of five maturity levels defined by special requirements that are cumulative.

Today, a vast number of maturity models have been designed for special purposes. Among others, Harmon (2004) developed a BPM maturity model based on the CMM (see also Harmon, 2003). An overview on BPM maturity models is given by Rosemann and vom Brocke (2010). The maturity levels being characteristic for these models are illustrated in Figure 6.8.

A process maturity analysis places the maturity level of a company's processes along a scale tailored to its business process requirements. The approach accounts for the context dependency of BPM. Hence, it is not intended that all companies reach the highest level of maturity in all processes. On the contrary, there is also good reason to remain on lower levels of maturity, considering, for example, the dynamics of a certain business area. Take for example a start-up company. A high level of maturity in terms of well-defined, organized and managed processes could be very dangerous for such an organization, since over-engineering could harm creativity and flexibility needed to leverage opportunities. Once the organization is growing, however, a greater need for rules and structures may be needed in order to safeguard quality in well-established areas of business and to coordinate a greater amount of people. However, once companies have reached an overall need for higher process maturity, we still need to consider that some areas might need less rules to foster creativity and flexibility. Typically, processes in research and design, to give an example, are considered such areas. The maturity assessment intends to picture the current maturity level processes in a certain area in order to learn how to evaluate and potentially further develop the processes.

Assessing the maturity level of processes, specific evaluations need to be carried out within the organization. Most CIOs and CPOs have a good understanding of different maturity levels of their processes even though no formal measurement system is used. Some companies distinguish levels other than the ones from CMM, also depending on the maturity of the process management approach itself. The longer the company is engaged in BPM, the more meaningful different stages of maturity become. In order to apply a more systematic approach to maturity level assessment, questionnaires and employee surveys can be used. Models such as CMM provide criteria to measure specific levels of maturity. As an example we refer to the BPM maturity by de Bruin (2007). Together with the comprehensive description available on this model, the BPM maturity model may also serve as a good starting point to develop an individual set of questions for maturity assessment in BTM^2. In Figure 6.8 we give an example of such a maturity model that has been further discussed in Chapter 3, Strategy Management.

Adapting questionnaires for maturity assessment allows considering specific requirements of certain domain or business areas. It is possible to derive specific measures for a process that is, for example, drawn from strategic measures of the organization. How mature is the process in the light of the company's overall strategy? These measures can be consolidated in an area-specific maturity level plan, which represents the sequence of the targeted measures and focuses on the company's long-term objectives. At the same time, building on a standard for maturity level assessment supports communication and allows for benchmarking. How mature is a process compared to partnering companies or competitors? Often a combination of standardized measures plus company specific measures is used in practice.

Considering the maturity level of processes is actually a vital element for all subsequent decisions on business transformation. For instance, implementing processes and process controlling in a specific business unit needs to consider whether the maturity is either level one (non-organized processes) or level four (managed processes). That said, we also need to account for lower levels of maturity in order to not force organizations to structures implemented in software systems that are too rigid for the organization. In fact, this is one of the big mistakes most BPM initiatives made in the past decades. We need to consider that a lower maturity level is not something negative per se but may well be grounded in the special requirements of the business and then, process implementation and management need to consider this. In particular, dealing with lower

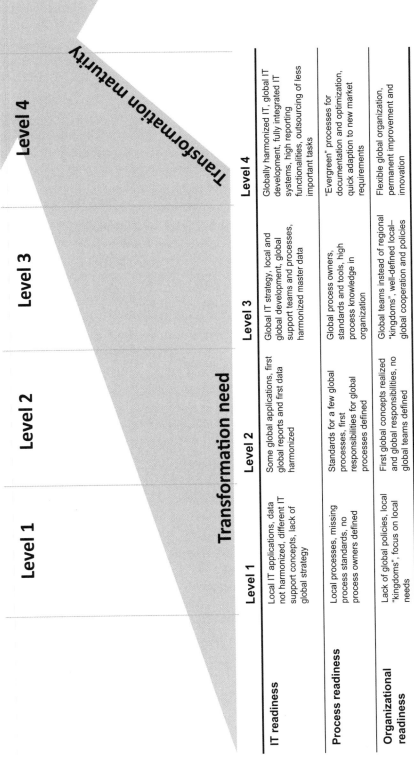

	Level 1	Level 2	Level 3	Level 4
IT readiness	Local IT applications, data not harmonized, different IT support concepts, lack of global strategy	Some global applications, first global reports and first data harmonized	Global IT strategy, local and global development, global support teams and processes, harmonized master data	Globally harmonized IT, global IT development, fully integrated IT systems, high reporting functionalities, outsourcing of less important tasks
Process readiness	Local processes, missing process standards, no process owners defined	Standards for a few global processes, first responsibilities for global processes defined	Global process owners, standards and tools, high process knowledge in organization	"Evergreen" processes for documentation and optimization, quick adaption to new market requirements
Organizational readiness	Lack of global policies, local "kingdoms", focus on local needs	First global concepts realized and global responsibilities, no global teams defined	Global teams instead of regional "kingdoms", well-defined local–global cooperation and policies	Flexible global organization, permanent improvement and innovation

Figure 6.8   Four stages of processes maturity and transformation readiness

levels of process maturity can be seen as one of the major challenge of today's process implementation. Often, we do not have the time to raise process maturity first before implementing or rolling out more automated processes (or we should actually not even intend to do it due to special requirements of a business unit). It is rather the challenge of learning how to provide sufficient IT support also for processes of low maturity and then, potentially further develop the process as it evolves. At Hilti, for instance, process management follows a *solid core and flexible boundary*-approach (vom Brocke et al., 2011). While core components are highly standardized, innovative and evolving solutions are integrated in information systems ecosystem at the same time. Software delivery models, considering highly specialized and work-related applications, provide promising means to dynamically support processes by selected IT-related services.

CHALLENGES CONCERNING THE PROCESS MATURITY MODEL:

1. Perform a process maturity analysis by placing the maturity level of a company's processes along a scale tailored to its business process requirements.
2. Assess the maturity level of processes by using questionnaires and employee surveys.
3. Consolidate the measures in an area-specific maturity level plan, which represents the sequence of the targeted measures and focuses on the company's long-term objectives.
4. Interpreting the measurement results by relating the maturity level to the specific requirements of an organization. A high level of maturity does not need to be a good thing. It is rather about finding the most appropriate level regarding a specific capability that supports the organizations' requirements best.

KEY MESSAGE:

The maturity assessment intends to picture the current maturity level processes in a certain area in order to learn how to evaluate and potentially further develop the processes. A lower maturity level is not something negative per se but may well be grounded in the special requirements of the business and then, process implementation and management need to consider this.

6.5 BPM Governance and Process Design (Engaging)

While modeling of processes marks a major part of BPM (Recker et al., 2009), we need to push BPM beyond modeling in order to successfully support business transformation. During the past years we witnessed companies investing in large-scale modeling projects with little (to no) value contribution. One major reason of this is that such companies neglected the organizational dimension of BPM (vom Brocke and Rosemann, 2010b). Among the organizational issues related to BPM, process governance plays an important role. It is essential to make processes "real" for people, comprising to assure processes are both meaningful and relevant in their daily work. Hence, as one major element of engaging into BPM we focus on BPM governance before we then cover issues of process design by modeling activities and methods.

6.5.1 BPM GOVERNANCE

In general, BPM governance refers to the institutionalization of BPM in an organization. In the literature both the governance of processes (Markus and Jacobson, 2010) and the governance of process management as such (Spanyi, 2010) are distinguished. So, the question is either (a) who is actually in charge of a process or (b) who is in charge of certain process management activities? As part of BTM², we refer to BPM governance simply as all organizational activities that are relevant when engaging in the transformation of business processes. This particularly comprises the following aspects:

- BPM roles and tasks: Make sure all activities relevant for a BPM initiative are planned and assigned.
- BPM terminology: Make sure all stakeholders speak the same language in terms of processes.
- BPM methodology: Make sure all stakeholders follow the same approach and produce valuable consistent results.
- BPM tools: Make sure appropriate tool support is available to facilitate BPM activities.

The management of BPM governance comprises taking according decisions and implementing measures to actually adopt such governance structures within an organization. So, on the one hand, roles need to be defined, a terminology needs to be agreed upon, a methodology needs to be chosen and tools need to be in place. On the other hand, however, management needs to make sure that such governance structures are actually lived by all employees. So, it is vital, for example, that roles are in fact taken and people are fully committed and empowered to their process-related tasks. The terminology needs to be understood and shared by all stakeholders and the methodology and tools, likewise, need to be perceived as useful and easy to apply by all employees.

While it may sound obvious that people actually need to adopt the governance structure, most BPM initiatives that fail, actually do fail because of a lack of adoption. Successful companies, on the contrary, have actually learned how to effectively set a good frame for BPM initiatives. In most cases, it has proven to start small. Considering the most relevant aspects it is important to take decisions and to go with these decisions allowing for continuous organizational learning processes. The more the organization is developing its maturity in BPM the more differentiated the governance structures can become. In most companies, this is quite a natural process once the organization starts learning and adapting these structures. In the following, we will discuss essential elements of BPM governance in more detail.

BPM roles and tasks

In order to define roles and tasks, a decision matrix can be applied. In general, roles such as the process owner, the process manager, the process participants, the process analysts and the process sponsor can be distinguished. The process owner is taking responsibility for a process. Process owners set target and budget for the process and report results on the corporate level. They closely collaborate with a process manager taking care of more operational issues related to the process (e.g. sales executive). The process manager is responsible for reaching performance targets in budget and to coordinate different resources related to the process accordingly (e.g. sales manager). As such, process participants play a special role as those employees essentially conducting work steps planned within the process (e.g. sales person). While these roles characterize a typical primary governance structure, secondary structures are added in order to support process innovation. Here, the process analyst plays a major role whose role is to consult process managers (and owners) in continuously reflecting and improving their business. Often, process analysts are situated either in IT or business units. Some companies start building so-called BPM centers of excellence, serving as independent competence centers for process expertise (Rosemann, 2010). Other companies also recruit so-called process coaches, who actually accompany and mentor process owners implementing change projects (Novotny and Rohmann, 2010). Since the alignment of both IT and business is a major issue in process management, also rotation schemes can be applied having process analysts and coaches move positions from IT- to business-related areas and vice versa. In the end, companies need to find a solution that actually fits their individual background and context. The roles illustrated here may help providing some sort of orientation.

BPM terminology

It is essential that all stakeholders speak the same language in terms of processes (Becker et al., 2003). We have to make sure that all employees actually share the same concept when using terms like *order* and *check*. Often, looking at process descriptions, however, variances in the wording can be found, like *check order* or *evaluate order* or *prove order*. Is there a difference in meaning? Actually, in process management it is essential to refer to items as precisely as possible. Synonyms (different words for the same meaning) and homonyms (same words with different meanings), in particular, shall be avoided. For that purpose organization need to build up a process glossary comprising the most relevant terms of business. Particularly, nouns and verbs need to be standardized in the sense that they have a definite meaning and that only those nouns and verbs are used (e.g. in process descriptions) that are part of the repertoire of standardized words. Building the terminology of an organization, standards can be used that are under continuous development in certain business areas and that can be adapted to a company-specific environment (Hofreiter and vom Brocke, 2010).

BPM methodology

It is essential that the BPM approach applied in an organization is clearly defined and communicated to all stakeholders. All employees need to know why the initiative is launched and what actions and results they can expect. Apart from informing employees, gaining their support for the methodology turns out to be very important. In a number of cases, however, employees keep reporting that the corporate BPM methodology is not applicable well in their specific business and does hardly deliver any value for their daily work. To some extent, this refers to challenges of standardization between centralization and decentralization in organizations (Tregear, 2010). More specifically, however, this also reveals a major challenge that needs to be taken seriously when defining the BPM methodology. This means that different context factors relevant for BPM in various business areas need to be taken into account. BPM methodologies need to make sense for special business areas and they also need to prove delivering value. BPM approaches ignoring this, by applying one standard approach throughout the organization are very likely to fail. At the same time, those approaches succeeding in being perceived as useful throughout the organization will find it easy to sustain and grow. Hence, it is recommended only to standardize to a certain degree but then also leave flexibility to adopt the BPM methodology to certain business requirements, whether you examine for example, the innovation process or the goods received process of an organization.

BPM tool selection

Once more and more business processes are analyzed within an organization, tool support is getting increasingly important. One aspect is to organize the various models captured within an organization. In this regard, tools offer services to archive process descriptions in form of a process repository (Hammer, 2010). Considering BPM as an ongoing management approach, also functions supporting the maintenance and further development of process knowledge play an important role. In this regard, it has been advocated that features supporting knowledge sharing and discourse need to be incorporated in BPM tools (vom Brocke and Thomas, 2006). To date, new developments in the field of social media offer new opportunities to support for collaborative BPM (Lind and Seigerroth, 2010; Richter et al., 2011) that are also discussed within the context of enterprise 2.0 (Kemsley, 2010). While selecting a tool for BPM is important, not too much time should be spent on evaluating alternative products. While a good preparation of BPM is basically recommendable, some companies actually spend too much time on selecting or implementing tools and then fall short in actual process-related work. The most important thing is to select a tool and start working with it. Following this notion, the criterion of global standards and the support by a wide range of experts becomes important. This ensures interoperability and also allows adapting tool support in line with the evolving maturity in BPM of the organization.

CHALLENGES CONCERNING BPM GOVERNANCE:
1. Apply a decision matrix in order to define roles and tasks.
2. Make sure that all employees actually share the same concept (by using e.g. a process glossary).
3. Define the BPM approach applied in an organization and communicate it to all stakeholders.
4. Organize the various models captured within an organization (by using a process repository).

KEY MESSAGE:
While it may sound obvious that people actually need to adopt the governance structure, most BPM initiatives that fail do so because of a lack of adoption.

These elements of the BPM governance set the frame for process-related work. This work is essentially characterized by process design, which is described in more detail in the next section.

6.5.2 PROCESS DESIGN

While we emphasize that BPM should not be limited to process modeling, the design of process models does certainly mark an essential element in BPM. Just like architects building houses and designing urban space do not start building right away, BPM architects also need to plan processes properly first. In fact, also looking into the emergence of BPM, capabilities of actually being able to engineer processes can be seen as a distinct element of the BPM discipline. Hence, BPM provides a sound package of methods to be applied in order to actually model processes before starting to implement them in practice.

The power of a process model is that it serves to analyze a process and to evaluate alternative ways of redesigning it. This is mainly because of three characteristics of a model that can be distinguished according to general model theory (Stachowiak, 1973):

1. Representation: a process model is a description of business, not the business itself; hence it allows playing around with the process before actually changing business.
2. Abstraction: a process model provides a description that is actually reduced to the most relevant aspects of processes; hence, it intentionally leaves out aspects that are perceived as less important and, thus, helps to focus in process-related studies.
3. Intention: a process model provides a description that is meant to fulfill a certain purpose. This purpose actually tells what aspects of a process are more or less important to be incorporated in the model. Hence, basically, process model are not wrong or right. They need to be designed in a way they are perceived to be useful by people working on certain process-related issues.

With these characteristics in mind, designing processes needs thorough support in practice in order to deliver value. According to BTM², the following phases are considered designing processes:

- Calibration: serves to prepare modeling in order to ensure value contribution through modeling.
- As-is analysis: serves to depict the current state of processes and thus provides a foundation for change activities.
- To-be design: services to describe an alternative process design the process that serves as a blueprint for the business transformation.
- Solution transformation: serves to ensure process implementation, particularly though mapping process models to software implementations.

Each phase will now be described in more detail. Given the limited space, we also refer to further publications providing more insight into specific aspects of process design.

Calibration

Since process modeling is not a means in itself a phase of process calibration is recommended to start with. This particularly means to choose your targets first before getting into detail extensively describing single processes. Methodologically, the process framework provides a first good orientation. It basically helps to focus on specific areas of the process landscape relevant for a specific business transformation. In addition, it is important to further specify the objectives of the transformation: What problem is addressed? What processes could be related to this problem? Is there a benchmark for the performance of these processes regarding the problem? What stakeholders are involved and what objectives do they have related to the processes at hand? These are guiding questions providing important information to both (a) identify processes for further evaluation and (b) derive criteria for evaluating alternative process design of these processes.

In order to support calibration, process portfolios can be designed according to multiple evaluation criteria. One example, as presented by Hammer and Champy (1993), is to distinguish between the need to reorganize and the process value (see Figure 6.9). In addition, further evaluation criteria may well be applied, such as cost, risk, strategic importance or frequency of processes (e.g. Becker et al., 2011).

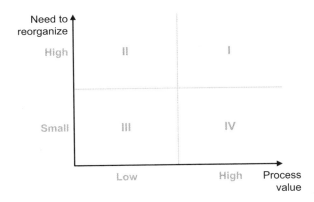

Figure 6.9   Process portfolio for process calibration

Source: Hammer and Champy, 1993

As a result the calibration phase provides the project team with a list of processes to be further analyzed along with criteria for process improvement.

As-is modeling

This serves to describe the current situation of a business process in the focus of interest. In BPM particularly graphical process modeling languages are applied in order to describe processes. The objective is to provide a description of the processes that is preferably clear and definite but easy to understand at the same time. Hence, so-called semi-formal languages are commonly applied that provide standardized constructs describing major elements of business processes, such as activities, flows and logical connectors. An overview of contemporary languages is available in Appendix D of this book.

According to an empirical study, the Event-driven Process Chain (EPC) is among the most commonly used languages in BPM projects (Davies et al., 2006). An example of an EPC model is given in Figure 6.10. The example particularly shows the intermediating

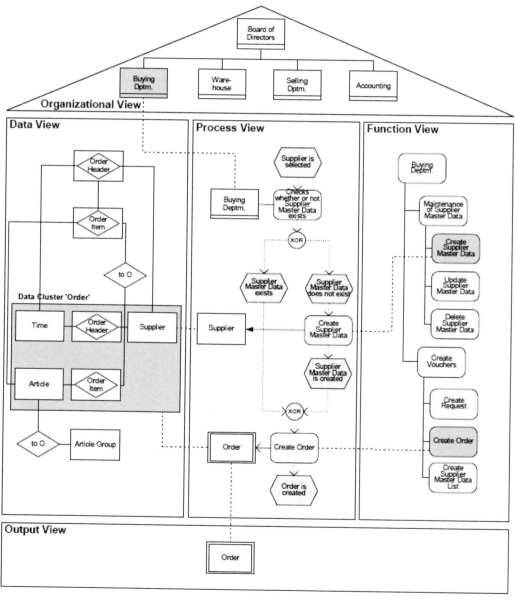

Figure 6.10 Process design using the ARIS framework

role of processes, with process models integrating enterprise models from various other views, i.e. data, functions, organizational and output view.

Selecting the right process modeling language, the specific context of process design activities in an organization needs to be considered. Once a greater amount of process models as to be designed, process integration, for instance, becomes a major issue. In addition, leveraging process models for multiple purposes, the adaptability and extendibility of process descriptions is a valuable characteristic. Last but not least, when considering process implementation, also vertical integration is highly important. In this regard, modeling languages should support reusing conceptual models for customizing and workflow management.

In general, good process modeling languages should provide both a core set of constructs applicable for most of the processes and options of extending the process description according to specific purposes. An emerging standard in BPM is the Business Process Modeling Notation (BPMN) that is currently available in the version 2.0 (see Object Management Group, 2011). The BPMN focuses on the modeling of the logical ordering of activities (Havey, 2005; Weske, 2007). Until the publication of version 2.0 the BPMN only provided a single diagram type for this task: the Business Process Diagram (BPD). Unlike other process modeling languages like the EPC or IDEF, the BPMN does not support multi-perspective process modeling, e.g. to describe value chains, organizational structures or data structures.

Since version 2.0 the BPMN provides means to model a *global view* on the interaction of multiple collaboration partners (i.e. to model distributed processes). For this purpose the BPMN has been extended with a conversation diagram (specifies the conversations within an interaction scenario) and the choreography diagram (specifies a single conversation between two partners). Both diagram types establish an external, inter-organizational perspective on the interplay of multiple collaboration partners. Internal processes of individual process participants are then modelled by means of BPD. The notation elements used in the BPD represent different object types, which can be used to describe business processes (Object Management Group, 2011). The BPMN distinguishes between flow objects, connecting objects, swimlanes, artefacts and data objects. Figure 6.11 provides an example.

BPMN comprises many more notation elements than used in the example. The elements considered here belong to the BPMN core and are the most frequently applied elements in business process modeling (cf. zur Muehlen and Recker, 2008):

- Flow objects are related to connecting objects. Sequence flows connect individual activities and specify the order of their execution.
- Swimlanes allow for the description of responsibilities for the activity execution.
- Artefacts serve to capture context specific particularities within a process model. *Annotations* are frequently used for this purpose.
- Data objects represent all information and documents which flow through a process.

The example shows two internal processes, which are defined within two pools. This is a typical scenario for the modeling of distributed processes (choreography). The processes or the process pools are connected by means of message flows. The choreography is initiated by the internal process of *Organization X*. After *Unit 1* has executed the first task, *Unit 2* continues the process execution and sends a message to *Organization Y*. The

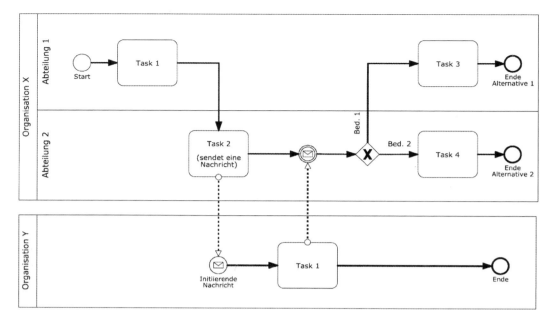

Figure 6.11 Example of a process model in BPMN

receipt of this message triggers the process execution in *Organization Y*. In the course of this process execution a new message is generated and sent back to *Organization X*. In the meantime, the internal process of *Organization X* has been waiting until the receipt of the response of *Organization Y*. On the receipt of the message, alternative tasks (*Task 3* or *Task 4*) are executed depending on the evaluation result of the conditions specified with the process model.

In general, as-is processes serve as a foundation to find options for process improvement. In BPM a wide range of techniques is available, actually supporting to craft ideas to further develop processes. A good set of examples is collected in the Six Sigma approach, including *cause and effect diagrams*, *pareto diagrams* and *root cause analysis* (e.g. Motorola, 2009; Conger, 2010). In BTM², however, we face a special situation, since results from strategic management, value management and risk management already predefine the direction for process (re)design in most cases. In addition, more substantial rather than incremental changes are the subject of interest. In this situation, the analysis of the as-is models needs to specifically focus on identifying specific areas in the processes affected by business transformation. As a deliverable, these areas need to be identified and the expected change to these areas needs to be outlined briefly. This sets the scene for the next phase of to-be modeling.

To-be design

The to-be phase is concerned with the future design of the processes. In principle, the phase seamlessly continues the analysis of the previous phase by crafting alternative future pictures of the processes of interest. Hence, from the modeling perspective, the same process modeling languages are used. In fact, most to-be models actually evolve from the as-is models through revision and extension.

One element, however, that is particularly challenging (while underestimated in most BPM approaches), is how to actually find the right to-be design. In fact, it is not the description of to-be models but rather the invention of the desirable to-be state that is demanding in practice. How can you actually assure that a to-be process is superior to another one? In conventional BPM literature, little guidance is provided for this essential task of BPM. Those recommendations that are available are mostly qualitative and remain rather abstract in a sense of avoiding unnecessary interfaces or changes in data formats. Those recommendations, as for example to be derived from lean management avoiding different types of waste (Ohno, 1988), help to find ideas on how to improve processes incrementally. They provide little decision support, however, in comparing alternative process designs regarding their contribution to strategy.

In contemporary BPM, however, complex design alternatives need to be evaluated that can hardly be taken based on an intuitive assessment. How to use the cloud? How to leverage mobile applications? Such decisions include a myriad of part decisions with diverse parameters relevant to be taken into account. Hence, decision models need to be designed helping decision makers to exemplary design and calculate alternative process variants. Since to-be models do not directly derive from as-is models, potential models help to evaluate further evaluate economic consequences of process design (vom Brocke et al., 2009). The concept of potentials models is illustrated in Figure 6.12.

The concept of potentials modeling intends to provide decision support in process redesign. These methods facilitate computing the actual return on process transformation for specific design alternatives taking into account specific parameters of process design. That way, so-called potential models are designed beforehand as candidates for to-be models result to further evaluation.

A potential model covers relevant design alternatives to be compared with each other in terms of their value proposition in a specific organizational situation. In terms of decision theory, an alternative represents one out of multiple exclusive decision choices (Grob, 1993). In the course of an information systems (re)design, thus, several potentials

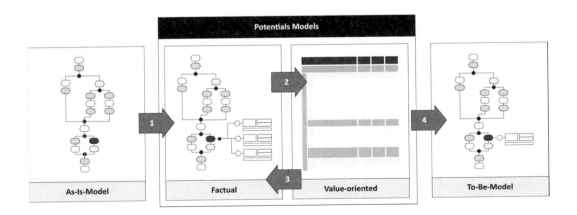

Figure 6.12 Finding to-be models via the evaluation of potentials models

models are compared in order to finally identify the most beneficial alternative. The concept of potentials modeling distinguishes factual and value-oriented potentials that are considered as follows:

- The factual specification of design alternatives forms the foundation for further analysis. Considering the SOA example, this means e.g. to capture alternative services for supporting individual functions – but also the various alternatives for business process redesign.
- The economic consequences associated with the design alternatives are documented and consolidated within value-oriented potentials models (e.g. by means of financial measures).
- On that basis, the alternatives can be compared and design decisions can successively be modified.
- Such an evolutionary approach makes it possible to create, compare and modify potentials models until – from a decision maker's perspective – a beneficial alternative has been identified. The latter finally represents the to-be model for the subsequent implementation.

As a key measure, the return on process transformation may serve as an example to evaluate the performance of an alternative process design (see Figure 6.13). In order to analyze the profitability of an alternative process redesign, both the potential return and the investment needed is to be taken into account.

- Assessing the return: Since a return can often hardly be quantified, both Total Payments of Process Ownership (TPPO) *with* (process p') and *without* (process p) redesign are computed (level 0 and 1). The Return is then operationalized exactly by the difference between the TPPO of p' and the TPPO of p.
- Assessing the investment: The investment is operationalized by the total payments needed to conduct the business transformation from p to p', the Total Payments of Process Transformation (TPPT). The TPPT include, for example, initial payments for licenses but also efforts for communicating and training new practices.

When assessing both TPPO and TPPT, long-term economic consequences need to be taken into account. Hence, a dynamic calculation needs to be carried out considering multiple periods in time. Often, a planning horizon of five years gives a good indication. Summing up both the return (TPPO p'– TPPO p) and the investment of payments in process transformation (TPPT), one representative series of payments is computed that is driven by a potential redesign of interest (level 2).

This series of payments – so-called original payments – builds the foundation for further computing the derivative payments resulting from the financial sector. These payments include, for example, interest rates and taxes. Since the economic effects of the process transformation have been aggregated in one representative series of payments, well-established methods from investment accounting can be applied here, like the net present value, the pay off period or the return on investment (Grob, 1993; vom Brocke and Grob, 2011).

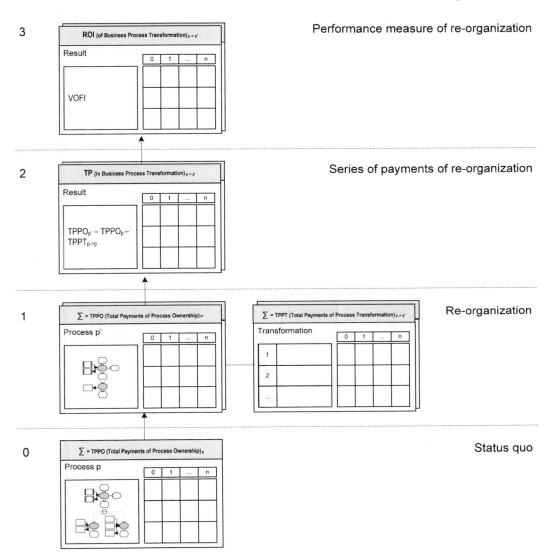

Figure 6.13 Framework for calculating the return on process transformation

Calculating the TPPO different levels of detail can be applied. In practice a two-staged approach is often useful. First, a rough assessment based on expert opinion can be conducted. Second, based on such first results, selected aspects of the calculation can be detailed on demand. For such detailed calculation, also process models can serve as a basis to further analyze resource utilization and frequencies of certain process branches (vom Brocke et al., 2010). Former research has provided models to evaluate the return of process transformation for a wide range of process transformation projects, including leveraging outsourcing and out-tasking (vom Brocke, 2007) and utilizing customer communities (vom Brocke et al., 2010).

The return on process transformation is one measure for decision support in process redesign. In practice, this information can well inform decision making, which indeed needs to take into account a wider range of decision criteria. Once a decision for a to-be process has been made, both the to-be state and the set of activities necessary to undertake business transformation are available. On that basis a detailed roadmap can be developed particularly including solution transformation.

Solution transformation

Most process management approaches actually fall short closing the loop by actually implementing to-be processes in an organization. Implementing processes needs to consider both people- and IT-related activities (e.g. Harmon, 2010). While, following BTM², the process transformation is covered in a special phase, the solution transformation step described here intends to prepare this transformation best. This is done by actually mapping the to-be process to both human and technical resources in order to make sure the to-be processes can actually be performed according to its specification. In order to support this step, a process implementation matrix can be designed showing the various relations (see Figure 6.14).

The process implementation matrix illustrated in Figure 6.14 applies the structure of so-called RA(S)CI models (Responsible, Accountable, Supportive, Consulted, Informed). The matrix has been extended in order to also assign IT resources. For a more detailed analysis, different views can be taken when mapping the process to IT resources:

- Component view: map to-be processes to SAP solution components using SAP solution composer.
- Process view: map to-be processes to SAP services from the repository of the SAP solution manager.
- Data view: map to-be processes to SAP data objects.

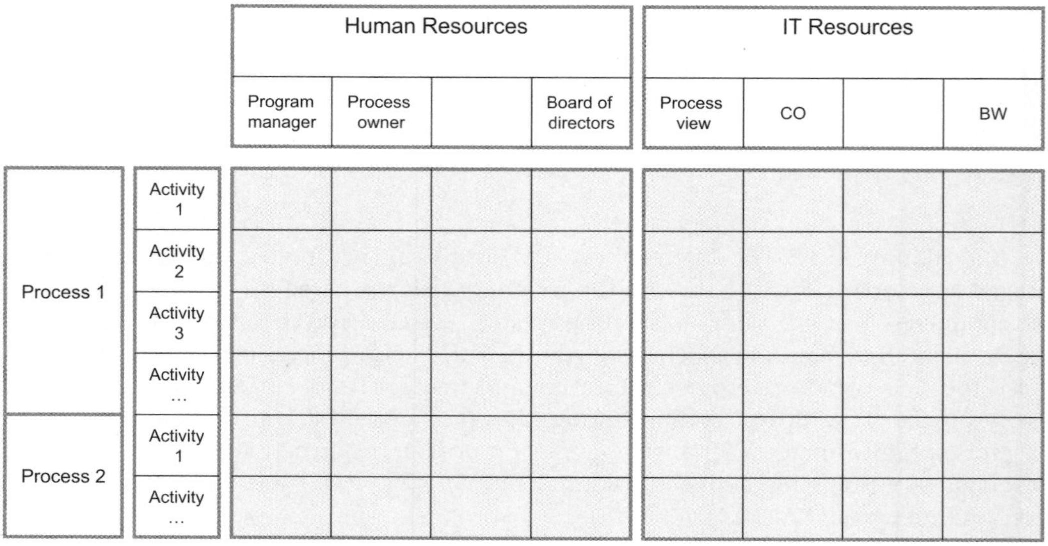

Figure 6.14 Process implementation matrix

CHALLENGES CONCERNING THE PROCESS DESIGN:
1. Choose your targets before getting into detail extensively describing single processes.
2. Design process portfolios according to multiple evaluation criteria.
3. Provide the project team with a list of processes to be further analyzed along with criteria for process improvement.
4. Select the right process modeling language for the specific context of process design in an organization.
5. Focus on identifying specific areas in the processes affected by business transformation.
6. Evaluate the economic consequences of alternative process designs by means of potential models.
7. Use the return on process transformation as an example to evaluate the performance of an alternative process design.
8. Compare several potentials models in order finally to identify the most beneficial alternative.
9. Design a process implementation matrix showing the various relationships between to-be processes and human and technical resources.

KEY MESSAGE:
The power of a process model is that it serves to analyze a process and to evaluate alternative ways of redesigning it. This is mainly because of the characteristics representation, abstraction and intention of a model. In addition to factual process flows, however, also the economic consequences driven by a process design need to be analyzed based on these processes models.

The solution transformation ensures that all factual considerations for the implementation of the to-be process are decided upon and prepared. This provides a good prerequisite for the implementation and controlling of processes.

6.6 Implementation of Processes and Controlling (Transforming)

With a focus on IT, this section describes the actual implementation of the to-be processes according to the implementation matrix. With respect to people, this particularly comprises to set up a controlling system. Actual execution of changes regarding technology and people's behavior are is a focus of two management disciplines of BTM², namely Transformational IT Management and Organizational Change Management. However, some related activities remain rounding up the BPM process.

6.6.1 DESIGN AND IMPLEMENT PROCESS CONTROLLING

What gets measured gets done. This, indeed, also holds true for processes. In particular, when it comes to changing the way people are supposed to do their work, measurement turns out to be essential. It is important to communicate clear targets and to also measure the results and take action on deviations. In BTM², this part of business transformation is referred to as process controlling.

Contributions on process controlling go back to early work in management accounting (Johnson and Kaplan, 1987). While the term process controlling is particularly used in the German-speaking community (Scheer and Breitling, 2000), on an international scale performance measurement, and *process* performance measurement in particular, are rather used instead (Heckl and Moormann, 2010). The topic has caught particular interest ever since Kaplan/Norton first published their paper on the balanced scorecard in the early 1990s (Kaplan and Norton, 1992). The idea is to define a set of comprehensive performance measures, also called Key Performance Indicators (KPI) or Process Performance Indicators (PPI) that are derived from the corporate strategy and that lead local action at the same time. Typically, not only monetary measures, but measures from different target dimensions are considered in order to assure long-lasting economic success. In fact, the definition of performance indicator is instrumental for every type of management system. So, most management disciplines in BTM² would present approaches to define specific KPIs related to their specific management area.

Designing and implementing a corporate performance measurement system follows a certain pattern (Kaplan and Norton, 2008). The steps considered in BTM² comprise the following:

- Define area of application: specify the process to be measured.
- Define process performance indicators: specify the measures to be used.
- Design reports and cockpits: specify the format of presenting measurement results.
- Implement reports and cockpits: technically realize the measurement system accordingly.

Among the various steps, finding the right process performance indicators (PPIs) actually turns out to be the most central task. Since *what gets measured gets done*, there is also the risk of measuring the wrong things and, thus, getting the wrong things done. There was, for example, a university, measuring the *amount of publications* published on a yearly basis; however, it did not consider the quality of these publications. The result was that a great amount of papers was published, most of them, however, in poorly ranked but easy-to-get formats. Obviously, this was not the desired result and, in fact, a serious threat to the university's reputation.

The process performance measurement matrix presented in Figure 6.15 helps to find appropriate PPIs:

The framework suggests defining performance measures in relation to (1) target dimensions and (2) as shown in figure 6.15 controlling objects. The essential element compared to the conventional approach is to explicitly consider (and model) tailor-made target dimensions. These target dimensions should be derived from the overall strategy and, thus, be kept consistent over different processes. Conventionally, such target dimensions comprise cost, time and quality of processes (Becker et al., 2011), also extended by the dimension of flexibility and referred to as the *devil's quadrangle* of BPM (Reijers and Limam Mansar, 2005).

Most companies, however, have their own very specific value system derived from the strategy that – following this framework – can be projected on each process to be measured. A lot of companies, for example, are currently concerned with integrating

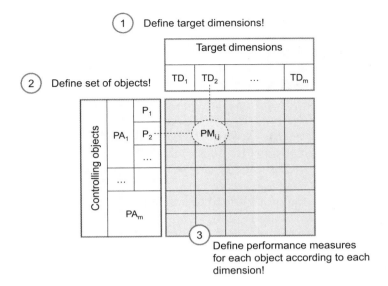

Figure 6.15 Process performance measurement matrix

sustainability measures in their corporate management system. Such an extension can be achieved by, for example, adding according value dimensions, e.g. for social and environmental sustainability (Hailemariam and vom Brocke, 2011; Seidel et al., 2011),

CHALLENGES TO BE ADDRESSED WITHIN DESIGN AND IMPLEMENT PROCESS CONTROLLING:

1. Specify the process to be measured.
2. Specify the measures to be used (process performance indicators vs. key performance indicators).
3. Specify the format of presenting measurement results.
4. Technically realize the measurement system accordingly.

KEY MESSAGE:

The measurement system needs to fit the individual strategy of an organization. In addition, measures need to be meaningful for single employees. The process performance measurement matrix can help to bring both perspectives together.

which ultimately led to the concept of Green BPM (vom Brocke et al., 2012). Given the individually designed structure of relevant target dimensions and process areas, (3) process performance indicators can be defined. In principle, each value dimension needs to be considered for each process. This ensures a maximum degree of strategy implementation in the processes.

Performance indicators are used to set targets. As such, they need to be defined in a *SMART* way:

- *Specific*: the measures and targets should be meaningful for both process executors and owners.
- *Measurable*: accomplishment rate and progress towards target values has to be measured.
- *Aligned*: PPIs should *be* aligned with strategies and higher goals, which is basically assured following the performance matrix framework.
- *Realistic*: process executers should be able to reach (and over perform) their targets at best performance.
- *Time-bound*: targets need to be bound to a time frame.

Once the PPIs are defined from a business perspective, the controlling cockpit can be designed and implemented accordingly.

6.6.2 IMPLEMENTATION OF DESIGNED PROCESSES

The implementation of the processes comprises both technical and non-technical aspects of the implementation. In concordance with the positioning of BPM in BTM² (see Figure 6.6), further details on process implementation are provided in Chapter 7 (Transformational IT Management), Chapter 8 (Organizational Change Management), Chapter 9 (Competence and Training Management) and Chapter 10 (Program and Project Management).

6.7 Run and Monitor (Optimizing)

An important success factor for BPM is to continuously revisit the processes designed and to also reconsider decisions taken before. Most BPM initiatives that have not proven sustainable, actually did not account for the continuous nature of BPM. Once an organization ran through the various stages described above, BPM is not over but it rather starts, since it is initiated and, now, needs careful management. Continuously revisiting the processes serves essentially two purposes:

1. It serves to evaluate the processes regarding potential changes in the process environment. Such changes regularly occur, e.g. due to technological development or changing business requirements.
2. Revisiting the processes essentially contributes to make processes real for employees. Hence, monitoring existing processes also achieves a strong influence on the commitment of people to the entire BPM initiative.

BTM² actually distinguishes four phases of optimizing business processes. A brief introduction into these phases may give an overview of the activities covered in this concluding and continuous phase of BPM.

- Executing and measuring the process: make sure that executed processes are measured regarding their performance. For that purpose process performance indicators defined in process controlling are used. To-be values and as-is values are compared providing valuable data for performance analysis.
- Analyzing the results: try to understand root causes of variances both in positive and negative direction leading to corrective action. While data analysis might not be sufficient for the identification of all root causes it can, however, provide first identifications of issues.
- Empower employees: make sure to align process performance to the management system of the organization. Process-oriented goals must be agreed upon in order to assure commitment and foster process-oriented thinking. Employees need to feel in charge, responsible and empowered for process performance. Recurring process audits help implementing such an empowerment.
- Process optimization cycle: finally, mechanisms for taking action need to be implemented. On the one hand, this means to take advantage of quick improvements. On the other hand, further improvement plans need to be developed and launched out of the continuous optimizing cycle.

CHALLENGES CONCERNING RUN AND MONITOR:
1. Evaluate the processes in order to support learning in process execution.
2. Regularly consider potential changes in the process environment that call for adaptations in the process.
3. Ask people about their processes and "talk process" on a daily basis in order to make processes meaningful and real for all employees.

KEY MESSAGE:
Once new processes are implemented and running, don't think BPM is over. It rather starts right over and over again. Research shows that those companies who have proven successful in BTM are those companies who have mastered the skill of building the capabilities needed to manage their business processes continuously.

6.8 Conclusion

In this chapter, we presented BPM as enablement type of BTM². We essentially described how to proceed implementing a transformation strategy in operational business. That said, we did not describe BPM as a standalone discipline but rather as a contributing set of competencies in BTM².

Hence, further considerations need to be taken into account, in order to successfully implement and manage business transformation that will be further illustrated in Chapters 7–10, namely on: Transformational IT Management, Organizational Change Management, and Competence and Training Management, and Program and Project Management.

Last but not least, we would like to make the point that, despite of all the good advice from research and practice, there is no blueprint or *silver bullet* to BPM. On the contrary, a successful BPM initiative needs to carefully take into account the specific organizational conditions. Hence, the methods we presented may rather serve as a toolbox that, however, still needs to be commanded carefully. A good assessment of the organization's specific situation and singularity is probably the most important key to BPM success.

Bibliography

Becker, Jörg and Kahn, Dieter (2011), The process in focus, in *Process Management: A Guide for the Design of Business Processes*, 2nd ed., edited by Jörg Becker, Martin Kugeler and Michael Rosemann (Berlin et al.: Springer).

Becker, Jörg, Dreiling, Alexander, Holten, Roland and Ribbert, Michael. Specifying information systems for business process integration – A management perspective, *Information Systems and E-Business Management* 1, no. 3 (2003): 231–263.

Becker, Jörg, Martin Kugeler and Michael Rosemann (eds) (2011), *Process Management: A Guide for the Design of Business Processes*, 2nd ed. (Berlin et al.: Springer).

Chandler, Alfred D. (1962), *Strategy and Structure: Chapters in the History of the Industrial Enterprise* (Cambridge, MA: MIT Press).

Conger, Sue (2010a), Six Sigma and business process management, in *Handbook on Business Process Management 1: Introduction, Methods, and Information Systems,* edited by Jan vom Brocke and Michael Rosemann (Berlin, Heidelberg: Springer).

Davies, Islay, Green, Peter, Rosemann, Michael, Indulska, Marta and Gallo, Stan (2006), How do practitioners use conceptual modeling in practice?, *Data & Knowledge Engineering* 58, no. 3, 358–80.

de Bruin, Tonia (2007), Insights into the evolution of BPM in organisations, in *ACIS 2007 Proceedings,* Paper 43: http://aisel.aisnet.org/acis2007/43 (accessed March 2012).

Grob, Heinz L. (1993), *Capital Budgeting with Financial Plans: An Introduction* (Wiesbaden: Gabler).

Hailemariam, Getachew and vom Brocke, Jan (2011), What is sustainability in business process management? A theoretical framework and its application in the public sector of Ethiopia, in *Business Process Management Workshops: BPM 2010 International Workshops and Education Track, Hoboken, NJ, USA, September 2010, Revised Selected Papers,* edited by Michael zur Muehlen and Jianwen Su (Berlin, Heidelberg: Springer).

Hammer, Michael (2010a), What is business process management?, in *Handbook on Business Process Management 1: Introduction, Methods, and Information Systems,* edited by Jan vom Brocke and Michael Rosemann (Berlin, Heidelberg: Springer).

Hammer, Michael and Champy, James (1993), *Reengineering the Corporation: A Manifesto for Business Revolution,* 1st ed. (New York, NY: Harper Business).

Harmon, Paul (2003), *Business Process Change: A Manager's Guide to Improving, Redesigning, and Automating Processes* (Amsterdam: Morgan Kaufmann).

Harmon, Paul (2004), Evaluating an organization's business process maturity: www.bptrends. com/publicationfiles/03-04%20NL%20Eval%20BP%20Maturity%20-%20Harmon.pdf (accessed March 2012).

Harmon, Paul (2007), *Business Process Change: A Guide for Business Managers and BPM and Six Sigma Professionals,* 2nd ed. (Amsterdam et al.: Morgan Kaufmann).

Harmon, Paul (2010), The scope and evolution of business process management, in *Handbook on Business Process Management 1: Introduction, Methods, and Information Systems*, edited by Jan vom Brocke and Michael Rosemann (Berlin, Heidelberg: Springer).

Havey, Michael (2005), *Essential Business Process Modeling* (Sebastopol, CA: O'Reilly).

Heckl, Diana and Moormann, Jürgen (2010b), Process performance management, in *Handbook on Business Process Management 2: Strategic Alignment, Governance, People and Culture*, edited by Jan vom Brocke and Michael Rosemann (Berlin, Heidelberg: Springer).

Henderson, John C. and Venkatraman, N.V. (1993), Strategic alignment: leveraging information technology for transforming organizations, *IBM Systems Journal* 32, no. 1, 272–84.

Hofreiter, Birgit and vom Brocke, Jan (2010), On the contribution of reference modeling to e-business standardization – how to apply design techniques of reference modeling to UN/CEFACT's modeling methodology, in *Business Process Management Workshops: BPM 2009 International Workshops, Ulm, Germany, September 2009. Revised Papers*: 671–682.

Johnson, H. Thomas and Kaplan, Robert S. (1987), *Relevance Lost: The Rise and Fall of Management Accounting* (Boston, Mass: Harvard Business School Press).

Kaplan, Robert S. and Norton, David P. (1992), The balanced scorecard: measures that drive performance, *Harvard Business Review* 70, no. 1, 71–9.

Kaplan, Robert S. and Norton, David P. (2008), *The Execution Premium: Linking Strategy to Operations for Competitive Advantage* (Boston, Mass: Harvard Business School Press).

Kemsley, Sandy (2010a), Enterprise 2.0 meets business process management, in *Handbook on Business Process Management 1: Introduction, Methods, and Information Systems*, edited by Jan vom Brocke and Michael Rosemann (Berlin, Heidelberg: Springer).

Kosiol, Erich (1976), *Organisation der Unternehmung*, 2nd ed. (Wiesbaden: Gabler).

Lind, Mikael and Seigerroth, Ulf (2010a), Collaborative process modeling: the Intersport case study, in *Handbook on Business Process Management 1: Introduction, Methods, and Information Systems*, edited by Jan vom Brocke and Michael Rosemann (Berlin, Heidelberg: Springer).

Luftman, Jerry (2005), Key issues for IT executives 2004, *MIS Quaterly Executive* 4, no. 2, 269–85.

Markus, M.L. and Jacobson, Dax D. (2010b), Business process governance, in *Handbook on Business Process Management 2: Strategic Alignment, Governance, People and Culture*, edited by Jan vom Brocke and Michael Rosemann (Berlin, Heidelberg: Springer).

McDonald, Mark P. and Aron, Dave (2010), Leading in times of transition: the 2010 CIO agenda, Gartner: www.gartner.com/id=1280013 (accessed March 2012).

Motorola, About Motorola University: the inventors of Six Sigma, Motorola Corporation: www.motorola.com/content.jsp?globalObjectId=3079 (accessed September 2009).

Nordsieck, Fritz (1955), *Rationalisierung der Betriebsorganisation*, 2nd ed. (Stuttgart: Poeschel).

Novotny, Stefan and Rohmann, Nicholas (2010b), Toward a global process management system: the ThyssenKrupp Presta case, in *Handbook on Business Process Management 2: Strategic Alignment, Governance, People and Culture*, edited by Jan vom Brocke and Michael Rosemann (Berlin, Heidelberg: Springer).

Object Management Group (2011), Business process modeling notation (BPMN): version 2.0: www.omg.org/spec/BPMN/2.0/PDF (accessed March 2012).

Ohno, Taiichi (1988), *Toyota Production System: Beyond Large-scale Production* (Cambridge, Mass: Productivity Press).

Paulk, M.C., Curtis, B., Chrissis, M.B. and Weber, C.V. (1993), Capability maturity model, version 1.1, *IEEE Software* 10, no. 4, 18–27.

Recker, Jan, Rosemann, Michael, Indulska, Marta and Green, Peter (2009), Business process modeling – a comparative analysis, *Journal of the Association for Information Systems* 10, no. 4, Article 1: http://aisel.aisnet.org/jais/vol10/iss4/1 (accessed March 2012).

Reijers, Hajo A. and Limam Mansar, Selma (2005), Best practices in business process redesign: an overview and qualitative evaluation of successful redesign heuristics, *Omega* 33, no. 4, 283–306.

Richter, Daniel, Riemer, Kai and vom Brocke, Jan (2011), Internet social networking: research state of the art and implications for enterprise 2.0, *Business & Information Systems Engineering* 3, no. 2, 89–101.

Rosemann, Michael (2010b), The service portfolio of a BPM center of excellence, in *Handbook on Business Process Management 2: Strategic Alignment, Governance, People and Culture,* edited by Jan vom Brocke and Michael Rosemann (Berlin, Heidelberg: Springer).

Rosemann, Michael and vom Brocke, Jan (2010a), The six core elements of business process management, in *Handbook on Business Process Management 1: Introduction, Methods, and Information Systems,* edited by Jan vom Brocke and Michael Rosemann (Berlin, Heidelberg: Springer).

Rosemann, Michael, Recker, Jan and Flender, Christian (2008), Contextualisation of business processes, *International Journal of Business Process Integration and Management* 3, no. 1, 47–60.

Scheer, August-Wilhelm and Breitling, Markus (2000), Geschäftsprozesscontrolling im Zeitalter des E-Business, *Controlling* 12, 8/9, 397–402.

SEI (2006), CMMI® for development, version 1.2, Software Engineering Institute, Carnegie Mellon University: www.sei.cmu.edu/reports/06tr008.pdf (accessed March 2012).

Seidel, Stefan, vom Brocke, Jan and Recker, Jan (2011), Call for action: investigating the role of business process management in green IS', in *Proceedings > Proceedings of SIGGreen Workshop. Sprouts: Working Papers on Information Systems,* 11(4): http://sprouts.aisnet.org/11-4 (accessed March 2012).

Snabe, Jim H., Rosenberg, Ann, Møller, Charles and Scavillo, Mark (2009), *Business Process Management: SAP Roadmap,* 1st ed. (Bonn, Boston: Galileo Press).

Spanyi, Andrew (2010b), Business process management governance, in *Handbook on Business Process Management 2: Strategic Alignment, Governance, People and Culture,* edited by Jan vom Brocke and Michael Rosemann (Berlin, Heidelberg: Springer).

Stachowiak, Herbert (1973), *Allgemeine Modelltheorie* (Wien, New York: Springer).

Taylor, Frederick W. (2006), *The Principles of Scientific Management* (New York: Cosimo).

Tregear, Roger (2010b), Business process standardization, in *Handbook on Business Process Management 2: Strategic Alignment, Governance, People and Culture,* edited by Jan vom Brocke and Michael Rosemann (Berlin, Heidelberg: Springer).

van der Aalst, Will M.P. and ter Hofstede, Arthur H.M. (2005), YAWL: yet another workflow language, *Information Systems* 30, no. 4, 245–75.

van der Aalst, Will M.P. and van Hee, Kees Max (2002), *Workflow Management: Models, Methods, and Systems,* 1st ed. (Cambridge, MA: MIT Press).

vom Brocke, Jan (2006), Design principles for reference modeling: reusing information models by means of aggregation, specialisation, instantiation, and analogy, in *Reference Modeling for Business Systems Analysis,* edited by Peter Fettke and Peter Loos (Hershey, PA, USA: Idea Group Publishing).

vom Brocke, Jan (2007), Service portfolio measurement: evaluating financial performance of service-oriented business processes, *International Journal of Web Services Research* 4, no. 2, 1–32.

vom Brocke, Jan (2011), Business process management (BPM): a pathway for IT-professionalism in Europe?, in *Emerging Themes in Information Systems and Organization Studies,* edited by Andrea Carugati and Cecilia Rossignoli (Heidelberg: Physica-Verlag).

vom Brocke, Jan and Grob, Heinz Lothar (2011), Profitability of business processes, in *Process Management: A Guide for the Design of Business Processes*, 2nd ed., edited by Jörg Becker, Martin Kugeler and Michael Rosemann (Berlin et al.: Springer).

vom Brocke, Jan and Michael Rosemann (eds) (2010a), *Handbook on Business Process Management 1: Introduction, Methods, and Information Systems* (Berlin, Heidelberg: Springer).

vom Brocke, Jan and Michael Rosemann (eds) (2010b), *Handbook on Business Process Management 2: Strategic Alignment, Governance, People and Culture* (Berlin, Heidelberg: Springer).

vom Brocke, Jan and Thomas, Oliver (2006), Reference modeling for organizational change: applying collaborative techniques for business engineering, in *AMCIS 2006 Proceedings*, Paper 88: http://aisel.aisnet.org/amcis2006/88 (accessed March 2012).

vom Brocke, Jan, Becker, Jörg, Maria Braccini, Alessio, Butleris, Rimantas, Hofreiter, Birgit, Kapočius, Kęstutis, Marco, Marco de, Schmidt, Günter, Seidel, Stefan, Simons, Alexander, Skopal, Tomáš, Stein, Armin, Stieglitz, Stefan, Suomi, Reima, Vossen, Gottfried, Winter, Robert and Wrycza, Stanislaw (2011), Current and future issues in BPM research: a European perspective from the ERCIS meeting 2010, *Communications of the Association for Information Systems* 28, no. 1, 393–414.

vom Brocke, Jan, Petry, Martin and Schmiedel, Theresa (2011), How Hilti masters transformation, *360° - The Business Transformation Journal* 1, no. 1, 38–47.

vom Brocke, Jan, Recker, Jan and Mendling, Jan (2010), Value-oriented process modeling: integrating financial perspectives into business process re-design, *Business Process Management Journal* 16, no. 2, 333–56.

vom Brocke, Jan, Seidel, Stefan and Recker, Jan (eds) (2012), *Green Business Process Management: Towards the Sustainable Enterprise* (Berlin: Springer).

vom Brocke, Jan, Sonnenberg, Christian, Lattemann, Christoph and Stieglitz, Stefan (2010), Assessing the total cost of ownership of virtual communities, in *Handbook of Research on Web 2.0, 3.0, and X.0: Technologies, Business, and Social Applications*, edited by San Murugesan (Hershey, PA, USA: IGI Global).

vom Brocke, Jan, Sonnenberg, Christian and Simons, Alexander (2009), Value-oriented information systems design: the concept of potentials modeling and its application to service-oriented architectures, *Business & Information Systems Engineering* 1, no. 3, 223–33.

Weske, Mathias (2007), *Business Process Management: Concepts, Languages, Architectures* (Berlin et al.: Springer).

Zairi, Mohamed (1997), Business process management: a boundaryless approach to modern competitiveness, *Business Process Management Journal* 3, no. 1, 64–80.

zur Muehlen, Michael and Indulska, Marta (2010), Modeling languages for business processes and business rules: a representational analysis, *Information Systems* 35, no. 4, 379–90.

zur Muehlen, Michael and Recker, Jan (2008), How much language is enough? Theoretical and practical use of the business process modeling notation, in *Advanced Information Systems Engineering 20th International Conference, CAiSE 2008 Montpellier, France, June 16–20, 2008 Proceedings*, edited by Zohra Bellahsène and Michel Léonard (Berlin, Heidelberg: Springer).

7 *Transformational IT Management*

ROBERT WINTER, PHILIPP GUBLER, FELIX WORTMANN
(University of St. Gallen), ANDREAS ELTING (SAP AG) and
WERNER SCHULTHEIS (Randstad Deutschland GmbH &
Co. KG)

7.1 Overview

Transformational Information Technology (IT) Management has different objectives. First of all, it evaluates the impact of current IT processes, IT competencies and IT systems on business transformation – and vice versa. Additionally, Transformational IT Management defines IT-related success criteria for business transformation. Transformational IT Management safeguards the design, implementation, roll-out and deployment of business transformation. It enables operations, maintenance and support of transformation deliverables. Last, but not least, Transformational IT Management also covers operations (continuous improvement).

Transformational IT Management within BTM² addresses the following steps (referring to the transformation lifecycle) for business transformation success:

1. Envision: assesses and enables solution readiness of the organization. For this purpose, an analysis of the organization's transformation maturity is conducted with special focus on IT and operational capabilities.
2. Engage: defines to-be IT analysis and assesses gap to as-is. Defines the application, data and technology architecture. Sets up a transformation roadmap.
3. Transform: deploys IT operations and services and implement IT governance.
4. Optimize: improves IT operations and services and manage IT lifecycle management.

OBJECTIVES OF THIS CHAPTER:
1. Understand activities that guide Transformational IT Management.
2. Learn about key success factors for Transformational IT Management.
3. Describe interdependencies between Transformational IT Management and other management disciplines of BTM².

7.2 Transformational IT Management in BTM²

Managing business transformation remains a key challenge for companies despite the fact that there are many methodologies and systematic approaches around. Business transformations are triggered by different causes, e.g. shifts on markets, technology innovations, economical changes such as globalization or changes of *soft* factors (Kotter, 1996). Regardless of the transformation trigger, it is crucial for business transformation to align IT transformation with organizational transformation (Ein-Dor and Segev, 1982). Such alignment is mutual because the relationship of IT and business is multifaceted. While many IT transformations might induce organizational change in order to be implemented successfully, most organizational changes require appropriate IT changes (Baumöl, 2005).

Transformational IT Management needs to consider the double role of IT, being sometimes the driver and sometimes the driven. Since both roles of IT are closely related to the business, Transformational IT Management needs to be closely connected to Organizational Change Management, Strategy Management, Processes Management and other relevant management disciplines of BTM². While the *enablement* type is focused on the context of BTM², many elements of the proposed methodology might also be applicable for an implementer role.

A key success factor for any form of business transformation is to ensure systematic and transparent, i.e. engineered transformation. The professional use of transformation techniques and the integration of well-trained transformation specialist facilitate this key challenge. Various generic concepts can be instantiated and combined to manage IT transformation. In the context of BTM², Transformational IT Management is part of the *enablement* type.

As depicted in Figure 7.1, Transformational IT Management covers the four phases of the transformation lifecycle.

- Envision is addressed via *Assess and enable solution readiness of the organization.*
- Engage is enabled via *Plan to-be IT architecture, operations and services* and *Create IT transformation roadmap.*
- Transform is implemented via *Deploy IT operations and services* and *Implement IT governance.*
- Optimize is addressed via *Optimize IT operations and services* and *Manage IT lifecycle.*

It should be noted that, like other management disciplines, Transformational IT Management focuses on enabling transformation, making transformation happen and managing transformation – the actual implementation of transformation projects is covered by existing development techniques from which only very few exemplary ones can be briefly summarized here.

Transformational IT Management has several interfaces to other disciplines of BTM². As shown in Figure 7.2, the following disciplines contribute to Transformational IT Management:

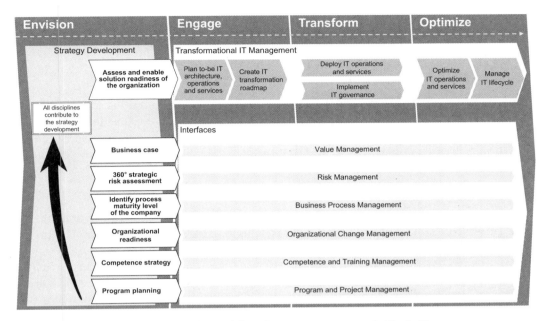

Figure 7.1   Interdependencies with other management disciplines

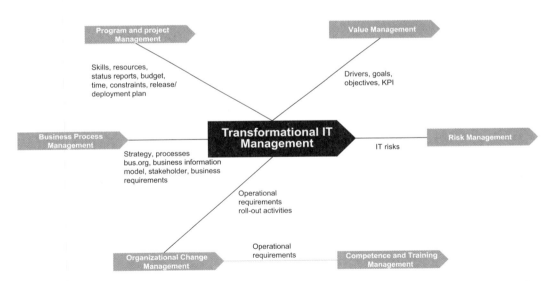

Figure 7.2   Transformational IT Management interfaces to other disciplines of BTM²

Program and Project Management is linked to Transformational IT Management by governing skills, resources, budget, time and other constraints. Transformational IT Management has to deliver status updates and adhere to the release/deployment plan supervised by Program and Project Management.

Business Process Management defines the dynamic (processes) and structural aspects of the organization. Most relevant business requirements for any Transformational IT Management initiative are derived from this discipline.

Value Management defines, monitors and manages goals and KPIs to assure that business targets are met. Transformational IT Management initiatives need to build upon the processes, frameworks, goals, SLAs and objectives of Value Management to ensure that transformation impact is achieved, and that business benefits are realized in a systematic approach.

Risk Management provides the fundamental structures and processes to manage IT risks. Transformational IT Management has to adhere to these fundamental concepts and manage its risks accordingly.

Organizational Change Management does not only support the roll-out activities and the organizational implementation of the Transformational IT Management initiatives, but does also prepare transformation impacts like capacity adjustments and competency changes. As a consequence, Organizational Change Management provides the link to Competence and Training Management.

7.2.1 PROCEDURE FOR TRANSFORMATIONAL IT MANAGEMENT

This chapter describes the activities that guide Transformational IT Management. As mentioned before, the transformation lifecycle is divided into the phases of envision, engage, transform and optimize. In Step 1, the readiness of the organization is assessed and the organization is enabled for implementing the solution. For this purpose, an analysis of the organization's transformation maturity is conducted with special focus on IT and operational capabilities. This maturity assessment covers the IT part of Enterprise Architecture (EA). Further activities of this step are IT maturity evaluation, development of an architecture vision and review of the business architecture. Step 2 covers planning of to-be IT architecture, operations and services. This includes the definition of the application, data and technology architectures. Based on these results, the transformation roadmap is created in Step 3. In Step 4, IT operations and services are deployed by leveraging the solution architecture and an IT deployment plan. The implementation of governance is the focus of Step 5. In the optimization phase of Step 6, IT operations and services are continuously improved. Step 7 implements IT lifecycle management by systematically managing IT architecture transformation requests and establishing a continuous improvement process for IT architecture.

Figure 7.3 summarizes the seven steps of Transformational IT Management. The following sections describe each step in detail. Please note that the different amount of text does not imply that certain steps are more important than others. The length of subsections is due to differences in the amount, complexity and generality of applicable techniques that are summarized here.

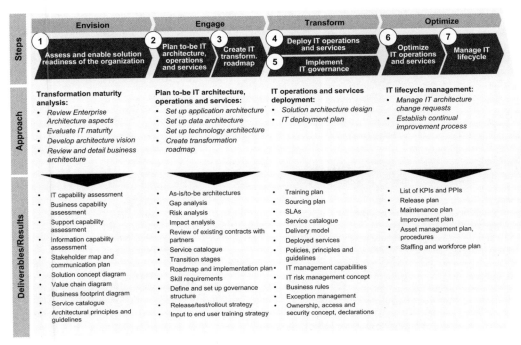

Steps	Envision		Engage		Transform		Optimize	
	1 Assess and enable solution readiness of the organization		**2** Plan to-be IT architecture, operations and services	**3** Create IT transform. roadmap	**4** Deploy IT operations and services **5** Implement IT governance		**6** Optimize IT operations and services	**7** Manage IT lifecycle

Approach				
	Transformation maturity analysis: • Review Enterprise Architecture aspects • Evaluate IT maturity • Develop architecture vision • Review and detail business architecture	**Plan to-be IT architecture, operations and services:** • Set up application architecture • Set up data architecture • Set up technology architecture • Create transformation roadmap	**IT operations and services deployment:** • Solution architecture design • IT deployment plan	**IT lifecycle management:** • Manage IT architecture change requests • Establish continual improvement process

Deliverables/Results				
	• IT capability assessment • Business capability assessment • Support capability assessment • Information capability assessment • Stakeholder map and communication plan • Solution concept diagram • Value chain diagram • Business footprint diagram • Service catalogue • Architectural principles and guidelines	• As-is/to-be architectures • Gap analysis • Risk analysis • Impact analysis • Review of existing contracts with partners • Service catalogue • Transition stages • Roadmap and implementation plan • Skill requirements • Define and set up governance structure • Release/test/rollout strategy • Input to end user training strategy	• Training plan • Sourcing plan • SLAs • Service catalogue • Delivery model • Deployed services • Policies, principles and guidelines • IT management capabilities • IT risk management concept • Business rules • Exception management • Ownership, access and security concept, declarations	• List of KPIs and PPIs • Release plan • Maintenance plan • Improvement plan • Asset management plan, procedures • Staffing and workforce plan

Figure 7.3   Seven steps of Transformational IT Management in BTM²

7.3 Assess and Enable Solution Readiness of the Organization

To assess and enable the solution readiness of the organization for Transformational IT Management, several tasks have to be accomplished (see Figure 7.4). Belonging to the envision phase, this step prepares the organization to build a broad overview of its capabilities and achieve the necessary transparency for business transformation.

In a first major activity, it has to be verified whether the organization is ready to deal with the specified scope of the intended business transformation. EA is instrumental as a point of reference here. Since the scope of EA understood as "the process of translating business vision and strategy into effective enterprise change by creating, communicating and improving the key requirements, principles and models that describe the enterprise's future state and enable its evolution" (Lapkin et al., 2008) comprises people, processes, information and technology of the enterprise, and their relationships to one another and to the external environment (Lapkin et al., 2008), it goes far beyond Transformational IT Management. In the context of Transformational IT Management, the use of EA documents and analyses assure that planned initiatives, programs and projects support the business strategy and do not induce major IT/business misalignment problems.

The evaluation of current IT capabilities and services form another fundamental activity. A comprehensive analysis of IT organization, IT support and IT operations is at the heart of this activity. The results of the maturity assessment are gaps between current and required capabilities, which build the basis for defining the transformation roadmap in Step 3.

Assess and Enable Solution Readiness of the Organization

Description	Methods, frameworks, tools and accelerators
Review Enterprise Architecture aspects • Facilitate business strategy and IT alignment • Scope of EA has to be in sync with stakeholder expectation • Establish Enterprise Architecture governance **Evaluate IT maturity** • Focus on capabilities of IT organization, IT support and IT operations • Define gaps between current and required maturity to absorb the change **Develop architecture vision** • Review architecture principles and best practices • Focus on a draft outline of as-is and to-be architectures (business, application, data, technology) • Define value proposition for stakeholders • Get stakeholder approval (sponsor, ops, others)	• Business capability assessment • IT capability assessment • SAP CoE assessment • SAP EAF framework • EA modelling and design • SAP EAF vision • SAP EAF business architecture • SAP solution manager • SAP ES workplace
Review and detail business architecture • Review business architecture of Business Process Management • Break business architecture down to the right level of service granularity, boundaries and contracts • Review existing internal and external service contracts • Identify gaps between as-is and to-be and prioritize together with BPM and stakeholders • Consider sourcing strategies for gaps	**Deliverables** • IT capability assessment • Business capability assessment • Support capability assessment • Information capability assessment • Stakeholder map and communication plan • Solution concept diagram • Value chain diagram • Business footprint diagram • Service catalog • Architectural principles and guidelines

Figure 7.4   Assess and enable solution readiness of the organization

Based on the EA review and the identification of the current maturity level, an architecture vision has to be developed. For this purpose, a review of architecture best practices and principles is a key activity to derive a solid architecture vision. Furthermore, comprehensive as-is and to-be architectures (business and technology) have to be reflected. In order to guarantee a successful business transformation, the value proposition for major stakeholders must be clearly defined and approved. This is also an important link to risk management from this step.

The business architecture is a key starting point for IT transformation. Hence, it must be reviewed and elaborated in sufficient detail. For this purpose, the business architecture has to be broken down into an appropriate level of granularity. The gap between as-is and to-be business architecture is identified in collaboration with business process owners. On this basis, existing internal and external service contracts have to be evaluated. Furthermore, sourcing strategies for filling gaps have to be considered.

Solution Readiness of an organization can be assessed with business capabilities and business capability maps. They depict what the business is doing to reach its goals and objectives. Business capabilities are a collection of functional facilities that are essential for the enterprise to conduct business (Gur, 2009). They are the functional equivalent to business processes. In contrast to fast changing business processes, the set of business capabilities is intended to be stable. Business capabilities are supported by applications and other IT resources and are thus an important link between business and IT architecture (Kurpjuweit and Winter, 2009). Figure 7.5 shows an example of how a business capability can be characterized in the course of assessing solution readiness.

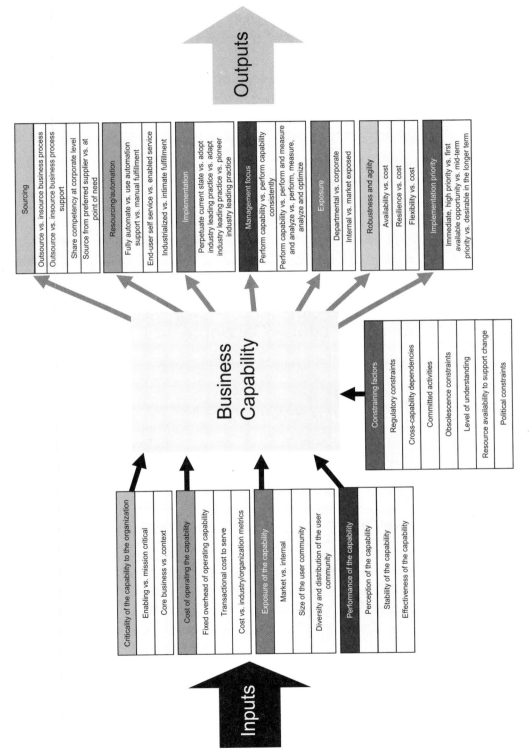

Figure 7.5 Business capability assessment dimensions

CHALLENGES CONCERNING THE ASSESSMENT AND ENABLEMENT OF SOLUTION READINESS OF THE ORGANIZATION:

1. Perform comprehensive analysis of IT organization, IT support and IT operations.
2. Plan an architecture vision based on a review of architecture best practices and principles.
3. Define and approve the value proposition for major stakeholders.
4. Break down the business architecture into an appropriate level of granularity and identify gap between as-is and to-be business architecture in collaboration with business process owners.
5. Evaluate existing internal and external service contracts.
6. Consider sourcing strategies for filling gaps.

KEY MESSAGE:

The use of EA documents and analyses assure that planned initiatives, programs and projects support the business strategy and do not induce major IT/business misalignment problems.

7.4 To-Be IT Architecture, Operations and Services Planning and IT Transformation Roadmap Development

This section outlines the two activities conducted in the engage phase of Transformational IT Management.

7.4.1 PLAN TO-BE IT ARCHITECTURE, OPERATIONS AND SERVICES

After the organization's as-is situation has been assessed, the to-be IT architecture, operations and services have to be specified. Therefore, Step 2 directly builds upon the results of Step 1. In practice, the to-be IT architecture covers three major areas: applications, data and technology. Figure 7.6 depicts typical activities, methods and deliverables of this step.

Following a top-down approach that also incorporates commercial off-the-shelf (COTS) software solutions, the application layer is defined first, determining the basis for the data and technology architecture. First of all, the application architecture baseline has to be documented as the transformation starting point. Internal and external reference models provide guidance on how to develop the application landscape and should therefore be applied if available. Building upon the results of the first phase, a more thorough gap analysis reveals the deviation between the desired to-be and the current as-is state.

Based on the findings of the application architecture assessment, the data and technology architectures are derived. Analyzing reference models and conducting a gap analysis are also key activities to determine the data and technology architecture. Evaluating sourcing options in more detail is another major activity in this context.

2 Plan To-be IT Architecture, Operation and Services

Description

Plan to-be IT architecture, operation and services
- *Set up application architecture*
  - Document application architecture baseline
  - Review IT operation requirements
  - Review reference models of to-be architectures
  - Detail application architecture vision (-> to-be architecture)
  - Develop draft data architecture
  - Evaluate sourcing options
  - Perform gap analysis
- *Set up data architecture*
  - Review application architecture requirements
  - Document data architecture baseline
  - Review reference models of to-be architectures
  - Detail data architecture vision (-> to-be architecture)
  - Evaluate sourcing options
  - Perform gap analysis and prioritize
- *Set up technology architecture*
  - Baseline current technology architecture
  - Consider service levels with hardware vendors
  - Consider IT operations requirements
  - Review reference models of to-be architectures
  - Design to-be technology architecture
  - Evaluate sourcing options
  - Perform gap analysis and prioritize

Methods, frameworks, tools and accelerators
- SAP ASAP accelerators
- SAP BPM accelerators
- SAP ES workplace
- SAP EAF application architecture
- SAP EAF data architecture (including data lifecycle management)
- SAP EAF technology architecture
- SLO accelerators
- AGS best practices
- SAP specific tools (PAM, s&c list, Solution Manager, Quicksizer)

Deliverables
- As-is/to-be application architectures
- As-is/to-be data architectures
- As-is/to-be technology architectures
- Gap analysis
- Risk analysis
- Impact analysis on existing/planned initiatives
- Review of existing contracts with partners (e.g. outsourcing partners, BPO)
- Service catalog to be used within the engagement

Figure 7.6   Plan to-be IT architecture, operations and services

CHALLENGES CONCERNING THE PLANNING OF THE TO-BE IT ARCHITECTURE, OPERATIONS AND SERVICES:
1. Document the application architecture baseline as the transformation starting point (apply internal and external reference models).
2. Derive the technology architecture based on the findings of the application architecture assessment.
3. Analyze reference models and conduct a gap analysis in order to determine the data and technology architecture.
4. Evaluate sourcing options in more detail.

KEY MESSAGE:
In practice, the to-be IT architecture covers three major areas: applications, data and technology.

7.4.2 CREATE IT TRANSFORMATION ROADMAP

Creating the IT transformation roadmap, i.e. the plan for implementing the to-be architecture, operations and services is the next step in Transformational IT Management. This step builds upon the to-be IT architecture, operations and services from Step 2. Key goal of this step is to develop a detailed transformation roadmap that outlines the upcoming transformation activities and enables a reliable execution. This activity involves lots of discussions with application specialists to provide the best to-be solution architecture.

In order to ensure a business case driven transformation process, the identified gaps must be prioritized and possible quick wins need to be elaborated. Addressing quick wins early is an important strategy in order to assure project success and support by all relevant stakeholders including sponsors and project members. Sourcing questions are key in creating the transformation roadmap. A critical question with respect to software is *make or buy*, which has to be answered carefully as there are severe consequences depending on this decision, e.g. maintenance and support costs as well as handling of upcoming change requests. Furthermore, the extension of custom development has to be determined. External support has to be determined, i.e. it has to be decided how many external resources will be leveraged for implementing the transformation roadmap. Key to successfully executing the roadmap is organizational readiness. First of all, it has to be assured that there is a comprehensive acceptance for the transformation project. Moreover, further organizational requirements have to be identified in order to later on successfully operate the solution.

Important activities of Step 3 are defining the build, the implementation and the deployment plan (see Figure 7.7). These plans have to be handed over to program management for monitoring and governance. Complementing these activities, a transformation management steering committee has to be set up. Summing up, this step covers the concrete project planning activities for subsequent steps.

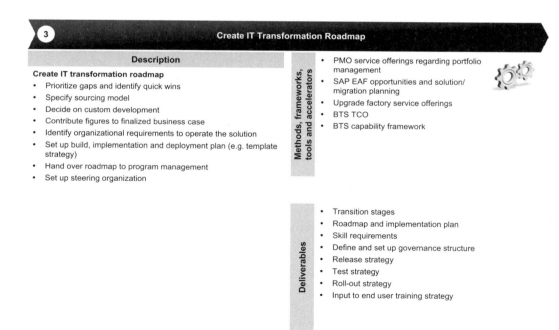

Figure 7.7　Create IT transformation roadmap

CHALLENGES CONCERNING THE CREATION OF THE IT TRANSFORMATION ROADMAP:

1. Prioritize identified and elaborated possible quick wins to ensure a business case driven transformation process.
2. Determine the extension of custom development.
3. Determine external support i.e. it has to be decided how many external resources will be leveraged for implementing the transformation roadmap.
4. Define the build, the implementation and the deployment plan.
5. Set up a transformation management steering committee.

KEY MESSAGE:

Addressing quick wins early is an important strategy in order to assure project success and support by all relevant stakeholders including sponsors and project members.

7.5 IT Operations, Service Deployment and IT Governance Implementation

This section outlines the two activities conducted in the transform phase of Transformational IT Management.

7.5.1 DEPLOY IT OPERATIONS AND SERVICES

Based on the transformation roadmap developed in Step 3, Step 4 follows the goal of developing IT services and putting them into place, i.e. of assuring appropriate IT Operations (see Figure 7.8). Two "extremes" of methods for IT Service Deployment are illustrated in the Appendix E of this book. 1) Rational Unified Process (RUP)[1] has its root in *development from scratch* (e.g. using JAVA, C++) and 2) Accelerated SAP (ASAP) (SAP AG, 2007) represents methods for implementing COTS (commercial off-the-shelf) software where certain standardized functionalities are already implemented by the package. Additionally, IT Infrastructure Library (ITIL)[2] is presented as an example for *IT service operations* (see also Appendix E).

Developing and deploying IT applications and services is a complex process. Hence, building upon well-proven process frameworks is state of the art practice. Iterative software development frameworks like RUP provide adaptable process frameworks, intended to be tailored by the individual organizations along their distinct needs.[3] More traditional development frameworks like the "V model" represent software development processes, which put less emphasis on iterative development but encourage linear development. There is also a growing number of evolving agile processes (like Scrum or Sprint) that

---

1   Wikipedia. "Rational Unified Process", 2012f: http://de.wikipedia.org/wiki/Rational_Unified_Process (accessed March 2012).

2   Wikipedia. "Information Technology Infrastructure Library", 2012d: http://en.wikipedia.org/wiki/Information_Technology_Infrastructure_Library (accessed March 2012).

3   More information is available at: Wikipedia. "IBM Rational Unified Process", 2012c: http://en.wikipedia.org/wiki/IBM_Rational_Unified_Process (accessed March 2012).

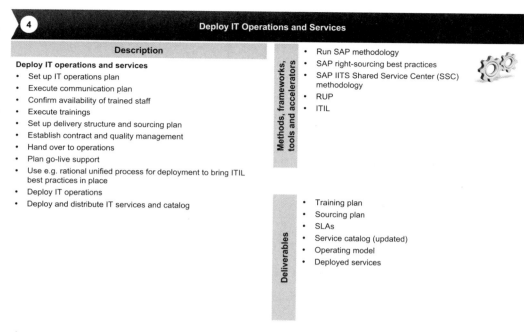

Figure 7.8 Deploy IT operations and services

promise to overcome shortcomings of traditional approaches like long cycle times and late discovery of design problems.

To operate IT services, approaches like ITIL provide a rich set of best practices on how to manage IT services. These IT Service Management (ITSM) approaches often follow a process perspective and therefore have a strong linkage to continuous improvement approaches like Six Sigma, Business Process Management or the Capability Maturity Model Integration (CMMI).[4] ITSM is generally concerned with the *back office* or operational concerns of information technology management – software development is not at the core of ITSM.

The basic idea behind ITSM is to offer IT applications and complementing IT services as well as other defined services to the business. As depicted in Figure 7.9, a well-defined service comprises functional requirements, such as the need to produce a service report or to generate an invoice, as well as non-functional requirements such as service availability, performance, accuracy and security. A service level agreement (SLA)[5] is a part of a service contract where the level of a service is formally defined.

ITSM covers domains such as service support, service delivery and infrastructure management. Service support focuses on the user of the services and on continuous and appropriate service delivery. Selected sub-processes are problem management, incident management and change management. Service support concentrates on the customer-focused development and provisioning of services by putting service level management,

---

4   Wikipedia. "IT service management", 2012e: http://en.wikipedia.org/wiki/ITSM (accessed March 2012).

5   Wikipedia. "Service level agreement", 2012g: http://en.wikipedia.org/wiki/Service_level_agreement (accessed March 2012).

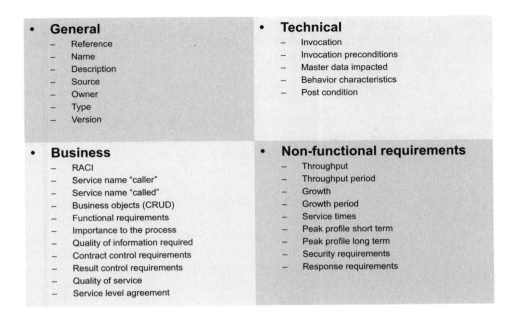

- **General**
  - – Reference
  - – Name
  - – Description
  - – Source
  - – Owner
  - – Type
  - – Version

- **Technical**
  - – Invocation
  - – Invocation preconditions
  - – Master data impacted
  - – Behavior characteristics
  - – Post condition

- **Business**
  - – RACI
  - – Service name "caller"
  - – Service name "called"
  - – Business objects (CRUD)
  - – Functional requirements
  - – Importance to the process
  - – Quality of information required
  - – Contract control requirements
  - – Result control requirements
  - – Quality of service
  - – Service level agreement

- **Non-functional requirements**
  - – Throughput
  - – Throughput period
  - – Growth
  - – Growth period
  - – Service times
  - – Peak profile short term
  - – Peak profile long term
  - – Security requirements
  - – Response requirements

Figure 7.9   Key aspects of a service definition

capacity management, service continuity management, availability management and financial service management processes into place. In general, ITIL will define additional requirements from a solution development perspective, e.g. definition of common interfaces.

CHALLENGES CONCERNING THE DEPLOYMENT OF IT OPERATIONS AND SERVICES:

1. Decide on a framework (e.g. V model, Scrum, Sprint) in order to develop and deploy IT applications and services.
2. Decide on an approach to operate IT services and potentially on a continuous improvement approach.

KEY MESSAGE:

Developing and deploying IT applications and services is a complex process; hence, building upon well-proven process frameworks is state-of-the-art practice.

7.5.2 IMPLEMENT IT GOVERNANCE

Governance covers decisions that define expectations, grant power or verify performance.[6] It relates to management, cohesive policies, guidance, processes and decision-rights for

---

6   See, Wikipedia. "Governance", 2012b: http://en.wikipedia.org/wiki/Governance (accessed March 2012).

a given area of responsibility. Complementing IT operations and services deployment, an adequate governance structure has to be set up to ensure successful Transformational IT Management. Step 5 addresses this topic and establishes the necessary governance structures and processes (see Figure 7.10). All these activities have to be based on an existing governance organization. The setup of this organization might require organizational change management activities up-front.

According to the IT Governance Institute (ITGI) there are five domains, which have to be addressed to ensure appropriate governance (Schwartz, 2007): strategic alignment, value delivery, resource management, risk management and performance measures. Linking business and IT together so that they work well is the goal of strategic alignment. The key challenge of strategic alignment lies in bringing together the corporate side of business with the line-of-business and IT leaders. Value delivery makes sure that the IT department delivers on the benefits promised at the beginning of a project or investment. Resource management is about achieving optimal use of resources. Two key aspects of resource management are creating the right organizational structures for high quality and efficient service delivery as well as ensuring a highly skilled and motivated employee base. Risk management puts a formal risk framework in place. This framework ensures sufficient rigor around how IT measures, accepts and manages risk, as well as the provision of reports on what IT is managing in terms of risk. Performance measurement is about measuring IT performance and corresponding business impact. The most widely applied concept in this context is the balanced scorecard, which examines where IT makes a contribution in terms of achieving business goals, being a responsible user of resources and developing people. Exemplary, one framework (namely COBiT) is presented in the Appendix E of this book, which supports implementing IT governance.

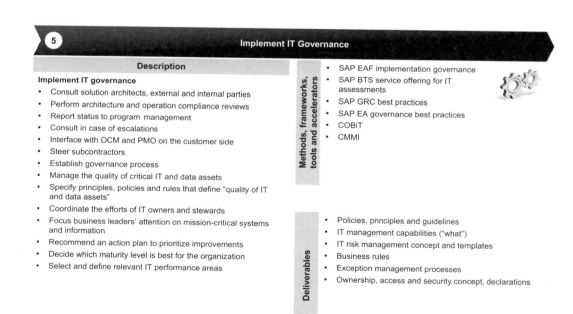

5 Implement IT Governance

Description

Implement IT governance

- Consult solution architects, external and internal parties
- Perform architecture and operation compliance reviews
- Report status to program management
- Consult in case of escalations
- Interface with OCM and PMO on the customer side
- Steer subcontractors
- Establish governance process
- Manage the quality of critical IT and data assets
- Specify principles, policies and rules that define "quality of IT and data assets"
- Coordinate the efforts of IT owners and stewards
- Focus business leaders' attention on mission-critical systems and information
- Recommend an action plan to prioritize improvements
- Decide which maturity level is best for the organization
- Select and define relevant IT performance areas

Methods, frameworks, tools and accelerators

- SAP EAF implementation governance
- SAP BTS service offering for IT assessments
- SAP GRC best practices
- SAP EA governance best practices
- COBiT
- CMMI

Deliverables

- Policies, principles and guidelines
- IT management capabilities ("what")
- IT risk management concept and templates
- Business rules
- Exception management processes
- Ownership, access and security concept, declarations

Figure 7.10 Implement IT governance

CHALLENGES CONCERNING THE IMPLEMENTATION OF IT GOVERNANCE:
1. Bring together the corporate side of business with the line-of-business and IT leaders.
2. Make sure that the IT department delivers on the benefits promised at the beginning of a project or investment.
3. Achieve optimal use of resources.
4. Put a formal risk framework in place.
5. Use performance measures.

KEY MESSAGE:
According to the IT Governance Institute (ITGI) there are five domains, which have to be addressed to ensure appropriate governance: strategic alignment, value delivery, resource management, risk management and performance measures.

7.6 IT Operations and Services Optimization and IT Lifecycle Management

The optimization phase covers IT operations and services optimization, as well as IT lifecycle management. Step 6 and Step 7 cover three major tasks, namely managing architecture requirements and transformation requests, establishing a monitoring and continuous improvement process and Application Lifecycle Management (ALM)[7] (see Figure 7.11).

In order to establish a formalized management of architecture requirements and change requests, several sources of inputs have to be taken into account: First of all, feedback from IT (e.g. from solution architects) has to be systematically gathered. In addition, a feedback loop to business and end users (e.g. via service/help desks) has to be established. To assure an adequate update policy, the deployment of solution updates must be restricted and defined appropriately. Furthermore, on the basis of a continuous management process, services have to be improved, modernized, replaced or retired on an ongoing basis.

To reach a next level in delivering IT services, the establishment of a continuous measurement and improvement process is necessary. Measurement requires the formal, planned monitoring of process execution and the tracing of results to determine the performance of a process. The information gained in the measurement process is then used to make decisions for improving or retiring existing processes and/or introducing new processes. For this purpose, monitoring tools and methods have to be put in place.

IT lifecycle management can be managed with the process of ALM. This is the process of managing applications continuously throughout their entire lifespan, i.e. including analysis and design, development, maintenance and decommissioning. ALM brings the ideas of continuous improvement to the discipline of software engineering and EA. ALM is enabled by processes and tools that facilitate and integrate requirements management, architecture, coding, testing, tracking and release management.

---

7   Wikipedia. "Application lifecycle management", 2012a: http://en.wikipedia.org/wiki/Application_lifecycle_management (accessed March 2012).

6-7   IT Operations and Services Optimization and IT Lifecycle Management

Description

Manage architecture change requests and requirements
- Get feedback from solution architects
- Enable feedback loop to service/help desk, prioritize feedback
- Steer updates of solutions
- Determine needs and plans to improve, modernize, replace or retire
- Coordinate skill demand and roles
- Standardize and automate operation and service delivery

Establish monitoring and continual improvement process
- Deploy monitoring tools and methods for IT operation
- Define and measure PPI and KPIs
- Conduct assessment to ensure requirements, quality, services, and performance is maintained and tied to business value
- Report back figures to management for actions
- Establish sourcing strategy
- Develop key factors for performance areas and survey stakeholders

Lifecycle management
- Operate, maintain and enhance the system landscape
- Build and deploy landscape into development, test, pre-production and production environments quickly, reliably and consistently
- Coordinate staff

Methods, frameworks, tools and accelerators
- SAP EAF architecture change management
- BTS CoE service offerings
- RunSAP methodology
- SAP ITTS SSC methodology
- ITIL
- CMMI

Deliverables
- List of KPIs and PPIs
- Release plan
- Maintenance plan
- Improvement plan
- Asset management plan, procedures
- Staffing and workforce plan

Figure 7.11 IT operations and services optimization and IT lifecycle management

CHALLENGES CONCERNING IT OPERATIONS AND SERVICES OPTIMIZATION AND IT LIFECYCLE MANAGEMENT:

1. Gather feedback from IT, e.g. from solution architects.
2. Establish feedback loop to business and end users, e.g. via service/help desks.
3. Restrict and define appropriately the deployment of solution updates in order to assure an adequate update policy.
4. Improve, modernize, replace or retire services on the basis of a continuous management process.
5. Establish a continuous measurement and improvement process in order to reach a next level in delivering IT services.

KEY MESSAGE:

ALM, which can be used to manage IT lifecycle management, is the process of managing applications continuously throughout their entire lifespan, i.e. including analysis and design, development, maintenance and decommissioning.

7.7 Key Success Factors for Transformational IT Management

Five factors affect the success of Transformational IT Management initiatives:

1. consider other frameworks and IT transformation relationship to it;
2. reuse proven and successful patterns, methods and principles;
3. use an appropriate level of detail to govern implementation;
4. apply the same framework on all levels; and
5. agree on KPIs to measure success.

These factors are described in the following.

7.7.1 CONSIDER OTHER FRAMEWORKS AND THEIR RELATIONSHIP TO TRANSFORMATIONAL IT MANAGEMENT

Well-accepted Transformational IT Management components exist in the domains of development, operations management, architecture development and project portfolio management (cf. Figure 7.12). Moreover, methods for business capability management complement the four core domains. The key challenge of Transformational IT Management is therefore to select appropriate components from different domains, adapt these to company specific requirements and integrate them into a comprehensive yet agile approach.

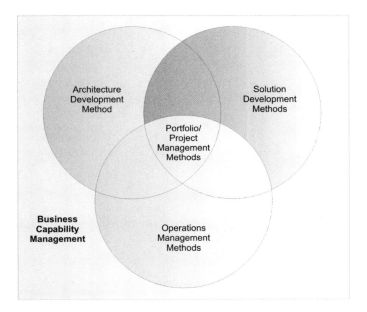

Figure 7.12 Intended overlap of method components for Transformational IT Management

Source: Reproduced with permission of The Open Group. TOGAF® Version 9. ©2005–2012 The Open Group.

For architecture development, frameworks such as TOGAF®[8] or EABOK (Hagan, 2004) can be used. A large number of development methods exist, e.g. waterfall type methods, various variants of the V model or agile development methods. These models provide guidance on how to structure and manage the realization of a solution. Operations management methods are dominated by ITIL.[9] Prominent portfolio/project management methods are the PMBOK[10] or PRINCE2.[11] Established business capability methods are Motion (Lloyd, 2006) or Component Business Modeling (Pohle et al., 2005).

7.7.2 REUSE PROVEN AND SUCCESSFUL PATTERNS, METHODS AND PRINCIPLES

The second success factor results from applying proven and successful concepts like patterns, methods and principles to ensure the reuse of best practices. This results in benefits from preliminary work, especially from successful projects and solutions. The experience captured in patterns, methods and principles helps project owners to realize planned actions more efficiently and effectively. This ultimately saves money and resources by not having to reinvent the wheel. Furthermore, using proven concepts fosters solution quality and prevents neglecting important solution aspects. Figure 7.13 presents a selection of such proven concepts subdivided into patterns, methods and principles.

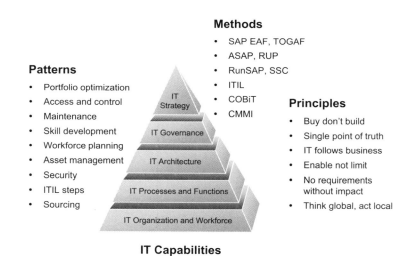

Figure 7.13 Proven and successful patterns, methods and principles for Transformational IT Management

---

8   TOGAF is a registered trademark of The Open Group in the United States and other countries. More information on TOGAF is available at *The Open Group. "Welcome to TOGAF®:Version 9.1 'Enterprise Edition'"*, The Open Group, 2012: www.opengroup.org/togaf (accessed March 2012).

9   ITIL. "Welcome to the Official ITIL® Website", ITIL® IT Service Management, 2012: www.itil-officialsite.com/home/home.aspx (accessed March 2012).

10   Project Management Institute. "PMBOK® Guide and Standards", Project Management Institute, 2012: www.pmi.org/PMBOK-Guide-and-Standards.aspx (accessed March 2012).

11   ILX Group. "What is PRINCE2? – PRINCE2 Definition", 2012: www.prince2.com/what-is-prince2.asp (accessed March 2012).

7.7.3 USE AN APPROPRIATE LEVEL OF DETAIL TO GOVERN IMPLEMENTATION

The third success factor is to use an appropriate level of detail to govern implementation. Clearly, it is not possible to govern every single project in full detail. This would result in an unmanageable amount of work. Therefore, it is essential to use an appropriate level of detail to govern implementation. Concerns of a large and diverse group of stakeholders must be addressed in business transformation. These include systems architects, project managers, sponsors, implementers and change agents who participate in the business transformation, as well as customers, employees, managers, system operators, outsourcing partners or the workers' council. For software and information systems engineering, catalogs of – mostly technical – concerns have been published. In the context of business transformation, also business concerns like business service implementation and business process efficiency should be considered. A transformation project must address the needs of its stakeholders. Following the criterion of width, all aspects required to address these needs should be covered. As a consequence, the scope of business transformation must be broader than solely the IT architecture of an enterprise.

Following the idea that EA is the blueprint for transformation projects, problems can arise from over-specifying design decisions that should better be made in the context of individual projects. Therefore, details such as class structures, detailed data structures, mapping information of network adaptors to servers, workflow specifications or product variant configuration should usually not be considered part of that task. The broader the scope needs to be, the less detail can be regarded. Using EA as an illustrative example, Figure 7.14 illustrates this wide and flat understanding.

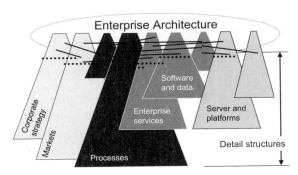

Figure 7.14 Using an appropriate level of detail to manage business transformation

Source: Aier, Stephan et al. 2008

7.7.4 APPLY THE SAME FRAMEWORK ON ALL LEVELS

The fourth success factor is to use the same framework for different levels of detail (capability architecture, segment architecture and strategic architecture). If one framework is used, the communication within the organization on different levels is much easier because identical terminologies are used and thinking along the same lines is fostered. This has the advantage that results can be exchanged between organizations and groups without causing "translation" problems. Furthermore, standardization and consistency are encouraged. Figure 7.15 illustrates the advantages of using the same framework on all levels.

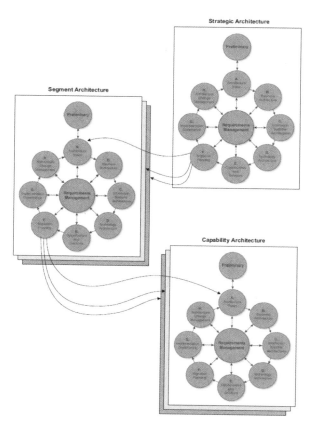

Figure 7.15 Apply the same framework on all levels

Source: Reproduced with permission of The Open Group. TOGAF® Version 9. ©2005–2012 The Open Group.

7.7.5 AGREE ON KPIs TO MEASURE SUCCESS

Measuring success during a project as the fifth success factor has multiple advantages. On the one hand, it allows having an overview over the project progress and to adhere to a chosen direction. On the other hand, a focused selection of measurements can strengthen staff's awareness to the project and motivate them to deliver high class deliverable. Therefore, a set of key performance indicators (KPIs) should be defined.

KPIs help measuring progress towards defined goals. Regarding an IT project, various kinds of KPIs can be distinguished, e.g. business KPIs, technology KPIs, application KPIs, operational KPIs, data KPIs or people-related KPIs. In fact, independent and isolated KPIs only have limited informative value. Therefore, systems of dependent KPIs have been developed in the past to reach an integrated and relevant overview of the project status.

One of the most popular and widespread KPI system is the balanced scorecard (Kaplan and Norton, 1992).

Measuring also asks for a systematic approach (Cooper, 2010). First of all, critical success factors have to be defined. Critical success factors are the few key levers where *things must go right* for the business to flourish: "Something that must happen if a Process, Project, Plan, or IT Service is to succeed" (ITIL, 2007). Based on the key success factors, KPIs are defined. They reflect the critical success factors of the organization. For KPIs to be effective, they must be specific, measurable, agreed, realistic and time-based. KPIs can use both financial and non-financial metrics. Metrics are used in conjunction with KPIs to measure the critical success factors. They implement KPIs and are numerical measures composed of one or more dimensions like time, application or organizational unit.

CHALLENGES CONCERNING KEY SUCCESS FACTORS FOR TRANSFORMATIONAL IT MANAGEMENT:

1. Select appropriate components from different domains, adapt these to company specific requirements and integrate them into a comprehensive, yet agile approach.
2. Apply proven and successful concepts like patterns, methods and principles, which ensures the reuse of best practices.
3. Use an appropriate level of detail to govern implementation.
4. Use the same framework for different levels of detail since the communication within the organization on different level is much easier because of identical terminologies.
5. Measure success during the project (use success factors, KPIs, metrics).

KEY MESSAGE:

The scope of business transformation must be broader than solely the IT architecture of an enterprise.

7.8 Conclusion

Transformational IT Management focuses on enabling transformation, making transformation happen and managing transformation – the actual implementation of transformation projects is covered by existing development techniques from which only very few exemplary ones were briefly summarized. The following seven steps guide Transformational IT Management:

1. Prepare the organization to build a broad overview of its capabilities and achieve the necessary transparency for transformation management.
2. After the organization's as-is situation has been assessed, the to-be IT architecture, operations and services have to be specified.
3. Develop a detailed transformation roadmap that outlines the upcoming transformation activities and enables a reliable execution.
4. Develop IT services and put them into place, i.e. of assuring appropriate IT operations.

5. Set up an adequate governance structure to ensure successful Transformational IT Management.
6. Manage architecture requirements and change requests, establish a monitoring and continuous improvement process and application lifecycle management.

This chapter also summarized the five key success factors of Transformational IT Management:

1. Consider other frameworks and IT transformation relationship to it.
2. Reuse proven and successful patterns, methods and principles.
3. Use an appropriate level of detail to govern implementation.
4. Apply the same framework on all levels.
5. Agree on KPIs to measure success.

Following the six steps above that guide Transformational IT Management and considering these five key success factors contributes to a prosperous business transformation.

Bibliography

Aier, Stephan, Kurpjuweit, Stephan, Schmitz, Otto, Schulz, Jörg, Thomas, André and Winter, Robert (2008), An engineering approach to enterprise architecture design and its application at a financial service provider, in *MobIS 2008: Modellierung Betrieblicher Informationssysteme; Modellierung Zwischen SOA und Compliance Management*; 27–28 November 2008, Saarbrücken, Germany: 115–30.

Baumöl, Ulrike (2005), Strategic agility through situational method construction, in *Proceedings of the European Academy of Management Annual Conference (EURAM2005)*, 4–7 May 2005, Munich, Germany.

Cooper, Larry (2010), CSFs, KPIs, Metrics, Outcomes and Benefits, itSM Solutions: www.itsmsolutions.com/newsletters/DITYvol6iss5.htm (accessed March 2012).

Ein-Dor, Phillip and Segev, Eli (1982), Organizational context and MIS structure: some empirical evidence, *MIS Quarterly* 6, no. 3, 55–68.

Gur, Natty, Business capabilities (a practical guide) – part 1: http://advice.cio.com/natty_gur/business_capabilities_a_practical_guide_part_1 (accessed March 2011).

Hagan, Paula J. (2004), Guide to the (evolving) Enterprise Architecture Body of Knowledge (EABOK): draft: 6 February 2004, The MITRE Corporation: www.mitre.org/work/tech_papers/tech_papers_04/04_0104/04_0104.pdf (accessed March 2012).

ITIL (2007), Glossary of terms, definitions and acronyms: V3, 30 May 2007, ITIL® IT Service Management: www.best-management-practice.com/gempdf/ITIL_Glossary_V3_1_24.pdf (accessed March 2012).

Kaplan, Robert S. and Norton, David P. (1992), The balanced scorecard: measures that drive performance, *Harvard Business Review* 70, no. 1, 71–9.

Kotter, John P. (1996), *Leading Change* (Boston, Mass: Harvard Business School Press).

Kurpjuweit, Stephan and Winter, Robert (2009), Concern-oriented business architecture engineering, in *Proceedings of the 24th Annual ACM Symposium on Applied Computing 2009*, Honolulu, Hawaii, USA, 8–12 March 2009: 265–72.

Lapkin, Anne, Allega, Philip, Burke, Brian, Burton, Betsy, Bittler, R. Scott, Handler, Robert A., James, Greta A., Robertson, Bruce, Newman, David, Weiss, Deborah, Buchanan, Richard and Gall, Nicholas (2008), Gartner clarifies the definition of the term "Enterprise Architecture", G00156559, Gartner Research: www.gartner.com/id=740712 (accessed March 2012).

Lloyd, Mike (2006), Motion business architecture methodology, Microsoft: http://download.microsoft.com/documents/uk/msdn/architecture/architectinsight/Day%201/Methods/QAd%20-%20Methods/MET0102%20AIC%20Motion%206%20WORDS.ppt (accessed March 2012).

Pohle, George, Korsten, Peter and Ramamurthy, Shanker (2005), Component business models: making specialization real, IBM Business Consulting Services: www-935.ibm.com/services/us/imc/pdf/g510-6163-component-business-models.pdf (accessed March 2012).

SAP AG (2007), Proven methodology for rapid implementation of SAP solutions – reduce costs, lower risks, and save time with ASAP", SAP AG: www.r3now.com/literature/Proven-Methodology-for-Rapid-Implementation-of-SAP-Solutions.pdf (accessed March 2012).

Schwartz, Karen D. (2007), IT governance definition and solutions, CXO Media Inc.: www.cio.com/article/111700/IT_Governance_Definition_and_Solutions (accessed March 2012).

8 *Organizational Change Management*

OLIVER KOHNKE (SAP AG), SEBASTIAN REICHE (IESE
Business School) and ERNST BALLA (Voestalpine AG)

8.1 Overview

People and their abilities and motivations are one of the main wild cards in business transformations (LaClair and Rao, 2002). Business transformation often involves a change of, or introduction of new elements to, the corporate culture which may lead to a misinterpretation of corporate signals and values, and a shift in power structures, both of which may entail serious constraints to the success of a business transformation unless adequately managed (Kotter, 2010). Addressing and managing these *human* elements through Organizational Change Management therefore forms an integral part of every business transformation. Specifically, *change management* deals with the people who have to change their ways of working because of a business transformation. It deals with their expectations, their needs, their abilities, their motivations, their concerns and their resistances. In general, we believe that Organizational Change Management efforts should involve specific interactions, interventions and coaching, as well as broad and personal communication with the aim of aligning executives, involving management, and engaging employees.

Organizational change management within BTM² addresses the following steps (referring to the BTM² transformation life-cycle) for business transformation success:

1. Envision: Set up a foundation for an effective organizational change management with respect to governance and assess organizational change readiness.
2. Engage: Initiate a definition of a comprehensive communication strategy and performance management that is related to both the particular transformation project team and the organization at large.
3. Transform: Apply and adopt stakeholder management, communication management, and performance management.
4. Optimize: Receive feedback about the level of success of already implemented interventions.

OBJECTIVES OF THIS CHAPTER:
1. Understand activities that guide Organizational Change Management.
2. Learn about organizational change monitoring methods.
3. Learn about an approach for communication management.

8.2 Importance of Organizational Change Management

Transformation projects usually impact on a company's different sets of resources, including organizational, financial, and human resources. What is distinct about the latter resource type is that it is able to *react* – in often unpredictable ways – to a particular business transformation, either by actively resisting a business transformation, failing to adapt to a new order, or simply walking out of the door.

Business transformation is likely to gain sufficient acceptance if core members of the organization can be united behind the initiative and empowered to act towards project milestones. This chapter outlines a comprehensive organizational change management approach that is highly integrated within BTM^2 and supports large-scale business transformation.

The relevance of Organizational Change Management can be assessed by analyzing the main reasons for why business transformations fail. Both our own studies (see Chapter 11 Case Study MotorStars and Chapter 12 Lessons Learnt) and existing research suggest that the majority of transformation projects continue to fail due to non-technical reasons such as non-acceptance of the new solution, skill problems, communication problems, or problems with project resources. In fact, failure rates of transformation efforts reported in the literature reach up to 70 percent (Beer and Nohria, 2000). According to Kotter and Cohen (2002) the high failure rate is seldom related to technical reasons, but is more often a result of human factors.

More importantly, evidence also suggests that effective organizational change management activities have a tangible effect on the success of business transformation. For example, one study identified a very strong correlation between the use of a set of change management best practices and the realized returns of transformation initiatives (LaClair and Rao, 2002). This indicates that companies with strong change management capabilities are able to capture the potential impact of planned transformation initiatives to a much greater extent.

An important characteristic of transformation projects is their complex and multi-faceted nature. This complexity stems from the different levels in an organization that are affected by the transformation and that call for a joint orchestration of different disciplines dealing with both tangible and intangible factors (see Figure 8.1).

The tangible factors are addressed by different disciplines of BTM^2, for example in the case of organizational processes (see Chapter 6 Business Process Management) or individual skills (see Chapter 9 Competence and Training Management). By contrast, Organizational Change Management mainly focuses on the intangible factors associated with business transformation. One key element that any organizational change management approach must address concerns the emotional processes that individual stakeholders experience as a result of a business transformation and that include emotions as divergent as fear, hope and active resistance (Vince and Broussine, 1996). The role of emotions can be explained by the fact that a business transformation reflects a transition from an existing state of comfort and security to an uncertain future state. Resistance is therefore a natural response of emotional adjustment during an unstable period. Unless properly addressed and managed, employees' emotions can easily trigger negative reactions and translate into open resistance to business transformation, as revealed by a lack of motivation, rumours, internal conflicts, absenteeism or sickness.

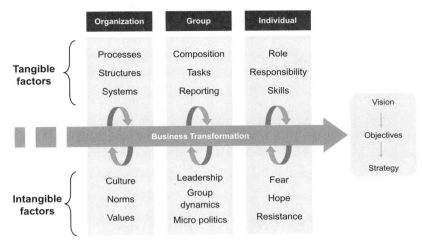

Figure 8.1   Levels of transformation processes

The negative emotional curve that organizational members pass through during the transition phase is commonly referred to as the *valley of tears* (Conner, 1992). Depending on the scale of business transformation, the negative reactions may be more pronounced and lasting. From this perspective, Organizational Change Management can be considered as an approach to actively reduce the scope of potentially negative reactions and leverage positive emotions inherent in business transformation (see Figure 8.2).

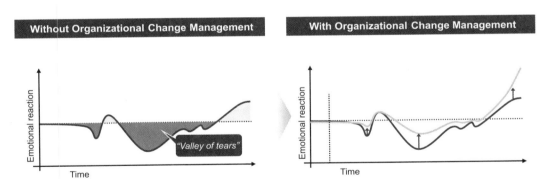

Figure 8.2   Reduction of the valley of tears

This requires four distinct dimensions of activities:

1. Communication: Making sure that people are informed and have the opportunity to formulate their wishes and concerns.
2. Motivation: Making sure that people accept the project and are willing to actively assist. This may also involve actions to provide confidence for the planned end state of business transformation.
3. Empowerment: Making sure that people are allowed to participate and become involved in business transformation.

4. Qualification: Making sure that people have the qualifications and skills to work in business transformation.

It is important to note that the emotional reactions to a transformation by different stakeholder groups may not always occur simultaneously and therefore require separate attention. For example, top managers pass through the valley of tears earlier than middle managers or employees because they are usually the first to become involved in change processes. By the time front line staff is finally involved, top and middle managers are likely to have already overcome their negative emotions, with the risk of reacting impatiently to the concerns and questions of their employees.

CHALLENGES CONCERNING THE IMPORTANCE OF ORGANIZATIONAL CHANGE MANAGEMENT:
1. Focus on intangible factors associated with business transformation.
2. Address the emotional processes that individual stakeholders experience as a result of a business transformation.
3. Reduce the scope of potentially negative reactions and leverage positive emotions inherent in business transformation.

KEY MESSAGE:
The majority of transformation projects continue to fail due to non-technical reasons such as non-acceptance of the new solution, skill problems, communication problems or problems with project resources. In fact, failure rates of transformation efforts reported in the literature reach up to 70 percent.

8.3 Organizational Change Management Approach of BTM²

Change management is a necessary discipline for any business transformation. However, the organizational change management approach outlined in this chapter is specifically targeted at large scale transformations that represent more radical changes where potential resistance towards the transformation may be more pronounced and the group of stakeholders potentially affected by the transformation is relatively large. At the same time, while the effects of business transformation reach beyond organizational boundaries and include external stakeholder groups such as shareholders, strategic partners or suppliers, organizational change management activities are mostly targeted at internal stakeholder groups.

The remainder of the chapter details a comprehensive methodology to deal with changes and the people side in business transformation, drawing from *best of breed* knowledge and experiences in the fields of organizational psychology, organizational behavior and human resource management. Briefly, the organizational change management approach detailed below deals with five key steps and requirements that need to be addressed in business transformation:

Set-Up and Governance

This initial step addresses the actions necessary to provide the foundation for an effective organizational change management. This includes defining the organizational change management charter, strategy and plan, as well as establishing the organizational change management team.

Stakeholder Management

The second step aims to assess existing attitudes among the relevant stakeholder (groups). Based on this stakeholder analysis, appropriate intervention strategies for stakeholders are derived.

Communication Management

This step deals with designing effective communication activities to create positive attitudes towards business transformation and increase acceptance levels. It involves both the definition of a comprehensive communication strategy and the design of a specific communication plan.

Performance Management

The fourth step concerns performance management activities that are related to both the particular transformation project team and the organization at large. First, it entails a set of instruments geared towards establishing a high performing project team. Second, it involves the systematic use and/or adaptation of HR practices with the aim of supporting business transformation.

Organizational Change Monitoring

The final step consists of applying appropriate monitoring tools to assess organizational change readiness and receive feedback about the level of success of already implemented interventions.

The five organizational change management steps comply with BTM[2] and the transformation life-cycle (*Envision, Engage, Transform,* and *Optimize*). Although the five steps build upon each other, our organizational change management approach should not be understood as strictly linear but rather as an iterative process in which the steps are often addressed simultaneously and need to be revisited at a later stage of business transformation (see Figure 8.3).

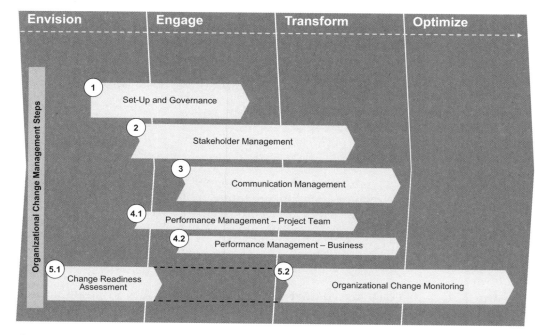

Figure 8.3   Overview and position of the Organizational Change Management approach within BTM²

8.4 Set-Up and Governance

Business transformation is too big to handle as a simple project. Therefore, a set-up and governance step is necessary to define the organizational change management approach, i.e. scope, activities, tools, roles, responsibilities and resources that are aligned with the overall project charter. The key objective is that the organizational change management team delivers value to meet the agreed expectations. Governance is an approach which is enterprise-wide and covers all activities to set-up, develop, integrate and adopt continuously the change activities. So what needs to be done to set the foundation for an effective organizational change management team? The following activities serve as a guideline to navigate through this first step of the organizational change management approach:

Involvement in Business Case Activities

The first activity is to provide input to the development of a business case to validate change management resources, budget, non-tangible business benefits and business resource requirements.

Initial Assessment

The second activity is to conduct interviews with key project stakeholders to gain an initial estimation of change management needs. The questions should cover the current situation, possible explanations, what should be changed, what must remain for a successful change, etc. The insights provided by these interviews lead to the requirements for the change management charter.

Organizational Change Management Charter

The third activity is to agree on the scope of work and deliverables that the change management team will deliver for the project. In a project sense this is the first step of project management, but filled with the initial insights of the interviews.

Organizational Change Management Strategy

The fourth activity is to document a high-level approach to change and training objectives, and guiding principles within a project. The strategy drives the plan.

Organizational Change Management Plan

The fifth activity is the definition of a detailed list of tasks and milestones to be able to track progress of change management activities. Furthermore, this provides a scope of work for the team and helps to align the expectations between change management team and project management.

Select & Build Organizational Change Management Team

After having decided on the plan, the next activity entails the appropriate identification and selection of people as change management resources to support the project.

Train Organizational Change Management Team

Depending on the gap between the competencies defined in the role description of a team leader or team member training sessions must be provided to deliver the right competencies.

The goal of these initial activities is to achieve a common understanding in a systemic sense. However, other deliverables are also important, including a defined plan of the change management activities and tasks, documentation of a high-level approach (with objectives and guiding principles), identification of resources to support, and provision of appropriate training to skill-up the team.

The following benefits could be achieved by ensuring a good Set-up and Governance:

- Increased understanding of expectations and deliverables, the alignment of project roles and responsibilities between the transformation project team and the change management team.
- Higher project buy-in, improved commitment, project team productivity and morale.
- Alignment of organizational change management project roles and responsibilities.
- Increased success rates of project efforts.
- Anticipation of project risks and definition of actions to mitigate risks.

To make this first step successful it is necessary to guarantee an early involvement of the organizational change management team in the strategy phase to understand the project requirements for the change management. The commitment from the project sponsor should lead to a commitment of the teams to follow the prescribed approach, standards and guidelines. Nevertheless the Set-up and Governance process is a joint effort between the project team and the change management team and results in a *contract* on which the scope of the deliverables within the project is based.

The critical success factor is a full commitment to the Set-up and Governance approach. This must be ensured by all contributing parties across the business including project sponsors, project managers and the project team. In addition, the clarity of the project vision and the overall objectives need to be defined in the organizational change management charter. On the planning-level a clear project plan and deployment strategy must be documented, allowing the organizational change management activities to be aligned with the overall project activities.

CHALLENGES CONCERNING SET-UP AND GOVERNANCE:

1. Provide input to the development of a business case.
2. Conduct interviews with key project stakeholders to gain an initial estimation of organizational change management needs.
3. Agree on the scope of work and deliverables that the change management team will deliver for the project.
4. Document a high-level approach to change and training objectives, and guiding principles within a project.
5. Define a detailed list of tasks and milestones to be able to track progress of organizational change management activities.
6. Identify and select people as organizational change management resources to support the project.
7. Provide training sessions to deliver the right competencies.

KEY MESSAGE:

To make this first step successful it is necessary to guarantee an early involvement of the change management team in the strategy phase to understand the project requirements for organizational change management.

8.5 Stakeholder Management

The stakeholder management step is one of the integral parts of the organizational change management strategy. Project stakeholders include any individual or group that may be impacted or influenced by project activities. Stakeholder are defined as individuals, groups or organizations that are actively involved in business transformation, or whose interests may be positively or negatively affected as a result of project execution or project completion (Project Management Institute, 2004).

Stakeholders are critical to project success because they can (and often do) significantly influence the development and outcome of a project. The effective identification and management of stakeholders is essential to the success of business transformation. It is therefore the responsibility of project leaders and sponsors to effectively manage these relationships within the organization's political environment, by identifying the appropriate project stakeholders early on within business transformation and to understand and address their capability and willingness to transform.

A project's success is related to stakeholder perceptions of the added value that is created in business transformation both at large and for themselves in particular, and the nature of their relationships as stakeholders with the project team. Therefore, stakeholder management is a critical success factor for any business transformation. If stakeholders are not fully engaged it is likely that there will be resistances to the implementation of the projects (Ward and Daniel, 2006).

The stakeholder management step has the following objectives:

- identifying and listing all stakeholders who are impacted by, or who can influence business transformation at the very beginning of the transformation project;
- conducting high-level change impact analysis that the project will have on the current organization and identified stakeholders;
- evaluating, analyzing and recording the degree of support and importance of each stakeholder;
- aligning communication activities to reflect the needs and demands of specific stakeholder groups;
- managing stakeholder (groups) individually along all project phases.

Stakeholder management enables the identification and analysis of all individual stakeholders or stakeholder groups that are affected by business transformation. It is the basis for developing a plan at the individual and group levels to achieve acceptance along the timeline of business transformation, to drive adoption and minimize resistance. The stakeholder management approach includes three key tasks (see Figure 8.4).

Stakeholder management helps to anticipate negative reactions to changes and supports to derive appropriate strategies to overcome potential resistances. At the beginning of business transformation all relevant project stakeholders have to be identified, described and listed. This information helps to understand how many people are affected by business transformation and where they are located (functionally and geographically). The second task is to assess the high-level organizational change impacts that business transformation will have on the current organization and different stakeholders. The high-level organizational change impact analysis provides information about the intensity of the changes for different stakeholder groups and supports the

Task 1: Identification of stakeholder groups*	Task 2: Organizational change impact analysis	Task 3: Stakeholder analysis	Organizational change management activities
• Who will/might be impacted by the change project? • Who are the decision makers in that area and who are the subject matter experts? • What is the number of identified stakeholders? • Where are these people located? • What are their expectations and needs with regards to the project?	• What will be the change for the identified stakeholder groups? • How intensive will the change be for them? • When will the change happen? • What are the impacts? • When do they occur? • How exactly does the impact affect the stakeholder?	• What is the stakeholder's power to influence the project and attitude towards the project? • What could be the reaction of stakeholder groups according to the planned changes? • What are the benefits for these stakeholder groups? • What are possible disadvantages for them?	• Plan and perform activities to overcome resistances • Manage resistances • Coordinate communication and training activities in terms of stakeholder (groups)

* A stakeholder is an employee, group or organization who is affected by the transformation project and/or is able to influence this project. Stakeholders with similar criteria could be grouped, e.g. end users.

Figure 8.4   Stakeholder management process

anticipation of possible reactions. During the third task all relevant stakeholder groups are evaluated and analyzed based on two dimensions.

The first dimension is related to the *level of influence*. This is the ability of the identified stakeholders to influence the project and is determined using a high to low scale. For example, a high level of influence can result in decisions or actions from this stakeholder being attributed to the success of the project and/or leading to delays in timing, or may influence the overall scope and/or resourcing of the project. A low level of influence means that the stakeholders have little or no influencing power over the progress or outcome of the change, although it is still important to capture their perceptions to minimize potential resistance.

The second dimension refers to the *attitude towards the project*. This is the attitude of the stakeholders to the project and can contribute to the successful adoption of the change project. For example, the stakeholder(s) may have a positive attitude to the project and is supportive of the project. A negative attitude to the project may lead the stakeholders to withdraw support for the project and actively seek ways of working around the changes. Each stakeholder can be rated according to these two dimensions, leading to four basic stakeholder classifications (see Figure 8.5, see also, Ward and Daniel, 2006).

The stakeholder portfolio matrix or stakeholder map (see Figure 8.6) helps to focus appropriate organizational change management activities that need to be taken to mobilize each stakeholder (e.g., management workshops, training).

The stakeholder portfolio matrix helps to derive organizational change management activities that need to be taken to mobilize specific stakeholders (especially opponents). organizational change management activities should be targeted at engaging these stakeholders in order to get their commitment and to overcome transformation resistance and to fully realize the business benefits as referenced within the business case. A revaluation of stakeholder groups on a continuous basis helps to consider the ever-

Stakeholder Portfolio Matrix		
I	Low level of influence Negative attitude towards project RESISTERS (monitor and respond)	Stakeholders with a low influence and a negative attitude should not be forgotten. Although their impact on the overall success of the project is not critical, these stakeholders should still be kept informed of the project's progress. However, stakeholders with a more positive attitude and higher influence may also be able to convert these stakeholders to have a more positive attitude through regular communication and information to ensure that these stakeholders understand the project and feel involved.
II	High level of influence Negative attitude towards project OPPONENTS (woo and win)	Stakeholders who have been identified as having a high level of influencing power and a negative attitude to the project are also likely to be critical to the successful adoption of the change project. However, as these stakeholders can directly influence the scope of the project and the progress to date, and can highly influence other people's views on the project, particular attention needs to be paid to these stakeholders to bring them on board with the project and ensure that the project does not face significant resistance. It may be that these stakeholders do not fully understand the project or do not feel suitably involved, in which case these issues need to be addressed to prevent a negative attitude spreading to other influencing stakeholders and employees.
III	High level of influence Positive attitude towards project PROMOTERS (keep informed)	Stakeholders who have been identified as having a high level of influencing power and a positive attitude to the project are also likely to be critical to the successful adoption of the change project. These stakeholders can directly influence the scope of the project and the progress to date; they can also highly influence other people's views on the project. These stakeholders should be used as much as possible to help promote the project to other employees and to ensure that a "positive voice" is being heard.
IV	Low level of influence Positive attitude towards project ENTHUSIASTS (maintain confidence)	Stakeholders who have low influence but a positive attitude can be used to help promote the project and to gain support from other employees.

Figure 8.5   Stakeholder classification based on portfolio matrix

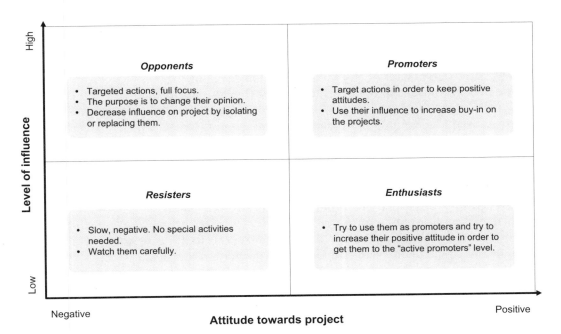

Figure 8.6   Stakeholder portfolio matrix and general stakeholder strategies

changing environments of projects that will affect stakeholder perceptions, interests, or priorities (Ward and Daniel, 2006). In addition, a reiteration of the stakeholder analysis supports the measurement of the impact of applied organizational change management activities on stakeholder attitudes. Therefore, it is strongly recommended to repeat the stakeholder analysis on a regular basis during the course of business transformation.

Stakeholder management activities can be supported by organizational change agents or a change agent network. An organizational change agent (or change champion) is the facilitator of the change. He or she acts as a communication conduit between the business and the project, facilitating two-way communication with message updates and feedback on impacts and project perceptions. An organizational change agent should be a well respected and influential team member with strong knowledge of functional systems and processes as well as excellent communication skills. They can be from any level in the organization. The stakeholder analysis could be used to identify appropriate change agents throughout the organization, e.g., promoters or enthusiasts.

The organizational change agent network is an internal network of enthusiastic and motivated organizational change agents that will generate awareness of the impending change and the impacts that it will have on the different business areas. It will support the management of organizational change issues on the ground while providing feedback to the relevant project leadership and organizational change management team.

The organizational change agent network builds an effective communications channel, enabling individuals to commit to the proposed transformation faster. The activities are focused on communicating consistent and timely messages to affected business areas using face-to-face communications wherever possible. The network helps to tailor communication language, style, message and methods to target audiences. In addition, the network assists with anticipating potential communication or acceptance issues and reports them to the project leadership team so that adequate mitigation activities can be developed. Establishing and maintaining an organizational change agent network throughout the overall project lifecycle can be considered as an important element and success factor of any stakeholder management.

The benefits of stakeholder management for the business include:

- increased understanding of expectations and required behaviors;
- engaged, involved and informed stakeholders;
- higher management buy-in, improved commitment, business and project team productivity and morale;
- faster response times enabled through the appropriate identification of stakeholders, from business requirements through delivery to embedment;
- increased success rates of project efforts;
- anticipation of project risks and definition of actions to mitigate risks;
- high and equal quality standard for all transformation projects.

The benefits of stakeholder management for the project management include:

- a standardized approach for stakeholder management activities ensuring a high and equal quality standard for all transformation projects;
- higher management buy-in, improved commitment, project team productivity and morale;
- better understanding of expectations and required behaviors and better management of stakeholders;
- faster response times enabled through the appropriate identification of stakeholders, from business requirements through delivery to embedment;
- increased success rates of project efforts;

- increased understanding of expectations and required behaviors;
- improved commitment, business productivity and project team member morale;
- stakeholder management helps to identify anticipated project risks, where actions can be anticipated and planned correctly on time, instead of reacting to issues.

It should be noted that achieving these benefits requires certain conditions that have to be fulfilled. Strong commitment from project sponsor and project teams regarding the organizational change management approach, standards and guidelines is necessary to conduct an effective stakeholder management. Stakeholder management activities are the basis for all subsequent organizational change management activities and, therefore, are mandatory for each business transformation. It should be clear that the project manager *owns* the stakeholder management process and the organizational change management team provides support to fulfil all related activities. These activities are a significant part of the project lifecycle and should be reassessed on a continuous basis, particularly when changes to project scope and/or timelines occur.

In general, the following three critical success factors are important for an effective stakeholder management with respect to a specific business transformation. Firstly, full commitment to the stakeholder management approach must be ensured from all contributing parties across the business including project sponsors, project managers, and project team. Secondly, a clear project vision, well defined objectives and project plan to enable stakeholder activities. Thirdly, an early identification and continuous review of stakeholder groups is necessary to optimize stakeholder acceptance during the overall project lifecycle.

CHALLENGES CONCERNING STAKEHOLDER MANAGEMENT:

1. Identify stakeholders, understand and address their capability and willingness to change.
2. Identify, describe and list all relevant project stakeholders.
3. Assess the high-level organizational change impacts that the transformation project will have on the current organization and different stakeholders.
4. Evaluate and analyze stakeholder groups based on their level of influence and attitude towards the project.
5. Repeat the stakeholder analysis on a regular basis.

KEY MESSAGE:

The organizational change agent network is an internal network of enthusiastic and motivated change agents that will generate awareness of the impending change and the impacts that it will have on the different business areas. It will support the management of organizational change issues on the ground while providing feedback to the relevant project leadership and change management team.

8.6 Communication Management

Communication is sometimes viewed as a very soft and vague topic. However, after having identified the stakeholders as described in the previous section and using the structure provided in this section it becomes a very powerful enabler for business transformation. The key objective is to rapidly generate involvement and build ownership of the process changes among the key stakeholder groups. It is about explaining the benefits and impacts in relation to the expectations of the different stakeholders.

A professional approach to communication requires the appropriate tools and templates which are mentioned in this section. These should also be provided for other departments and functions to enable a consistent approach. Furthermore, an efficient feedback process for all stakeholder groups should be established to have a strong two-way communication. The following tasks guide through the framework (see Figure 8.7).

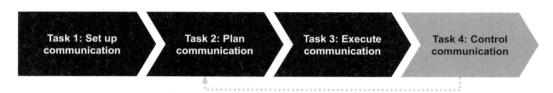

Figure 8.7   Communication management process

Task 1: Set-up Communication

It is crucial to set-up the communication activities in a structured way. This means reviewing existing material, defining the communication objectives, assessing the current communication resources, creating the infrastructure for ongoing communication, etc. A communication needs analysis is a useful initial tool to identify the needs and desires of the stakeholders and translate them into communication needs within several contexts. This could be combined with identifying the current knowledge of the stakeholder groups.

To assess the current communication resources a communication channel analysis is very helpful (see Figure 8.8). Since there are many channels that can be used for communication, it has to be decided which means is appropriate. Depending on their reach and their scope of influence, the channels may entail video messages or e-mail from the CEO, coffee talk with executives up to using an internet/intranet portal and face-to-face dialogue with managers. Following the formal structure of the chain of command, the managers would be informed first. A more informal way is to use organizational change agents that are local colleagues supporting the local needs.

As in every strategic work the goals, approach and outcomes of all communication activities should be defined clearly to ensure guidance and coherence across the business.

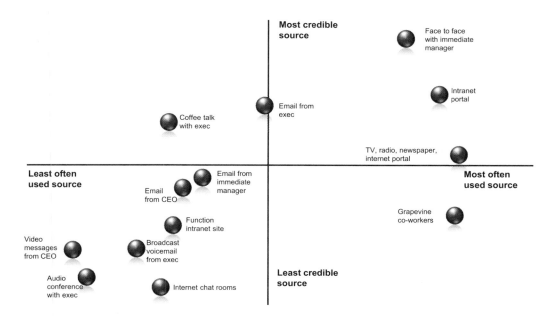

Employees seek multiple channels of communication to find information that they deem the most credible.

Figure 8.8   Credibility of communication tools

Source: Reproduced with permission from Whitworth, Brad, and Riccomini, Betsy. "Management Communication" in Communication World March/April, no. 2 (2005)

Task 2: Plan Communication

This task is about establishing communication activities for the project itself (according to the program management). Putting the steps above into a plan ensures specific communication and a necessary overview of all activities. The key messages and channels have to be identified. The developed communication plan (see Figure 8.9) supports the

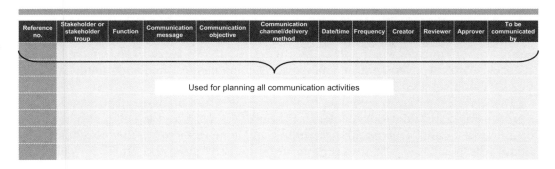

Figure 8.9   Communication plan

development and planning of specific communication activities for stakeholders. It provides an overview of the communication activities. The most important element of this plan is to establish a mechanism for obtaining feedback. The following communication plan is an example for which information should be included.

Task 3: Execute Communication

While a communication plan is an important condition for executing the communication activities, in reality there will be several obstacles that need to be addressed. This step is to develop content for events and actions. Selecting and preparing the communicators, using different channels to reinforce the same message and providing the communication plan within the project team lead to a very structured and powerful way of delivering the right message at the right "point of change". This is the precondition for the success of the events that are promoted and launched. With the help of a communication activity log (see Figure 8.10) a solid documentation of the activities is possible. It is also necessary to ensure timely responses for the established feedback channels.

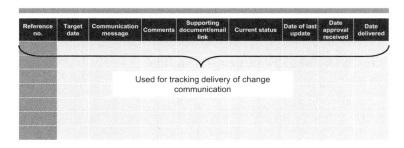

Figure 8.10 Communication activity log

Task 4: Control Communication

Controlling the communication activities is an ongoing process which should be initiated when the first activities start. This entails the use of the communication activity log (see Figure 8.10) combined with reviewing and reporting on quantity and quality of feedback. This feedback should be supported by feedback events with sponsors, conducting focus groups with employees to air issues and the scheduling of regular Q&As recording the feedback. With the given control data the success can be measured and modifications of the plan can be implemented as required.

The deliverables are stakeholder-specific messages and activities. This standardized approach for communication management ensures a high and equal quality standard for all projects and a better understanding and management of the stakeholders. It should lead to a faster response time from business requirements through delivery to embedment and therefore to an increased success rate of project efforts. Understanding the expectations and required behaviors result in improved commitment, productivity and project team member morale.

To ensure these benefits, it is necessary that the stakeholder analysis has been performed and the ownership of the communication activities has been agreed on, because the organizational change management team is not the communication *owner* and as such it should not be seen as representing the business in the messages being developed and delivered. Therefore, the content of the key communication and training materials must be developed and provided by an appropriate business representative, e.g., a subject matter expert. The communication activities are considered a significant part of the project lifecycle and should be reassessed on a continuous basis. This ensures that any amendments to project scope and/or the timeline are reflected in realigned communication activities.

The critical success factors include the clarity of the project vision and overall objectives, and a clear project plan and deployment strategy that enable communication management activities to be aligned with the overall project activities. Full commitment must be ensured from all contributing parties including management sponsors at the top and line levels. An early identification and continuous review of stakeholder groups combined with an effective, frequent and proactive two-way communication both top-down and bottom-up will optimize this communication approach. It is also necessary to have the full business support and endorsement to ensure an appropriate level and skill of resources to support the communication activities.

CHALLENGES CONCERNING COMMUNICATION MANAGEMENT:

1. Identify the needs and desires of the stakeholders and translate them into communication needs within several contexts.
2. Perform a communication channel analysis to assess the current communication resources.
3. Establish a mechanism for obtaining feedback of the communication activities.
4. Use a communication activity log to avoid obstacles during execution.
5. Use a communication activity log combined with reviewing and reporting on quantity and quality of feedback for controlling of communication activities.

KEY MESSAGE:

The change management team is not the communication owner and as such it should not be seen as representing the business in the messages being developed and delivered. Therefore, the content of the key communication and training materials must be developed and provided by an appropriate business representative, e.g. a subject matter expert.

8.7 Performance Management

The fourth step of our Organizational Change Management methodology concerns performance management. In general, performance management can be understood as the process of establishing a work context in which people are enabled to perform to the best of their abilities. It entails the entire work system that begins with the definition of required jobs and ends with an employee leaving the organization. In the context of a transformation project, performance management activities are related to the particular project team and the affected organization at large. Both sets of activities are mainly situated along the second and third stage of BTM^2 (see Figure 8.3). The following sections will discuss each dimension in turn.

8.7.1 PERFORMANCE MANAGEMENT – PROJECT TEAM

The transformation project team is resourced and wholly accountable for the project deliverables. How project teams perform throughout the project lifecycle will have an impact on the success of the project. It is therefore necessary to ensure that the project team is a cohesive unit from the outset and that its collective success is recognized and celebrated. To ensure a high performing project team throughout the entire project lifecycle, the scope of performance management entails four areas of interventions.

A first aspect concerns the formation of the project team. This requires the identification of individuals with complementary skills and role preferences in order to assemble a balanced team. Self-assessment tools such as the Belbin team inventory (Belbin, 1993), which measures an individual's relative preference across nine distinct team roles, may help with deciding on the team composition. It is also important to conduct team building events with the entire project team to encourage relationship building, develop acceptance for different individual character types, identify and resolve potential conflicts, and highlight areas for improving collective performance. A second requirement refers to the provision of appropriate team recognition. It is essential that key milestone achievements are identified and celebrated. Similarly, high performance, especially if it collectively achieved, needs to be properly acknowledged while also communicating achievements with the business to attract positive PR across the wider organization. Third, through its operation the transformation project team builds a relevant stock of knowledge about key transformation challenges, potential resource constraints or crucial interfaces in the organizational structure. Given the temporary nature of the project team, it is important to establish an explicit process that allows knowledge to be codified and shared between internal and external project team members to ensure that the intellectual property is retained in the business upon project closure. Fourth and finally, it is necessary to continuously refresh and check project team relationships, collective performance levels and knowledge transfer to maintain best practice throughout the whole project lifecycle. This can be achieved through regular project check questionnaires that are to be filled out by project members. The results of these project checks need to be presented to the team and should lead to recommendations for how project management can be improved.

There are additional performance management activities targeted at the transformation project team that may foster high team performance levels. For example, large-scale transformation projects tend to have an emergent nature that makes it difficult to plan all necessary activities at the outset. Therefore, individual team members need to receive continuous training and development to be able to face changing project needs. It is also important to provide tangible incentives and rewards that are linked to a regular performance feedback process in order to motivate and positively influence the project team members. Similarly, it is helpful for other parts of the organization to contribute to and actively support the project team work. Further, roles and responsibilities, as well as goals and incentive plans need to be aligned to ensure that all project members are fully accountable and execute their work consistent with the project deliverables.

Following from the above, a systematic performance management targeted at the transformation project team entails three distinct benefits. First, the measures described above help to optimize the project team relationships which will translate into a higher quality of performance and team outputs, thereby increasing project success. Second, the measures facilitate both the internal and external transfer of knowledge with the aim of developing internal capabilities of the organization. This is specifically important if future transformation projects are conceivable. Third, explicit support for the project team will lead to improved commitment, productivity and project team member morale. It should be noted that achieving these benefits assumes that certain conditions can be met by the wider organization:

- The communication regarding the adoption of performance management KPI's with respect to the project is actively supported and delivered by project management and its sponsors.
- The annual HR mechanism that underpins the performance management strategy already exists within the HR business process.
- A project budget is available for the capability development and recognition activities that were identified above.

CHALLENGES CONCERNING THE PERFORMANCE MANAGEMENT – PROJECT TEAM:

1. Identify individuals with complementary skills and role preferences in order to assemble a balanced team.
2. Identify and celebrate key milestone achievements.
3. Establish an explicit process that allows knowledge to be codified and shared between internal and external project team members to ensure that the intellectual property is retained in the business upon project closure.
4. Refresh and check project team relationships, collective performance levels and knowledge transfer to maintain best practice throughout the whole project lifecycle.
5. Align incentive plans to ensure that all project members are fully accountable and execute their work consistent with the project deliverables.

KEY MESSAGE:
It is important to provide tangible incentives and rewards that are linked to a regular performance feedback process in order to motivate and positively influence the project team members.

At a broader level, the following critical success factors can be derived on which effective performance management activities regarding the transformation project team rely:

- Full commitment of the project/program manager to the performance management strategy.

- Provision of development and recognition activities within the project budget forecast.
- Regular communication with the project team to feedback stakeholder perception.
- Regular review to validate and identify further interventions to optimize the efficacy of development and recognition activities.

8.7.2 PERFORMANCE MANAGEMENT – BUSINESS

While it is important to ensure an effective functioning of the project team over the course of the whole transformation, performance management activities reach beyond the team context. In particular, performance management should also involve the active use and adaptation of the existing HR infrastructure in an organization to support the transformation project and create ownership and acceptance within the business. At a general level, this requires a detailed review of the entire set of HR processes and practices to understand which of the existing ones could be used more systematically and which new instruments would need to be adopted.

Performance management in this broader sense may involve a variety of practices to support business transformation. For example, it is important to align transformation-related objectives with goal-setting and incentive systems, as well as with feedback schemes that are able to systematically evaluate desired behavior. In this regard, 360° feedback serves as a multi-source appraisal mechanism that can provide detailed information about project-related progress and goal achievement. Other practices include the systematic use of job rotations to move employees with positive attitudes and potentially high influence into critical and highly visible positions while relocating resisting employees into less critical/visible positions. Similarly, for those employees that are made redundant due to the transformation, specific (out-)placement strategies need to be devised and implemented. Furthermore, suggestion schemes encourage employees to actively share suggestions and/or voice concerns related to the planned transformation, thereby signalling to staff that their involvement is valued. Overall, it is important to consider the entire talent management system that covers the acquisition of adequate people for the transformation initiative, their continuous development, and their long-term retention in the organization. Below, two exemplary practices are reviewed in greater detail.

Key to any organizational change effort is that it requires a review and adaptation of the existing compensation systems because incentives act as a powerful signal of what is considered desired behavior within the organization. Depending on the phase of the change or transformation project, different incentives may gain in relative importance (Lawler, 2000). During the initial stage of unfreezing existing routines, processes and behaviors and opening up the organization for change, it is important to foster a motivation for developing change efforts. From the perspective of the incentive system, this requires the design and adoption of profit sharing, stock ownership or other forms of variable pay that explicitly reward company performance. In comparison, the change implementation phase focuses primarily on encouraging employees to develop new skills and adopt the change. To support these objectives, the incentive system can introduce bonus programs specifically geared towards change implementation or the achievement of new performance targets. Similarly, rewards may be allocated based on the acquisition of new skills and knowledge, or entirely new employment contracts need to be designed to better reflect changing job and task requirements. The final phase that consists of ensuring the ongoing operation under the changed end state focuses on creating the necessary motivation and capabilities to perform effectively. Compensation practices such as pay-for-performance systems that focus on strategic performance targets and are directed at the attraction, development and retention of high performers can support these objectives.

The challenge in devising incentive system change is to combine and sequentially introduce temporary compensation system changes that will prompt the implementation of business transformation, and permanent ones that are intended to become part of the organization's ongoing operation. It is the permanent incentive system changes that are necessary to have a lasting impact and facilitate the potential implementation of future changes. The specific design of compensation practices should be guided by the transformation project-related objectives and their translation into a goal-setting system:

1. Definition of project-related objectives: In a first step, it is essential to develop performance and behavioral objectives that support the key milestones within the project life cycle. This also entails an identification of the target stakeholder groups to be included in the performance management strategy.
2. Review and alignment of objectives and incentives: In a second step, the identified objectives need to be translated into tangible and relevant KPI targets that may be valued by the individual and can be measured and rewarded by the business. The identified KPIs need to be validated and signed off by the project sponsors.
3. Integration of objectives and incentive systems: Finally, it is important to work with the appropriate business function and stakeholders to integrate the approved KPI targets into individual performance scorecards. In addition, mid-point scorecard review check point needs to be established to ensure that the KPI targets continue to be aligned with project scope.

Large-scale transformations have numerous repercussions for the existing talent management system. For example, the nature and scope of required competences may change as roles and responsibilities are altered during business transformation. Performance management therefore needs to re-configure the entire talent management cycle to reflect organizational change efforts. This requires interventions concerning talent acquisition, talent development, and talent retention. From the perspective of talent acquisition, it is important to attract and select the right people that can implement and "live" the organizational change efforts. To reflect changing needs in talent acquisition, existing job descriptions need to be modified and new responsibilities defined. The output is then to be translated into existing selection methods to ensure that the new skills and competencies are explicitly considered during the selection process. It may also be necessary to revise the recruitment and selection strategy if other channels of talent acquisition need to be tapped into. For example, it is possible that the transformation creates the need for jobs with an interdisciplinary scope which can only be filled by candidates with expert training from specific institutions. Further, existing employer branding activities need to be reviewed to assess whether they adequately address the modified candidate pool.

Talent development is concerned with ensuring that all required competencies and skills are available within the organization. During organizational change efforts, talent development also plays an important role in signalling what is considered as the new shared values and exemplary behaviors. First, this requires the definition of modified and/ or new competences as well as the design of a training and development infrastructure that allows employees to develop these competences in a timely and ongoing manner. Similarly, performance evaluations need to be adapted to reflect the development and application of the new skills and competences. It is important that these changes are clearly communicated to employees at the outset of the performance review cycle to create realistic expectations. If talent development requirements change more radically as a result of the transformation project, it may also be necessary to establish revised development and career tracks for employees. For example, it may be necessary to maintain a separate career track for technical experts that are essential to the implementation and future operation of the transformed organization.

Finally, talent retention aims at ensuring that high performers and key promoters of the organizational change efforts remain in the organization. This not only requires an adaptation of the incentive system described earlier but may also involve explicitly differentiating between core and peripheral employees to help focus and prioritize retention efforts, especially at the outset of the transformation initiative. Talent retention practices may differ in their scope and time frame depending on whether additional transformation projects are to be envisioned in the near future. Talent retention practices can also be more responsive in nature, for example in the case of specific retention bonuses, or of a preventive type such as fostering a supportive working environment and providing opportunities for employees to become actively involved in the transformation project (Reiche, 2008).

CHALLENGES CONCERNING THE PERFORMANCE MANAGEMENT – BUSINESS:

1. Align transformation-related objectives with goal-setting and incentive systems as well as with feedback schemes that are able to systematically evaluate desired behavior.
2. Design and adopt profit sharing, stock ownership or other forms of variable pay that explicitly reward company performance.
3. Reconfigure the entire talent management cycle to reflect organizational change efforts.

KEY MESSAGE:

It is important to consider the entire talent management system that covers the acquisition of adequate people for the transformation initiative, their continuing development and their long-term retention in the organization.

8.7.3 OUTCOMES AND SUCCESS FACTORS FOR PERFORMANCE MANAGEMENT

For performance management activities related to the use and adaptation of HR practices to effectively support the transformation project, it is crucial to establish continuous alignment with the wider context of the project. This alignment involves three distinct dimensions:

1. Alignment with the transformation project itself: The performance management activities need to be aligned with key performance indicators and milestones as derived from the transformation project to positively influence stakeholder enrollment.
2. Internal consistency among HR practices: The various elements of the HR infrastructure need to be aligned with each other to send consistent messages to the different stakeholders and can be leveraged to promote behavioral changes. For example, if the transformation leads to the establishment of separate development and career tracks, their different requirements need to be reflected in the organization's recruitment and selection activities.
3. Fit with overall corporate strategy: Performance management needs to ensure a fit and re-alignment of the HR system with the new strategy of the organization. To that end, the HR infrastructure serves as the necessary set of tools and instruments that facilitate achievement of the organization's strategic objectives. For example, the new strategy that emerges from business transformation will translate into different talent requirements.

Given the complexity of large-scale transformation projects, ensuring this alignment is not limited to a single point in time but requires continuous review and interventions to reflect the changing needs during business transformation.

Through its various activities, performance management entails three distinct benefits. First, leveraging the HR infrastructure helps to embed the project *ownership* within the organization, thereby ensuring greater sustainability of the transformation initiative. Second, performance management activities geared towards the business allow a better prioritization of project activities vis-à-vis competing initiatives because potential goal conflicts can be detected more easily and hence avoided. Third, a systematic consideration of HR processes will provide the support tools necessary to facilitate project success. Again, achieving these benefits assumes that certain conditions can be met by the wider organization, including clear communication concerning the adoption of performance management KPIs by key management stakeholders and a general availability of an underlying HR infrastructure to support the performance management strategy. At a broader level, the following critical success factors can be derived on which effective performance management activities regarding the business rely:

- Full commitment to the performance management strategy from all participating stakeholders across the organisation including project sponsors, line management, and HR.
- Importance of the right timing to change incentive systems. If the incentive system is changed too early, *right* behavior may be induced, but for the *wrong* reasons, i.e. required behavior is incentivized without changing the necessary cultural values and norms. Changing the incentive system has to go hand-in-hand with instilling new values, it cannot precede culture/value change.
- Tangible and relevant KPIs are aligned with project plan objectives, deliverables and timeline.
- Timely review of milestones to ensure continued relevance of KPIs and alignment with the project scope.

> **CHALLENGES CONCERNING THE OUTCOMES AND SUCCESS FACTORS FOR PERFORMANCE MANAGEMENT:**
> 1. Align performance management activities with KPIs and milestones as derived from the transformation project to positively influence stakeholder enrollment.
> 2. Align various elements of the HR infrastructure with each other to send consistent messages to the different stakeholders.
> 3. Ensure a fit and realignment of the HR system with the new strategy of the organization.
>
> **KEY MESSAGE:**
> Given the complexity of large-scale transformation projects, ensuring the three dimensions of alignment is not limited to a single point in time but requires continuous review and interventions to reflect the changing needs during business transformation.

8.8 Organizational Change Monitoring

Organizational change monitoring focuses on general monitoring activities, e.g., business readiness. It provides the opportunity to check the transition of impacted stakeholders by gathering and analyzing feedback and specific information on the project situation. It answers the following questions:

• Are the impacted stakeholders transitioning in the right direction?
• Are they transitioning within the planned time frame?
• Are any extra activities or redirection necessary?

Readiness for organizational change of the affected stakeholders is a major success factor to any transformation program. To ensure the change readiness, a change management strategy has been established and specific change management activities have been defined during the whole transformation project lifecycle. The evaluation of the impact of organizational change management activities delivered and of the recommended organizational change management strategy requires a specific monitoring approach, e.g., definition of meaningful measurement categories. If the results provided by the organizational change monitoring activities are ignored, a significant success factor will be disregarded.[1]

Furthermore, scheduling organizational change monitoring activities avoids typical failures derived from lessons learnt from transformation projects (see Table 8.1). In addition, organizational change monitoring will ensure that unambiguous, specific and operational goals are set; highlighting the seriousness and stability of the intended change as well as confirming the value of having organizational change management activities in business transformation.

An objective and reliable evaluation of the change process enables continuous improvement, early adaptation of the organizational change management strategy and

---

1   We refer to Cohen and Kotter (2005) for an example of a change readiness questionnaire.

Table 8.1   Typical lessons learned from other transformation projects

Failure	Recommendation
No change monitoring concept defined and no monitoring measures conducted in the transformation program.	Organizational change monitoring activities should be an integral part of the change management strategy and defined at the beginning of the project.
KPIs are focused on typical project aspects (e.g. budget, time and scope or business case related). No measurement of people-related aspects to evaluate the impact of organizational change management activities.	Organizational change monitoring must be goal-oriented. Therefore, it is important to clearly define the change management goals, e.g. increase of acceptance, level of information, commitment and development of appropriate KPIs.
Even if organizational change monitoring measures are applied, no alignment with project risk management exists.	Organizational change monitoring could be a valuable source for the overall risk and issue management. Ensure alignment with project risk management approach.
Evaluation of the organizational change readiness/user acceptance/satisfaction was measured only once and too late (e.g. after go-live).	Measure goal achievement on a regular basis right from the start of the project and during the whole project lifecycle.
Only single measures are applied that are not covering all stakeholder groups and perspectives.	Use a mix of organizational change monitoring measures to cover all stakeholder groups and different perspectives.

is considered as a key success factor. In addition, it is vital to have project leadership's commitment to the organizational change monitoring approach.

The scope of the organizational change monitoring is to measure the impact of organizational change management activities (e.g., stakeholder management, communication management, or performance management). Organizational change monitoring activities are linked to the people related aspects of the project (e.g., readiness, acceptance, motivation, commitment). They should be seen as complementary to the project controlling activities that are traditionally focused on *hard* project aspects (e.g., budget, time, and scope). Organizational change monitoring has three main objectives:

1. Evaluation of the organizational change management strategy:
   - Assessing the level of overall business acceptance and readiness of impacted stakeholders.
   - Reviewing the quality and effectiveness of the organizational change management strategy and specific organizational change management activities (e.g., stakeholder, communication, competency, and skill management) for the project.
2. Regular feedback on the project:
   - Providing the organizational change management project team advisor as well as the project manager with regular and general feedback on stakeholders' perception of the transformation project.
   - Ensuring "softer" feedback comes back to the project (e.g., informal conversations, general thoughts, coffee machine corner discussions).

3. Continuous improvement process:
   - Deriving and prioritizing appropriate activities to improve organizational change management strategy, e.g., better communication of business benefits.
   - Facilitating a continuous improvement process (measuring the impact of follow-up activities).
   - Ensuring knowledge transfer and usage of experiences for developing best practices for subsequent projects.

The organizational change monitoring approach combines different methods and tools to evaluate the impact of organizational change management activities and the overall strategy. These methods and tools are structured along two dimensions:

1. Focus of organizational change monitoring activity:
   - Evaluation of the organizational change management situation: Assessing the current situation of business transformation with regard to the organization's readiness to accept the change, the achievement of organizational change management objectives (attitude changes, e.g., acceptance, satisfaction) and organizational change management related risks.
   - Evaluation of a specific organizational change management activity: Evaluating the effectiveness and efficiency of specific organizational change management activities applied, e.g., a specific event or workshop.
2. Frequency of organizational change monitoring activity:
   - Once: The monitoring activity will be applied only once during the implementation process, e.g., after a specific activity.
   - From time to time: The monitoring activity will be applied more than one time, e.g., to make attitude changes visible.

Based on these two dimensions it is possible to structure common change management monitoring activities in a general approach (see Figure 8.11). The application of the right mixture of organizational change monitoring tools avoids *blind spots* and enriches overall organizational change monitoring.

Typical organizational change monitoring methods are described in Appendix F of this book.

Organizational change monitoring has several benefits for the change management team as well as for the project manager and project sponsor of a transformation program:

Benefits for the change management team:

- Enables immediate feedback about the effectiveness of organizational change management activities and the overall organizational change management strategy.
- Supports the refinement of the organizational change management strategy and the alignment of organizational change management activities.
- Ensures continuous improvement processes during the project implementation as well as for subsequent business transformation.

Benefits for project managers and project sponsors:

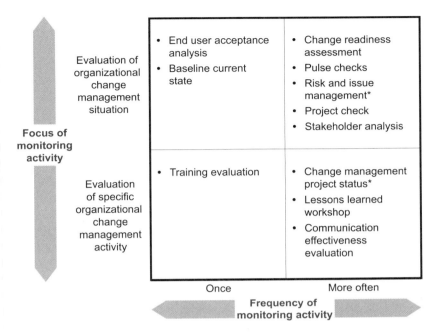

	Once	More often

* Depending on Project Management Office (PMO) standards

Figure 8.11 Organizational change monitoring approach

- Supports the evaluation of the overall organizational change management effort on the basis of predefined organizational change management success criteria, KPI's and milestones during the project charter preparation.
- Contributes to the overall project risk and issue management and status reporting.
- Avoids blind spots during the project by covering the people side of business transformation.

There are several assumptions and critical success factors that should be considered for the organizational change monitoring step. The organizational change management team has agreed the success criteria, KPI's and milestones at the beginning of business transformation with the project manager and project sponsor. The effectiveness of the organizational change management strategy and activities will be evaluated against these criteria during the project life cycle. Senior project leaders must be open for receiving feedback about stakeholder's project perception. Any kind of project feedback should be treated in a constructive and action oriented way, i.e. *no disregard of negative feedback, no finger pointing, and using feedback for improvement activities. In addition, the change management team should have access to all relevant project stakeholders in order to involve them in appropriate* organizational change monitoring activities.

Most of the applied organizational change monitoring methods are based on interviews and/ or questionnaires. In order to get the most reliable information from the people involved, it is important to follow four basic quality standards (see Table 8.2).

To evaluate the benefits of Organizational Change Management, it is mandatory to define specific and measurable organizational change management objectives before the transformation project begins. A broad range of different key performance indicators (KPIs) is available to measure the impact of Organizational Change Management in business transformation. In Figure 8.12, possible KPIs are structured according to the project phase in which they might be used.

Before go-live, most KPIs focus on awareness of the transformation project within the organization as well as on monitoring the project's progress from a organizational change management perspective. During go-live, the KPI focus is on end-user readiness. After go-live, most KPIs focus on the acceptance of new processes and applications as well as the satisfaction of different stakeholders. Other indicators are targeted at the sustainability of change after go-live, such as the number of requested process changes and reduction of support efforts.

Defining the right KPIs to measure the benefits of Organizational Change Management is an important precondition, but it is also necessary to define the right tools or methods to obtain this information. The following list summarizes several tools or methods:

- surveys and interviews covering different topics, such as change readiness and acceptance;
- workshops with the business and/or organizational change agents;
- pre- and post-go-live evaluations – Finding out the expectations of people before the project and asking them again after the project is six months live;
- benchmarking against own projects and/or other companies' projects (if data is available).

Surveys are considered an appropriate tool for evaluating the acceptance of end users with respect to new business processes and IT applications. Furthermore, in contrast to interviews, surveys offer the possibility of involving a large group of end users in transformation projects. Especially after go-live or during global rollouts impacting several assets the project management gains broad feedback about the implementation process. This feedback can then be used for a subsequent continuous improvement process. Nevertheless, the use of surveys requires a strong management commitment and a professional methodology.

Table 8.2   Quality standards for organizational change monitoring activities

Quality standard	Description
Anonymity	The participation in any survey (questionnaires, interviews) follows strictly the standard of anonymity. It should not be possible to attribute any kind of result to a specific person.
Voluntariness	The participation in any survey should be considered as voluntary.
Transparency	Results of the monitoring activities should be made available to all the participants.
Strive for improvements	All monitoring activities should be accompanied by a strong commitment to improving the project situation if necessary. The activity plan has to be communicated to all people involved in the monitoring activities.

Before Go-Live	Go-Live	After Go-Live
• Level of knowledge about the project within the organization • Level of confidence of different stakeholders with respect to the project • Level of involvement of business functions in project work (percentage of project team, attendance rate at workshops) • Number of meetings or time required to make decisions • Achievement of CM milestones	• Readiness of business to work with new processes and use new systems • Error rate of users during go-live (e.g. monitor log files)	• Acceptance or satisfaction with new processes and systems • Reduction of support efforts/requests • Number of requested process changes in a period of time • Number of system user error rates • Number of additional training requests • User knowledge and use of the system • Indicators of user performance

Figure 8.12 Sample KPIs for evaluating the benefits of Organizational Change Management

Source: Kohnke, 2006.

CHALLENGES CONCERNING ORGANIZATIONAL CHANGE MONITORING:

1. Establish a change management strategy and define specific change management activities during the whole transformation project lifecycle.
2. Assess the current situation of business transformation with regard to the organization's readiness to accept the change.
3. Evaluate the effectiveness and efficiency of specific organizational change management activities.
4. Apply monitoring activity during the implementation process.

KEY MESSAGE:

Before go-live, most KPIs focus on awareness of the transformation project within the organization as well as on monitoring the project's progress from an organizational change management perspective.

8.9 Conclusion

This chapter has outlined a comprehensive organizational change management approach that aims to support the planning and preparation, implementation and execution, as well as continuous monitoring of business transformation. Its distinct benefit lies in a focus on managing the intangible factors that are inherent in and have the potential to derail business transformation. Successfully addressing the *human* side of business transformation to achieve far-reaching acceptance and buy-in of the proposed transformation is critical for the overall success of any transformation initiative.

Bibliography

Beer, Michael and Nohria, Nitin (2000), Cracking the code of change, *Harvard Business Review* 78, no. 3, 133–41.

Belbin, R.M. (1993), *Team Roles at Work* (Oxford: Butterworth-Heinemann).

Cohen, Dan S. and Kotter, John P. (2005), *The Heart of Change Field Guide* (Boston, Mass: Harvard Business School Press).

Conner, Daryl (1992), *Managing at the Speed of Change: How Resilient Managers Succeed and Prosper Where Others Fail*, 1st ed. (New York: Villard Books).

Kohnke, Oliver (2006), How effective change management works: results of a European study 2006, SAP Business Consulting: www.docstoc.com/docs/14980084/How-effective-Change-Management-works (accessed March 2012).

Kotter, John P. (2010), *Leading Change: Why Transformation Efforts Fail* (Boston, Mass: Harvard Business Press).

Kotter, John P. and Cohen, Dan S. (2002), *The Heart of Change: Real-life Stories of How People Change Their Organizations* (Boston, Mass: Harvard Business School Press).

LaClair, Jennifer A. and Rao, Ravi P. (2002), Helping employees embrace change, *McKinsey Quarterly*, no. 2, 17–20.

Lawler, Edward E. (2000), Pay system change: lag, lead, or both?: A commentary on Wruck, Ledford and Heneman, in *Breaking the Code of Change*, edited by Michael Beer and Nitin Nohria (Boston, Mass: Harvard Business School Press).

Project Management Institute (2004), *A Guide to the Project Management Body of Knowledge: Third Edition (PMBOK Guides)*, 3rd ed. (Newtown Square, PA: Project Management Institute).

Reiche, B.S. (2008), The configuration of employee retention practices in multinational corporations' foreign subsidiaries, *International Business Review* 17, no. 6, 676–87.

Vince, Russ and Broussine, Michael (1996), Paradox, defense and attachment: accessing and working with emotions and relations underlying organizational change, *Organization Studies* 17, no. 1, 1–21.

Vogt, Peter (2004), Awareness to action: connecting employees to the bottom line, *Communication World* March/April, no. 2, 22–6.

Ward, John and Daniel, Elizabeth (2006), *Benefits Management: Delivering Value from IS & IT Investments* (Chichester: Wiley).

Whitworth, Brad and Riccomini, Betsy (2005), Management communication, *Communication World* March/April, no. 2.

9 *Competence and Training Management*

CHRISTOPH PIMMER (University of Applied Sciences and Arts Northwestern Switzerland), JÜRG HAEFLIGER (Sulzer Ltd) and FLORIAN BLUMER (University of Applied Sciences and Arts Northwestern Switzerland)

9.1 Overview

Business transformation requires a longer-term and often major change in the competences of team members and the management. For example, when transforming an HR department from an administration-oriented unit to one providing strategic consulting, not only the competences for transformation, for example, in the area of leadership, must be trained. Numerous team members previously working primarily in administrative roles must first be prepared and suitably trained with regard to their new strategic consulting competences (see also Chapter 11, Case Study).

Competence and Training Management provide qualification and enablement of selected key groups with respect to (1) the competences required for business transformation and (2) the strategic core competences vital for the company's future success.

Competence and Training Management within BTM^2 addresses the following phases (referring to the BTM^2 transformation lifecycle) for business transformation success:

- Envision and engage: During these phases, the company's need and objectives are specified with respect to business transformation strategy implementation. The need and objectives are then compared with the results of the as-is analysis.
- Engage, transform and optimize: These phases develop training measures for the identified gaps, foster the "learning transfer" and, eventually, analyze the success of the measures.

OBJECTIVES OF THIS CHAPTER:
1. Understand major influence on learning and the development of competences.
2. Learn how to acquire particular competences that are needed for business transformation.
3. Understand the significance of an appropriate working environment.

9.2 Significance, Definition and Scope

Our own experiences, as well as numerous literary examples, show the major significance of team members in business transformation projects. For example, a broadly based McKinsey study came to the following conclusion: "When organizational transformations succeed, managers typically pay attention to people issues" (Keller et al., 2010). People issues are examined as part of BTM² both from an organizational change management as well as a competence and training management perspective; whereas Organizational Change Management – to put it simply – focuses primarily on the will and attitudes of team members and management towards business transformation, Competence and Training Management in this section concentrates on the knowledge, ability and skills of these target groups. For a business transformation project to succeed, the work between managers and team members, and in particular the building of capacities, for example, in the area of leadership skills, are of enormous significance. Preparing and training the team members for their new tasks within the context of a transformation project are also highlighted as factors in the success of a business transformation (Dingens and Bach, 2009).

Competence management is significant for the whole of personnel development, and includes tasks from restructuring, long-term qualification and career planning to the assessment of team members and the management. Principally, it is about realizing measures for the promotion of strategically important competences resulting from the planned/actual analysis comparison. In this chapter, however, we will focus on competence and training management measures in business transformation projects. Accordingly, we introduce methods that we deem suitable in such specific contexts. A detailed methodological engagement, though desirable, would go well beyond the scope of this chapter. Readers will find, however, references to more extensive discussions of the methods described.

In the context of a business transformation the methods cannot generally be used in a non-selective way. The necessary measures are used specifically and selectively, that is, on certain individual target groups. However, the discipline of Competence and Training Management is not only restricted to qualifications that are necessary for the transformation process itself, but also targets those who must cope with the company and team members after the transformation.

Competence and Training Management in the context of business transformation involve the following key questions:

- Current and future tasks: Which tasks are being tackled in the company, now and in the future?
- Current and future competences: Which competences are needed for this? Which competences are required to achieve the desired objective?
- Gaps and measures: What is the gap between current and future competence requirements? Which measures enable this gap to be bridged?
- Transfer and evaluation: How can the acquired competences be applied and successfully evaluated?
- Work environment: How must the working and transformation environments be configured so that they promote the development of competences?

In this chapter, typical competence and training management processes and their associated methods are presented. Here too, however, the proposed approaches must on no account be perceived as rigid instructions in the sense of a recipe, but should be correspondingly adapted with regard to the specifics of the respective business transformation – every business transformation is different – such as the targets, focus, magnitude, duration or urgency. For this reason, those methods presented in the chapter are to be seen as a set that should be applied and used in a specific context. The level of competence management and training offerings that exist in the company are also crucial. The more extensive they are, the easier the systemic application is, also within the context of a complex and possibly turbulent business transformation. We are fully aware that even the best training measures can only influence competences of team members to a certain degree. At least as important are the working environment and structures, as well as the personal and biographical prerequisites of the team members, who can prove to be a great help or hindrance to learning. Here, we can devote only a certain amount of time to this topic (see Section 9.3). The working environment and the whole transformation context, however, are discussed at length in Chapter 2, Meta Management.

The competence and training management process within the context of a business transformation can summarily be characterized as follows: First, in the strategy development step strategic objectives and focal points must be described in terms of the identified target group competences (step 1). In the subsequent steps of strategy implementation, first, the needs and objectives are specified in the need analysis step (2) and then compared with the results of the as-is analysis (3). For identified gaps, training measures are developed in step 4. After all, the aim of this training is to address identified gaps. The success of training (5) depends largely on the application and use of the acquired knowledge in various working contexts. The *learning transfer* must be fostered and, eventually, the success of the measures has to be analyzed (step 6). Throughout all steps, the circumstances of the working and transformation environment must be considered as they have a major influence on learning and the development of competences. Figure 9.1 summarizes the process and illustrates how the various steps from Competence and Training Management fit into the BTM² transformation lifecycle.

When applying the whole model, flexibility is required with respect to the characteristics of the company, the size and type of transformation process, and the respective target group. For example, if it involves communicating leadership competences to the business transformation manager responsible, this must be done relatively quickly in the engage phase. If, however, team members are being trained to operate an HR IT platform, for example, as part of an HR transformation, this measure is carried out at a much later stage.

9.2.1 PREPARATION AND STRATEGY DEVELOPMENT

As established at the outset, transformation projects are often associated with changes in the team members' competence requirements, which should be worked out as part of a strategy at the beginning of a transformation project. For this purpose, target groups must be identified at a "high level" in view of the company's future value chain and associated tasks and competences have to be specified. This can be done based on the stakeholder groups that are ascertained in the organizational change management

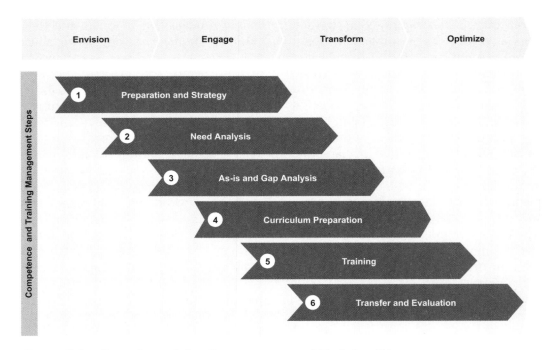

Figure 9.1   Overview of the Competence and Training Management process

discipline (see Chapter 8, Organizational Change Management). The two dimensions to be distinguished according to the definition must again be considered here:

1. those competences that are needed to change the company – that is, to even enable it to be successful in the future; and
2. those strategic core competences that are changed by the business transformation and are becoming increasingly important in achieving future success in the market – that is, after the business transformation.

The following metaphor should help to explain this difference: If a Formula One racing car spins off the track, a team's specialist expertise, for example, making speedy repairs, is needed to get the car back on course. As soon as this has been achieved, other competences – for example, quick reactions or skillful driving – are needed to manoeuvre the car back into pole position. However, this distinction is sometimes only analytic in nature because, for example, leadership competences, which are to be given particular consideration during a business transformation, should continue to be fostered after the transformation has ended.

This is particularly valid in view of the fact that business transformation does not represent a one-off, isolated process that is to be concluded once and for all, but has much more the character of a recurring cycle that takes place at many levels.

The competence strategy is an independent part of the transformation strategy, although this is primarily developed on the basis of important findings from the other management disciplines. Because only from a forecast of the market development and of the company's targeted future position can the future team members' tasks and resulting necessary competences be derived. Development of the competence strategy is also based on the results of the stakeholder analysis in accordance with the organizational change management discipline. In the "performance management" step of this discipline, the HR systems are also aligned with the change objectives, thereby supporting sustained behavioral change.

Developing a competence strategy as part of business transformation does not differ in terms of its methodology from elaborating other competence and HR strategies, and is done using the usual tools, for example, holding interviews, workshops and meetings, as well as including various stakeholder groups, such as educational managers, customers, team members, employees' representatives and experts from the areas of competence management, training management and HR.

CHALLENGES CONCERNING PREPARATION AND STRATEGY DEVELOPMENT:
1. Identify target groups to define team members' competence requirements.
2. Derive future team members' tasks and resulting necessary competences based on company's targeted future position.
3. Develop a competence strategy.

KEY MESSAGE:
The competence strategy is an independent part of the transformation strategy, although this is primarily developed on the basis of important findings from the other strategic subdisciplines.

9.2.2 NEED ANALYSIS

In the need analysis, the competence strategy is specified and operationalized: with the help of the job families and job profile cards tools, the target groups can be specified in accordance with the competence strategy and attributed with corresponding competence requirements.

Job families

To better structure future competence requirements and target groups, the job families tool can be used. job families consolidate different job positions or roles using similar competence areas. This means that from a company's perspective, resources can be grouped together and effective training programs devised to further develop these specific competences. For team members, core areas of their (future) development, which they need for their career planning, become transparent. Examples of structuring factors that can be considered for the development of job families are roles (such as project manager, business transformation manager, technical expert or general management), functional areas (such as research and development, production, logistics, finances, HR and so on), hierarchies (such as division managers, institute directors, employees, assistants and so on) or geographical criteria (global, national, regional).

With competence structuring, we focus on a comprehensive competence concept that includes cognitive competences (knowledge), functional competences (skills), as well as meta and social competences (for example, leadership skills or general problem-solving skills) (Winterton et al., 2006). Figure 9.2 shows an example of how various hierarchical positions with comparable competence areas (but different parameters) can be structured.

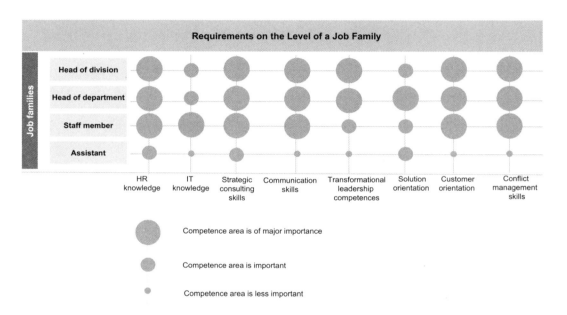

Figure 9.2　Example of competence requirements at a job family level

Job profile card

While job families provide an overview display of target groups, job profile cards enable the requirements at a position level or individual level to be selectively visualized (see Figure 9.3). Job profile cards help to determine the necessary core competences at an individual protagonist level and can also be used for recruiting measures. They also ensure the consistent description and comparability of future job profiles. Determining the requirements at this individualized level is recommended for core groups involved in the business transformation, such as a business transformation manager.

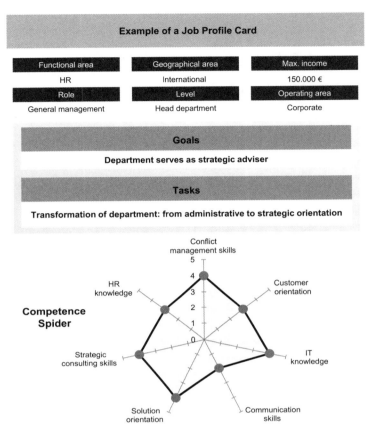

Figure 9.3   Job profile cards

CHALLENGES CONCERNING THE NEED ANALYSIS:

1.   Group resources together in order to devise effective training programs.
2.   Determine the necessary core competences at an individual protagonist level and use them for recruiting measures.
3.   Structure competence requirements and target groups.
4.   Selectively visualize the requirements at a position level or individual level.

9.2.3 AS-IS AND GAP ANALYSIS

In the next step, the defined requirements are compared with the actual situation at present and important gaps and training needs are identified for the respective target groups. The process can be split into two steps as follows:

Analysis of the current competence landscape in accordance with the defined target groups and competence requirements

Application of the methodology when determining competences depends on the current competence management level. The higher the quality, the more data can be directly retrieved from it. Other HR sources, for example, information from employee and management assessment, quality reports, yellow pages or supervisor reports, can also be used and analyzed. The less information can be retrieved from the existing systems, the more crucial it is to generate primary data. For this purpose a methodological repertoire is available, which can be used depending on the transformation context, such as the resources, company size and scope of the transformation. While group interviews (focus groups) can be sufficient for carrying out job analysis and for determining the currently existing competences in small organizations, to achieve usable results, quantitative procedures, such as questionnaires, tend to be used in larger organizations in addition to qualitative data collection. Transformational and transactional leadership competences can be determined quantitatively (Avolio et al., 1999; Bass, 1990; Bryant, 2003). Managers with transformational competences can motivate and inspire their team members without explicit incentive systems such as reward and punishment. For key positions in a transformation program, for example, when determining the competences of a business transformation manager, considerably more time-consuming methods such as 360° feedback or in-depth interviews are appropriate.

Actual/planned situation comparison and gap analysis

When comparing the actual situation with the results of the previously carried out need analysis, job families (on a generic level) and job profile cards (for an individual level) can again be used for identifying and visualizing differences (see Figure 9.4). Representations such as these make it easier to complete the identification of qualification requirements.

At this point, it should be noted that in addition to using the right competence tools, the manner of implementation also plays a major role. In business transformation at an HR organization of a major telecommunications company, the following implementation factors in particular were viewed critically: Integration with organizational processes, rewards and recognition mechanisms (cf. performance management in Chapter 8, Organizational Change Management), the close involvement of participating individuals not only in the planning and structuring phases but also the implementation phase, the use of numerous information channels, as well as measuring and evaluating the competences (Morris, 1996).

With major strategic changes, it might not be possible to offset all changed competence requirements with training measures. In this case, job profile cards can also prove very useful when recruiting new team members who bring with them the required competences. There are also numerous examples where, in the scope of transformation projects (such as acquisition and merger), not only individual new team members were taken on but completely new companies were purchased to fill "competence gaps" (Pollack, 2009).

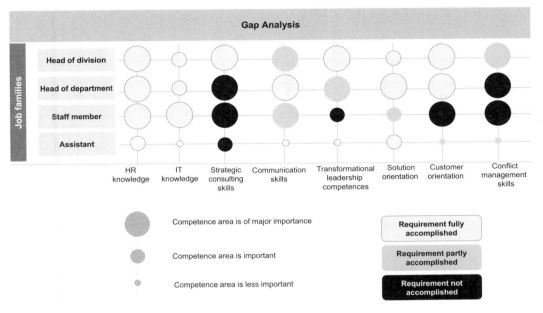

Figure 9.4 **Gap analysis at job family level**

CHALLENGES CONCERNING THE AS-IS AND GAP ANALYSIS:

1. Analyze information from employee and management assessment, quality reports, yellow pages or supervisor reports.
2. Determine qualitatively and quantitatively transformational and transactional leadership competences.
3. Compare the defined requirements with the actual situation at present.
4. Identify important gaps and training needs for the target groups.

KEY MESSAGE:

For key positions in a transformation program, for example, when determining the competences of a business transformation manager, considerably more time-consuming methods such 360° feedback or in-depth interviews are appropriate.

9.2.4 CURRICULUM PREPARATION AND TRAINING

Once competence gaps and training requirements have been identified at job families and job profile cards level, the next step involves preparing the training curriculum. A number of aspects and issues must be considered here:

- Specify learning objectives and scope: What should be learned? What should the learners be able to do/know after training?

- Identify internal/external training products/providers or develop new training offerings.
- Structure and compile training and create a curriculum.
- Prepare (individual) training plans and time schedules.

First, the competence differences should be converted into concrete learning objectives at a curriculum level and later at a course level. It must be ensured that the learning objectives address the identified gaps. The next step involves analyzing whether training products exist in the company itself or on the market that can ensure that the learning objectives will be achieved.

This decision must be taken in view of strategic company objectives and transformation objectives, the available budget, and other prevailing conditions, such as learning prerequisites or media competences of the team members, trainer experience, cultures and technological factors, for example, software architecture or hardware equipment (Gröhbiel and Schiefner, 2002). If the competences are very specific and of major significance for the company's future success, outsourcing the training to an external training provider would entail considerable risks, even in spite of any cost-saving potential. In this case, the training is carried out by internal providers, who might still have to develop or expand the training courses.

However, attention must be paid to an appropriate level of didactic quality, both when developing the company's own training and purchasing external training. This includes taking a balanced and varied combination of methods, learning forms, processes, social and communication forms, and media into account (Bachmann et al., 2004; Leclercq and Poumay, 2005). Attention must also be paid to a balanced didactic portfolio in view of the proximity to the working process; while abstract, decontextualized knowledge can also be conveyed in seminars and training courses away from the workplace, business transformation in particular requires practical competences and therefore didactic measures that are close to the working process, for example, coaching or mentoring programs or action learning – group-based "actions" and the subsequent discussion using authentic problem scenarios (Revans, 1982).

The various elements that are developed and/or purchased on the market are combined as overall curricula in accordance with the desired granularity and specific training plans are drawn up for the target groups. The team of trainers, mentors and e-learning authors must also be assembled. Since trainers for complex training tasks in the context of business transformation usually also have to be trained, this must be considered and scheduled as early as the start of step 4.

If the business transformation is linked to the implementation of software, training sessions should be carried out a week before using the system. Particular attention should be paid to ensuring that, during IT training, not only the operating steps are conveyed, but that "subject matter experts" explain and embed the applications in the respective business contexts. While piloting is also recommended for non-IT-based training, its significance is essential when it comes to e-learning training – for example, in the form of usability tests.

It is important that the training measures are coordinated centrally and uniformly. However, the ownership should be anchored in the respective business area. Critical factors for success can be classified into three categories: resources, time and budget. First, the management must be sufficiently committed and provide the relevant "human resources", such as trainers, authors and subject matter experts. The latter should also carry out a training review or provide expert input even before this is done. Second, the timescale must not be too restricted. The time required for planning and implementing training measures is often underestimated and the organizational benefits of the training measures are generally communicated too late. Third, there is also the risk of underestimating the costs of carrying out the training – for example, hiring rooms and providing training (information) systems and tools.

CHALLENGES CONCERNING THE CURRICULUM PREPARATION AND TRAINING:

1. Convert competence differences into concrete learning objectives at a curriculum level and later at a course level.
2. Analyze whether training products exist in the company itself or on the market.
3. Take care of an appropriate level of didactic quality, both when developing the company's own training and purchasing external training.
4. Pay attention to a balanced didactic portfolio in view of the proximity to the working process.
5. Assemble the team of trainers, mentors and e-learning authors.
6. Coordinate training measures centrally and uniformly.

KEY MESSAGE:
Business transformation requires practical competences and therefore didactic measures that are close to the working process, for example, coaching or mentoring programs or action learning – group-based "actions" and the subsequent discussion using authentic problem scenarios.

9.2.5 TRANSFER AND EVALUATION

In the preceding sections, we have already mentioned the application and so-called *transfer problems*, and in this part, we will take another more in-depth look at these issues. The challenge of *transferring* the acquired knowledge and the skills from the training to everyday (transformation) situations is conveyed in the following statement:

> Most current training efforts do not result in a significant transfer of new skills or knowledge to the job.
>
> (Broad, 1997)

The transfer gap model (Wilkening, 2002) expresses this problem in a simplified way as it shows how, immediately following the training phase, the "actual" knowledge curve falls sharply as the *target* curve rises (see Figure 9.5). Although the model is simplistic, it still clearly visualizes the competence gap between the actual and target values and the significance of taking appropriate measures.

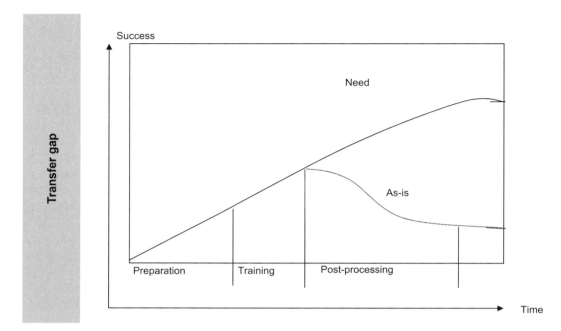

Figure 9.5   Transfer gap model

Source: Reproduced with permission from Wilkening, Otto S. (2002), Bildungs-Controlling
– Erfolgssteuerungssysteme der Personalentwickler und Wissensmanager, in *Strategien der
Personalentwicklung: Mit Praxisberichten von Bosch*, Gore, Hamburg-Mannheimer, Opel, Philips, Siemens,
Volkswagen, Weidmüller und Weka. 5th ed., edited by Hans-Christian Riekhof (Wiesbaden: Gabler).

There is a range of factors that influence transfer and application of knowledge. The most important organizational influencing variables include the organization's commitment to the training, the correlation between the department's objectives and the learning content, and an open team environment for communication. At an individual level, there are three important factors that influence the successful application of what has been learned. First, discussions with the supervisor that focus on directly applying this new knowledge and the skills acquired, the supervisor's positive feedback and the degree of his or her involvement. Second, the team members' feedback to the learner plays a part. And third, there is simply the opportunity to put all that has been learned into practice in everyday working situations (Lim and Johnson, 2002).

Especially during complex phases of business transformation, training in general and ensuring the transfer in particular tend to be neglected. In view of the major challenges and the practical transformation competences that these urgently necessitate, this can lead to particularly negative consequences. To avoid making a mockery of investments for training and to support their influence in practice, a range of measures need to be defined and implemented in addition to workplace-oriented training measures. This ideally begins even before a specific training session and only ends some considerable time after the training has been concluded. These measures include managing the learning transfer in both the field of learning as well as the field of application (Solga, 2011). The former envisage, for example, the use of practical and authentic materials as a prerequisite for successfully applying what has been learned to everyday working situations. Case studies or role plays can ensure that transformation problems, for example, for the training of transformation planning and leadership behavior, are authentically conveyed. To increase motivation and a sense of personal responsibility, for example, learning contracts can be agreed individually with the participants even before the training measure begins.

The degree to which they have been achieved is discussed after the training, for example, with a coach. "Follow-up meetings" or "transfer days" specially arranged for this purpose at which seminar participants repeat topics in a structured manner and discuss the previous transfer and application of knowledge are also worthwhile. The significance of transfer coaching by supervisors arises from the aforementioned influencing factors and, together with the support of line managers and colleagues, is ultimately critical to the level of success. Another measure worth mentioning is the integration of learning objectives in the regular performance review to ensure that the transfer is followed through as necessary and its degree of success is evaluated.

The ultimate level of success of a training measure is gauged during the evaluation. Typical mistakes that are made here lie in restricting the evaluation to participant satisfaction and the cost of the training. An evaluation of the effect at a business level as suggested, for example, by Kirkpatrick (1998) is also often left out. During one broadly based study, a third of the participants were unable to make any statement about the effect of the company's training investment (Gryger et al., 2010). In accordance with comprehensive controlling approach, i.e. the planning, realization and evaluation of educational measures, an overall distinction should be made between the three dimensions of *monetary*, *quantitative* and *qualitative* benefit and cost factors. Monetary controls should include the cost and benefit factors that can be measured in monetary terms – for example, training costs, savings and, if possible, the calculation of the monetary business impact. Factors that cannot be measured in monetary terms but are quantifiable are also considered. These could be, for example, time spent on the training and also time

CHALLENGES CONCERNING TRANSFER AND EVALUATION:

1.   Understand the most important organizational influencing variables (e.g. organization's commitment to the training or the correlation between the department's objectives and the learning content).
2.   Define measures that manage the learning transfer in both the field of learning as well as the field of application.
3.   Agree individually learning contracts with the participants even before the training measure begins.
4.   Analyze the degree to which the learning contracts have been achieved after the training, for example, with a coach.
5.   Evaluate the effect of the training at a business level.

KEY MESSAGE:

Ensuring that training sessions are oriented to higher-level transformation objectives is much more meaningful than simple monetarization, even if evaluating these objectives does not always result in something quantifiable.

savings, which are specified in hours or days. After all, criteria will emerge that can only be determined on a qualitative basis but are no less important as a result. The satisfaction or acceptance of learners, team members or customers are examples of this (Gröhbiel et al., 2010). It would be very oversimplified and foolhardy within the context of a business transformation to consider only short-term monetary aspects and to restrict the focus, for example, to the costs. Ensuring that training sessions are oriented to higher-level transformation objectives is much more meaningful than simple monetarization, even if evaluating these objectives does not always result in something quantifiable.

9.3 The Significance of a Working Environment

Instructional training measures can only influence the competence development and learning of the team members to a certain extent. Whereas the learners' biographical and personal characteristics or experiences are decisive in their competence development (Bates et al., 2005), even the definition of work-based learning as learning *for*, *at* and *through* work (Evans, 2011) shows the limited scope of training. Classical training offerings (*for work*) usually take place away from the workplace in specially constructed training and further education centers. In addition, however, there are also informal and implicit forms of learning in a more immediate work context – for example, learning from being accompanied by a coach at the workplace (*at work*) – or the development of competences resulting from work itself (*through work*) – for example, by solving a problem or working together with colleagues. For all these forms, the context of work – which can be characterized by social, cultural, temporal, spatial, technological or thematic dimensions – is vital; working conditions that promote learning need to be created (e.g. Hardwig, 2006). Taking the work context into consideration for competence development and learning is especially relevant against the background of a business transformation that is characterized by particularly unstable conditions and uncertainty. Although putting an environment into practice that promotes learning and transformation is complex and can scarcely be managed by individual positions or even individual educational managers and trainers; it is of such significance for competence development that it seems important at this point to identify some key basic principles of favorable working and learning conditions. Further information about the context of business transformation can be found in Chapter 2, Meta Management.

In view of the complex dynamics of a rapidly changing working world (Hagel and Brown, 2010), competence development and learning are firmly anchored in the processes of experimenting with and trying out new things, solving problems together and sharing knowledge with talented team members in authentic working contexts. Collaboration that has an influence on learning takes place in a variety of extensive and rather loosely structured networks or communities (Fuller and Unwin, 2008) beyond company boundaries. According to Hagel and Brown (2010), this learning can be fostered by technological support in the form of flexible pull platforms. For example, IBM has implemented a search engine tool that enables informal and network-like learning by also linking search requests to experts, projects, discussions and so on (Veen et al., 2009). By using mobile devices such as smartphones, the company has also improved the networking of and cooperation between team members. What is remarkable is that the team members did hardly use their devices to complete the devised HR training units, but to obtain necessary information directly in the working process or to consult experienced colleagues. In particular, this stimulated contact and networking between the learners and people beyond their own working groups, with *weak ties* (Ahmad and Orion, 2010). This can promote the dissemination of ideas and innovations beyond the team and the organizational unit. Ideally, the flow of information takes place according to the just-in-time respectively *pull principle* (Hagel et al., 2009), as the above IBM example shows. Also the pull platform from Toyota can be considered as an initial, albeit still limited approach to these principles.

> *Pull platforms are essential to fostering learning on the job, since they make it easier to access unexpected resources in unexpected ways and thereby encourage participants to try new approaches.*
>
> (Hagel et al., 2009)

The management's attitude to the team members and to cross-company cooperation is also of pivotal importance for the development of competences. If cooperation and the sharing of knowledge are perceived as a *zero-sum game* or even as a potential loss of personal property, the conditions for learning and the development of talent are extremely unfavorable. In contrast, they are greatly facilitated when open cooperation in the form of a *collaboration disposition*, even beyond company boundaries, is taken for granted and perceived as an opportunity from which everyone involved can learn and profit (Hagel et al., 2009).

CHALLENGES CONCERNING THE SIGNIFICANCE OF A WORKING ENVIRONMENT:

1. Facilitate an open working and learning culture characterized by the sharing of knowledge across institutional boundaries.
2. Foster collaboration that has influence on learning by technological support in the form of flexible pull platforms.

KEY MESSAGE:

If cooperation and the sharing of knowledge are perceived as a "zero-sum game" or even as a potential loss of personal property, the conditions for learning and the development of talent are extremely unfavorable.

9.4 Conclusion

Competence and training management mainly address qualification and enablement of peers required to fulfill the business transformation. Competence and Training Management consists of six steps:

1. Identify target groups at a high level in view of the company's future value chain and specify associated tasks and competences.
2. Specify and operationalize the competence strategy.
3. Compare the defined requirements with the actual situation at present and identify important gaps as well as training needs for the respective target groups.
4. Prepare the curriculum.
5. Train the curriculum.
6. Transfer the acquired knowledge and the skills from the training to everyday (transformation) situations.

Finally, this chapter discussed the significance of a working environment and in particular of pull platforms, which foster learning.

Bibliography

Ahmad, Nabeel and Orion, Peter (2010), Smartphones make IBM smarter, but not as expected, *Training & Development*.

Avolio, Bruce J., Bass, Bernard M. and Jung, Dong I. (1999), Re-examining the components of transformational and transactional leadership using the Multifactor Leadership, *Journal of Occupational and Organizational Psychology* 72, no. 4, 441–62.

Bachmann, Gudrun, Dittler, Martina and Tesa, Gerhild (2004), Didaktik und Lernen, *UNI NOVA Wissenschaftsmagazin der Universität Basel, Neues Lernen,* no. 98, 15–17.

Bass, Bernard M. (1990), From transactional to transformational leadership: learning to share the vision, *Organizational Dynamics* 18, no. 3, 19–31.

Bates, P., Hunt, Will and Hillage, J. (2005), Learning at work: strategies for widening adult participation in learning below Level 2 via the workplace: a scoping study, Report 052230, Learning and Skills Development Agency.

Broad, Mary L. (1997), Overview of transfer of training: from learning to performance, *Performance Improvement Quarterly* 10, no. 2, 7–21.

Bryant, Scott E. (2003), The role of transformational and transactional leadership in creating, sharing and exploiting organizational knowledge, *Journal of Leadership & Organizational Studies* 9, no. 4, 32–44.

Dingens, Angelika and Bach, Norbert (2009), Ziele definieren – sicher Ankommen. Professionelle Steuerung von Veränderungsprozessen und der Beitrag des Human Resource Managements, *KPMG Studie*, KPMG AG.

Evans, Karen (2011), Work-based learning – setting the scene, in *Work-based Mobile Learning: Concepts and Cases,* edited by Norbert Pachler, Christoph Pimmer and Judith Seipold (Oxford: Peter Lang).

Fuller, Alison and Unwin, Lorna (2008), Towards expansive apprenticeships: a commentary by the teaching and learning research programme, TLRP.

Gröhbiel, Urs and Schiefner, Mandy (2002), Die E-Learning-Entscheidungsmatrix, in *Handbuch E-Learning,* edited by Andreas Hohenstein and Karl Wilbers (Köln: Dt. Wirtschaftsdienst).

Gröhbiel, Urs, Stoller-Schai, Daniel and Plimmer, Christoph (2010), E-Learning: Den Mehrwert steuern, *PERSONAL*, no. 1.

Gryger, Liz, Saar, Tom and Schaar, Patti (2010), Building organizational capabilities: McKinsey Global Survey results, *McKinsey Quarterly* (McKinsey & Company).

Hagel, John and Seely Brown, John (2010), Six fundamental shifts in the way we work, *Harvard Business Review*: http://blogs.hbr.org/bigshift/2010/08/six-fundamental-shifts-in-the.html (accessed March 2012).

Hagel, John, Seely Brown, John and Davison, Lang (2009), Talent is everything, The Conference Board Review: www.johnseelybrown.com/talentiseverything.pdf (accessed March 2012).

Hardwig, Thomas (2006), Worauf kommt es bei der betrieblichen Gestaltung lernförderlicher Rahmenbedingungen eigentlich an?, in *Arbeitsprozessorientierte Weiterbildung: Lernprozesse gestalten, Kompetenzen entwickeln*, 1st ed., edited by Claudia Loroff, Katja Manski and Walter Mattauch (Bielefeld: Bertelsmann).

Keller, Scott, Meaney, Mary and Pung, Caroline (2010), What successful transformations share: McKinsey Global Survey results, *McKinsey Quarterly* (McKinsey & Company).

Kirkpatrick, Donald L. (1998), *Evaluating Training Programs: The Four Levels*, 2nd ed. (San Francisco, CA: Berrett-Koehler).

Leclercq, Dieudonné and Poumay, Marianne (2005), The 8 Learning Events Model and its principles, LabSET, University of Liège: www.labset.net/media/prod/8LEM.pdf (accessed March 2012).

Lim, Doo H. and Johnson, Scott D. (2002), Trainee perceptions of factors that influence learning transfer, *International Journal of Training and Development* 6, no. 1, 36–48.

Morris, Deborah (1996), Using competency development tools as a strategy for change in the human resources function: a case study, *Human Resource Management* 35, no. 1, 35–51.

Pollack, Andrew (2009), Roche agrees to buy Genentech for $46.8 billion, *New York Times*: www.nytimes.com/2009/03/13/business/worldbusiness/13drugs.html (accessed March 2012).

Revans, Reginald W. (1982), What is action learning?, *Journal of Management Development* 1, no. 3, 64–75.

Solga, Marc (2011), Förderung von Lerntransfer, in *Praxishandbuch Personalentwicklung*, edited by Jurij Ryschka, Marc Solga and Axel Mattenklott (Wiesbaden: Gabler).

Veen, Wim, Lukosch, Heide and de Vries, Pieter (2009), Improving organizational learning through networked learning, in *Fifth Conference Professional Knowledge Management, Experiences and Visions: [WM 2009]*, March 25–27, 2009 in Solothurn, Switzerland: 22–31.

Wilkening, Otto S. (2002), Bildungs-Controlling – Erfolgssteuerungssysteme der Personalentwickler und Wissensmanager, in *Strategien der Personalentwicklung: Mit Praxisberichten von Bosch, Gore, Hamburg-Mannheimer, Opel, Philips, Siemens, Volkswagen, Weidmüller und Weka*, 5th ed., edited by Hans-Christian Riekhof (Wiesbaden: Gabler).

Winterton, Jonathan, Delamare-Le Deist, Françoise and Stringfellow, Emma (2006), *Typology of Knowledge, Skills and Competences: Clarification of the Concept and Prototype* (Luxembourg: Office for Official Publications of the European Communities).

10 Program and Project Management

MICHAEL ROSEMANN, JAN RECKER, NORIZAN SAFRUDIN
(Queensland University of Technology) and
RONALD MARKETSMUELLER (SAP AG)

10.1 Overview

Program Management serves as an overall vehicle for the transformation effort (Pellegrinelli, 2011). It aims to support the implementation of the decided strategy in order to achieve the expected benefits in business transformations. A *program* is defined as a group of related projects managed in a coordinated way to obtain benefits and control unrealized when they are managed individually (Project Management Institute, 2008). A *project*, on the other hand, is a temporary endeavor undertaken to create a unique product, service or result. Projects tend to have definite start and finish points, with the aim of delivering a predetermined output, giving them relatively clear development paths from initiation to delivery. Programs, on the contrary, exist to create value by enriching the management of projects in isolation (Lycett et al., 2004). Programs typically have a more strategic vision of the desired end goal, but no clearly defined path to get there. Therefore, Program Management is expected to deal with the uncertainty surrounding the achievement of the vision, whereas projects work best where the outputs can be well defined. As Project Management is embedded within Program Management, this chapter will predominantly focus on Program Management, with Project Management being discussed as a tangential topic.

Program and Project Management mainly address the engage phase, with some also playing a role in the transform phase for business transformation success:

1. Engage: During this phase, programs are set up and executed to deliver the specific benefits identified by Value Management. Furthermore, programs are coordinated and its components and projects are integrated. Last, quality requirements are identified and the need for additional capacity and skills is evaluated.
2. Transform: This phase monitors the allocated budget and time to ensure that they are not exceeded throughout the business transformation. It also considers realistically how much effort it would take to complete a business transformation in terms of duration and cost.

OBJECTIVES OF THIS CHAPTER:
1. Understand the processes of Program and Project Management.
2. Understand the similarities and differences of skills between a project and program manager.
3. Learn about success factors for achieving the objectives of Program and Project Management.

10.2 The Role of Business Transformation Program and Project Management

Program and Project Management is part of the *enablement* type of BTM² (see Figure 10.1). Where the *direction* type provides the common vision and overarching course of action for business transformation, *enablement* ensures that the endeavor is executed in alignment with the goals and objectives of the business transformation. As such, program and project management function to provide a comprehensive methodology to deal with program and project management in business transformation by including the *best of breed* knowledge and experience in the field of managing scope, teams and human resources. The approach, at an operational level, can be complemented by known Program and Project Management methodologies.

Although programs provide benefits through better organization of projects, they do not in themselves deliver individual project objectives. Generally, the goal of project management (ILX Group, 2012) is to ensure that such projects are organized and controlled from initiation through to completion by organizing and planning things properly prior to commencement. Once this has been established, it is imperative to ensure that it continues to be organized and controlled, and when the project is finished, all loose ends need to be tidied up. By contrast, the two fundamental goals (ILX Group, 2012) of Program and Project Management are:

1. Efficiency and effectiveness goals – Incorporating an integrated approach to particular aspects of management in business transformation, including improving coordination, improving dependency management, utilizing resources effectively, effective knowledge transfer and greater senior management visibility.
2. Business focus goals – Aligning projects with the requirements, strategy, goals, business drivers and culture of the wider organization, by defining an appropriate direction for the embedded projects within a program, as well as for the program as a whole via a more coherent communication to stakeholders involved.

Many organizations struggle to execute major transformation programs successfully due to a range of reasons. Firstly, priorities and accountabilities are often not clear to the involved participants (Morello and Olding, 2008). Also, bureaucratic, ineffective and often manual management processes often hinder the ability to manage transformation programs successfully. Furthermore, overstretched resources and fragmented middle managers with lack of focus on what really matters can also pose as a barrier (Spreitzer, 1996). The lack of up-front preparation and thinking, as well as insufficient planning prevents structured reporting, thereby resulting in a *garbage in – garbage out* syndrome. As

Orchestration of individual disciplines:
guidelines, leadership, culture, values and communication

Meta Management	Direction			Enablement				
	Strategy Management	Value Management	Risk Management	Business Process Management	Transformation IT Management	Organizational Change Management	Competence and Training Management	Program and Project Management
	As-is data collection	Baseline analysis	360° strategic risk assessment	Determine scope of analysis	Business and IT capability assessment	Set-up and governance	Competence strategy	Program planning and governance
	Analysis of needs and maturity level	Value estimation	Risk identification	From template to bespoke inventory	To-be analysis	Stakeholder management	Training need analysis	Program/project integration management
	Design business vision	Detailed business case	Risk evaluation	Identify improvements/ add attributes	Gap analysis	Change agent network	As-is analysis	Program/ project scope management
	Design business model	Agree ownership for realization	Define risk response plan	Map selected processes	IT roadmap plan	Communication management	Gap analysis	Program/ project time and cost management
	Integrated transformation plan	Plan benefit realization	Execute risk mitigation plan	Plan process implementation	Solution architecture design	Performance management – project team	Curriculum development	Program quality management
	Business case	Execute benefit realization	Risk monitoring and reporting	Implement processes	IT deployment plan	Performance management - business	Training preparation	Program human resource management
	Organizational model	Review and evaluate results	Risk management review	Evaluate processes	IT operations and service optimization	Change readiness assessment	Training	Program procurement management
	Align with risk management	Establish potentials for further benefits	Risk management improvement	Establish improvement process	IT lifecycle management	Change monitoring	Evaluation and improvement	Program reporting

Figure 10.1 Program and Project Management as an enabler in business transformation

a consequence, problems identified in program and project management are often too late to deal with in the process of transforming the organization.

In response, Program and Project Management seeks to answer the following questions:

- What is the schedule, the involved resources and how should they work together?
- How do we coordinate the different projects within a program and make sure that they are aligned with the overall business transformation goals?
- What are the scope and objectives of the underlying programs and projects?
- How do we track time and costs and make sure that we are in line with the budget and value?
- How do we make sure that we follow best practices in terms of quality of work and the deliverables?
- How do we make sure that we have the right people, and the right place and at the right time?
- How do we ensure delegation to outside providers and optimize the invested capital?
- How do we track progress and inform our stakeholders?

This chapter will proceed as follows. We will first outline the eight steps for program and project management in business transformation. Next, a description of the roles and responsibilities for program and project managers is presented, followed by a discussion of the key skills required for these roles. The chapter then concludes by outlining lessons learned, providing a list of dos and don'ts of program management in business transformations, and summarizing the main results.

CHALLENGES CONCERNING THE BUSINESS TRANSFORMATION PROGRAM AND PROJECT MANAGEMENT:
1. Communicate priorities and accountabilities to involved participants.
2. Disburden resources and middle managers and communicate focus on what really matters.
3. Tackle up-front preparation and thinking, as well as planning.

KEY MESSAGE:
Program and Project Management provide a comprehensive methodology to deal with program and project management in business transformation by including the "best of breed" knowledge and experience in the field of managing scope, teams and human resources.

10.3 The Process of Business Transformation Program and Project Management

We define a business transformation program and project management framework that comprises of eight steps, which address the abovementioned challenges pertaining to the management of business transformation and the inherent projects. As can be seen in

Figure 10.2, the eight activities are mainly involved in the engage phase, with some also playing a role in the transform phase (see Chapter 2, Meta Management, for a detailed description of the transformation lifecycle):

1. Program planning and governance – primarily seeks to bring operational strategies in alignment with the vision of business transformation and define governing principles that establish the program structure.
2. Program and project integration management – focuses on establishing coordination measures to manage business transformation, its components and projects towards the transformation goal.
3. Program and project scope management – ensures that all key stakeholders involved approve of the extent to which the transformation effort will be executed.
4. Program and project time and cost management – defines the budget and time frame required.
5. Program quality management – establishes an environment that identifies and fulfills the quality requirements of the program.
6. Program human resource management – assembles the right people with the required skills to fulfill their respective responsibilities and value delivery.
7. Program procurement management – evaluates the need for additional capacity and skills, whether potential areas could be outsourced to.
8. Program reporting – ensures that the documentation of all changes, updates and performances are registered in a manner that is known to involved stakeholders.

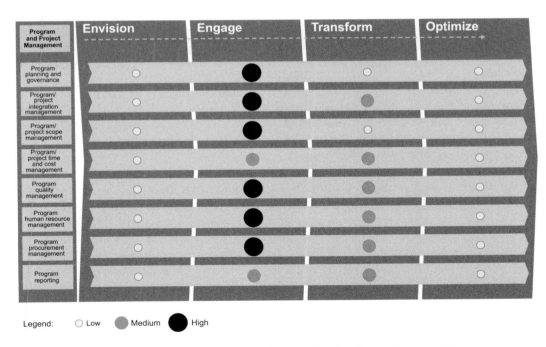

Figure 10.2 Activity level per process themes in the four phases of the transformation lifecycle

Details of these eight steps are outlined in the following subsections.

10.3.1 PROGRAM PLANNING AND GOVERNANCE

In this first key step, the basic structure for the program needs to be established. Before a program can be executed, program managers need to define the program organization and roles, define the procedures and communication channels between different entities and so forth. Tools and accelerators that can facilitate such engagement include program organization charts, standard roles, program escalation procedure sample and program organization templates. Thus, the approach can simply be seen as relying primarily on previous project and program experience. Indeed, our own studies on business transformation project roles in the United States and Asia-Pacific (Safrudin et al., 2011) show that the minimum number of years taken to be considered as an experienced program manager is five to ten years, while a project manager requires a minimum of three to eight years of experience.

The deliverables for program planning include:

- program management plan;
- program goals, benefits and values;
- program roadmap updates;
- governance plan;
- updated organization charts;
- defined roles; and
- escalation process.

Program and project management integrate all subsidiary program plans into a cohesive overall program management plan. It also updates the program roadmap accordingly if necessary. This is an iterative process, as competing priorities, assumptions, dependencies and constraints are resolved to address critical factors, such as business goals, deliverables, benefits, time and cost. The program management team, in conjunction with major stakeholders, establishes the key governance principles and ensures that the correct structure is in place to encourage effective and appropriate governance.

Governance structures ensure that the program goals and objectives are aligned with the strategic goals and objectives of the enterprise for which the program is being developed. Effective governance ensures that the strategic alignment and the value that has been promised are realized and benefits are delivered (Project Management Institute, 2008):

Program governance is the process of developing, communicating, implementing, monitoring, and assuring the policies, procedures, organizational structures and practices associated with a given program. The result is a framework for efficient and effective decision-making and delivery management focused on achieving program goals in a consistent manner, addressing appropriate risks and stakeholder requirements.

Program governance ensures that decision-making and delivery management activities are focused on achieving program goals in a consistent manner. This includes addressing appropriate risks and fulfilling stakeholder requirements. Governance for programs is different than governance for most projects, because the scope and impact of a program is typically complex and spans across multiple projects and therefore project governance structures. Examples of factors contributing to this complexity are multi-year timelines, competition between projects for scarce resources, diverse stakeholder requirements, as well as inter-project and enterprise-level risks and issues.

As can be seen in Figure 10.3, the task of program planning is to orchestrate the inherent projects in alignment with the business transformation strategy. Therefore, tools and methods such as, but not limited to, program governance, multi-project steering,

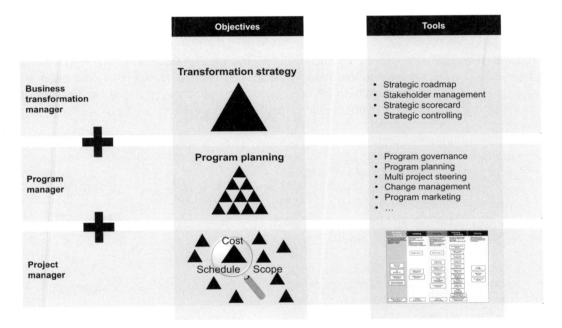

Figure 10.3 Programs link projects with the strategy of an organization

---

CHALLENGES CONCERNING THE PROGRAM PLANNING AND GOVERNANCE:

1. Integrate all subsidiary program plans into a cohesive overall program management plan.
2. Update the program roadmap if required.
3. Orchestrate the projects inherent in a program in alignment with the organizational business transformation strategy.
4. Ensure that decision-making and delivery management activities are focused on achieving program goals in a consistent manner.

KEY MESSAGE:

The minimum number of years taken to be considered as an experienced program manager is five to ten years, while a project manager requires a minimum of three to eight years of experience.

change management, program marketing and others can facilitate the deployment of multiple projects. Objective factors such as cost, schedule and scope of the projects, will need to be aligned with the business transformation strategy as delivered by the business transformation manager. Associated tools and methods that may benefit such communication include strategic roadmap, strategic scorecard, stakeholder management, strategic controlling and others.

10.3.2 PROGRAM AND PROJECT INTEGRATION MANAGEMENT

Program and project integration management is a critical step because many organizations do not integrate these two disciplines together well (Lycett et al., 2004). This step ensures that the program, its components and projects, and all the program activities from the program processes are well coordinated and integrated (see Figure 10.4), in order to achieve the expected program benefits in a consistent way. This process aims at planning the support structure that will enable the program to successfully achieve its goals (Project Management Institute, 2008):

> The Program Integration Management Knowledge Area includes the processes and activities needed to identify, define, combine, unify, and coordinate multiple components within the program as well as coordinate the various processes and program management activities within the program management process groups.

To that end, a program support structure consists of:

- core program management and governance teams;
- resource planning and management (personnel, tools, facilities and finances);
- program management framework (selected processes);
- program management office; and
- integration into the meta management structure of business transformation, especially value management.

Specifically, program and project integration management describes an important interface to BTM^2 (see Chapter 2, Meta Management) and also needs to correspond with value management (see Chapter 4, Value Management). Moreover, integration management also takes care of tactical issues and risks. Such issues are unplanned events, concerns or disputes that may have an impact on cost, schedule, technical architecture or other program areas. Therefore, issue management and control at the program level also includes addressing the issues escalated from the constituent projects that could not be resolved at the project level. These unresolved project issues can impact the overall progress of the program and must be tracked. Examples of methods and accelerators that can be used in this step include:

- project management office start-up roadmap;
- program change logs;
- program change requests;
- issue log files or databases; and
- program risk management.

Deliverables that arise from program and project integration management typically include:

- program management plan;
- update the program roadmap;
- program roadmap updates;
- governance plan;
- updated organization charts;
- defined roles; and
- escalation process.

Figure 10.4 summarizes how program management performances the linkage between the overall transformation management and the management of the individual projects within this initiative.

Transformation Management	Program Management	Project Management
• Identifies drivers for transformation	• Builds bridge between strategy and realization	• Initiates and oversees the project
• Supports transformation strategy development	• Plans and develops the overall program plan	• Provides the program management recommendations on requirements, costs and schedule
• Analyzes transformation readiness	• Provides policy and program direction	
• Plans programs together with program managers	• Aligns programs and projects with corporate goals and objectives	• Defines the project objectives and how the project will be organized, staffed and managed
• Establishes transformation governance including guidelines and principles	• Conducts multiple year program planning and identifies annual milestones	• Defines the program management approach and optimizes the procurement strategies
• Supports and steers transformation strategy execution until strategic objectives are achieved	• Establishes and justifies need for project within the program	• Develops the project execution plan
• Acts as trusted adviser for senior management	• Supports strategic and mid-term transformation planning efforts	• Understands transformation strategy and program goals and strategies
• Updates strategy if needed	• Is valid until program objectives are achieved	• Provides input for the program strategic plan

Figure 10.4 The link between transformation, Program and Project Management

CHALLENGES CONCERNING THE PROGRAM AND PROJECT INTEGRATION MANAGEMENT:

1. Plan the support structure that will enable the program to achieve its goals successfully.
2. Address key tactical issues and risks.

KEY MESSAGE:

Unresolved project issues (unplanned events, concerns or disputes that may have an impact on cost, schedule, technical architecture or other program areas) can impact the overall progress of the program and must be closely monitored.

10.3.3 PROGRAM AND PROJECT SCOPE MANAGEMENT

While the high-level program scoping is done in the envision phase, the detailed program scope is defined and benefits analyzed in the engage phase of business transformation. In this phase, the step program and project scope management seeks to reach a consensus with key stakeholders on the program plan and benefits, as well as on staffing key resources. The preliminary program scope is the first formulation of the program scope statement, which will be finalized in the program charter. This common acknowledgment among several stakeholders can be managed with scoping workshops, with the aim of managing and adjusting the scope of program and related projects over time.

The essential task of program scoping is to ensure that all key stakeholders of the program achieve a common understanding of the program mandate and approve it. Typical program key stakeholders include:

- sponsors;
- program manager (if already named);
- CxOs; and
- future steering committee members.

Examples of tools, techniques and accelerators that can facilitate program and project scope management include:

- the SAP roadmap global ASAP template, for preliminary program scope definition;
- the SAP FS project management methodology, for preliminary scope statement development; and
- the program charter, for commencing implementation planning for the program.

This step provides deliverables such as an approved program scope statement (also called program charter) in relation to the vision, goals and objectives. The program charter is the summary document that provides a solid foundation, which helps to reduce risk and ensure a successful implementation.

CHALLENGES CONCERNING THE PROGRAM AND PROJECT SCOPE MANAGEMENT:

1. Formulate the program scope statement, which will be finalized in the program charter.
2. Manage and adjust the scope of the program and its related projects over time.
3. Ensure that all key stakeholders of the program achieve a common understanding of the program mandate and approve and commit to it.

KEY MESSAGE:

Deliverables of program and project scope management is a program charter, which is a summary document that provides a solid foundation, which helps to reduce risk and ensure a successful implementation.

10.3.4 PROGRAM AND PROJECT TIME AND COST MANAGEMENT

This fourth step aims to define the budget and time constraints for the different components of the program and the involved projects. Managing time and cost are of importance specifically in the engage and transform phases (see Figure 10.2). In the engage phase, Program and Project Management is responsible for setting up and executing programs that deliver the specific benefits identified by Value Management. During the transform phase, program and project management is responsible that the allocated budget and time are not exceeded throughout business transformation, but also to consider realistically how much business transformation would take to complete in terms of duration and cost. In doing so, management needs to plan a project time frame in order to assign budgets to projects. This will facilitate time reporting, costs providing and monitoring of expenses for business transformation managers, as well as plan budgets for subsequent phases. In turn, these activities support value management (see Chapter 4) by estimating the boundaries of value achievement.

Some tools and accelerators that may assist in this step include program controlling tools, program plans and budget planning procedures. The outcome of these tools will provide deliverables such as:

- capacity planning;
- program controlling procedures;
- actual and forecast charts; and
- burn rate charts.

CHALLENGES CONCERNING THE PROGRAM AND PROJECT TIME AND COST MANAGEMENT:
1. Plan a project time frame in order to assign budgets to projects.
2. Initiate time reporting, costs providing and monitoring of expenses for business transformation managers, as well as plan budgets for subsequent phases.

KEY MESSAGE:
A project time frame will facilitate time reporting, costs providing and monitoring of expenses for business transformation managers, as well as plan budgets for subsequent phases.

10.3.5 PROGRAM QUALITY MANAGEMENT

The objective of program quality management is to implement a program environment that ensures that quality requirements are identified, understood and fulfilled through all parts of the program and through all program activities and related projects. Program quality management is thus the process of meeting the quality required to ensure that not only deliverables of all projects are of adequate quality, but that they can be combined to create the necessary capabilities that will deliver the long-term objectives of the program. Therefore, quality management activities include those at the program level, plus all relevant and related activities within the component projects. In practice, it is common for component projects to have their own quality management function with individual management plans, quality audit and control activities, deliverable checklists and quality metrics. For this reason, some elements of quality management may be delegated from the program level to the project level. Program quality planning is the process of identifying the quality standards of the program and determining how to adhere to those standards within each of the involved projects. One way of doing so, for example, is by means of SAP's quality management plan, which identifies relevant quality assurance services within a program and describes how to achieve quality throughout the program.

As depicted in Figure 10.5, program quality management entails a series of inputs and outputs, where the input entails a value realization plan, program scope management, stakeholder management plan and program management plan. The process outputs include a quality management plan, program cost of quality and process quality improvement

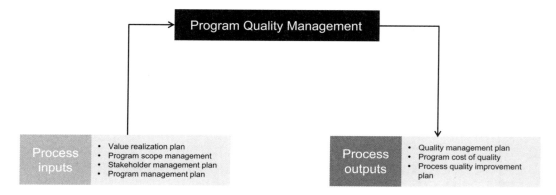

Figure 10.5 Program quality management

plan. Tools that can be utilized in this step include program quality management plan template, program cost of quality template and process quality improvement plan template. The anticipated deliverables include quality management plan, program cost of quality and a process quality improvement plan. Three dimensions are defined to substantiate the program quality management step, namely: program quality assurance, program quality audits and program quality management control. These dimensions are described in the following.

Program quality assurance

This is the process of executing quality audits at key milestones in the program, with a focus on ensuring the delivery of business benefits. The purpose of performing quality assurance is to evaluate overall program performance regularly to provide confidence it complies with the relevant quality standards. Quality assurance is a prevention-driven process to prevent mistakes from entering into the program and its component projects. Quality assurance control inspects both program and project work to ensure that the deliverables are of quality to keep mistakes from entering in the client's hands. Findings as an output lead to the need to issue a change request that are needed for:

- quality improvement – increase effectiveness of policies, procedures and processes for added benefits to stakeholders;
- corrective action – bring expected future performance in line with the program management plan; and
- preventive action – reduce the probability of negative consequences associated with risk.

Program quality audits

The objective of quality audits is to ensure that the program achieves its business benefits. This stems from the agreement and implementation of improvement plans in response to the findings from the audits. Specific areas at the program level to audit are:

- effectiveness of risk management (see Chapter 5, Risk Management), particularly in relation to the risks to deliver the long-term business benefits;
- interfaces among projects and other initiatives within the organization that may compete for limited resources or generate inter-project risk;
- engagement with stakeholders, including proactive consideration of their interests in the program and the impact of the changes on them; and
- exploitation and use of lessons learned across projects.

Program quality management control

This is the process of ensuring that program work and activities meet the defined quality objectives and attributes. The purpose of program quality management control is to monitor specific program deliverables and results to see if they fulfill quality requirements, identify faulty outcomes and eliminate causes of unsatisfactory performance at all stages of the quality loop. This is typically carried out throughout the program delivery and closure phases, whereby quality reviews and checklists are used to see that the quality plans are executed at the project level. Quality management control covers:

- solution and services;
- deliverables;
- program and project management results;
- cost, schedule and scope performance; and
- achievement of defined values.

> ## CHALLENGES CONCERNING THE PROGRAM QUALITY MANAGEMENT:
>
> 1. Execute quality audits at key milestones in the program, with the focus being on ensuring the delivery of business benefits.
> 2. Agree and implement improvement plans in response to the findings from the audits.
> 3. Ensure that program work and activities meet the defined quality objectives and attributes.
>
> ## KEY MESSAGE:
>
> It is common for component projects to have their own quality management function with individual management plans, quality audit and control activities, deliverable checklists and quality metrics. Some elements of quality management may be delegated from the program level to the project level.

10.3.6 PROGRAM HUMAN RESOURCE MANAGEMENT

This step ensures that companies have the right people, at the right place and at the right time in order to execute a successful business transformation. In doing so, program managers have to balance the available resources in order to deliver the optimized value to the program and set achievable targets and KPIs to the program team members. As part of program human resource management, performance procedures and metrics are defined and feedback is given to the line organization. Simply put, this step manages and addresses human factor issues where post-program roles and responsibilities are defined, relocations are managed and adequate career path are proposed. In essence, program human resource management seeks to create the right working environment in order to manage business transformations.

Examples of tasks that fall under this step include working with relevant HR departments, relevant resource management, departments and the organizational change management (OCM) leader, where applicable. As a result, deliverables will typically include:

- feedback reports;
- work certificates;
- capacity and load planning;
- KPIs;
- metrics;
- communications; and
- team events.

CHALLENGES CONCERNING THE PROGRAM HUMAN RESOURCE MANAGEMENT:

1. Balance the available resources in order to deliver the optimized value to the program.
2. Set achievable targets and key performance indicators to program team members.
3. Define performance procedures and metrics, and give feedback to the line organization.

KEY MESSAGE:

Program human resource management seeks to create the appropriate working environment in order to manage business transformations.

10.3.7 PROGRAM PROCUREMENT MANAGEMENT

The purpose of the program procurement management step is to evaluate the need for additional capacity and skills, as well as the selection of potential suppliers based on needed skills and resources. In doing so, this step evaluates potential areas to outsource or offshore, and also creates and negotiates all contracts for service providers and suppliers. Guidelines and frame agreements are communicated to project managers, which further requires the team to track progress as well as open issues. Other management tasks include managing the budget and make cost control, as well as to manage quality of services and deliverables.

Some examples, tools and accelerators that can be used in this step are using contract templates, involving purchasing and legal departments, make use of existing frame agreements and utilizing SAP ERP systems. The deliverables include:

- contracts;
- estimations;
- invoice checking;
- program controlling;
- budget tracking.

CHALLENGES CONCERNING THE PROGRAM PROCUREMENT MANAGEMENT:

1. Communicate guidelines and frame agreements to project managers, and require the team to track progress as well as open issues.
2. Manage the budget and implement cost controls, and manage quality of services and deliverables.

10.3.8 PROGRAM REPORTING

Based on component project work results, program reporting collates and defines program performance reports, incorporating the results from program audits and project audits. This reporting is required so that program governance can evaluate the program progress compared to the strategic plan, and raise any potential risk, identified issues or necessary change requests, at program or component level. This process aims to manage the program, according to the program management plan, in order to ensure that its components remain aligned with the program's strategic directives and business case.

Monitoring should be performed throughout the program lifecycle, and should include collecting, measuring and disseminating performance information, and assessing overall program trends. In turn, this process provides program management with the data necessary to determine the program's state and trends. Such information is key to identifying areas in potential need of correction. Considering potential changes to the program scope, the program reporting process examines the cost, schedule, quality, human resources, communications, risk and procurement impacts of the proposed change. If the change is approved, impacts of the approved change must be taken into consideration in the other program areas. This process assesses the issues and escalates where necessary.

Techniques and accelerators that can be used in this step are program change request, program change request log and templates for program performance report. Typical deliverables provided by program reporting include:

- approved change requests;
- update change request log;
- risk register updates;
- issue log updates;
- program performance report; and
- benefit/value reporting.

CHALLENGES CONCERNING THE PROGRAM REPORTING:

1. Evaluate program progress compared to the strategic plan, and raise any potential risks, identified issues or necessary change requests, at program or component level.
2. Monitor the program throughout its lifecycle, and collect, measure and disseminate performance information, and assess overall program trends.

10.4 Roles and Responsibilities of Program and Project Managers

Having defined the steps and deliverables of Program and Project Management, we now examine the key roles and responsibilities of both program and project managers in charge of these steps. The differences between program and project management are not simply one of scale – the management processes are fundamentally different (Pellegrinelli, 2011). The program manager's responsibility is to balance resources between projects in order to optimize the program benefit delivered. Program management embodies a group of interlinked projects to achieve defined business objectives. Project management on the other hand, encompasses a series of inter-related activities to achieve a business objective. Thus, the project manager's responsibility is to achieve three different goals for a given project: quality, cost and time. We define the two key roles below.

10.4.1 ROLE OF THE PROGRAM MANAGER

The program manager is often directly responsible to senior management such as the executive sponsor, steering committee and business transformation manager. The program manager is the management focal point between the organization and the solution implementation partner during the whole business transformation period, across multiple sites and multi-project business processes and solutions. In that capacity, the program manager leads the program through its lifecycle, initiating projects to achieve the objectives and resulting benefits agreed upon in the program management plan. Managing a program thus involves providing direction and guidance to the project managers, who are responsible for developing the products and/or services, and implementing the solutions that will produce the program benefits. The program manager manages the interdependencies of projects within the program and other programs across the organization (see also leadership skills mentioned in Chapter 2, Meta Management). They tend to draw from a strong foundation of project management knowledge and ability. Working with customers as a key and influential member of their business planning teams helps to ensure a continuing delivery of outcomes. Another key task is to manage risks proactively for the overall program.

Figure 10.6 illustrates an overview of the program manager's role throughout the four phases of the transformation lifecycle, namely in the envision, engage, transform and optimize. Throughout these phases, the program manager is responsible for the following:

- Direct the program and arbitrate conflicts with line management.
- Ensure complete integration and timeliness of all activities.
- Ensure that the implementation is on time and within budget.
- Identify and supply required resources and approve team staffing in alignment with project manager.
- Manage change, clarify and release change requests, if necessary with involvement of executive sponsor.
- Be the guardian of project scope and gap analysis.
- Provide project management, methodology and approach support
- Coordinate project planning and execution.
- Ensure coordination with project and core teams.
- Organize and participate in audits, gate reviews and interviews.

Examples of the typical tasks a program manager would do include the following:

- Ensure overall team understanding and deployment of project approach.
- Report program progress to steering committee.
- Ensure quality of deliverables.

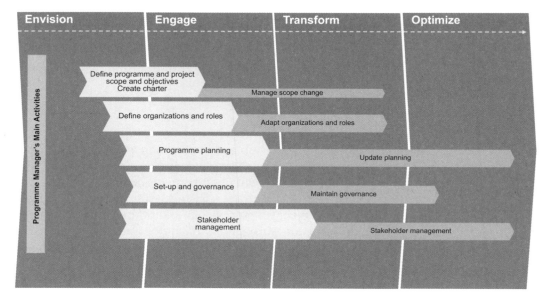

Figure 10.6 Main activities of the program manager

- Initiate corrective actions with regards to results, time, priorities, budget and quality.
- Ensure day-to-day management of achievements, issues, deliverables execution.
- Ensure team is trained and staffed to succeed.

CHALLENGES CONCERNING THE ROLE OF THE PROGRAM MANAGER:

1. Manage the interdependencies of projects within the program and other programs across the organization.
2. Lead the program through its lifecycle, initiate projects to achieve the objectives and resulting benefits agreed upon in the program management plan.
3. Manage the interdependencies of projects within the program and other programs across the organization.

KEY MESSAGE:

The program manager is the management focal point between the customer and the organization during the whole customer engagement lifecycle, across multiple sites and multi-project business processes and solutions.

10.4.2 ROLE OF THE PROJECT MANAGER

The project manager is directly responsible to the program manager, particularly in terms of the overall management of the planning, implementation and direction of the project throughout the lifecycle from project initiation to go-live and support. The project manager not only has to lead the project team, but is also responsible for implementation, quality, deadlines and costs of the project. Furthermore, they are also responsible for the planning, organization, coordination and direction of the project, including risk management for the project. Other duties include providing clarification and release of change request, if necessary with the involvement of the program manager. Key responsibilities for a project manager therefore, include the following:

- Define project organization in agreement with program manager.
- Be responsible for planning, organization, coordination and direction of the project.
- Be responsible for functionality, results, implementation, structure, quality, deadlines, costs and values.
- Clarify and release change requests, if necessary with the involvement of the program manager.
- Define and verify work packages together with team leads.
- Escalate issues early to program management.
- Manage and mitigate project risks.
- Manage team leads.
- Define and control project standards, performance and ensure compliance.

Several instances of the tasks carried out on the project level are as follows:

- Ensure overall team understanding and deployment of project approach.
- Ensure quality of deliverables.
- Initiate and coordinate detailed phase planning.
- Ensure day-to-day management of achievements, issues, deliverable execution.
- Be responsible for testing, appoint key-users for regression testing, training and support in alignment with program manager.
- Establish a single point of contact for program manager.

CHALLENGES CONCERNING THE ROLE OF THE PROJECT MANAGER:
1. Plan, organize, coordinate and direction of a project, which also includes project risk management.
2. Provide clarification and release of change requests, if necessary with the involvement of the program manager.

KEY MESSAGE:
The project manager is directly responsible to the program manager, particularly in terms of the overall management of the planning, implementation and direction of the project throughout the lifecycle from project initiation to go-live and support.

10.5 Key Skills of Program and Project Managers

Having understood the tasks and responsibilities of those in charge of program and project management, we now discuss the required skills and capabilities. This is based on an analysis of 140 business transformations within the United States and Asia-Pacific to identify the key skills in demand for program and project managers in business transformation (Safrudin et al., 2011). Our findings indicate that the top five skills for both a program and project manager are similar yet distinguished from one another.

The main similarities between program and project managers in terms of skills required include transactional leadership experience, transformational leadership skills, collaborating in cross-functional management disciplines and having individual abilities that meets the requirements of the business transformation. Firstly, both program and project managers must have transactional leadership (Bryant, 2003) experience at the organizational level – that is, the effective process of coordinating a particular project, or parts of a larger project – in achieving the overall business transformation objective. They are required to have a proven track record in coordinating the transition of an organization, technical and domain knowledge. Secondly, both managers should encompass both functional and non-functional skills, including leadership, interpersonal (soft) skills, communication, presentation and negotiation, active listening and the ability to influence employees. In other words, they are required to have transformational leadership skills (Eisenbach et al., 1999), to drive motivation, commitment and beyond-average organizational performance. Third, both managers would have had experience in pertinent management disciplines such as IT, human resource, financial, change, risk and so forth, plus communicating and dealing with both vertical and horizontal levels of management. Another sought skill from both program and project managers are the personal or individual capabilities that meets the company's requirements, such as flexibility in travelling, creative and analytical abilities, work ethics that adhere to the organizational values and so on.

The main difference identified from the analysis is that the program manager requires business acumen, which relates to the knowledge, aptitude and capacity to deal with stakeholders in order to deliver value towards business transformation. This is in line with one of the main goals of Program and Project Management (stated in Section 10.2), i.e. *business focus goals*. The project manager on the other hand, must possess the exposure and competency in specific project management methodology such as Six Sigma or PMI certification, leading projects and utilizing project management tools, which is congruent with the other program management goal, viz. *efficiency and effectiveness goals*.

In essence, the key skills of both program and project managers are required to meet the goals of program and project management as a whole. Furthermore, both transformational and transactional leadership skills coexist together in business transformation. The following sections will brief the capabilities and formal qualifications required from the program and project managers in business transformation.

10.5.1 SKILLS OF THE PROGRAM MANAGER

Program managers differ from transformation managers in a sense that, the role of a transformation manager is to manage the vision and value (value capturing), while a program manager looks at the management of scope, budget and quality of business transformation. Program managers need to be able to take a strategic business capability direction and translate them into a roadmap of projects and work tracks in order to execute and deliver the intended value. This requires the experience (typically five to ten years minimum) and the ability to evaluate broad business issues by having strategic thinking and analytical problem-solving skills. They must have the capability to break down complex problems in a simplified way, foster creativity of ideas and innovation by developing and conducting analytical assessments to test out and refine the various strategies where necessary. The program manager also needs to have effective conflict resolution and influencing skills to help establish good rapport, and also the ability to clearly communicate in an open and authentic manner in all situations with both business and technical audience (at all levels). Thus, the program manager is charismatic, and must be an exceptionally strong communicator, equally adept at communicating strategy and execution by means of crafting a full range of clear, high-impact communication. Proven ability to confidently package and present ideas, information and results for senior executives, as well as experience in significant senior management interaction is highly regarded.

Stakeholder management is crucial in ensuring good client-relationship, including business and negotiation skills to work with clients and business analysts to determine what features the project team will deliver, given constraints of time, staff and quality. This requires the program manager to have thorough experience in identifying and addressing client needs, including: developing and sustaining strong client relationships using networking, negotiation and persuasion skills to identify and introduce potentially new service opportunities; preparing and presenting complex written and verbal materials; and defining resource requirements, project workflow, budgets, billing and collection. Thus, financial and analytical skills both at strategic and functional levels are required, where program managers must be effective in making high-quality decisions and taking decisive action.

A solid understanding of how people go through a transformation and the transition process is required from a program manager. The program manager has solid experience as a team leader and a strong passion in supporting people and aligning their values with that of the organization (Herold et al., 2007). This involves leading teams to generate a vision, establish direction and motivate members, create an atmosphere of trust, leverage diverse views, coach staff, and encourage improvement and innovation. Thus, the ability to mentor less experienced project managers in a highly decentralized and customer-facing environment is essential to create open environment conducive to freely sharing information and ideas. Prior experience in implementing transformation management, innovation and creativity initiatives will be an advantage. In other words, program managers require creativity skills in defining approaches to program activities or overcoming program execution hurdles.

Solid process, program and project management skills are required for this role, including the ability to manage numerous priorities simultaneously while maintaining a sense of urgency. Program managers need to be able to operate effectively in an unstructured environment, and have strong time management and multitasking skills, including the ability to handle changes in business requirements and set priorities across multiple projects. The program manager will have experience in redesigning business processes with the ability to analyze poorly defined areas and processes within a cross-functional organization. They are effective in implementing new and improved processes, preferably ones which are of complex and global nature with a proven track record in successfully managing and delivering large-scale and diverse programs of change.

Typically, the program manager functions as an individual contributor role. As such, the ability to balance program management with day-to-day hands-on implementation is essential. Strong business acumen, exceptional project management and multitasking skills and the ability to interact and engage across all levels of staff will be key success factors. Due to the complex nature of business transformation, program managers should have high level of initiative, is self-driven, motivated, independent and comfortable working in a fast-paced, results-oriented environment.

With regards to formal qualifications, our analysis on program management roles indicate that companies typically require a Bachelor's degree (BA/BS) relevant to the transformation discipline, with a preference for a Master's or MBA degree. PMP certification or PMO background is useful, and strong Six Sigma experience, ideally at a black belt level, is also a strong plus.

10.5.2 SKILLS OF THE PROJECT MANAGER

Project managers need to be able to work with customer and internal teams to manage and deliver transformation projects on schedule, within budget and with a high level of customer satisfaction. Therefore, the project manager should have project management skills and experience of successful project lead (minimum three to eight years) would be ideal, including an in-depth understanding of project management best practices/ methodologies, techniques, tools and project lifecycle. Project managers are to update and improve the methodology based on learning and customer requirements and feedback.

CHALLENGES CONCERNING THE SKILLS OF THE PROGRAM MANAGER:
1. Take a strategic business capability direction and translate them into a roadmap of projects and work tracks in order to execute and deliver the intended value.
2. Determine what features the project team will deliver, given constraints of time, staff and quality.
3. Understand how people go through a transformation and the transition process.
4. Lead teams to generate a vision, establish direction and motivate members.
5. Create an atmosphere of trust, leverage diverse views, coach staff, and encourage improvement and innovation.
6. Handle changes in business requirements and set priorities across multiple projects.

KEY MESSAGE:
Strong business acumen, exceptional project management and multitasking skills and the ability to interact and engage across all levels of staff will be key success factors.

Our analysis of the project management roles indicates the demand to practically apply Six Sigma concepts, methods and tools to solve business problems. Further skills include budget accountabilities for project capital and expense budgets, as well as experience in establishing effective metrics and measures for project portfolios. The ability to provide sound governance, a performance framework and clear direction the project team will be paramount as the project manager deliver projects in alignment with the business transformation.

Business transformations embody projects to facilitate change. As such, change management principles are conceptually integrated into project management methods to drive results and support organizational change (Cowan-Sahadath, 2010). In effect, project managers work as change agents who will lead the organization through the transformation, including ability to influence and gain alignment with people at all levels in the organization. They require the skills to drive key initiatives from concept to delivery and craft transition plans to be executed in projects. The project managers must also have the desire to work in a rapidly changing environment, the ability to deal with ambiguity, and the ability to challenge upwards and influence without direct authority, knowing when to escalate to ensure alignment and timely completion of projects. Thus, multitasking skills in fast-paced deadline intensive environment are essential, as is the ability to anticipate obstacles and plan contingencies accordingly. This requires sound problem-solving capabilities to formulate approaches to problems in a rational manner by using strategies that ensure comprehensive understanding and effective resolution.

As a magnitude of risks are susceptible in projects during the transformation process, risk and process management capabilities are critical skills to be sought from project managers. They will be quick in responding and providing resolution to issues during the project, offering close acceleration and/or risk remediation by utilizing root cause or gap analysis. Hence, project managers must have a thorough knowledge of project controls processes such as change control, risks and issues management, resource management, document control and progress measurement techniques, etc. Project managers will also possess knowledge of planning and scheduling processes with the ability to define, implement and maintain project process guidance. This further requires process documentation and process assessment skills in order to identify process short-comings. Project managers will also work with others to improve or transform processes. They will possess broad cross-functional knowledge of business organizational processes to ensure that processes are not viewed as silos in that the organization does not remain fragmented.

Similar to program managers, project managers too require supervision experience. They must have the ability to develop others through providing timely coaching, guidance and feedback to help others excel on the job and meet key accountabilities. Project managers must have the demonstrated ability to teach, facilitate and communicate effectively, including coaching and mentoring of team members to successful completion of projects. It is also critical to be able to influence and gain alignment with people at all levels in the organization, to partner with peers, team members and demonstrate collaborative, effective teamwork. A required experience is the ability to successfully lead multiple teams working on different transformational projects, as they will be significantly involved in workforce planning and development. Therefore, project managers value the role of human capital and strive to optimally develop this resource for the benefit of the corporation, and are flexible with changing priorities.

The ability to communicate technical issues in a clear and concise manner is a critical skill required from project managers. Strong verbal and written communication skills, with an ability to express complex concepts effectively in simple business terms across all levels of the organization, are essential. Project managers must have a proven ability to make tough decisions and to provide delivery parameters. This is in addition to stakeholder management and all round reporting experience whereby project managers are to develop an own transition communication plan to ensure consistent understanding of the transition progress within key stakeholders. The project manager will collaborate effectively with others to ensure shared commitment to an enterprise and mutually beneficial result, build executive business-oriented relationships at the highest levels in pursuit of alliances that will advance or protect corporate interests.

Our findings from the analysis of project manager skills show that a Bachelor's degree (BA/BS) in a relevant discipline is demanded by transforming organizations. Professional qualifications such as CISA, CISM, PMP, IT audit or IT risk management experience with a professional services firm or equivalent will be advantageous. Other listed qualifications include MBA or other tertiary qualifications such as CPA, CMA, CFA or CA, dependent on the transformation discipline. The project manager would ideally have a good understanding of lean Six Sigma concept, and green or black belt certification in lean Sigma will be a plus, i.e. proven proficiency with Six Sigma methodology (Lean, DMAIC, DMADV, Kaizen).

10.6 Lessons Learned about Program and Project Management

Having defined activities, roles, responsibilities and key skills required to perform Program and Project Management, we now define the essential success factors for

---

CHALLENGES CONCERNING THE SKILLS OF THE PROJECT MANAGER:

1. Respond and provide resolution to issues during the project, offering close acceleration and/or risk remediation by utilizing root cause or gap analysis.
2. Provide timely coaching, guidance and feedback to help others excel on the job and meet key accountabilities.
3. Influence and gain alignment with people at all levels in the organization, to partner with peers, team members and demonstrate collaborative, effective teamwork.
4. Develop an own transition communication plan to ensure consistent understanding of the transition progress among key stakeholders.
5. Collaborate effectively with others to ensure shared commitment to the enterprise and mutually beneficial results.
6. Build executive business-oriented relationships at the highest levels in pursuit of alliances that will advance or protect corporate interests.

KEY MESSAGE:

Project managers value the role of human capital and strive to optimally develop this resource for the benefit of the corporation, and are flexible with changing priorities.

achieving the objectives of Program and Project Management. We encapsulate our view of these success factors, derived from industry practical experience and academic research, in Figure 10.7.

As depicted, we identify eight key success factors for Program and Project Managementin BTM[2]. First, having a defined strategic vision and business objectives is an imperative prerequisite for managing business transformation. This will enable program and project managers to align their activities in accordance with the organizational goals, specifically with the strategic direction (Wischnevsky and Damanpour, 2006) that will drive the transformation. Upon doing so, business capabilities are to be analyzed as the second step. This ensures that the organization has the resources and capacity to support and execute the steps required in Program and Project Management. Once the capabilities are identified, the best options are then determined to provide managers with a range of feasible avenues to execute their steps. As every business transformation is unique (Morgan and Page, 2008), the decision will need to be made based on business requirements, and subsequently be divided into manageable and focused modules. This will ensure that work packages are feasible enough to be executed within the allocated time and budget.

Another important factor is to carefully consider the risks involved and mitigation strategies to manage the risks, roadblocks or obstacles (Kotter, 2010) throughout the business transformation. Strong leadership is also a fundamental success factor (Cowan-Sahadath, 2010), as this will provide employees and co-workers with the required direction and motivation to carry out the activities in a complex endeavor. Finally, the eighth success factor looks at revising progress and identifying the need for intervention

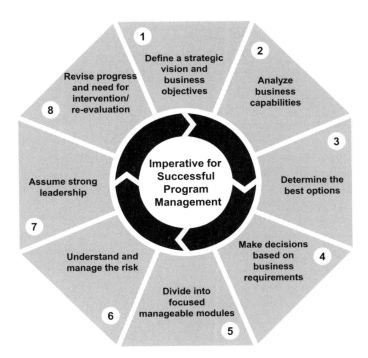

Figure 10.7 Critical success factors for Program and Project Management

or re-evaluation, as it is imperative to shape and coordinate projects in accordance with the context of a dynamic organizational environment (Pellegrinelli et al., 2007).

In conclusion, a summary of dos and don'ts of Program Management in business transformation are summarized in Table 10.1:

Table 10.1 Dos and don'ts of Program and Project Management in business transformation

Dos	Don'ts
Make sure you get strong sponsors at CxO level.	Accept non-estimated deadlines.
Have one project location (at a time).	Compromise on quality.
Build a strong project team.	Say "it's just an IT project" (for IT/IT-enabled business transformation).
Define clear common objectives.	Try to achieve perfection.
Understand the politics.	Run over budget.
Balance scope, resources and timing.	Fail to update the business case.
Plan for "neutral" ongoing quality assurance reviews to manage risks.	Delay a milestone more than once.
Use state of the art tools (project management, testing, documentation, etc.).	
Plan for regular steering committee (to validate decisions early).	
Define clear scope change procedures.	
Define business benefits and value to be achieved.	

10.7 Conclusion

Program and Project Management provide a comprehensive methodology in business transformation by including the *best of breed* knowledge and experience in the field of managing scope, teams and human resources. The two fundamental goals of Program and Project Management are *business focus goals* and *efficiency and effectiveness goals*. Program and Project Management consist of eight steps in business transformations:

1. Establish the basic structure for the program.
2. Ensure that the program, its components and projects, and all the program activities from the program processes are well coordinated and integrated.
3. Reach a consensus with key stakeholders on the program plan and benefits, as well as on staffing key resources.
4. Define the budget and time constraints for the different components of the program and the involved projects.

5. Implement a program environment that ensures that quality requirements are identified, understood and fulfilled through all parts of the program and through all program activities and related projects.
6. Ensure that companies have the right people, at the right place and at the right time in order to execute a successful business transformation.
7. Evaluate the need for additional capacity and skills, as well as the selection of potential suppliers based on needed skills and resources.
8. Define program performance reports, incorporating the results from program audits and project audits.

Program and Project Management further provides a description of the roles and responsibilities for program and project managers and discuss key skills required for these roles. Based on the eight activities, roles, responsibilities and key skills required to perform business transformation, success factors for achieving the objectives of Program and Project Management were introduced.

Bibliography

Bryant, Scott E. (2003), The role of transformational and transactional leadership in creating, sharing and exploiting organizational knowledge, *Journal of Leadership & Organizational Studies* 9, no. 4, 32–44.

Cowan-Sahadath, Kathy (2010), Business transformation: leadership, integration and innovation – a case study, *International Journal of Project Management* 28, no. 4, 395–404.

Eisenbach, Regina, Watson, Kathleen and Pillai, Rajnandini (1999), Transformational leadership in the context of organizational change, *Journal of Organizational Change Management* 12, no. 2, 80–9.

Herold, David M., Fedor, Donald B. and Caldwell, Steven D. (2007), Beyond change management: a multilevel investigation of contextual and personal influences on employees' commitment to change, *Journal of Applied Psychology* 92, no. 4, 942–51.

ILX Group (2012), What is PRINCE2? – PRINCE2 definition: www.prince2.com/what-is-prince2.asp (accessed March 2012).

Kotter, John P. (2010), *Leading Change: Why Transformation Efforts Fail* (Boston, Mass: Harvard Business Press).

Lycett, Mark, Rassau, Andreas and Danson, John (2004), Programme management: a critical review, *International Journal of Project Management* 22, no. 4, 289–99.

Morello, Diane and Olding, Elise, (2008), Rethinking change: practical realities of successful transformation, G00154663, Gartner Research: www.gartner.com/id=597614 (accessed March 2012).

Morgan, Robert E. and Page, Kelly (2008), Managing business transformation to deliver strategic agility, *Strategic Change* 17, 5–6, 155–68.

Pellegrinelli, Sergio (2011), What's in a name: project or programme?, *International Journal of Project Management* 29, no. 2, 232–40.

Pellegrinelli, Sergio, Partington, David, Hemingway, Chris, Mohdzain, Zaher and Shah, Mahmood (2007), The importance of context in programme management: an empirical review of programme practices, *International Journal of Project Management* 25, no. 1, 41–55.

Project Management Institute (2008), *The Standard for Programme Management*, 2nd ed. (Newtown Square, PA: Project Management Institute).

Safrudin, Norizan, Recker, Jan and Rosemann, Michael (2011), The emerging management services of business transformation management, in *PACIS 2011 Proceedings*, Paper 160: http://aisel.aisnet.org/pacis2011/160 (accessed March 2012).

Spreitzer, Gretchen M. (1996), Empowering middle managers to be transformational leaders, *The Journal of Applied Behavioral Science* 32, no. 3, 237–61.

Wischnevsky, Daniel J. and Damanpour, Fariborz (2006), Organizational transformation and performance: an examination of three perspectives, *Journal of Managerial Issues* 18, no. 1, 104–28.

11 Case Study: MotorStars – Implementation of a Global HR System in an Automotive Company

CHRISTOPH PIMMER (University of Applied Sciences and Arts Northwestern Switzerland), AXEL UHL (SAP AG), MICHAEL BRANDENBURG (IESE Business School) and ROBERT GÜNTHER (SAP AG)

11.1 Overview

Using a fictitious case study as a basis, this chapter describes the protracted, challenging and costly attempts of an automotive company to transform the strategic alignment of its HR department by implementing a shared service center and HR IT system. Faced with historically grown, organizational and sociocultural transformation problems, as well as personal animosities and the resulting micropolitical tactics of leading players, the group is on the verge of failing again in its efforts. After an initial presentation of the evolutionary history and background, the second part of this chapter discusses the overall complexity of the situation and focuses on the conflict-ridden relationships between the players involved. The subsequent description of the strategic planning concept then presents a realistic method of resolution that is based on the envision phase of BTM^2. We describe how the undertaking is implemented further from the perspective of the strategic planning team in charge. Although this story is fictional, it does combine a number of elements that typically characterize an undertaking of this kind; it can, therefore, in a sense be regarded as an authentic case.

The case study presented in this chapter primary addresses the envision phase of BTM^2 with the following steps: identification of scope and a rough project plan, examination of triggers and drivers for the planned business transformation, evaluation of benefits of the objectives from a strategic perspective and definition of a transformation plan.

OBJECTIVES OF THIS CHAPTER:
1. Understand problems and challenges of business transformation projects.
2. Understand how to use the management disciplines of BTM^2.
3. Understand the application of BTM^2 in the envision phase.

11.2 The Case History

This section summarizes the company's history and the company's goal. The case study is built on the following company background.

MotorStars is an important player in the global automotive market. It develops and offers vehicles and components and related automotive services. The company operates in the fields of cars, busses and trucks, and motorcycles. These also form its divisions. In 2010, the three divisions generated a combined revenue of 35 billion euros. Headquartered in Berlin, Germany, the company currently employs 100,000 associates who work in over 120 countries worldwide. Its main operating areas are Germany, France and the USA.

11.2.1 COMPANY HISTORY

The company originated from the merger of PremiumDrive and CheapVehicle, two German automotive companies, in 2000. Through the merger, two companies with different histories, strategies and cultures were united into one global organization: while PremiumDrive was perceived as a trusted, high-quality provider of automotive-related products and services, CheapVehicle had a relatively poor image due to several environmental scandals; CheapVehicle pursued its business goals through an aggressive pricing strategy. The new and emerging culture of MotorStars was increasingly dominated by the norms and values of CheapVehicle. Although the financial results after the merger were satisfactory, the company was challenged by the clash of these different cultures and by a working atmosphere that was filled with tensions and distrust. In addition to the cultural difficulties, the situation was further complicated by heterogeneous and non-standardized processes, policies and systems that varied across the company. The organization was further characterized by high local autonomy and slow-moving functional silos.

CHALLENGES OF THE COMPANY'S HISTORY:
1. Merger of a high-quality provider with a low-quality provider.
2. Combining different cultures and working atmospheres.
3. Introducing heterogeneous and non-standardized processes, policies and systems.

11.2.2 THE OUTSET OF A GLOBAL HR PROJECT

The human and intellectual capital and, thereby, the recruitment, professional development and retention of motivated and high-performing employees was perceived as crucial for MotorStars' success. However, in view of this policy and with regard to the 70,000 associates working in the company at that time, the global and local HR departments had limited personnel. A total of 700 people were working in the different HR departments after the merger. There was no overall HR concept but rather a heterogeneous mixture across the company. The HR processes were not harmonized on a global scale. Instead, they were supported individually by a number of different regional, local or business-unit-specific IT systems. There was a lack of common standards and of a consolidated database. For example, the PeopleSoft HR solution was used in the USA, UK and France, while SAP solutions were in place in Germany, Switzerland and Japan. This resulted in a lack of transparency. It was – as we will show – not possible to determine exactly the number of employees working in the company at any given time; and it was difficult to fill vacant management positions quickly or to fulfill compliance requirements consistently.

CHALLENGES OF THE GLOBAL HR PROJECT:

1. Only limited HR staff available.
2. No overall and global HR concept available.
3. HR processes are not harmonized on a global scale.

11.2.3 INITIAL IDEA AND GOALS

In order to address these challenges, the Head of Corporate HR started a project in 2005 that was aimed at standardizing the HR processes and implementing a global, web-based HR information system. For the planned duration of three years, a budget of 80 million euros was approved by the executive board. After a planning and blueprint phase and the development of a prototype, the roll-out was planned to take place in France and would be followed by the company's other main locations in Germany and the USA.

The project's overall goals included:

- implementation of standardized HR processes;
- timely provision of accurate HR data;
- improvement of the decision-making processes; and
- reduction of HR operating costs.

Across the organization, a global HR information system would provide accurate data on jobs, positions and related information in order to support the organization and talent review processes. The company's strategy of international expansion and associated organizational change processes were expected to be supported through harmonized HR processes and a multi-lingual and web-enabled system on a global scale. The establishment of an organizational service structure was intended to increase organizational efficiency and to reduce operational costs. Employees would enter their data in online forms in real time and managers would be able to compile precise and timely reports. While HR employees up until then had spent more than half of their time dealing with administrative processes, the envisioned system was expected to drastically reduce these kinds of activities. Instead, the solution would enable them to devote their time to more strategic issues. This, in turn, was expected to help transform and extend the traditional role of HR in the organization from an administrative service provider to a more strategic consulting partner for the business units.

From a technical standpoint, the IT solution was planned to include:

- SAP R/3 as a core transaction processing system;
- SAP Business Warehouse for HR data in order to facilitate reporting and analysis and, eventually, to improve managerial HR decisions; and
- web-based enterprise HR portal solution that allows the personalization of data and of the graphical user interface.

The initiative was set up as a pure HR project with limited involvement of the Corporate IT department. The idea was to delegate the overall responsibility for the technical part to an external partner: the mandate for the IT part was given to BusinessComp, a multinational computer, technology and IT consulting company. Even the software licensing was outsourced: acting as an intermediary, BusinessComp had acquired software licenses from SAP with the intention to resell these to MotorStars. The project office was established in the USA with the idea to closely involve this important, but relatively independent area of the company. For this reason, however, the team was relatively isolated from the rest of the global areas.

GOALS OF THE GLOBAL HR PROJECT:
1. Standardization of HR processes.
2. Implementation of a web-based HR information system.
3. Reduce administrative work and focus on strategic issues.

11.2.4 TRANSFORMATIONAL CHALLENGES

The project was considered complex because of its sheer scope; in addition, the project team had relatively little knowledge with respect to an effort of this size and scale. At the outset, the team analyzed benchmarks and comparable cases in order to identify best practices and expected challenges. Across the reviewed cases, the challenge of convincing local players, re-engineering existing processes and transforming mindsets became evident. Analyzing the challenges ahead, the project team recognized technical complexities to be tackled and the importance of diligent, culture-specific communication. The biggest problem, however, was seen in the acceptance of the system by the various local players. These parties wanted to preserve their local way of working. In the initial planning and preparation phase, the project team was troubled by a number of additional analytical tasks burdened by local HR departments. The team had to prove that their global system would also work in the regional markets and outperform existing systems. From the very beginning, they were confronted significant tension and power struggles. Particular difficulties were faced when trying to establish a corporate compensation and performance management system. The underlying motives originated from the unresolved cultural tensions from the merger and from the established matrix organization with associated dual reporting lines which lead to unclear hierarchical relationships. The main conflict occurred between the Corporate HR management and the HR management of the Car

Division. *Car* was by far the largest and, from a political perspective, the most powerful product line. Its division covered 80 percent of the profit and employed 50 percent of the company's workforce. The Head of Car HR had to report primarily to the Car CEO and, secondarily, to the Corporate HR management (see dotted reporting line on Figure 11.1 below).

After a period of unproductive power struggles and quarrels, so-called *white smoke meetings* were arranged. The conflicting parties were invited to meetings and were only permitted to return to work once they had worked out a solution accepted by all parties. However, even this method did not result in the desired outcome. The measures that had been agreed upon were not followed by the parties afterwards. There was an overall lack of senior leadership support that did not go beyond the funding of the project: senior management did not drive the overall implementation and did not help to overcome the organizational tensions. Approaches such as the redefinition of the project scope, enforced commitment of local HR organizations, increased budget or extended project length were not given serious consideration.

The situation became more and more problematic. An internal IT manager, who was at that time successfully implementing a global finance management system, was asked for his opinion on the issue. The manager (who later became the Head of ERP) recommended the project be halted and restarted from scratch at a later time.

CHALLENGES DURING THE BUSINESS TRANSFORMATION:
1. Overall size, scope and technical complexity of the project.
2. Lack of experiences project members and unclear responsibilities.
3. Lack of acceptance by local players and missing guidance from senior management.

11.2.5 A FAILED BUSINESS TRANSFORMATION

Instead of following the principles of *promise less and deliver more*, the project team had merely created high expectations with regard to project goals in order to secure the approved budget. This turned out to be a mistake, particularly in view of the project's slow progress. After one and a half years a total of 40 million euros had been spent while the defined targets had not been reached in any significant way. The solution had not been implemented in any country and there was not even a blueprint available. As a consequence, the overall project was cancelled. In the meeting where this decision was made, the Head of HR Car commented that he "had always been aware that this project had been doomed to fail". The Head of Corporate HR was dismissed and a manager with a background of production management was nominated as his successor. The project stop was also a financial disaster for BusinessComp, which was then unable to resell its previously acquired licenses from SAP to MotorStars. The complete failure strengthened the power of the local and regional departments, and fostered the growth of local HR IT solutions. As a consequence, some of the local players did not only increase their local impact; they even expanded it geographically.

REASONS FOR FAILURE:
1. Expectations with respect to project goal were set to high.
2. Definition of a too wide and complex project scope.
3. Lack of commitment from management.

11.3 Problems Faced by Key Players

Against the background of aggravated tensions it is discussed in the following, how interest and power of the key players involved affect, and further complicate, the situation.

11.3.1 PROBLEM STATEMENT AND CASE FOR ACTION

Three years after the project failure, the problems still remain unresolved. Significant inefficiencies exist in most back office functions, whereby staff are tied up in unnecessary manual tasks and resources are wasted. Many local HR processes comprised of out-dated practices, procedures and information systems. MotorStars does not conform to required standards or best practices. Inadequate information systems exist that are vulnerable to failure, functionally insufficient and technically unstable. Information is unmanageable, inaccessible and often inaccurate. It is also fragmented throughout different systems and maintained sporadically. Reporting is difficult and both internal and external staff and managers are poorly informed. This problem is further aggravated by the fact that the company has expanded: turnover, profit, as well as the number of employees and affiliations have increased. This is a development that made a global HR approach even more important.

11.3.2 THE KEY PLAYERS

Currently, there is a controversial and wide-ranging debate on a new approach. While the main three competing parties are Corporate HR, Car HR and IT, a number of personal conflicts between the actors also have to be taken into account (see Figure 11.1).

Executive board members

The top management of the company demands this issue be solved. The CEO believes that a global HR IT system is more efficient than many individual installations. In addition, the CEO favors a global solution also for reasons of prestige. While he recognizes the importance of cultural issues, his perception of HR is focused on leadership development, performance, incentive and talent systems; he is not so much interested in employee administration.

The CFO's interests are centered on a well-performing enterprise. He feels personally offended by the immense waste of money in the first project and is sceptical with regard to the ability of the HR Department to run such a global project. He is, however, aware of the need to establish a global reporting system. One event in particular caused

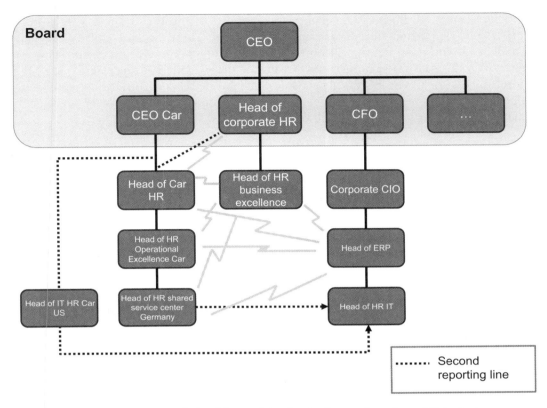

Figure 11.1 Description of the hierarchical relations of and conflicts between the main players

alarm bells to ring: at an analysts' conference, he and the Head of Corporate HR were expected to present the latest facts and figures. Discussing their slides shortly before their presentation they realized that they had calculated a different number of employees: while the CFO's presentation featured 100,000 employees, the Head of Corporate HR was about to announce a total of 90,000 employees. The CFO is extremely interested in diligent headcount reporting and realizes that this can be only achieved with an IT-based solution. However, he doubts that an overall HR system is needed for this purpose. He considers this a "waste of money" and, in an informal meeting, he was heard to say, "Why do we need an HR system in Timbuktu?"

Corporate HR

The new Head of Corporate HR is a cooperative manager. As a manager with a strong background in production, he has only limited experience of HR matters. His moderating role is, however, respected across many organizations. In general he tries to avoid conflicts, as the following statement shows: "Why should I get a bloody nose if the organization is not ready for the system?"

The Head of HR Business Excellence is a member of the HR Council. The Head of Corporate HR poached him from another company. There he had already had bad experience with implementing a global HR project. He was hired to establish a new HR delivery model and to harmonize and streamline the existing HR processes. Due to the short time that he has been working at MotorStars, his network within the company and, in particular, his access to local HR representatives is limited. He is, however, engaged in establishing relations with the IT and Car departments.

Car Division

The Head of Car HR is the main antagonist of the Head of Corporate HR and also opposed to the Head of ERP. He reports to the CEO of Car with whom he also maintains a close relationship. He is by no means willing to leave the project leadership to the Head of Corporate HR – a task he claims for his division. Although he has been held partly accountable for the first project, he blames his *limited responsibility* as the main reason for its failure. While the Head of Car HR places centrality on top management issues, he has only limited knowledge of administrative HR processes. In order to gain control over the new HR project, he has internally recruited the Head of HR Operational Excellence Car as a tactical measure.

The Head of HR Operational Excellence Car was entrusted to achieve the same goals as the Head of HR Business Excellence: winning control over the HR system. While she comes from the field of quality management and also has limited knowledge about HR. She reports to the Head of HR Operational Excellence Car and maintains a good personal relation also with the Head of Corporate HR. However, she would like to secure the mandate as project leader and is reluctant to share this with the Head of HR Business Excellence, with whom she is at odds. Another player in the reporting line of Car is the Head HR Shared Service Center Germany. Starting from Germany, she has successfully expanded her shared service center concept to countries such as Italy or Switzerland. She aims to expand further and become the Head of the Shared Service Center Europe. She has formed a coalition with the Head of HR Operational Excellence Car. Although she operates in the field of IT, she is in the reporting line for Car and, therefore, is in conflict with the Head of ERP systems from IT as well as with the Head of HR Business Excellence.

IT

Although the Corporate CIO heads the IT department, he is not on the Executive Board. He reports to the Corporate CFO, who also controls the IT budget. The CIO favors SAP because the global financial processes are already based on SAP's finance component (SAP ERP FI/CO). Moreover, the CIO was told to stay as close as possible to the standard processes so as to keep the cost of maintenance and further development low. However, the CFO set other IT priorities for the CIO such as outsourcing of basic IT infrastructure in order to cut costs. The CIO has only limited experience of and interest in ERP systems.

The Head of ERP is a manager who implemented the global finance system (as indicated above). Although he had several escalating conflicts during the project due to his aggressive communication style, he managed to complete it successfully. This was largely due to the support of a second, more moderate and careful manager. As he has recently managed to get his job title changed to *Head of Corporate ERP*, he is adamant about wanting to become the *CIO of ERP*. He is more than eager to be in charge of the project. However, due to his lack of knowledge in the field of HR, he has hired the Head of HR IT, who is a former consultant with both HR and IT skills. He is obliged to cooperate with the Head of HR Operational Excellence Car and with the other actors to find a jointly accepted way of managing the project.

In brief, there are protracted power fights between the Head of Corporate HR and the Head of HR Business Excellence both from Corporate HR and the Head of Car HR and the Head of HR Operational Excellence from the Car Division. The Head of ERP (IT) is – due to his offensive style – in conflict with nearly all of the other players. All the involved parties want to gain control over the transformation project.

11.4 Strategic Approach

This section describes how a method of resolution is planned from a strategic perspective. In doing so, we will follow MotorStars' Business Transformation Strategy team, which will base its approach on the six steps outlined in the BTM^2 envision phase (see Figure 11.2).

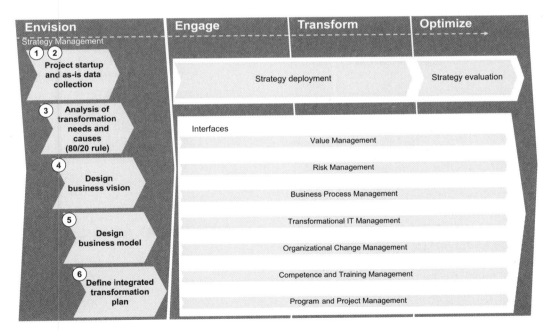

Figure 11.2 Envision phase in the BTM^2 context

11.4.1 PROJECT STARTUP AND AS-IS DATA COLLECTION (STEPS 1 AND 2)

The relatively small team is staffed with representatives from the various parties involved. It comprises of the Head of HR Business Excellence, the Head of HR IT, the Head of HR Operational Excellence Car and the Head of the Shared Service Center Germany (Car). The initiation commenced with identifying the scope, a rough project plan and a budget of 120 million euros allocated to achieve the following revised goals:

- Implementation of a global HR IT system that is based on one single trusted source of HR Data in order to improve the quality of reporting.
- Implementation of a shared service model for HR in order to improve the overall quality of HR processes.

In addition, the plan envisages a greater role for HR as a strategic consulting partner for the business units. To obtain a clearer impression of the current situation, the team conducts a series of interviews with the representatives from Corporate HR, the local HR managers from all three divisions, and with top management, which serve as awareness-building measures. As part of the as-is data collection step, the wrong decisions taken in the past are also identified. The team starts by examining the mistakes of the previous project using the BTM² management disciplines. It soon becomes evident that the strategic focus was too broad and too vague with little differentiation. This was compounded by the fact that neither a business case nor a risk assessment had been conducted. Against this background, exaggerated goals were communicated that gave rise to expectations that could not be fulfilled. Similarly, a stakeholder analysis and management were also neglected and the potentials for conflict and existing tensions (organizational readiness) were significantly underestimated. Additional factors that had a negative impact included the wrong leadership approach with regard to third parties as well as an incorrect estimate of the costs involved and a misjudgment of the required time frame.

While mistakes were also made in the implementation phase, this analysis clearly shows that key omissions and wrong decisions taken early on in the strategy phase prevented the objectives of the project from being achieved. Consequently, this section focuses on this phase, which, as already stated, is equivalent to the BTM² envision phase.

KEY ACTIVITIES WITHIN PROJECT STARTUP AND AS-IS DATA COLLECTION:

1. Identify the scope, a rough project plan and a budget.
2. Conduct a series of interviews with representatives.
3. Identify wrong decisions taken in the past based on the management disciplines of BTM².

11.4.2 ANALYSIS OF TRANSFORMATION NEEDS AND CAUSES (STEP 3)

In the next step, the team examines the triggers and drivers for the planned transformation: A key driver is the need for greater support from HR for the company's expansion strategy

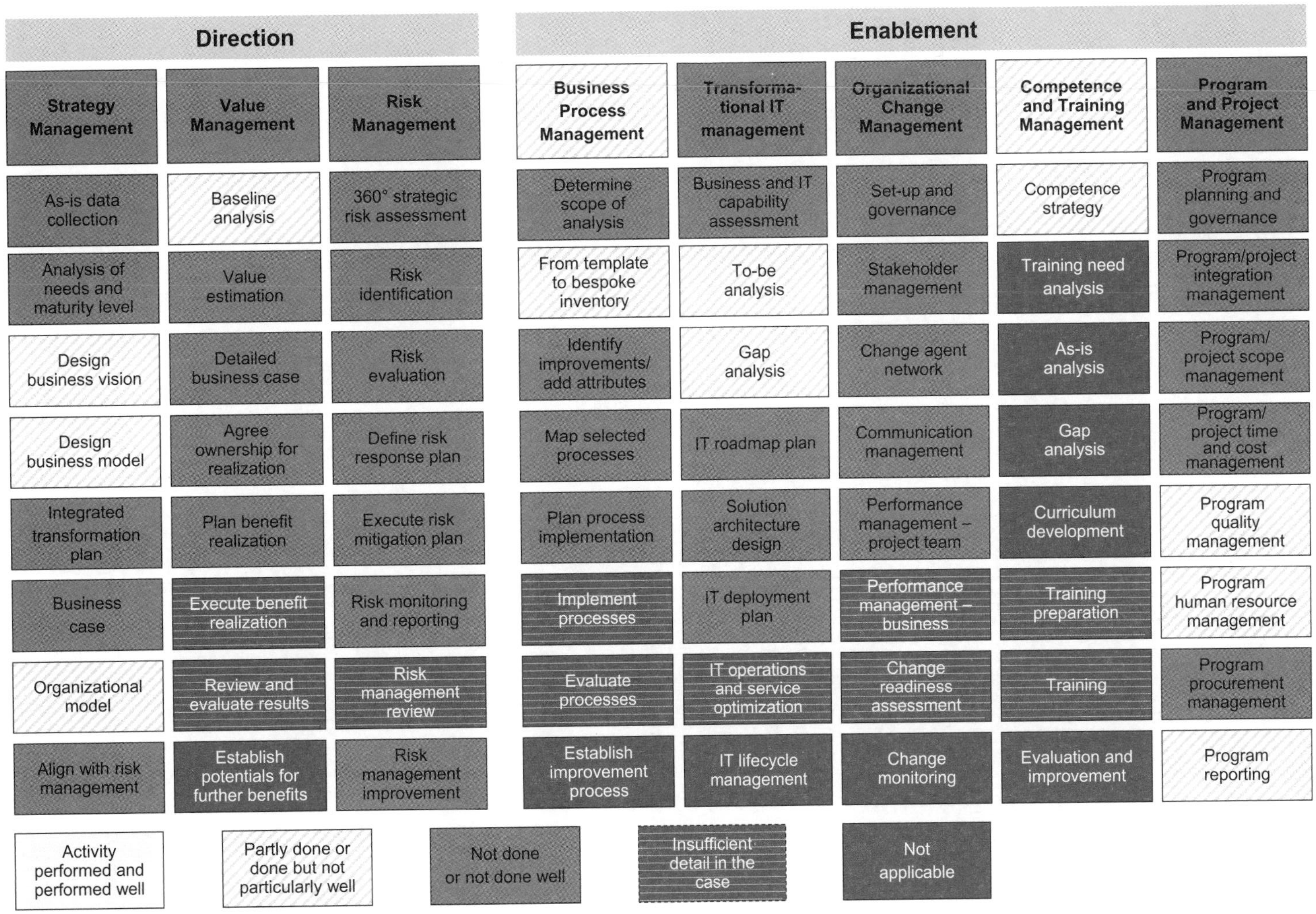

Direction | Enablement

Strategy Management	Value Management	Risk Management	Business Process Management	Transformational IT management	Organizational Change Management	Competence and Training Management	Program and Project Management
As-is data collection	Baseline analysis	360° strategic risk assessment	Determine scope of analysis	Business and IT capability assessment	Set-up and governance	Competence strategy	Program planning and governance
Analysis of needs and maturity level	Value estimation	Risk identification	From template to bespoke inventory	To-be analysis	Stakeholder management	Training need analysis	Program/project integration management
Design business vision	Detailed business case	Risk evaluation	Identify improvements/add attributes	Gap analysis	Change agent network	As-is analysis	Program/project scope management
Design business model	Agree ownership for realization	Define risk response plan	Map selected processes	IT roadmap plan	Communication management	Gap analysis	Program/project time and cost management
Integrated transformation plan	Plan benefit realization	Execute risk mitigation plan	Plan process implementation	Solution architecture design	Performance management – project team	Curriculum development	Program quality management
Business case	Execute benefit realization	Risk monitoring and reporting	Implement processes	IT deployment plan	Performance management – business	Training preparation	Program human resource management
Organizational model	Review and evaluate results	Risk management review	Evaluate processes	IT operations and service optimization	Change readiness assessment	Training	Program procurement management
Align with risk management	Establish potentials for further benefits	Risk management improvement	Establish improvement process	IT lifecycle management	Change monitoring	Evaluation and improvement	Program reporting

Legend:
- Activity performed and performed well
- Partly done or done but not particularly well
- Not done or not done well
- Insufficient detail in the case
- Not applicable

Figure 11.3 Error analysis based on BTM²

in emerging markets. This is accompanied by pressure from top management to simplify the complex process landscape by using IT-supported processes and boost efficiency through the resulting standardization effects. The current condition of the HR data is also unsatisfactory in that it is imprecise and therefore makes decision making at executive level extremely difficult. Since the incident with the discrepancy regarding the headcount figures, the CFO in particular is immensely dissatisfied with the performance of HR.

Following the analysis of the business transformation needs and causes, the team rates MotorStars HR at Stage 3 of the BTM^2 model (see Figure 11.4). Apart from the financial disaster of the initial attempt, there has been no significant negative impact on HR's core business. Nevertheless, a strategy is still lacking and the scope for internal solutions is becoming more and more restricted as customers and other key stakeholders have lost confidence. There is an immediate need for action as otherwise there is a risk that the next transformation stage (Stage 4) will be reached, thereby jeopardizing operative objectives.

MotorStars' readiness for the pending business transformation is determined using the BTM^2 transformation readiness analysis. The process readiness is rated at Level 2. While most of the HR processes are not harmonized at global level, some standardized processes, such as in performance management, exist that are at least performed globally in paper form. The IT readiness with regard to the HR systems is clearly at the lowest level (Level 1). There are a variety of different, local applications ranging from Excel sheets to SAP or PeopleSoft installations. There are no consolidated data records or standards. As a result of the various systems involved, the information is imprecise and fragmented. The organizational readiness too must be classified at the lowest level (Level 1). Due to the previous failed harmonization projects, the local HR departments are in an even stronger position compared to Corporate HR. There are certain regional *kingdoms* that are even about to expand geographically.

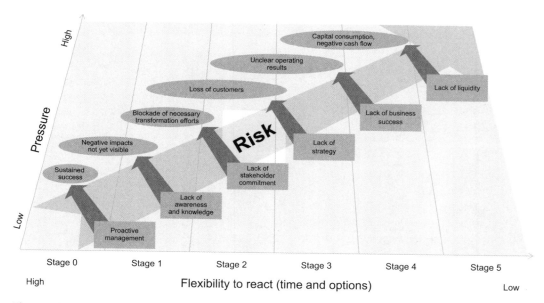

Figure 11.4 Stages of transformation needs

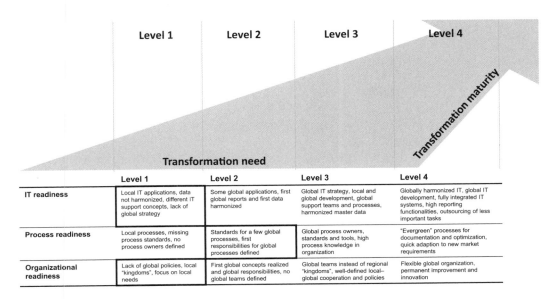

	Level 1	Level 2	Level 3	Level 4
IT readiness	Local IT applications, data not harmonized, different IT support concepts, lack of global strategy	Some global applications, first global reports and first data harmonized	Global IT strategy, local and global development, global support teams and processes, harmonized master data	Globally harmonized IT, global IT development, fully integrated IT systems, high reporting functionalities, outsourcing of less important tasks
Process readiness	Local processes, missing process standards, no process owners defined	Standards for a few global processes, first responsibilities for global processes defined	Global process owners, standards and tools, high process knowledge in organization	"Evergreen" processes for documentation and optimization, quick adaption to new market requirements
Organizational readiness	Lack of global policies, local "kingdoms", focus on local needs	First global concepts realized and global responsibilities, no global teams defined	Global teams instead of regional "kingdoms", well-defined local–global cooperation and policies	Flexible global organization, permanent improvement and innovation

Figure 11.5 Transformation readiness

KEY ACTIVITIES WITHIN ANALYSIS OF TRANSFORMATION NEEDS AND CAUSES:

1. Simplify the complex process landscape by using IT-supported processes and boost efficiency through the resulting standardization effects.
2. Determine the readiness for the pending business transformation with the transformation readiness analysis.

11.4.3 DESIGN BUSINESS VISION AND BUSINESS MODEL (STEPS 4 AND 5)

After completing the Transformation Readiness Analysis, the team evaluates the benefits of the objectives from a strategic perspective. Given the current availability problems of global HR data, inconsistent processes and lack of IT-supported performance or compensation management, implementing an HR IT platform harbours significant potential for boosting quality and transparency. The perceived immediate benefits include the simplification of the global HR processes and reporting as well as ensuring minimum technical and process standards in HR – even in smaller countries. From a purely monetary perspective, however, the business case for the HR IT solution is less compelling. Even though managing and maintaining IT systems centrally does offer certain economic potentials, the costs caused by the small, local IT solutions – in many cases Excel sheets – are insignificant anyway.

In contrast, the purpose of introducing a shared service center is to leverage potential cost savings rather than boost quality. At 1:60, MotorStars' HR-to-employee ratio is now relatively low compared to the international benchmark of 1:80. From this perspective, cost savings could be achieved with the company's current 1,700 HR employees. However, due to political reasons and the company's overall positive performance, dismissing the employees is not under consideration. Instead, the aim is to achieve a growth in productivity through the rising number of employees throughout the company with the same number of HR employees. Furthermore, by using the shared service center in Eastern Europe, labor arbitrage advantages could be leveraged. Sharp price increases in these countries, however, have to be taken into consideration. Due to the significant cultural and language differences involved, MotorStars is not considering the option of transferring its operations to India.

Using the previous analysis as a basis, the current situation at MotorStars HR can be clearly graded in the business model. In short, the transformation need is medium to high with a deep transformation readiness (Figure 11.6, top left quadrant). The primary maxim of business transformation, therefore, is overcoming the stakeholder crisis. As we will see later, this problem holds the key to solving the case.

As well as the various strategic methods, the prioritization and sequencing of the two underlying objectives have to be defined. From a strategic perspective, the following options are available in terms of when the shared service center and HR IT solution are implemented:

1. Big bang: From a purely monetary perspective, it is advisable to implement the shared service center and HR IT system at the same time because a shorter project duration will reduce costs. This approach, however, represents a strategic redirection that requires many resources to be managed in parallel, increases complexity and thus heightens the risk of the project failing again. In view of the failure of the last project, the willingness to take risks within the company and in the project team is low. Instead, solutions that are less drastic are required.

2. A second option would also be a strategic redirection by prioritizing the introduction of the shared service center with subsequent implementation of the new HR IT solution by its staff. However, this approach is risky because the staff do not have the know-how of designing these processes. The day-to-day work in the center and implementation of the HR IT solution at the same time would result in a dual burden. Similarly, it is questionable whether the local HR organizations would support a shared service center due to fear of losing their jobs and petty rivalries.

3. Implementing the IT system and then setting up the shared service center seems to be the most viable solution for the team. By doing so, the team hopes to reduce complexity and be able to use the global HR IT platform to implement the shared service center; it regards setting up a shared service center using local solutions as scarcely possible. While the complexity, risks and number of staff involved in the project are lower, higher costs must be accepted due to the longer project duration. Since HR is not exposed to any significant cost pressures at present, however, the strategy team is in favor of this option.

KEY ACTIVITIES WITHIN DESIGN BUSINESS VISION AND BUSINESS MODEL:

1. Evaluate the benefits of the objectives from a strategic perspective.
2. Design business model using the four strategic options.
3. Analysis of different realization methods.

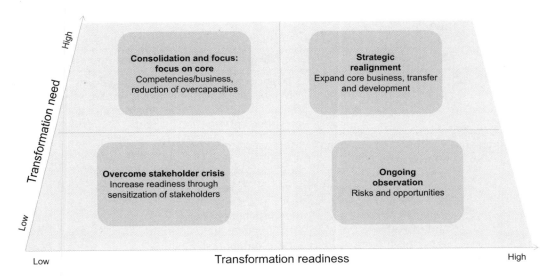

Figure 11.6 Strategic options

11.4.4 DEFINE INTEGRATED TRANSFORMATION PLAN (STEP 6)

In the following, we summarize the major milestones during the transformation planning of the presented case study:

Organizational implementation planning and business case elaboration

Following the decision presented in the previous section, a separate business case is prepared for the HR IT system and the shared service platform. Given that the greatest monetary saving potentials will not be realized until the shared service center is set up, the business case for the HR IT solution is prepared first. As already indicated, the savings are considerably less and result from the shutdown of local solutions and avoidance of future, local investments in new IT infrastructures. However, these are offset by the implementation costs and cost of the ERPs. From a purely monetary perspective, it is evident that this investment does not pay off. Instead, it must be regarded as a strategic investment and consolidation (see Table 11.1).

When planning the HR IT system, the strategy team opts for a cautious, selective and focused approach that initially centers on the core aspects of the HR IT (HR Core), such as HR administration and organizational management, since these are easily standardized and also represent the prerequisites for global reporting and other global processes. To demonstrate that global processes can also be realized, the team plans to implement global, IT-based performance management. This course of action appears to be favorable in that this process already works on a paper basis and *merely* needs to be modelled electronically and (partially) automated. Other areas such as learning, training and compensation management, which are handled very differently at a local level,

Table 11.1   Classification of benefits: adapted according to Ward and Daniel (2006)

	Do new things	Do things better	Stop doing things
Financial		Efficiency gains in HR result in a slight reduction in HR operating costs.	Shutting down local systems saves maintenance and repair costs.
Measurable/ Observable	Repositioning regarding strategic consulting leads to greater visibility. A higher level of satisfaction amount (internal) customers and management is expected as a result.	More accurate reporting is expected to lead to fewer errors and higher transparency; fewer integration gaps result in prompt and high-quality HR data. A further non-quantifiable aspect is the improvement in data security.	

have been excluded initially by the project team. The plan is based on a step-by-step implementation covering various modules over a period of five years.

Geographical sequencing

With respect to implementing the system in the different regions, the team makes the following considerations taking the stakeholder and organizational change management aspects into account: The pilot implementation serves to demonstrate the general feasibility of the project as well as to identify problem areas, such as processes that have not been defined clearly enough or technical difficulties. This is to ensure that these *lessons learned* can be used for subsequent implementations. Since the success of the initial roll-out is extremely significant for the entire project, Italy is selected as it provides the most favorable prerequisites. All of the MotorStars divisions are represented in Italy. On the one hand, the country is not too small and thus can be accepted as a valid *proof of concept* should the implementation succeed. On the other hand, since the political and organizational situation is not overly complex, initial successes can be anticipated in the short term. Italy also has processes that are relatively easy to standardize and also requires a new IT HR solution. Countries that already have functioning, established local IT HR systems and where resistance is expected are scheduled last. In this way, France will be the last country in which the system will be implemented this time, as it was here that the initial attempt failed.

Germany, Switzerland and then the other European countries are scheduled to follow Italy. Finally, the HR IT solution will be rolled out in Asia and then North America. This regional focus is intended to prevent work from being conducted in parallel in more than two time zones.

Budgeting and distribution of costs

The company plans that the local offices will contribute to the budget, which will be allocated centrally. During the initial implementation in Italy, the costs will be distributed in such a way that Corporate HR too will contribute financially to absorb any additional costs that arise from the pilot implementation. Even though the finance plan allows for the entire project to be budgeted, an overall budget will not be proposed for the complete duration of the undertaking. Instead, the individual subprojects will be budgeted sequentially. To prevent delays in releasing the budget, it has been agreed that the budget for the next sequence will be released automatically as long as the milestones are met and no other problems arise. This sequential budgeting and execution is intended to ensure that the successful implementation of effective IT systems in certain countries can be recognized if the project is cancelled.

Standardized roll-out

A standardized roll-out is planned using the predefined template and a uniform methodology. Only those aspects that cover the requirements of several countries will be integrated in the standard system. For this purpose, the standard processes of the SAP HR component will be defined as a basis. Purely nice-to-have requirements will not be included and local specifics only considered if these are either necessary from a legal perspective or are justifiable by providing a unique business advantage. The onus of proof is on the local offices, which must substantiate why the standard template does not meet their requirements. Any local special requests that are not included in the template must be financed exclusively by the local offices.

Various standards are defined, however, depending on the size of the country involved. Certain modules, for example, are mandatory for large countries and optional for smaller ones. A readiness analysis is scheduled prior to each roll-out and will be used by the country organizations to verify their readiness with respect to the pending transformation. The results will allow each country to rectify any deficits identified by the time the implementation begins.

Governance and implementation team

The governance structure insists on effective collaboration between local as well as global IT and HR teams. For this reason, the HR IT implementation team comprises both global and local employees. The global team collects, aggregates and transfers knowledge and experience of the various implementations. At the start of a country roll-out, the global team performs a fit-gap analysis in conjunction with the local team based on the global template and taking local specifics into account. During the course of the roll-out, the tasks are gradually transferred to the local team. Transferring the data from the legacy to the new systems, testing, on-site training and so on, are typical responsibilities that are performed entirely by the local team.

Resolution of stakeholder conflicts

After a brief working period of two months, the strategy planning team presents the high-level strategy to 80 managers at a global HR manager meeting. After the Head of HR IT has presented the strategy in the plenary session, all four members of the project team provide a detailed explanation of the strategy in a series of workshops. During the course of this meeting, the team succeeds in securing buy-in from the entire HR organization. It is decided that the outlined concept is on the right track and should be elaborated further. The meeting enables the team to obtain and reinforce the support of the entire organization – even if it is still at a relatively abstract level.

At this point, however, the old rivalries between Corporate HR, the Corporate Lead Division Car and IT resurface. Each party wants to secure ownership and thus control of the project. The local offices as well as the members of the project team, the Head of HR Operational Excellence Car and the Head of the Shared Service Center Germany (Car) realize that their influence is threatened by the planned implementation. The further project lead would come under Corporate due to the involvement of the Head of HR Business Excellence. For this reason, the Car Division increasingly begins to undermine the further course of the project. Ultimately, the situation ends in a very emotional project team meeting that is called by the Head of Corporate HR and to which the Head of ERP is also invited. In the meeting, the Head of Corporate HR reemphasizes the significance of the project. He is fully aware that past differences have to be smoothed over if the project is to be a success and the roles of the parties involved have to be uniquely defined. During the course of the meeting, however, it transpires that, with the current team constellation, the project threatens to fail for exactly the same reasons as the first attempt did. Consequently, the Head of the HR Shared Service Center Germany is removed from the project team and assigned other responsibilities internally. The Head of ERP too is transferred to a different business function and replaced by an external IT specialist.

Next, the project is approved by the Finance department and finally Car can be won over after the business case is presented by the Head of HR IT in an executive board meeting. However, this required the following clarification and role allocation prior to the meeting and was primarily initiated by the Head of Corporate HR: it was agreed that the Car Division would act as project lead. Car leads the project that it is implementing as a vendor in conjunction with IT. Corporate HR assumes a control and monitoring function in the steering committee, which consists of the Head of Corporate HR, the Head of Car HR, the Head of HR Business Excellence, as well as the CFO and CIO. By doing so, the team was able to secure the strongest division within MotorStars as a driver for the project and thus settle the stakeholder conflicts between Corporate HR and Car. Even though Corporate HR is taking a step back as a result and is performing merely a steering role, given the original personal and micropolitical situation, a solution has been found whereby no side has to lose face. The objective of this strategy is thus to overcome the stakeholder crisis first, then aspire to a consolidation with the IT solution, and only then complete a strategic redirection by implementing a shared service center (see Figure 11.6).

KEY ACTIVITIES WITHIN DEFINE INTEGRATED TRANSFORMATION PLAN:

1. The first proof-of-concept implementation is realized in the region with the most favorable prerequisites.
2. Plan and distribute costs to individual subprojects.
3. Define a standardized roll-out scenario using predefined templates and a uniform methodology.
4. Shift responsibilities from the global team to the local team in the course of project execution time.
5. Present intermediate project results and resolve stakeholder conflicts.

11.5 Conclusion

This chapter demonstrates the importance of a comprehensive approach to business transformation. Even seemingly simple projects, such as the implementation of a new information system, can have transformational impact and, accordingly, entail unexpected and complex challenges. As shown, these are often rooted in *people issues* such as micropolitical tactics of leading players than in technological matters. Consequently, efforts that are solely focused on the implementation of an IT system are likely to fail. Instead, a systematic approach that includes knowledge and methods related to strategy, values, risk, processes, program, technology and in particular organizational change and learning needs to be taken into consideration. By following a business transformation team in the strategic phase (envision), we have exemplified the application of BTM^2 in a complex situation. In addition, this contribution clearly shows the complexity of business transformation that more often than not is circular rather than linear. It also illustrates the importance of reflecting on past mistakes and of incorporating the lessons learned into the new roadmap. Sometimes a winner-loser situation is inevitable. In this case, every effort should be taken to ensure that the *losers* are removed fairly so that new attempts are not undermined by old rivalries.

Bibliography

Ward, John and Daniel, Elizabeth (2006), *Benefits Management: Delivering Value from IS & IT Investments* (Chichester: Wiley).

CHAPTER 12 Lessons Learned from the Business Transformation Case Studies

JOHN WARD (Cranfield University, School of Management) and AXEL UHL (SAP AG)

12.1 Overview

As part of the development of BTM², 13 case studies of different types of business transformation in large European corporations across a range of industries were conducted. The industries were: automotive, pharmaceuticals, construction, food, oil and chemicals, financial services, telecommunications and IT. The cases included transformations to develop new products and services as well as restructuring and reorganizing core business functions and introducing global processes and systems.

All the transformations involved changes in organization structures and individuals' roles, responsibilities and behaviors. In a few of the cases this led to large-scale staff relocations and redeployments. All the cases included new and significant investments in IT to enable the business transformation, but, in all but one of the cases, IT benefits were not the main rationale for the transformation.

The cases were used to test, validate and enhance BTM². This was possible because the cases demonstrated different levels of success:

- Four were very successful achieving all the main objectives of the transformation.
- Five cases were partially successful as some expected benefits were achieved, but not all.
- Four were unsuccessful, achieving none of the transformation objectives or were not completed. Most incurred substantial costs.

This ratio is typical of the overall statistics of success rates for projects, programs and business transformations.

The cases were developed and analyzed by teams consisting of experienced academics, researchers, consultants and senior company managers. They involved interviews with those involved in the business transformation and reviews of relevant documentation. Each case was written up in detail by the team and verified as an accurate record of events by the organizations concerned. Some have already been published in *360° – The Business Transformation Journal*[1] and others will be published in future editions.

---

1   Business Transformation Academy. *360° – The Business Transformation Journal, 2011*: www.bta-online.com/360degree (accessed March 2012).

The cases have been analyzed using a number of the BTM² models described in earlier chapters in this book. Initial assessment considered the strategic positioning of the business transformation, then each was analyzed in terms of how extensively and how well the eight BTM² disciplines, such as Value Management and the subdisciplines within each, were performed. The analyses for all the cases were compared to identify significant aspects which appeared to affect the level of success achieved. Summaries and examples of these analyses are included in this chapter. The companies have not been named since the details are confidential.

OBJECTIVES OF THIS CHAPTER:

1. Demonstrate how the evidence from a range of business transformation case studies was used to develop and evaluate BTM².
2. Understand the lessons learned from case studies of successful and unsuccessful transformations.
3. Learn how each of the BTM² management disciplines can influence the success of a business transformation.

12.2 An Overview of the Cases and Outcomes

12.2.1 THE SUCCESSES

Case 1

Global HR system and reorganization, implemented top-down in response to external criticism of the company's corporate governance. Organizational changes preceded the IT implementation. The organization had learned from a previous expensive failure to achieve the same transformation.

Case 2

IT enabled sustainability program which has been successful so far in creating initiatives and structures to address sustainability issues and reduce environmental impact for the company and its customers.

Case 3

Global customer service process transformation through new IT foundations and business changes to act consistently as one global organization. It was an extended change program, which was based on collaborative process redesign and implementation through compromise not confrontation.

Case 4

Reorganization and rationalization into shared service centers for support functions and implementation of new operational model with standardized processes and common systems. The reorganization preceded the introduction of the new systems and processes.

12.2.2 THE PARTIAL SUCCESSES

Case 5

The implementation of a corporate HR database, but the roll-out across all business units was deferred due to lack of local benefits and increasingly difficult trading conditions. Project is seen as a relatively low cost, learning experience.

Case 6

Implementation of global HR excellence function, new HR database and systems: 50 percent of HR tasks worldwide supported by the new systems and further benefits have been identified. Initial programr was IT-led and achieved little until taken over by HR function as part of global business transformation.

Case 7

The development of a service business capability to complement a successful product strategy by creating a global center of excellence, sharing knowledge with customers to develop high-quality valued services.

Case 8

The creation of a new product concept to meet demands of a different customer segment, to be manufactured and delivered through a new business model: the product proved popular, but the business model could not be made profitable.

Case 9

The reintegration of the new product (Case 8 above) into the main manufacturing, logistics and sales organization to exploit traditional competences through the adoption of standard processes and systems, to stabilize costs and reduce losses.

12.2.3 THE UNSUCCESSFUL

Case 10

A very expensive investment in a global HR system, functionally led, aimed at reducing systems costs. There was no real business justification, few achievable benefits and it was abandoned before completion.

Case 11

Another failed global HR system: overspent, late and only partially implemented prior to abandonment; it was a system few parts of the business wanted and the benefits were very limited (the failed transformation that preceded the success described in Case 1).

Case 12

Rationalization and centralization of finance and accounting functions across Europe, accompanied by new systems and processes. The program was abandoned due to lack of business buy-in to a weak business case. A second attempt is now underway, adopting a different approach.

Case 13

Introduction of common production planning and control processes and systems across global manufacturing units. There was no real business case, due to variations in products and manufacturing processes, no stakeholder buy-in and no internal transformation capability. Pilot implementations failed and the project was abandoned.

In the figures used to summarize some of analyses that follow, the cases are known by the numbers above.

12.3 Strategic Positioning of Business Transformations

The transformation portfolio matrix shown in Figure 4.2 in Chapter 4, Value Management, was used to position the transformations based on the expected strategic impact as expressed in the transformation objectives. Figure 12.1 shows the results of that analysis.

Figure 12.1 shows that those considered as both strategic and high potential, aimed at creating or identifying competitive advantages were all at least partially successful. It could be concluded that the "positive" nature of the business transformation intentions meant that there was little stakeholder resistance to the initiative and hence the organization was able to deploy its most capable resources.

Conversely all three that best fit the support definition – to reduce costs or remove inefficiencies – were all unsuccessful. As will be argued later, in each case what could be considered as operational problems should not have become the argument for a major

Strategic	
Level of success	Case
Successful	1
Partly successful	7
Failed	

High potential	
Level of success	Case
Successful	2
Partly successful	5, 8
Failed	

Key operational	
Level of success	Case
Successful	3, 4
Partly successful	6, 9
Failed	13

Support	
Level of success	Case
Successful	
Partly successful	
Failed	10, 11, 12

Figure 12.1 The cases positioned on the transformation portfolio matrix

transformation, which increased the scope of the changes but not the business benefits. Senior management engagement and support was limited and the initiatives were given little priority, except in the functional area concerned.

The five key operational transformations, aimed at overcoming or preventing real or potential disadvantages, had mixed fortunes and the reasons for this are in the detail of how they were managed, not in the *strategic* intent.

12.4 Transformation Need and Readiness

The importance of a clear understanding of the *need to transform* – the drivers and objectives – and the timescale within which it has to be achieved is discussed in detail in Chapter 3, Strategy Management. Then assessing the organization's readiness or capability to make the changes is essential to decide not only the best approach to the business transformation, but also to define the transformation scope so that the chances of success are increased. An adapted version of the Strategic Options model (see Figure 3.9 in Chapter 3, Strategy Management) was used to describe each case in terms of the importance of the business transformation and the organization's apparent readiness as shown in Figure 12.2. How the transformation need and readiness can be assessed is described in detail in Chapter 3, Strategy Management.

Figure 12.3 shows the positioning of each of the cases on this matrix to describe the situation at the start of each transformation, based on the evidence provided.

This analysis shows vividly that in all the unsuccessful cases the need for transformation was relatively low; either there was no pressing need or there was little agreement, at a senior level, that it was a business priority. In three of the cases the need was argued only by one business function or the IT department. As a consequence the rest of the organization was unwilling to do the low priority, but demanding and complex work involved: readiness was also low. Had the organizations undertaken such an analysis early in the business transformation, failure and the significant resulting waste of money and resources could have been avoided.

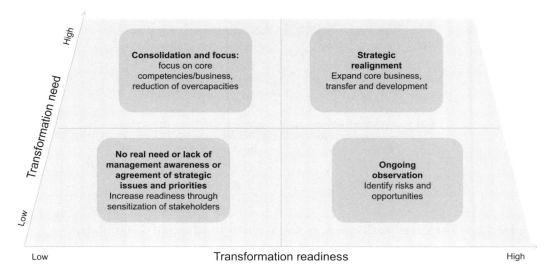

Figure 12.2 Strategic options: need and readiness

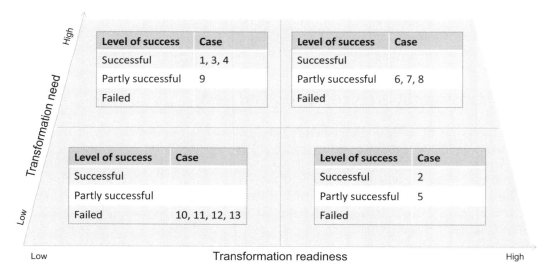

Figure 12.3 Transformation need and readiness in the cases

In three of the four successful transformations the need was *high* – clearly recognized as a priority – but initially the readiness was *low*. In these cases the argument for change was endorsed at executive level and time and effort spent in the engagement phase to achieve the buy-in of the rest of the organization and develop the organization's ability to undertake the changes.

In the majority of those that were partially successful the transformation readiness appeared to be *high* as well as the need. The reason they were not entirely successful is perhaps best explained as over ambition or even over enthusiasm, due to rather too many "positive" assumptions being made at the start and little assessment of the potential risks involved. In one case this was compounded by the program team providing only positive feedback to management about progress and not reporting aspects that would cause concern. In some cases assumptions about the business environment were too optimistic and in other the envisioned new business model proved not entirely viable.

One "outlier" – Case 9 – shows that the analysis is not always precise and that a *high* does not always lead to increased transformation readiness: in this case due to major concurrent changes in senior personnel and the loss of key staff. The other – Case 2 – suggests that high readiness does enable opportunistic initiatives to explore new business options and prove the value they may deliver.

Some initial conclusions can be drawn from these analyses to suggest why some business transformations are more successful than others:

- Business transformation needs to be driven by clear imperatives – the strategic reasons to do it – which should be easy for everyone to understand. If there is no clear strategic imperative, it is likely to get stopped or lose priority, as there is no real motivation to change.
- All the successful ones had business imperatives that affected the whole corporation's future not just a function – a clear need to "transform the business". These imperatives were communicated throughout the organization. A lack of strategic alignment creates risks which cannot be addressed later in the program. Therefore initiatives need to be selected carefully.
- The business drivers provide the "case for action": strategic, tactical and operational issues should not be confused during the envision and engage phases. In some cases, what were initially operational efficiency issues were developed (sometimes with the help of the IT implementation partner) to become "strategic opportunities", which were not justified. None of these were successful. There can be a tendency to make operational problems strategic, just to get them solved.
- In most of the unsuccessful cases the complexity of the transformation was underestimated and the adaptability, or readiness to adapt, of the organization overestimated. Understanding the organization's readiness to transform is crucial to deciding the transformation strategy. Transformation requires a lot of energy and resources and the amount of dedicated resource required increases when readiness is less.
- The successful transformations had CEO sponsorship and a C-level executive leading or directing the transformation. Involvement should be real and visible: if not, other executives will not see it as important and not spend time on it. Leading the transformation involves communication of clear, consistent messages, time spent on the program details and being actively involved in solving issues that arise.

12.5 Analyzing the Cases Using the BTM² Management Disciplines

In each of the sections that follow, how effective or ineffective management practices across the eight BTM² management disciplines (which are described in detail in the preceding chapters) affected the evolution of the transformation and the eventual outcome, in terms of the level of success achieved are discussed.

An overview model of the discipline relationships is shown in Figure 12.4.

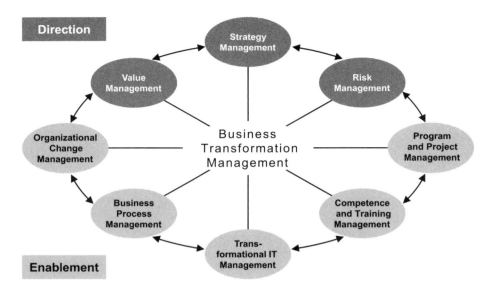

Figure 12.4 The direction and enablement discipline relationships (please also refer to Figure 2.1)

Figures 12.5–12.7 show the BTM^2 disciplines and how they were performed in three typical, example cases – one successful, one partially successful and one unsuccessful. The analysis is based on the evidence presented in the case study write up and in some cases evidence about a particular subdiscipline was not available. In others a subdiscipline was "*not applicable*" normally because the transformation was not completed. The performance of the individual activities in each discipline is highlighted according to the color code at the bottom of each figure.

We differentiate between activities, which:

- were performed and performed well;
- were performed either only to some extent or not particularly well;
- were either not performed or performed poorly;
- do not provide any evidence in the case in order to decide; and
- were not applicable.

The pattern of the extent and quality of the discipline and subdiscipline performances are typical of the cases in each of the three levels of success.

Findings for each of the eight management disciplines are now discussed, in turn, before considering findings regarding the Meta Management aspects.

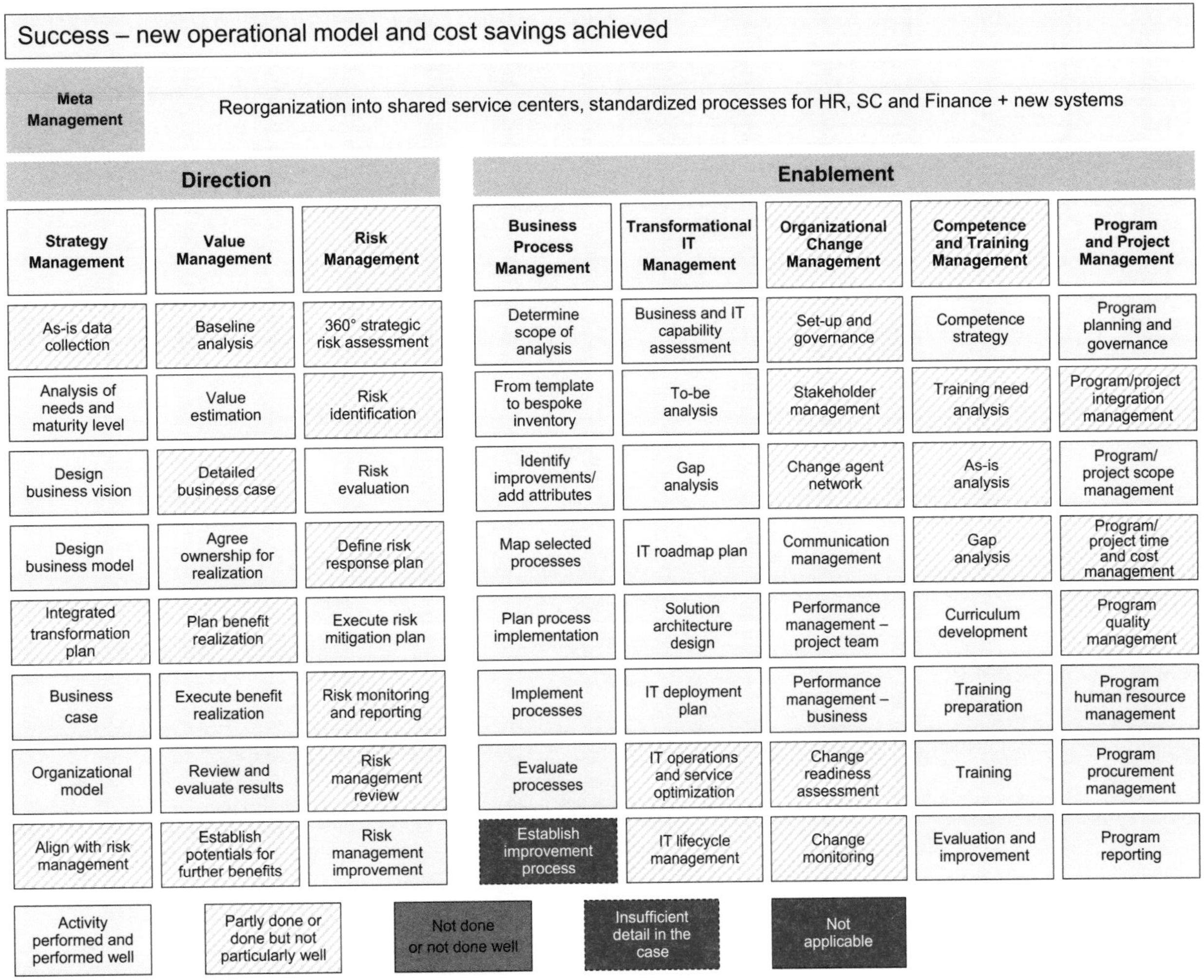

Success – new operational model and cost savings achieved

Meta Management: Reorganization into shared service centers, standardized processes for HR, SC and Finance + new systems

Direction

Strategy Management	Value Management	Risk Management
As-is data collection	Baseline analysis	360° strategic risk assessment
Analysis of needs and maturity level	Value estimation	Risk identification
Design business vision	Detailed business case	Risk evaluation
Design business model	Agree ownership for realization	Define risk response plan
Integrated transformation plan	Plan benefit realization	Execute risk mitigation plan
Business case	Execute benefit realization	Risk monitoring and reporting
Organizational model	Review and evaluate results	Risk management review
Align with risk management	Establish potentials for further benefits	Risk management improvement

Enablement

Business Process Management	Transformational IT Management	Organizational Change Management	Competence and Training Management	Program and Project Management
Determine scope of analysis	Business and IT capability assessment	Set-up and governance	Competence strategy	Program planning and governance
From template to bespoke inventory	To-be analysis	Stakeholder management	Training need analysis	Program/project integration management
Identify improvements/add attributes	Gap analysis	Change agent network	As-is analysis	Program/project scope management
Map selected processes	IT roadmap plan	Communication management	Gap analysis	Program/project time and cost management
Plan process implementation	Solution architecture design	Performance management – project team	Curriculum development	Program quality management
Implement processes	IT deployment plan	Performance management – business	Training preparation	Program human resource management
Evaluate processes	IT operations and service optimization	Change readiness assessment	Training	Program procurement management
Establish improvement process	IT lifecycle management	Change monitoring	Evaluation and improvement	Program reporting

Legend:
- Not applicable
- Insufficient detail in the case
- Not done or not done well
- Partly done or done but not particularly well
- Activity performed and performed well

Figure 12.5 The pattern that is typical for a successful case

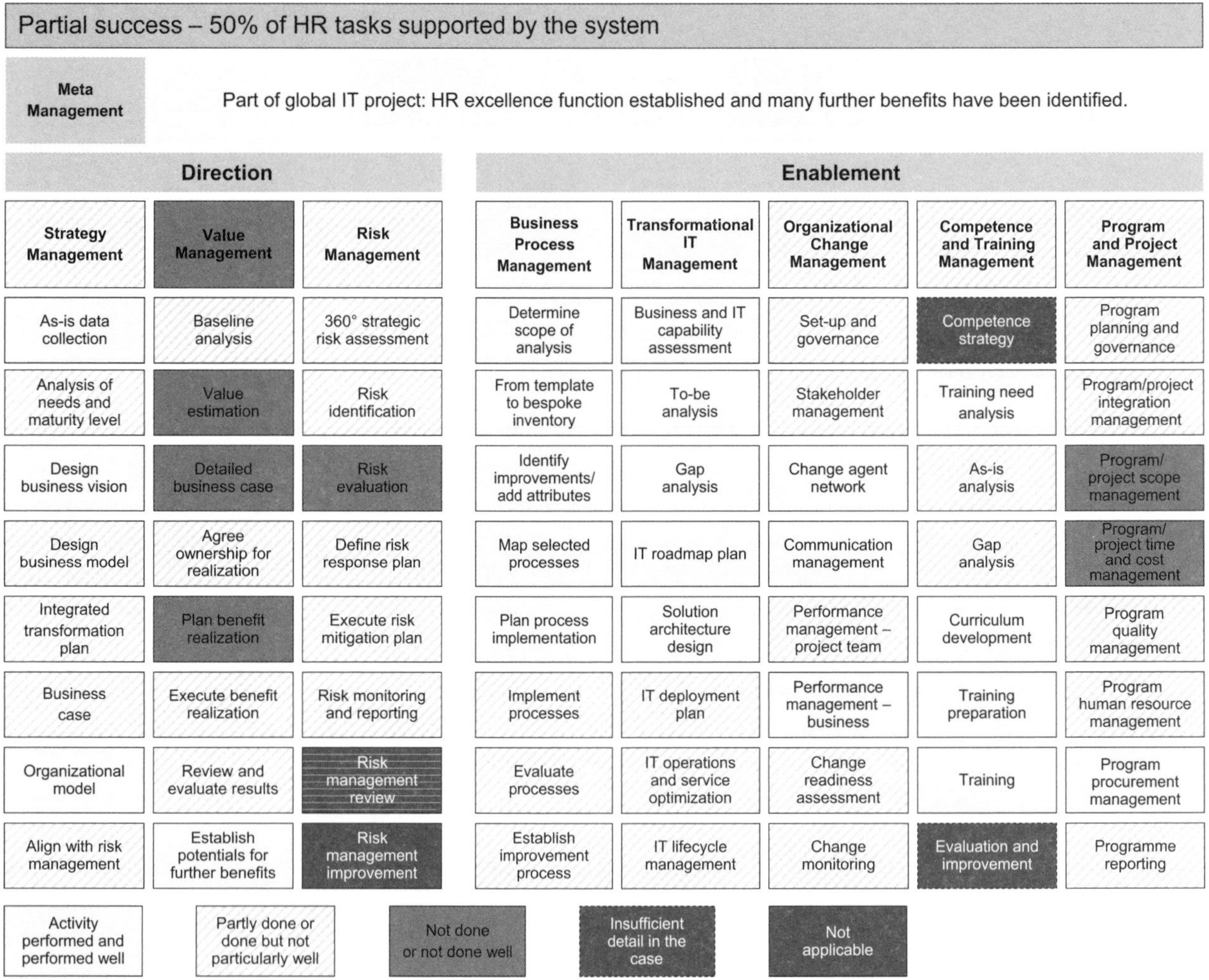

Partial success – 50% of HR tasks supported by the system

Meta Management — Part of global IT project: HR excellence function established and many further benefits have been identified.

Direction

Strategy Management	Value Management	Risk Management
As-is data collection	Baseline analysis	360° strategic risk assessment
Analysis of needs and maturity level	Value estimation	Risk identification
Design business vision	Detailed business case	Risk evaluation
Design business model	Agree ownership for realization	Define risk response plan
Integrated transformation plan	Plan benefit realization	Execute risk mitigation plan
Business case	Execute benefit realization	Risk monitoring and reporting
Organizational model	Review and evaluate results	Risk management review
Align with risk management	Establish potentials for further benefits	Risk management improvement

Enablement

Business Process Management	Transformational IT Management	Organizational Change Management	Competence and Training Management	Program and Project Management
Determine scope of analysis	Business and IT capability assessment	Set-up and governance	Competence strategy	Program planning and governance
From template to bespoke inventory	To-be analysis	Stakeholder management	Training need analysis	Program/project integration management
Identify improvements/add attributes	Gap analysis	Change agent network	As-is analysis	Program/project scope management
Map selected processes	IT roadmap plan	Communication management	Gap analysis	Program/project time and cost management
Plan process implementation	Solution architecture design	Performance management – project team	Curriculum development	Program quality management
Implement processes	IT deployment plan	Performance management – business	Training preparation	Program human resource management
Evaluate processes	IT operations and service optimization	Change readiness assessment	Training	Program procurement management
Establish improvement process	IT lifecycle management	Change monitoring	Evaluation and improvement	Programme reporting

Legend:
- Activity performed and performed well
- Partly done or done but not particularly well
- Not done or not done well
- Insufficient detail in the case
- Not applicable

Figure 12.6 Typical pattern for a partially successful case

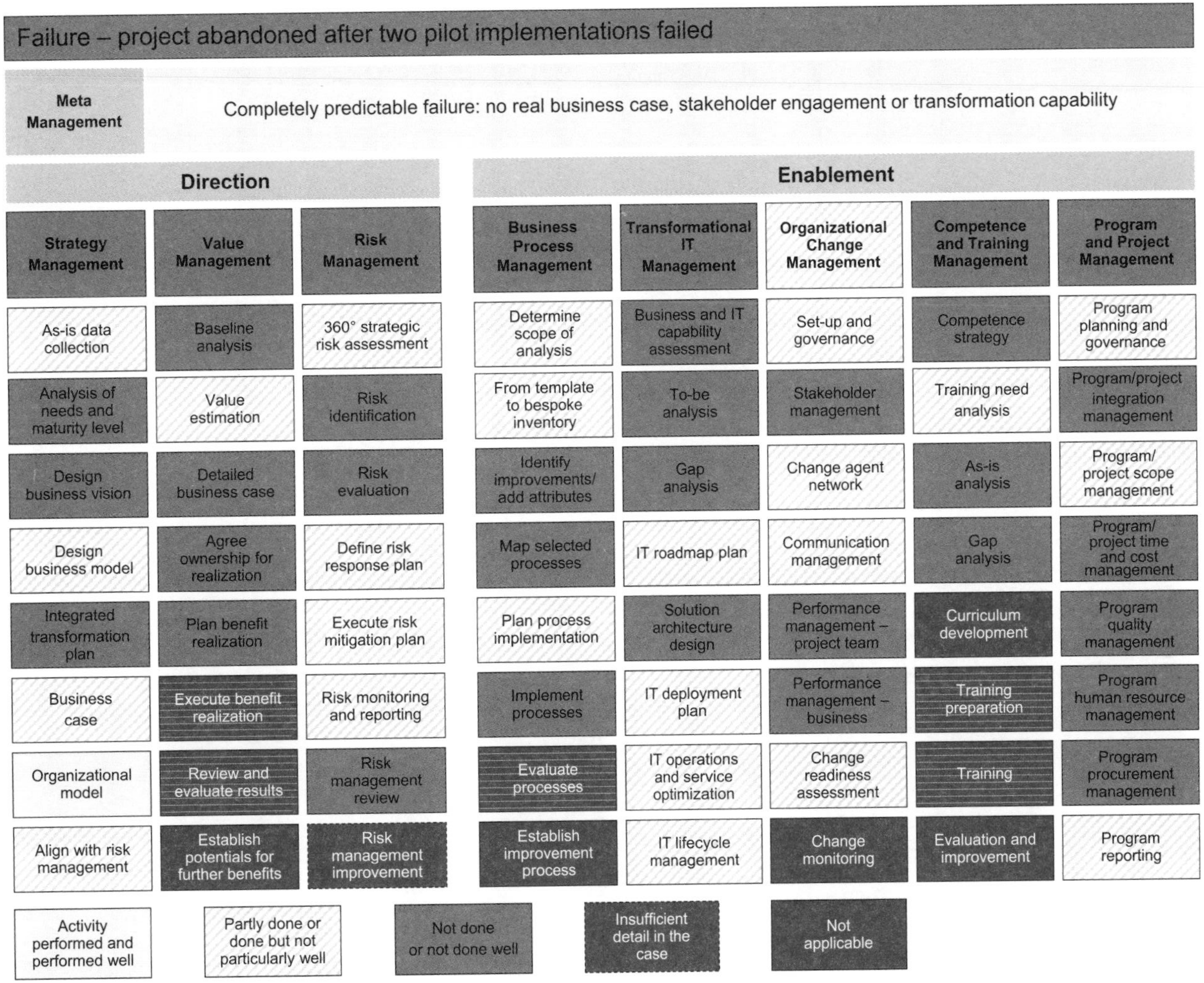

Failure – project abandoned after two pilot implementations failed

Meta Management: Completely predictable failure: no real business case, stakeholder engagement or transformation capability

Direction

Strategy Management	Value Management	Risk Management
As-is data collection	Baseline analysis	360° strategic risk assessment
Analysis of needs and maturity level	Value estimation	Risk identification
Design business vision	Detailed business case	Risk evaluation
Design business model	Agree ownership for realization	Define risk response plan
Integrated transformation plan	Plan benefit realization	Execute risk mitigation plan
Business case	Execute benefit realization	Risk monitoring and reporting
Organizational model	Review and evaluate results	Risk management review
Align with risk management	Establish potentials for further benefits	Risk management improvement

Enablement

Business Process Management	Transformational IT Management	Organizational Change Management	Competence and Training Management
Determine scope of analysis	Business and IT capability assessment	Set-up and governance	Competence strategy
From template to bespoke inventory	To-be analysis	Stakeholder management	Training need analysis
Identify improvements/add attributes	Gap analysis	Change agent network	As-is analysis
Map selected processes	IT roadmap plan	Communication management	Gap analysis
Plan process implementation	Solution architecture design	Performance management – project team	Curriculum development
Implement processes	IT deployment plan	Performance management – business	Training preparation
Evaluate processes	IT operations and service optimization	Change readiness assessment	Training
Establish improvement process	IT lifecycle management	Change monitoring	Evaluation and improvement
		Not applicable	

Program and Project Management

Program and Project Management
Program planning and governance
Program/project integration management
Program/project scope management
Program/project time and cost management
Program quality management
Program human resource management
Program procurement management
Program reporting

Legend:
- Activity performed and performed well
- Partly done or done but not particularly well
- Not done or not done well
- Insufficient detail in the case
- Not applicable

Figure 12.7 An unsuccessful case – not completed

12.5.1 THE DIRECTION DISCIPLINES

These three examples clearly demonstrate a pattern that was consistent across almost all the cases:

- If the majority of the *directional* disciplines were neglected or performed poorly, the transformation was either unsuccessful or not completed.
- With one exception, even if a minority of the disciplines were neglected or performed poorly, or many were not carried out well or thoroughly the best that was achieved was partial success.

In essence, the outcome of the business transformation could be predicted from predominant color in the assessment of the *directional* disciplines. Hence an appraisal during the envision and engage phases of how clearly and comprehensively the transformation strategy, value and risks have been understood and communicated, will provide a strong indication of likely success.

Strategy Management

- Transformations should start top-down with a vision of what the future will be, but decide the actual content and process for change from the "middle out", during the engage phase, to make sure it's doable, while also "keeping the shop open" and maintaining business performance during the transformation.
- Having a clear vision of the intended future business and organizational models and then allowing compromises and trade-offs in the detail of how they are implemented, is more likely to achieve stakeholder commitment than imposition. In some cases, when the drivers demand urgent action a top-down, mandated approach to implementation can also work, but tends to achieve stakeholder compliance or acceptance rather than positive commitment.
- Most business transformations involve at least two distinct and different phases – first to create a new capability and second to exploit it. In most cases the capability was created, but was not (yet) always exploited, hence the benefits achieved were often less than those originally envisaged. This is because creating a new capability can be done "off-line", separately from business as usual, but using and exploiting it usually competes with other operational priorities.

Value Management

- In those that were not successful the transformation objectives and business cases were often vague, based on a "benefits vision" rather than an evidence-based set of benefits and an understanding of how to realize them. This makes it difficult for some stakeholders to believe the transformation is worthwhile and commit the required time and resources.

- In some of the cases there was confusion between *changes* and *benefits*: for example introducing common global processes is a change, not a benefit. It may create the potential for benefits, such as reducing costs or higher service levels.
- Very often business benefits were overestimated, while the risks and the problems in making the changes were underestimated, because otherwise it would be difficult to get funds and resources. Realistic and evidence-based benefits are needed.
- Like many (so-called) *strategic projects*, instigated by senior management, the development of a detailed business case seems unnecessary. However, transformations are business investments so investment board/governance bodies should demand realistic business cases and also assess how successful the investments have been, by reviewing the benefits actually achieved. The successful ones all did this and most reviewed the progress of the investment, not just the change program during implementation.

Risk Management

- Risk Management was often glossed over, but given that a high percentage of such programs "fail", it is best to identify and anticipate what could go wrong, before it happens. The distinction between strategic and operational risks was often not clear. As a result many risks only became apparent during implementation leading to increased costs, delays, scope reductions and even abandonment. This reluctance to explore the risks earlier may have been influenced by executive instigation of the transformation, which can discourage negative feedback, making it inadvisable or even career limiting to point out the potential risks.
- To reduce risks, the transformation should be planned in short deliverable stages if possible. This provides the following advantages:
  - Earlier delivery of some benefits.
  - Reduced vulnerability to changing business conditions.
  - Easier to adjust the transformation to retain strategic alignment.
  - Earlier learning of the implications of the changes.
  - More manageable interactions with related programs.
  - Reduced risk of wasting resources, if the transformation scope has to change.
  - It provides more opportunities to review the expected value to be realized.
  - Governance structures are more effective and can be adjusted as the transformation evolves.
- Some business transformations are unduly influenced by changes in senior management personnel rather than changes in business strategy. The interests and priorities of individuals should not "corrupt" the organizational purpose of the transformation. However, this could be observed in a number of the less successful cases, especially where the transformation objectives could be interpreted in different ways.

12.5.2 THE ENABLEMENT DISCIPLINES

Business Process Management

- The IT and process changes tend to be performed more successfully than organizational changes, resulting in some benefits being delivered, even in some of the less successful cases. But this rarely is enough to enable the transformation to achieve its strategic objectives and the majority of the benefits.
- Established or proven methodologies were applied in most of the cases; however, in some the IT or process methodology dominated the overall implementation approach, making the implementation of other changes more difficult.
- In two of the unsuccessful cases the IT function followed a "traditional" needs analysis approach and tried to satisfy all the expressed user needs, irrespective of whether the associated process changes would deliver business benefits. This increased the scope to the point where the costs considerably outweighed the benefits. In other cases, operational process issues were discovered (or deliberately introduced) during implementation causing a reduction in potential benefits or increased complexity and costs.

Program and Project Management

- Transformations cannot be fully planned in advance and have to adapt to both changing business conditions and program achievements: this is not necessarily a comfortable position for senior management and requires a knowledgeable, accountable and empowered steering or governance group to oversee and, where necessary, adapt the transformation program.
- Effective management of the change content and benefits delivery is more important than the efficiency of the process. The process should reflect not only the transformation required but the organization's values, experience, capabilities and culture.
- The transformation manager needs to have expert knowledge in the area that is being changed and also how to manage change in the specific organization. A key skill is being able to reconcile the differing views of the change and resource implications between senior managers and operational line management. Figure 12.8 shows the relationship triangle and research (Peppard and Ward, 2005) suggests that the priority early in the program should be to gain agreement between senior and line management as to what the transformation entails, before "negotiating" with senior management for the funds and dedicated resources required. In some of the less than successful cases the "contract" between the project team and senior management was agreed before the views of line managers had been taken into account.
- In some failure cases the organization relied heavily on the generic knowledge and capabilities of a third party supplier throughout both the directional and enablement activities. In some cases this changed the nature of the transformation towards what the supplier could do, not what was required. External suppliers can only complement and not replace internal, organization specific knowledge and capabilities.

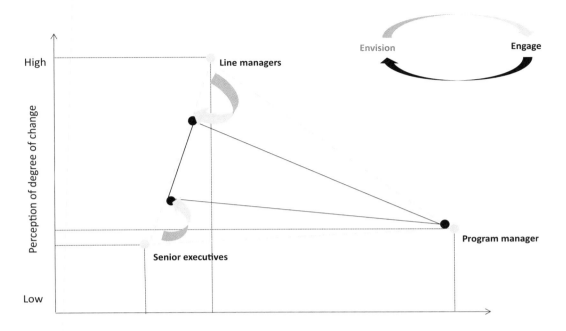

Figure 12.8 The relationship triangle: transformation program manager, line managers and senior management

- In other failures the organization relied too much on the existing IT project management approaches and hence did not effectively balance the IT and business aspects of the transformation.

Transformational IT Management

- IT change cannot be entirely delegated to a partner. An implementation partner is actually a supplier of products or services so there is always a potential conflict of interests.
- The transformations whose main benefits were seen as IT cost reduction or rationalization or are led by IT (including the CIO) were not successful. Some business transformations become only IT transformations, as the first phase is about replacing old IT and exclusively IT methodologies and approaches are used. The result is that a transformation becomes just "IT replacement project", with little or no business involvement (Ward et al., 2005). Transforming the organization's IT, should be considered as an enabler of business transformation – not an end in itself (Gregor et al., 2006).
- IT is often in a weak position in the context of a business transformation, due to a real lack of business knowledge, but a perception that they know how it works: but they only know how the IT systems work. This created conflict in some of the transformations. When IT "won" the argument the transformation was unsuccessful, but when it was clearly "business-led", any potential conflict was easily resolved.

Organizational Change Management

- These cases suggest that organizations should manage business transformations as orchestrated, continuous, incremental sets of changes – co-evolving and co-existing with business as usual priorities.
- The successful transformations usually addressed the organizational, people and capability aspects of the first, then the process and IT aspects. The less successful tried to do the reverse. As mentioned earlier, in all the unsuccessful cases only a very limited or unrealistic organizational change readiness assessment was carried out.
- Understanding and addressing stakeholder issues and having a strategy for accommodating or dealing with them as early as possible in the transformation is vital – it is the core activity of the engage phase. The longer the time available to transform, the more the stakeholder views can and should be included in how the transformation is conducted.
- Stakeholder engagement is a critical success factor in almost every business transformation and early alignment or reconciliation of multi-stakeholder interests is very important. Getting this wrong will cause major problems throughout the implementation due, for example, to dominance by the interests of a minority of stakeholders or destructive negotiations between dissenting groups.
- The methodologies used should enable all the main stakeholders to directly contribute their knowledge and plan their involvement, not rely on expert knowledge and interpretation of their "needs". Outside or specialist parties are there to enable the organization to transform, not transform it.
- The well-known "transition curve" describing how people and organizations experience major change should be respected in the change management approach adopted. The curve is shown in Figure 12.9 and Figure 12.10. A comprehensive and

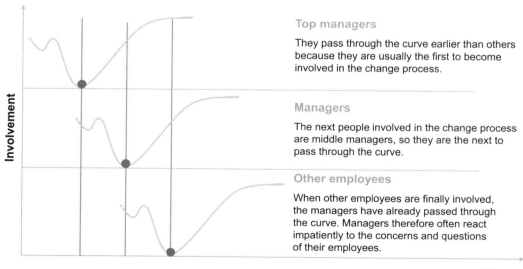

Top managers
They pass through the curve earlier than others because they are usually the first to become involved in the change process.

Managers
The next people involved in the change process are middle managers, so they are the next to pass through the curve.

Other employees
When other employees are finally involved, the managers have already passed through the curve. Managers therefore often react impatiently to the concerns and questions of their employees.

● "Valley of tears"

Figure 12.9 The transformation experience curve (1)

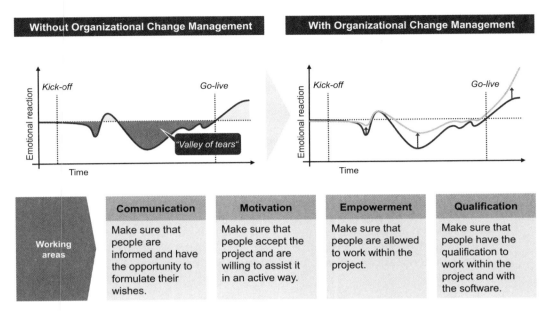

Figure 12.10   The transformation experience curve (2)

sustained approach (as summarized in Figure 12.10) should ensure that the period that people spend in the valley of tears characterized by uncertainty and even disillusionment, is reduced to a minimum. The other curve also shows that different groups reach this point at different times in the transformation: senior management concerns may have moved on, just at the time many line managers and staff are under stress, usually due to change and business as usual pressures colliding.

- In some cases the performance measures used to assess the program teams' performance were too supply-side biased – looking at costs and timescales – which did not allow sufficient flexibility to address unexpected change management issues sufficiently during implementation. This led to a protracted "shakedown" or optimization phase when aspects of the changes had to be reworked or further changes made. This even occurred in some of the successful cases, increasing the costs and causing delays, but not preventing eventual success.

Competence and Training Management

- Assessing existing competences as part of the readiness analysis is important to determine the strategy, because what can be achieved is a function of the amount of work required to make the changes and the knowledge and skills that can be made available at the required time. If some essential competences or skills are limited or absent a strategy for developing them is needed early in the transformation. Insufficient "gap analysis" was a contributory reason for the failure in at least two of the cases.

- In the successful transformations informing and educating people about what the intended future business should look like, helped them apply their existing knowledge to determining how it could be achieved, but also exposed where that existing knowledge was inadequate.
- Where suppliers are providing essential competences those also need to be appraised and managed – suppliers tend to both overstate and overestimate their capabilities. Organizational and individual experience cannot always be transferred from other projects, especially in other organizations. And the transformation may compete with other priorities for the supplier, which can result in the substitution of less competent staff (the "B-team") to replace the initial team that was expected to last the duration. And when people change, knowledge is always lost.
- Suppliers, especially IT suppliers, can have undue influence over what is done rather than just how it is done. Clearly the supplier wants their role in the transformation to be seen as successful, but also profitable. As a consequence however, sometimes even when the supplier only provides the "how" (technology, methods, etc.) this can in effect determine what can actually be achieved – the how drives the what.

12.6 Lessons Learned in Relation to the Meta Management Key Themes

Chapter 2 (Meta Management) introduced the structure, rationale and key elements of BTM² and meta management. It also considered higher-order organizational constructs or themes, which influence the performance of any type of business transformation and also each other: leadership, communication and organization culture and values. The underlying philosophy for the development of the approach described in this book to managing transformations is shown in Figure 12.11.

From the case studies a number of lessons can also be learned about these more general organizational topics.

Our View on Business Transformation and the Role of Meta Management

" Every business transformation is different. The success depends on the complex interplay of actors in a multifaceted ecosystem. According to this understanding, the focus of Meta Management lies in:

a) providing a framework to manage the aspects of the business strategy that requires significant changes;

b) the delegation of responsibilities for the realization to the appropriate organizational levels; and

c) the creation of the appropriate culture and organization for feedback, learning and change. "

Figure 12.11   The underlying philosophy of BTM²

Leadership

- While the successful transformations demonstrated the importance of involvement and leadership by a "C-level" executive, the cases also show that neither dictatorial or autocratic leadership nor micro-management from the top work well and can create resistance.
- The early transfer of "ownership" to a consortium or coalition of business managers, who will actually deliver the changes or benefit from them and the establishment of the core transformation team is the best way to develop the capability to change. The leadership role is to provide a context for those groups to build the business case for the transformation and to trust and support their decision making. One key decision that needs to be taken by the transformation leader in consultation is the mode of "change agency" to be adopted. Our cases show that either an "expert task force" or devolving responsibilities, usually supported by peer-to-peer networks, can work, but a lack of role clarity is likely to cause fragmentation and even disintegration of the initiative. This is discussed further below.
- The leadership role is particularly critical in the envision and engage phases, during which it is essential to achieve credibility for the program. A transformation leader who, due to role or reputation, has little personal credibility in the context of what is intended, is unlikely to achieve the necessary buy-in from other stakeholders. This was clearly a problem in three of the unsuccessful cases – two have been restarted under new leadership.
- Probably the most testing challenge for the leadership role is identifying and resolving any power or interest conflicts among the key stakeholders and the business transformation team. This is never pleasant work but it often has to be done to prevent or limit the damage discordant relationships can cause.
- Many studies have shown that senior management "commitment" is essential in transformation projects, but commitment is a vague term. The evidence from these cases suggests sustained, continuous personal involvement in the governance of the transformation is what it really means but it is not always easy for a busy, ambitious executive to sustain that over the extended period required for most transformations.
- The business transformation leader, director or manager – many titles are used – needs explicit and visible public support from the executive team. Some executive teams are dysfunctional with individuals pursuing different agendas. As our case studies suggest, in such situations, undertaking a major business transformation is probably unwise.

Communication

- A common lesson from many of the cases – even the successful ones – is that no amount of communication is ever enough. When asked, "What would you do differently next time?", more and better communication was the most common response.
- Informing everyone in the organization why change is needed and the consequences of not changing is one of the most important messages and needs regular repetition. Being equally open about what the transformation is going to mean, even if it will be

unpopular with some stakeholders, is important if the credibility of the transformation is to be maintained. Evasiveness builds distrust or suggests ignorance, both of which reduce credibility and commitment.

- In addition, ensuring the communication strategy explains what is going on and intended in the language of the recipients is essential – tailoring the messages to the different audiences. Delivering it at the appropriate times when it is meaningful in the working context of the recipients is also critical if it is to be effective. In a number of cases this was poorly done, creating undue expectations, unexpected concerns and even suspicion.
- Remembering that communication is a two-way process is often a weakness in the transformation process and in a number of the less successful cases little attention was paid to questions, concerns or feedback that the project team felt were distracting or unimportant. It became clear later that if more attention had been paid, serious problems could have been avoided.

Culture and values

- All the transformations included significant changes in organizational roles, responsibilities and behaviors, and in the process changed aspects of the culture at least in some parts of the organizations. In many cases the changes were counter to the prevailing culture or organizational norms. The successful transformations recognized this was either desired or inevitable and addressed the organizational issues first to create a new context within which to bring about further changes. As mentioned earlier, the less successful deferred those changes until the new processes and systems were defined. As a result the organizational changes and behaviors had to fit the new processes, causing a steep and difficult learning curve for the staff and managers involved or effective rejection of the new processes as unnecessary or not fit for purpose.
- In a minority of cases the new business strategy that drove the transformation also demanded a change in the organization's values: for example, loss of autonomy and reduced discretion for opportunistic and tactical investment, consolidation to achieve corporate control of resources and practices and the adoption of standard processes to achieve corporate rather local business advantages. Inevitably these changes created tensions and exposed cultural and value differences across the business units and functions, which had to be either reconciled or overridden to succeed with the transformation. In the less successful transformations these tensions either could not or were not addressed and existing power structures prevented or subverted the changes.
- The structure and mode adopted to bring about the transformation should normally reflect the organization's overall culture unless cultural change is essential to achieve the business changes. This concerns both formal and informal roles and the purposes of those roles in the exercise of power or the use existing or the creation of new organizational relationships during the transformation. The "task force" approach, which exercises the use of power, worked well when the need to transform was urgent, the objectives were very clear and the means of achieving them were known. In the opposite situations a more devolved approach enabled at least one organization

to extend the ambition of the transformation through embedding learning and knowledge sharing processes into the program.

- As the transformation proceeds it may be necessary to change modes and in turn the governance of the program. In particular the creation of a new capability can be carried out by a task force largely separated from day-to-day operations, but to exploit the new capability can require different types of changes especially in a multi-unit, multinational organization where the units are of different sizes and maturities. This "transfer of ownership" from the transformation team to the business units has to be planned carefully and, as in some of the successful cases, tested through pilot implementations.

12.7 Conclusion

Every business transformation is different but not unique and lessons can be learned from the experiences of others. While it is not possible to prescribe a methodology that will meet the requirements of every transformation, the approach to developing BTM^2 combined the knowledge of leading academics and experienced consultants and business managers plus lessons learned from studying a range of different types of transformations in different organizations and contexts.

Business transformation management is the holistic management of extensive, complex changes on which the organization's future success strongly depends.

Put another way: transformation is a way of achieving accelerated business evolution whilst not damaging the current business performance. BTM^2 not only includes theoretically sound and recognized best practices in each discipline, but also how those practices can be combined and integrated into an overall approach to successful transformation management.

The evidence from the case studies shows that the organizations whose approach to managing transformations included management attention to the majority of the BTM^2 management disciplines were more successful than those that did not.

Bibliography

Business Transformation Academy (2011), *360° – The Business Transformation Journal*: www.bta-online.com/360degree (accessed March 2012).

Gregor, Shirley, Martin, Michael, Fernandez, Walter, Stern, Steven and Vitale, Michael (2006), The transformational dimension in the realization of business value from information technology, *The Journal of Strategic Information Systems* 15, no. 3, 249–70.

Peppard, Joe and Ward, John (2005), Unlocking sustained business value from IT investments, *California Management Review* 48, no. 1, 52–70.

Ward, John, Hemingway, Christopher and Daniel, Elizabeth (2005), A framework for addressing the organisational issues of enterprise systems implementation, *The Journal of Strategic Information Systems* 14, no. 2, 97–119.

Appendices

Appendix A
BTM² Strategy Management

A.1 Methods for Strategy Development

Name	Description
SWOT	A SWOT analysis is a strategic planning method that systematically records a company's strengths, weaknesses, opportunities and threats (in terms of capital, sales, procurement and personnel). The analysis of the company's strengths and weaknesses is based on its current, internal situation and forms the basis for identifying opportunities or threats in relation to its own business model while taking external factors (such as technology or shifting business conditions) into account.
Lifecycle	Alongside diffusion models, lifecycle models describe growth and saturation processes. They assume that the analyzed time series (such as sales) approaches a saturation limit in the long term. In contrast to diffusion models, lifecycle models explicitly show the degeneration. By using mathematical models, the factors influencing the growth process and the position of products in their lifecycle can be derived and used as a basis for sales forecasts, planning and strategic decisions.[1]
GAP	In business and economics, gap analysis is a management tool that helps a company identify strategic and operative gaps by analyzing the difference between the target and probable development of its basic business – in case the business policy is not going to be changed. The gap analysis is a derived analysis that graphically relates the environmental and company analysis. The principle of gap analysis is based on future projections that are compared with one another. On the one hand, quantifiable elements of the corporate goals (such as sales, profit, or Return on Investment (ROI)) are projected as target values with their desired future development. On the other hand, the expected development of the target values is calculated by extrapolating historical data. Both results are then divided into milestones. A detailed understanding of statistical forecasting methods is thus essential to conduct a gap analysis.
Benchmarking	Benchmarking is applied in many different areas and with many different methods and objectives. Benchmarking in business economics is the systematic and ongoing process of comparing one's business processes, products, services and performance metrics to industry bests and/or best practices from other industries. Dimensions typically measured are quality, time and cost. Improvements from learning mean doing things better, faster and cheaper.

---

1   See Wikipedia, "Produktlebenszyklus", 2012: http://de.wikipedia.org/wiki/Produktlebenszyklus (accessed March 2012).

Portfolio techniques	Portfolio techniques in marketing or strategic corporate planning help companies to gain an overview of their own products and are useful whenever a company has a wide variety of products. Portfolio overviews essentially compare factors external to the company with internal ones. Using the BCG matrix as an example, an external factor is market growth, over which the company itself has little influence. An internal factor is the relative market share – that is, the company's actual share of the market compared to the strongest competitor. Unlike market growth, this internal factor can directly be influenced by the company – for example, through appropriate marketing measures. Next, the company's products are entered in the portfolio overview in the form of circles of various sizes representing their sales significance. The products are then assigned to one of the four fields in the portfolio. Each field now has certain standard strategies, which the company should not pursue without conducting additional analyses. The standard strategies for the individual fields are (1) Stars – invest, (2) Question marks – select, (3) Cash cows – milk and (4) Poor dogs – divest. Additional analyses can include contribution margins, for example, because there is an entire range of products that, despite being classified as "poor dogs", still generate high contribution margins and, therefore, do not merit outright divestment.[2]

2   See Teia, "Portfoliotechnik", 2009: www.teialehrbuch.de/Kostenlose-Kurse/Marketing/15195-Portfoliotechnik.html (accessed March 2012).

Appendix B
BTM² Value Management

B.1 Template for Benefits – With Examples

Benefit no., type and description	Benefit owner(s)	Required changes and responsibilities	Measures	Expected value (if applicable)	Due date	Revised value and date of revision	Reasons for revision
B2: Financial Eliminate invoice errors	Financial Controller	C1 – Distribution Manager	1. Number of customer invoice queries: Baseline: 400 per week	Reduce by 90%	Oct 20xx	80% (May 20xx)	More queries than expected not due to inaccurate invoices
			2. Admin time on corrections and reconciliations Baseline: 60 hours/week	Reduce by 40 hours per week (1 FTE salary saving)	Sept 20xx		
B4: Financial Reduced costs of stock holding – including inventory reductions	Product Managers	C4 – Production Planners C5 – Purchasing Manager E3, E4 and E5 – Operations Director	1.Stock holding by product type for: a) Raw Materials (RM) Baseline: £300,000 b) Packaging: £250,000	Reduction of holding RM by 20% and Packaging by 25%: One off saving of £125,000	Oct 20xx	May be higher up to £140,000 (June 20xx)	Underestimated level of overstocking in packaging
			2. Value of stock write-offs: £200,000 in 20xx	Annual saving of 75%: £150,000	Nov 20xx	Maybe 10–20% lower (Aug 20xx)	Increased demand could use more old stock of packaging.

Change no. and description and dependent benefits	Responsibility (and involvement)	Prerequisite or consequent changes	Evidence of completion	Due date	Resources required	Revisions to date or resources and reasons for them
Enabling Change 8: Develop new KPIs based on balanced scorecard B7, B9 and B10	Executive Directors	P: None C: C6 Implement Performance Management Process	Balanced Scorecard and KPIs agreed by board and published	April 20xx	2/3 Executive Meetings + 1 day per Dept Manager.	(May 20xx) CEO sick when first meeting due – start postponed 2 weeks
Business Change 2: Implement new raw material stock Replenishment Algorithms B3, B4	Purchasing Manager (and Product Managers)	P: E1 Restructure Stock Coding C: None	Tested and agreed algorithms for all A and B class materials	June 20xx	20 days of inventory controllers 10 days of Product/ Purchasing Managers + 4 days of Accounts staff/	May be able to complete earlier with external help

Appendix C
BTM² Risk Management – Methods and Tools

C.1 Methods and Tools

Tool or method*	Purpose and description	Risk class applicability	Risk process applicability	Usage considerations
360° risk assessment	Systematically and holistically identifies major risks and opportunities across the organization by involving a wide range of stakeholders who are capable of offering internal and external perspectives.	Strategic risk	Identification	Involves interviews with analysts, transformation specialists, customers and other key stakeholders to provide independent and unbiased views on key risks and interdependencies. Based on the Delphi Method, this approach is best suited to circumstances where sufficient, suitable expertise is available.
Business case analysis	Detailed inspection of business case including anticipated costs and benefits can highlight important features of the transformation that are expected to drive success.	Strategic risk Operational risk	Identification Response planning	A bottom-up approach that is dependent on the quality of the business case being analyzed.
Cash flow at risk (CaR)	A measure that represents how much an organization's cash flow would be expected to decrease, within a set confidence interval, in response to a risk event.	Operational risk	Analysis and evaluation	Relatively high-level, quantitative metric that can be difficult to apply to evaluating business transformation risk.

Tool or method*	Purpose and description	Risk class applicability	Risk process applicability	Usage considerations
Checklists	Pre-established lists of potential risk drivers, similar to risk maps, that can be used to identify or inspect risks.	Operational risk	Identification Monitoring and reporting	The use of checklists is dependent on experience with prior initiatives that are similar to the transformation being assessed. This can limit the extent to which they are relevant to understanding transformation risk, particularly at the strategic level.
Cluster analysis	Aggregates risk drivers into related clusters that represent business regimes or scenarios. Helps to discern important risks that must be regularly monitored from those that must be scanned/monitored on an occasional basis.	Strategic risk	Identification Analysis and evaluation Response planning Monitoring and reporting	Quantitative technique that requires some degree of expertise. Can be used to support scenario planning.
Earnings at risk (EaR)	A measure that represents how much an organization's earnings would be expected to decrease, within a set confidence interval, in response to a risk event.	Operational risk	Analysis and evaluation	Relatively high-level, quantitative metric that can be difficult to apply to evaluating business transformation risk.
Expert opinion (**Delphi Study**)	Formal method for independently collecting and aggregating the opinions of experts and establishing consensus among these experts. Facilitates the assembly of insights from potentially large, diverse groups of individuals.	Strategic risk Operational risk	Identification Analysis and evaluation	Relies on anonymous input and, as such, may be useful for circumstances where people are uncomfortable publicly expressing their views or where there is a risk of groupthink. The technique typically relies on the use of questionnaires.
Industry benchmarks	Comparison of an initiative with similar initiatives undertaken by other organizations.	Operational risk	Identification Analysis and evaluation Monitoring and reporting	Dependent on other organizations having undertaken a similar initiative which can limit relevance of the approach to business transformation.

Tool or method*	Purpose and description	Risk class applicability	Risk process applicability	Usage considerations
Key risk indicators	Leading indicators that mark the possible emergence of a risk event. Provide an early warning system that can be used to trigger proactive responses.	Strategic risk Operational risk	Response planning Monitoring and reporting	Pilot testing is necessary to ensure that risk indicators are truly indicative of the emergence of risk events.
Monte Carlo or probability simulation	A quantitatively based method for estimating expected outcomes based on probabilistic sampling. Capable of generating quantitative confidence intervals around individual estimates. Can be used to validate assumptions made in relation to future scenarios.	Strategic risk Operational risk	Analysis and evaluation Monitoring and reporting Response planning	Depends on the availability of suitable, quantitative estimates for the probability distributions underlying the parameters that drive the outcome(s) of interest. PERT analysis can be used as a simpler, less rigorous alternative to Monte Carlo simulation.
PERT analysis	A simple method of quantitatively expressing the range of variability associated with estimates.	Strategic risk Operational risk	Analysis and evaluation Monitoring and reporting Response planning	Depends on the availability of suitable, quantitative estimates. PERT analysis can be used as a simpler, less rigorous alternative to Monte Carlo simulation.
Porter's five forces model[1]	Identifies suppliers, customers, new entrants, product substitutes and industry competition as the five key threats to an organization's competitive position. These categories can be used to elicit risk drivers and they provide a framework for inspecting risks.	Strategic risk	Identification Analysis and evaluation Response planning	SWOT analysis is a related approach that can be used in a manner similar to Porter's Five Forces Model.

1 Porter, Michael E. (1979), How competitive forces shape strategy, *Harvard Business Review* 57, no. 2, 137–45.

Tool or method*	Purpose and description	Risk class applicability	Risk process applicability	Usage considerations
Prediction markets[2]	Draws on the knowledge and insight of a large number of individuals (a "crowd") to forecast or predict future outcomes. Provides an early warning system that permits early, rapid adjustments in response to emerging issues. Also capable of generating quantitative confidence intervals around individual estimates.	Strategic risk Operational risk	Analysis and evaluation Monitoring and reporting	Currently suitable for large organizations that have access to a sufficiently informed crowd. Best used only for key uncertainties to avoid "crowd fatigue". Relies on anonymous input and, as such, may be useful in circumstances where people are uncomfortable publicly expressing their views or where there is a risk of groupthink.
Risk breakdown structure	Provides a hierarchical, categorically oriented depiction of potential risks that might be encountered in a predetermined domain such as business transformation.	Operational risk	Identification Analysis and evaluation	The hierarchical nature of risk breakdown structures means that they can be used to gain some understanding of underlying causes. However, they are typically developed based on prior initiatives. This can limit the extent to which they are relevant to understanding transformation risk, particularly at the strategic level.
Risk driver map	Provides a consistent, comprehensive, qualitative overview of risk drivers that might merit consideration. Permits exploration of risk drivers that share a potential for wider systemic impact with either positive or negative implications for achieving objectives. Can serve as input to 360° risk assessments and scenario planning.	Strategic risk Operational risk	Identification	Risk driver maps can be developed with a mid- to long-term perspective in mind or in relation to short-term operational risks. Development of a risk driver map can draw on a wide range of internal and external sources. Ongoing attention is, however, required to ensure that it remains current.

2   Malone, Thomas W. (2004), Bringing the market inside, *Harvard Business Review 84*, no. 4, 106–14.

Tool or method*	Purpose and description	Risk class applicability	Risk process applicability	Usage considerations
Risk matrix	Prioritizes risk based on likelihood of occurrence and magnitude of impact.	Operational risk	Analysis and evaluation	Widely used approach to assessing operational risk. Can be based on quantitative or qualitative assessments of likelihood of occurrence and magnitude of impact.
Root cause analysis	Identifies the causes that underlie risks that have been identified via other mechanisms.	Strategic risk Operational risk	Identification Response planning Monitoring and reporting	A number of approaches are available to conduct root cause analysis including the five whys technique, Failure Mode and Effects Analysis (FEMA), Fishbone or Ishikawa diagrams and root cause mapping.
*Scenario planning*³	Supports the generation of insights on emerging risks and helps to identify possible future scenarios. Can be used to "stress test" assumptions and plans. Identifies the major contingencies that can impact plans. Can also be used to identify key risks, thereby ensuring that attention is only directed to those risks that are particularly salient.	Strategic risk	Identification Analysis and evaluation Response planning	Can be performed informally using heuristics or in a more formal manner that is supported by formal statistical methods such as cluster analysis. Use of statistically based scenario planning requires a certain level of expertise. Can be used in conjunction with Monte Carlo simulation.
Stakeholder analysis	Analysis of stakeholder needs and their influences within the context of an organizational governance structure.	Strategic risk Operational risk	Identification Response planning Monitoring and reporting	Particularly important in organizations characterized by a high degree of politically oriented decision making.

3   Schoemaker, Paul J. (1995), Scenario planning: a tool for strategic thinking, *Sloan Management Review* 36, no. 2, 25–40.

Tool or method*	Purpose and description	Risk class applicability	Risk process applicability	Usage considerations
SWOT analysis	A strategic framework that identifies strengths, weaknesses, threats, and opportunities as four categories for assessing the competitive position of an organization. These categories can be used to elicit risk drivers and they provide a framework for inspecting risk.	Strategic risk	Identification Analysis and evaluation Response planning	Porter's five forces model is a related approach that can be used in a manner similar to SWOT analysis.
Transformation plan review	Detailed analysis of work breakdown structure, critical path, dependencies, timelines, effort and resource allocations, and assumptions.	Operational risk	Identification Response planning Monitoring and reporting	A bottom-up approach that is dependent on the availability of detailed planning. As a result, this approach is likely to be less useful during the early stages of a transformation.
Value at risk (VaR)	A measure that represents how much the value of an asset or group of assets would decrease, within a set confidence interval, in response to a risk event.	Operational risk	Analysis and evaluation	Relatively high-level, quantitative metric that can be difficult to apply to evaluating business transformation risk.

*Italic methods have been reported as being used by more than 40 percent of organizations.[4]

4   Carpenter, Guy and Wyman, Oliver (2010), *Excellence in Risk Management VII: Elevating the Practice of Strategic Risk Management* (Marsh Inc).

Appendix D
BTM² Business Process Management

D.1 Modeling Languages for Process Design

Language	Description
EPC[1]	The EPC (Event Driven Process Chain) is part of the ARIS-Architecture (Architecture of Integrated Information Systems). It serves to model processes, integrating different views in enterprise modeling, such as data-view, function-view, organizational view and output view. Processes, as such, are modelled as sequences of events and functions and can be extended by further information objects describing, for example, data flow and organizational responsibility. EPCs are particularly used for reference modeling and customizing in SAP.
Activity diagram[2]	Activity diagrams are part of UML (Unified Modeling Language). They substantiate the dynamic aspects of individual use cases. Activity diagrams include start events and end events. Like BPMN 2.0, activity diagrams adopt the semantics of Petri nets. Usually, activity diagrams are combined with other UML diagram types, e.g. to capture business as well as technical requirements of application systems (by means of a use case diagram) or to express relationships between relevant economic entities that participate in a process (by means of a class diagram).
Petri nets[3]	Petri nets represent a formal graphical process modeling notation, which can be used to describe the behavior of application systems as well as to model business processes. Petri nets are based on the concept of tokens, places (correspond to events) and transitions (correspond to functions or activities). However, they cannot be used to describe different views of business processes. Tokens and transitions are a means to formally describe and analyze the semantics of control flows. Many contemporary process modeling languages build on the Petri net semantics in order to allow for analyzing processes with regard to cycles, deadlocks or reachable process regions.

---

1 See Scheer, August-Wilhelm (2000), *ARIS–Business Process Modeling*. 3rd ed. (Berlin, New York: Springer) or Keller, Gerhard, Nüttgens, Markus and Scheer, August-Wilhelm (1992), Semantische Prozeßmodellierung auf der Grundlage Ereignisgesteuerter Prozeßketten (EPK), in *Veröffentlichungen des Instituts für Wirtschaftsinformatik*, edited by August-Wilhelm Scheer (Heft 89. Saarbrücken).

2 See Object Management Group, Unified Modeling Language: www.uml.org (accessed March 2012).

3 See Petri, Carl A. (1962), Kommunikation mit Automaten, dissertation (Technische Universität Darmstadt, Darmstadt) or van der Aalst, Will M.P. (1998), The application of Petri nets to workflow management, *The Journal of Circuits, Systems and Computers* 8, no. 1, 22–66.

BPEL[4]	The OASIS standard "Business Process Execution Language for Web Services" (BPEL4WS, BPEL) is an XML-based machine readable process description language. A BPEL process is conceived of a web service, which can be called by other web services or can call web services by itself. BPEL can be used to describe both internal processes as well as inter-organizational processes. The BPMN standard defines mapping rules to transform graphical BPMN process models into a BPEL model.
ebXML BPSS[5]	Similar to BPEL, the ebXML Business Process Specification Schema is an XML-based standard hosted by the OASIS to describe processes in a machine readable way. ebXML-based process descriptions specify what business partners, roles, collaborations, choreographies and business documents are required for a process execution. ebXML process descriptions focus on inter-organizational exchanges of business documents.

---

4   OASIS (2007), Web services business process execution language version 2.0 OASIS standard: http://docs.oasis-open.org/wsbpel/2.0/OS/wsbpel-v2.0-OS.pdf (accessed March 2011).

5   OASIS (2006), ebXML business process specification schema technical specification v2.0.4: http://docs.oasis-open.org/ebxml-bp/2.0.4/OS/spec/ebxmlbp-v2.0.4-Spec-os-en.pdf (accessed March 2011).

Appendix E
BTM² Transformational IT Management

E.1 Methods for IT Service Deployment

E.1.1 RATIONAL UNIFIED PROCESS[1]

Rational Unified Process (RUP) provides a knowledge base, i.e. guidelines, templates and tools for all critical activities of the software development process. Within the development of RUP in 1998, the founders agreed on a consistent notation language for modeling, the Unified Modeling Language (UML). RUP therefore provides guidance for an effective use of UML. RUP is built upon six key guidelines: develop software iteratively, manage requirements, use component-based architectures, model software visually, verify software quality and control changes to software. As illustrated in Figure E.1, RUP's process model is built upon two dimensions. The horizontal axis represents the software project's progress dimension and is expressed in terms of cycles, phases, iterations and milestones. The vertical axis represents the various disciplines that are relevant for the development process.

Software development projects are broken down into cycles. Figure E.1 illustrates one such cycle. A development cycle is divided into four consecutive phases, the "inception phase" (project setup and project scoping), the "elaboration phase" (domain analysis and derivation of basic architecture), the "construction phase" (software implementation) and the "transition phase" (training and deployment). RUP phases can themselves be broken down into iterations. An iteration is a complete development loop with an internal or external release as a result. This release is an executable product, i.e. a subset of the product under development, which grows incrementally from iteration to iteration. The advantages of such an iterative approach are that risks are mitigated earlier, changes are more manageable, the level of reuse is higher and the project team is able to learn along the way.

In RUP, nine disciplines are regarded as relevant for software development. Six core engineering workflows are complemented by three core supporting workflows. In *business modeling* (core engineering workflow), business processes are documented on the basis of UML in order to establish a common problem understanding for software engineers and business people. The goal of the *requirements* workflow (core engineering workflow) is to define what the software system should do. Uses cases are the means to depict requirements. *Analysis and design* (core engineering workflow) show how the software system will be

---

1 The overview about the Relational Unified Process in this section, as well as the image of Figure E.1 originates back to the following references: Rational Software Corporation (1998), Rational Unified Process – best practices for software development: www.augustana.ab.ca/~mohrj/courses/2000.winter/csc220/papers/rup_best_practices/rup_bestpractices. pdf (accessed March 2012), Wikipedia (2012a), IBM Rational Unified Process: http://en.wikipedia.org/wiki/IBM_Rational_Unified_Process (accessed March 2012) and Wikipedia (2012c), Rational Unified Process: http://de.wikipedia.org/wiki/Rational_Unified_Process (accessed March 2012).

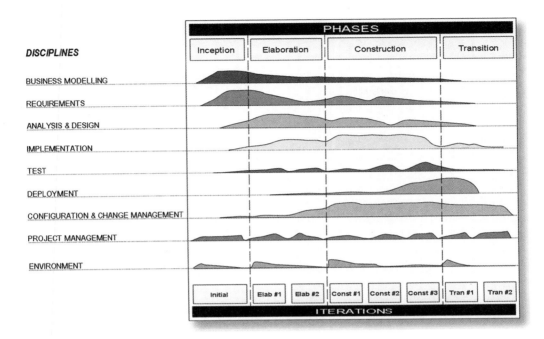

Figure E.1   The two dimensions of RUP

Source: Reprint Courtesy of International Business Machines Corporation, © 1998, 2012 International Business Machines Corporation

realized. This workflow results in a design model being an abstraction of the source code. At the core of design models are design classes. *Implementation* (core engineering workflow) covers the organization of the code (subsystems, layers), the implementation of components via classes and objects, the test of components and the integration of the individual produced results into an executable system. *Test* (core engineering workflow) is an iterative activity that is performed throughout the whole project. Major aspects of testing are to verify the proper integration of all software components and to check that all requirements have been correctly implemented. The *deployment workflow* (core engineering workflow) produces product releases, and delivers the software to the end users. This includes activities like software packaging, distribution, installation, and providing help and assistance to users. *Configuration and change management* as a core supporting workflow handles the control of the numerous artefacts produced by different people and teams working in the project. It avoids problems like conflicting changes. This workflow also covers change request management. The goal of *project management* (core supporting workflow) is to provide a framework for managing software-intensive projects, as well as practical guidelines for project planning, staffing, executing, and monitoring. The *environment* workflow (core supporting workflow) ensures the availability of processes and tools that are necessary to enable team-based software development.

E.1.2 ACCELERATEDSAP (ASAP)[2]

The ASAP methodology is a comprehensive set of content, tools and knowledge provided by SAP for rapid implementation, upgrade or enhancement of SAP solutions. Although ASAP has been developed specifically for SAP solutions, many components of the approach (e.g. the roadmap) can also be applied to other standardized business software solutions. ASAP includes three key elements designed to deliver rapid and reliable results: the Solution Composer tool, the SAP Solution Manager application management solution and the ASAP roadmap. The Solution Composer is a tool for planning, defining, documenting and communicating business solution requirements. SAP Solution Manager is the SAP product for SAP application management and administration. Thereby, it facilitates solution design, documentation, testing, operations and monitoring of SAP solutions. The ASAP roadmap details the activities involved in implementing, upgrading and enhancing SAP solutions. It is enriched with sets of deliverables, accelerators, role descriptions and checklists. Every ASAP project is divided into five phases that cover the entire software project lifecycle (cf. Figure E.2).

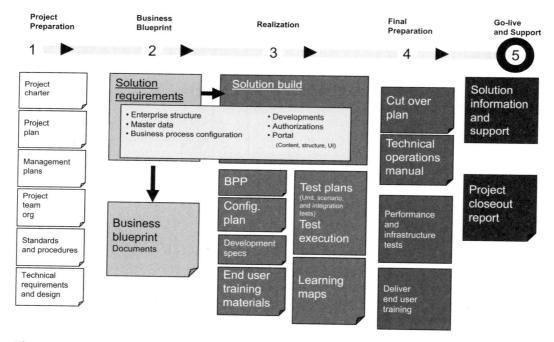

Figure E.2   ASAP phases and key deliverables[3]

2   The overview about the AcceleratedSAP methodology in this section originates back to the following reference: SAP AG (2007), Proven methodology for rapid implementation of SAP solutions – reduce costs, lower risks, and save time with ASAP: www.r3now.com/literature/Proven-Methodology-for-Rapid-Implementation-of-SAP-Solutions.pdf (accessed March 2012).

3   See Musil, Jan, and Raimar Hoelinger (2010), The new ASAP methodology: overview of the new ASAP methodology for implementation 7.x and ASAP business add-ons, SAP AG: www.sdn.sap.com/irj/scn/go/portal/prtroot/docs/library/uuid/1026829e-7169-2d10-05b6-b5dd7042d446?QuickLink=index&overridelayout=true&48438641495058 (accessed March 2012).

Project preparation is the first ASAP phase covering project planning and preparation. During this phase, project goals are set, the high-level project scope is defined, resource requirements are estimated and the project plan is documented. This phase assesses key aspects before implementation begins: the degree of readiness, current business processes, risks and opportunities among others. Major activities are securing executive sponsorship, agreeing on roles and responsibilities, and validating project plans and objectives. SAP Solution Manager can be set up in this phase as a repository for solution implementation documentation.

The purpose of phase two (*Business blueprint*) is to gather business requirements and achieve a common understanding of how the company intends to run SAP to support their business. The result is the business blueprint, a detailed documentation of the results gathered during requirements workshops. This phase is characterized by two milestones. "Business scenarios defined" is the point in time where high-level requirements for the business scenarios are identified and described. "Business blueprint completion" is the point in time when the detailed business blueprint is available, i.e. business scenarios and their corresponding business processes, process steps and transaction requirements are identified and documented.

During *Realization* the functional and technical requirements are implemented based on the business blueprint. The goal is to have a solution built and integration tested, with end user training and documentation material prepared, and the production environment designed and set up. Key deliverables of this phase are baseline configuration, key development specifications, test plan, training materials and plans, as well as plans for change and risk management. The baseline configuration is the configuration of the organizational structure, master data and key business processes. Key development specifications cover interfaces, data conversion programs, reports and required enhancements. The test plan includes an integration test plan and test cases to ensure all processes integrate and run smoothly before the data cutover.

The *Final preparation* procedures are completed during phase four to ensure readiness to go live. The activities include end user training and preparing for the cutover. During this phase, volume and stress tests are conducted. Furthermore, user acceptance tests ensure a smooth transition to go-live. This phase also serves to resolve all critical open issues. On successful completion of this phase, the business is ready to run with the new solution.

In *Go-live and support* (phase five) the implementation moves from project-oriented preproduction to live operation. First of all, a support organization has to be set up. It has to be ensured that high-quality user support is available during the first critical days of production. Also, this organization plays a vital role in supporting and improving operations on an ongoing basis. Moreover, continuous software monitoring and optimization has to take place during this phase as well. SAP Solution Manager is a key means for performing this support and is moved from the implementation project organization to the IT support organization.

E.2 Best Practices for IT Service Management[4]

The IT Infrastructure Library (ITIL) is a collection of best practices for IT service management and the leading approach in this domain. Services in the ITIL terminology are understood as an instrument that brings additional value to customers by realizing their requirements. Service management therefore requires a set of specialized, organizational skills to bring customers additional value by delivering services. By now, ITIL is available in version 3 and can be seen as a de facto standard for IT service management. Figure E.3 illustrates the latest version of the ITIL framework.

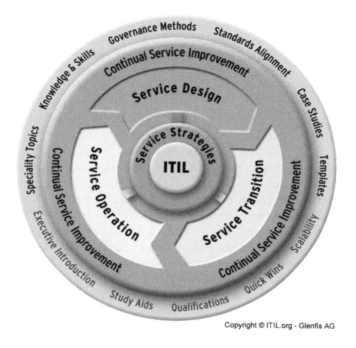

Copyright © ITIL.org - Glenfis AG

Figure E.3   The ITIL framework[5]

Reprint Courtesy of Glenfis AG, www.itil-forum.ch

    The ITIL framework consists of five core areas that cover all stages of the service lifecycle from the initial definition to service operation and optimization. Version 2 of the ITIL framework focuses on specific activities directly related to service delivery and support and therefore the versions should not be considered in isolation. The five stages of the current ITIL version 3 are service strategies, service design, service transition, service operation and continual service improvement.

---

4   The overview about the ITIL framework in this section originates back to the following reference: Wikipedia (2012b), Information Technology Infrastructure Library: http://en.wikipedia.org/wiki/Information_Technology_Infrastructure_Library (accessed March 2012).

5   See Glenfis AG, ITIL® knowledge – overview: www.itil.org/en/vomkennen/itil/index.php (accessed March 2012).

At the center of ITIL service lifecycle management is service strategy. Service strategy provides guidance on prioritization of service-provider investments in services. Service strategy builds upon a market-driven approach. Selected key tasks in this regard are service value definition, business case development and market analysis. This book of ITIL has some overlaps with the IT strategy work stream.

Service design provides best practices on the design of IT services, processes and other aspects of service management. In ITIL, design is understood to encompass all elements relevant to service delivery, rather than simply focusing on design of technology. Service design addresses how a planned solution interacts with the business and technical environment. Key processes of service design are service catalog management, service level management, IT service continuity management, IT architecture management and supplier management. Here we have overlaps with business processes activities.

The objective of service transition is to build and deploy IT services. Furthermore, service transition assures that changes to services are carried out in a systematic and professional way. Major processes of service transition are change management, project management, application development and customization or release and deployment management.

Service operation describes best practices for ensuring the delivery of agreed levels of services to end users and business customers. It is the part of the lifecycle where the services and their value are actually delivered and realized. Monitoring of problems and managing the adequate balance between reliability and costs are key in service operation. Service operation includes activities such as technical management, application management, operations management and service desk.

Continual service improvement aims to align IT services to changing business needs. This is realized by identifying improvements and implementing them into the service portfolio. The focus of improvement is put on service quality from a business perspective. However, process efficiency and improvements concerning costs of IT processes are addressed as well. Key processes of continual service improvement are service level management, service measurement and reporting as well as continual service improvement.

E.3 Framework for IT Governance[6]

Control Objectives for Information and Related Technology (COBiT) is one of the most widely applied frameworks for IT controlling. Its best practices and toolsets have been developed and updated by the Information Systems Audit and Control Association (ISACA) and ITGI since 1996. COBiT provides an internal control system that helps to ensure that an organization's IT successfully delivers against business requirements. To that end, delivery is linked to business requirements, IT activities are organized into a generally accepted process model, the major IT resources are identified that are to be leveraged and the management control objectives are defined that should be considered.

---

6   The overview about the IT governance framework in this section, as well as the image in Figure E.4, originate back to the following reference: IT Governance Institute (2007), COBiT® 4.1: *Framework, Control Objectives, Management Guidelines, Maturity Models* (Rolling Meadows, IL: IT Governance Institute).

In order to satisfy business goals, information needs to conform to certain control criteria, which are referred to as business requirements for information. Seven distinct yet overlapping information criteria are defined: effectiveness, efficiency, confidentiality, integrity, availability, compliance and reliability.

The IT organization delivers against business goals by a set of processes that use resources like people, skills and technology infrastructure to run automated business applications while leveraging business information and performing business processes (efficiency and effectiveness). These resources, together with the processes, constitute an Enterprise Architecture for IT.

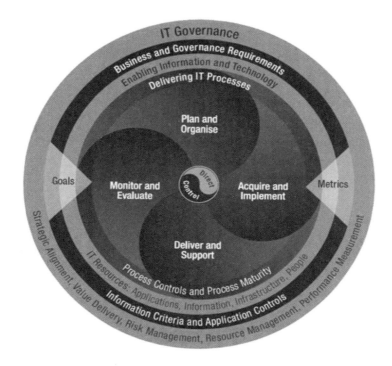

Figure E.4   The COBiT framework

COBiT is based on applications, information, infrastructure and people as "IT resources". Applications are automated systems and manual procedures that process information. Information is the data, in all forms, entered, processed and reported by the information systems in whatever forms. Infrastructure is the underlying technology and the facilities that enable information processing. People are the staff required to plan, organize, acquire, implement, deliver, support, monitor and evaluate information systems and services.

COBiT defines four domains of IT activities in a generic process model. These domains are *plan and organize*, *acquire and implement*, *deliver and support*, and *monitor and evaluate*. This classification maps to IT's traditional responsibility areas of planning, building, running and monitoring. The overall framework of COBiT is illustrated by Figure E.4.

Plan and organize addresses strategy and tactics in terms of how IT can best contribute to the accomplishment of business objectives. A proper IT organization as well as technological infrastructure has to be put in place. Therefore, processes like *define a strategic IT plan and direction, define the information architecture, assess and manage IT risks* or *manage projects* have to be established.

In order to implement the IT strategy, IT solutions have to be identified, developed or acquired, as well as implemented and integrated into business processes. Additionally, changes in existing systems or in its maintenance have to be addressed. All these aspects are addressed in the *acquire and implement* domain.

Deliver and support covers the actual delivery of services. This includes service delivery, management of security and continuity, service support for users, and management of data and operational facilities.

All IT processes need to be assessed regularly for their compliance and quality with control requirements. Therefore, the *monitor and evaluate* domain handles performance management, monitoring of internal control, regulatory compliance and governance.

Index

If you have found this book useful you may be interested in other titles from Gower

Solutions
Business Problem Solving
Eric Bolland and Frank Fletcher
Hardback: 978-1-4094-2687-5
e-book: 978-1-4094-2688-2

The Evolution of Strategic Foresight
Navigating Public Policy Making
Tuomo Kuosa
Hardback: 978-1-4094-2986-9
e-book: 978-1-4094-2987-6

International Operations Management
Lessons in Global Business
Alberto F. De Toni
Hardback: 978-1-4094-0329-6
e-book: 978-1-4094-0330-2

Creating Collaborative Advantage
Innovation and Knowledge Creation in Regional Economies
Hans Christian Garmann Johnsen and Richard Ennals
Hardback: 978-1-4094-0333-3
e-book: 978-1-4094-0334-0

Participative Transformation
Learning and Development in Practising Change
Roger Klev and Morten Levin
Hardback: 978-1-4094-2378-2
e-book: 978-1-4094-2379-9

Visit **www.gowerpublishing.com** and

- search the entire catalogue of Gower books in print
- order titles online at 10% discount
- take advantage of special offers
- sign up for our monthly e-mail update service
- download free sample chapters from all recent titles
- download or order our catalogue